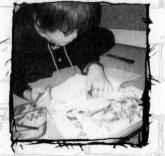

For starters, I'd like to say that I read all of my fan letters (of course!). Some of you write to me every week, and some even include gifts. I'm really touched! I just regret that I don't have the time to reply to all of you. One of these days, I intend to do something about it. But for now, my way of repaying your kindness and generosity is to produce my very best work. I hope you'll forgive me!

—Kentaro Yabuki, 2001

Kentaro Yabuki made his manga debut with *Yamato Gensoki*, a short series about a young empress destined to unite the warring states of ancient Japan and the boy sworn to protect her. His next series, *Black Cat*, commenced serialization in the pages of *Weekly Shonen Jump* in 2000 and quickly developed a loyal fan following. *Black Cat* has also become an animated TV series, first hitting Japan's airwaves in the fall of 2005.

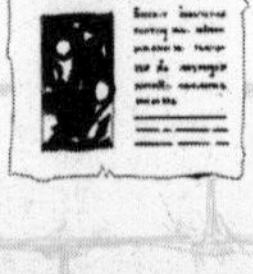

TRAIN HEARTNET

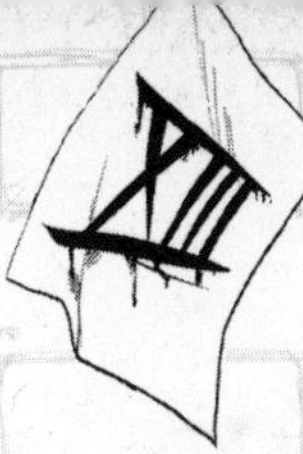

BLACK CAT VOL. 1
The SHONEN JUMP Manga Edition

STORY AND ART BY
KENTARO YABUKI

English Adaptation/Kelly Sue DeConnick
Translation/JN Productions
Touch-up Art & Lettering/Gia Cam Luc
Design/Courtney Utt
Editor/Frances E. Wall

Editor in Chief, Books/Alvin Lu
Editor in Chief, Magazines/Marc Weidenbaum
VP of Publishing Licensing/Rika Inouye
VP of Sales/Gonzalo Ferreyra
Sr. VP of Marketing/Liza Coppola
Publisher/Hyoe Narita

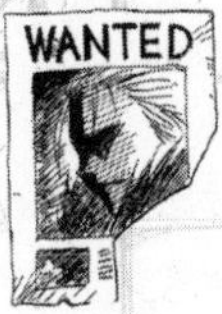

Printed in the U.S.A.

Published by VIZ Media, LLC
P.O. Box 77010
San Francisco, CA 94107

SHONEN JUMP Manga Edition
10 9 8 7 6 5
First printing, March 2006
Fifth printing, November 2007

THE WORLD'S
MOST POPULAR MANGA

VIZ media
www.viz.com

SHONEN JUMP
www.shonenjump.com

RATED
T+
FOR OLDER TEEN

PARENTAL ADVISORY
BLACK CAT is rated T+ for Older Teen and is recommended for ages 16
and up. This volume contains tobacco use and graphic, realistic violence.

ratings.viz.com

SHONEN JUMP MANGA EDITION

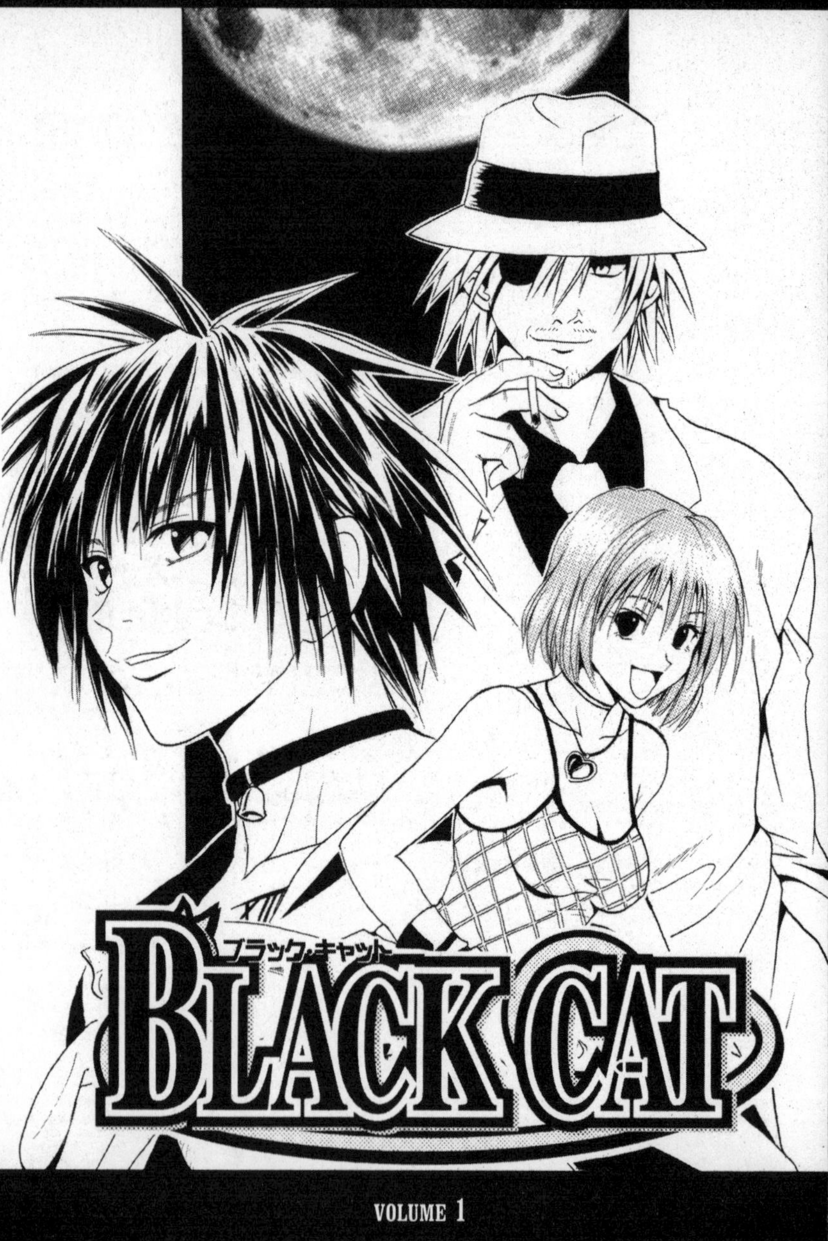
ブラック・キャット
BLACK CAT

VOLUME 1

THE MAN CALLED BLACK CAT

STORY & ART BY KENTARO YABUKI

BLACK CAT

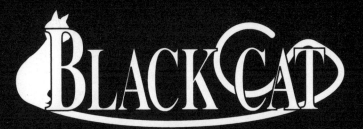

VOLUME 1 THE MAN CALLED BLACK CAT

CONTENTS

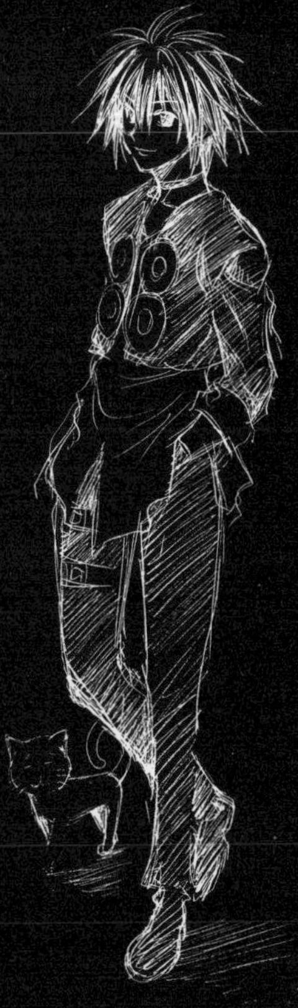

CHAPTER 1: THE MAN CALLED BLACK CAT

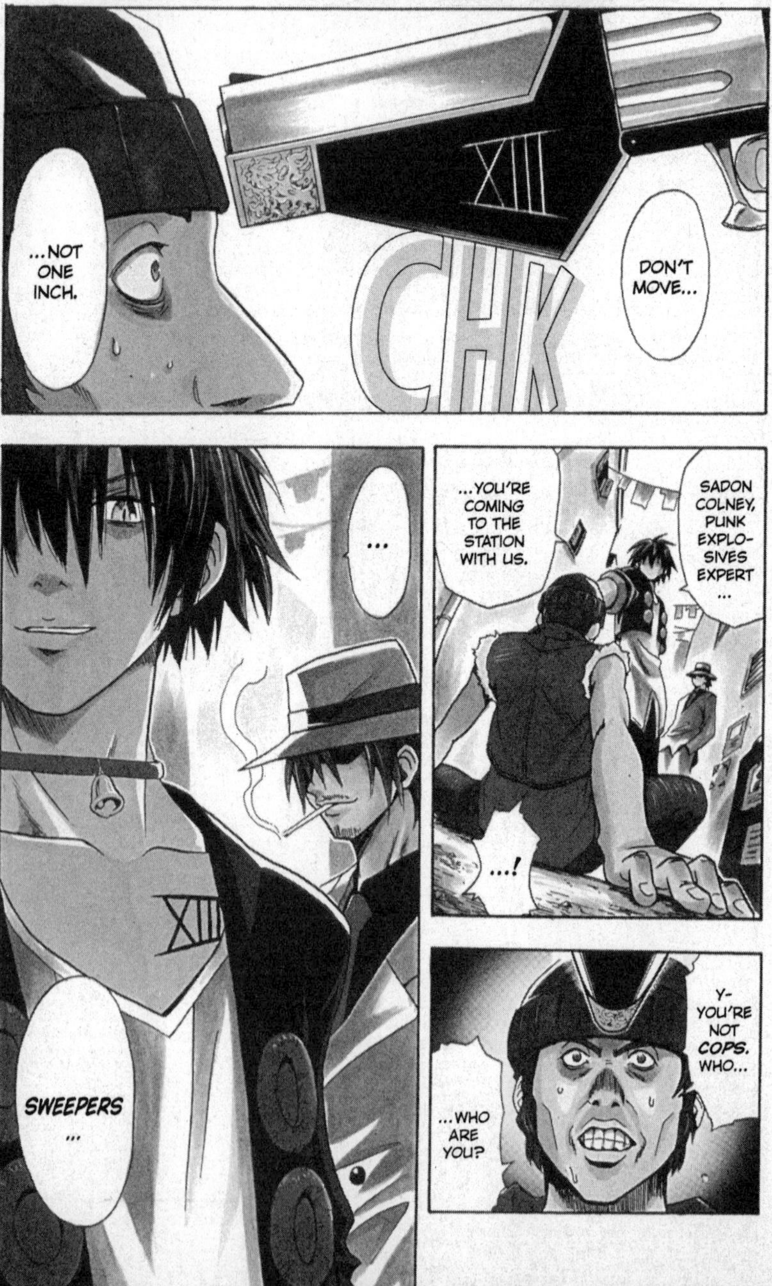
DON'T MOVE...
...NOT ONE INCH.
CHK
SADON COLNEY, PUNK EXPLO-SIVES EXPERT...
...YOU'RE COMING TO THE STATION WITH US.
...!
Y-YOU'RE NOT COPS. WHO...
...WHO ARE YOU?
...
SWEEPERS...

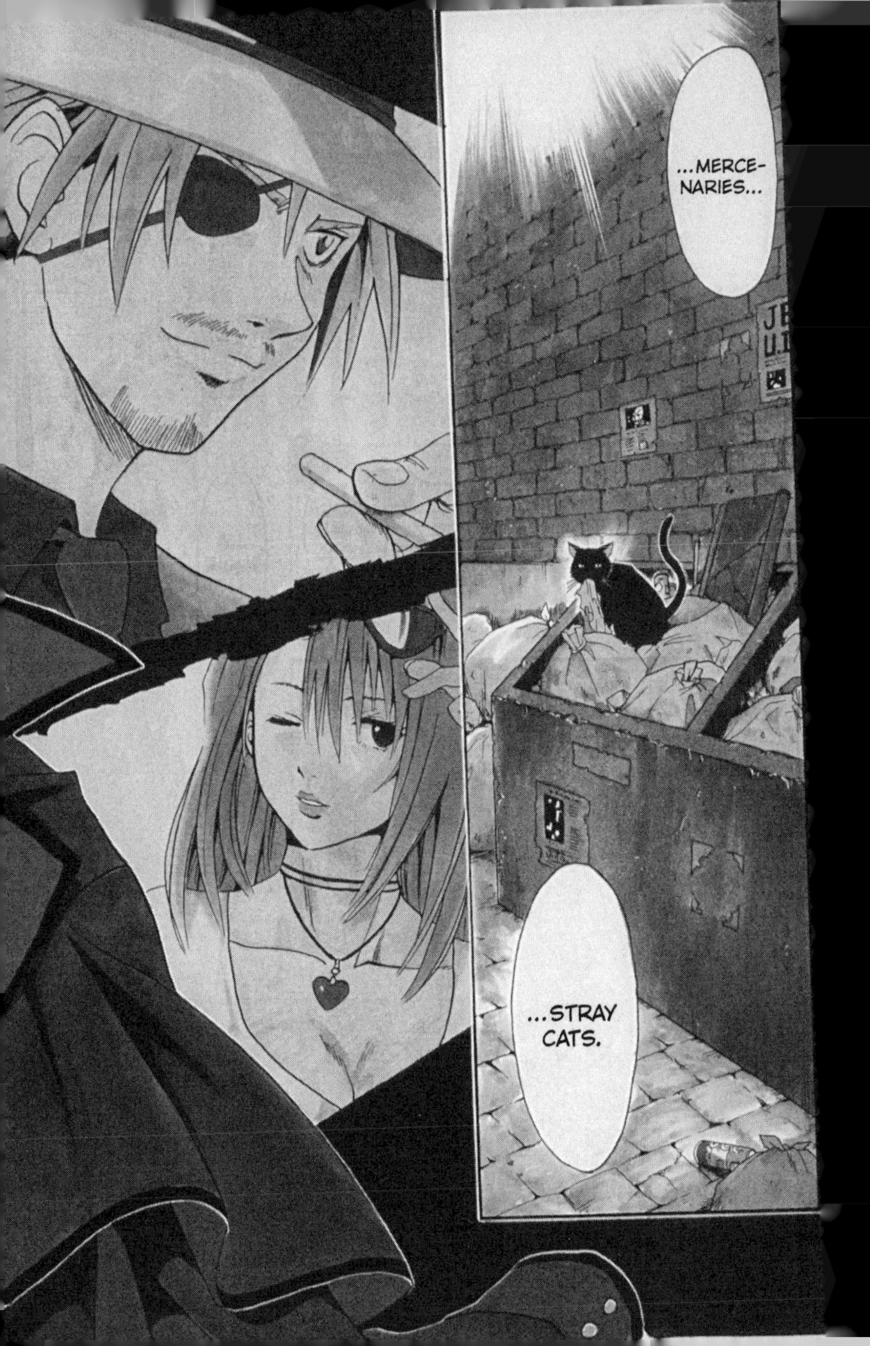
...MERCE-NARIES...
...STRAY CATS.

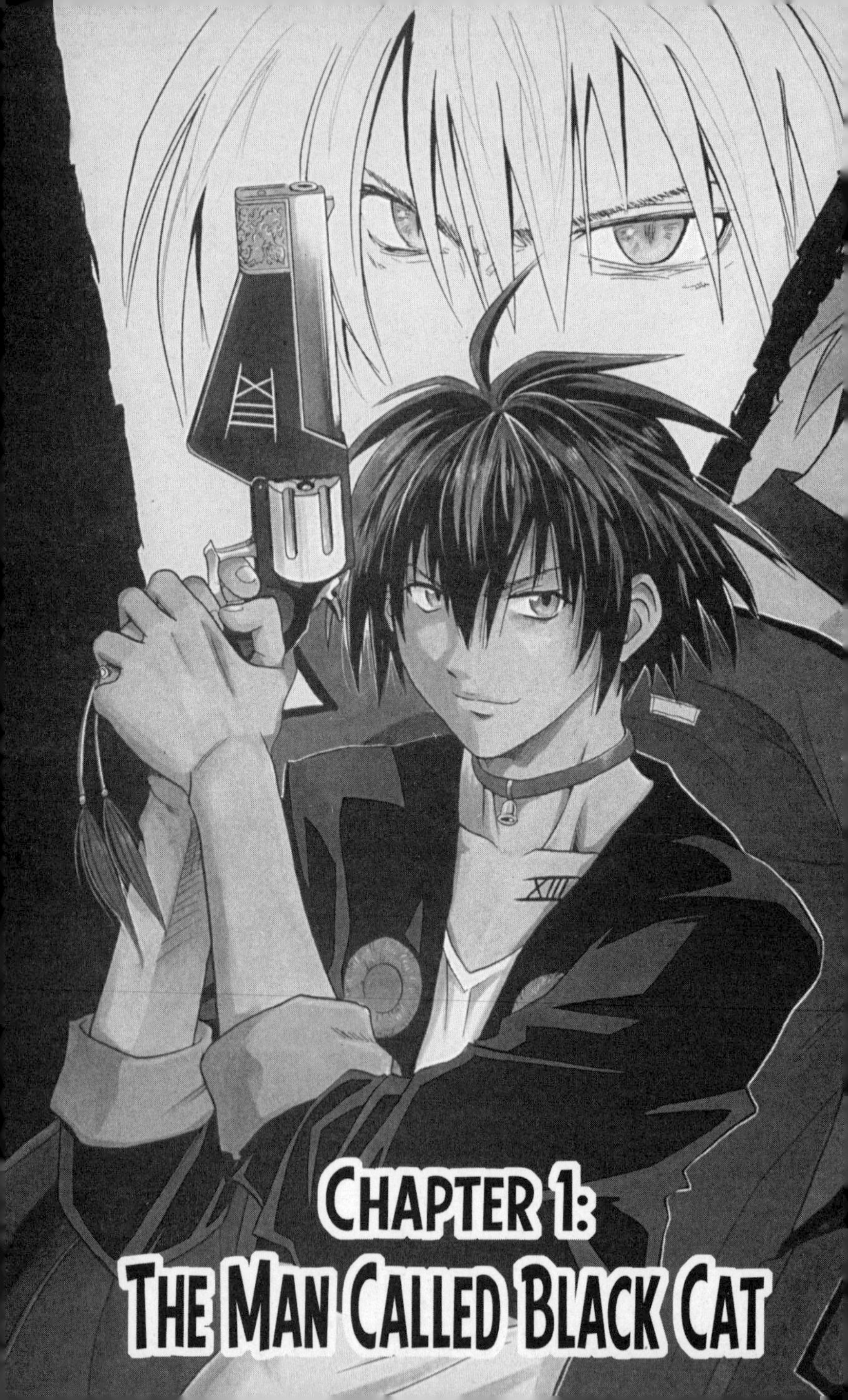
CHAPTER 1:
THE MAN CALLED BLACK CAT

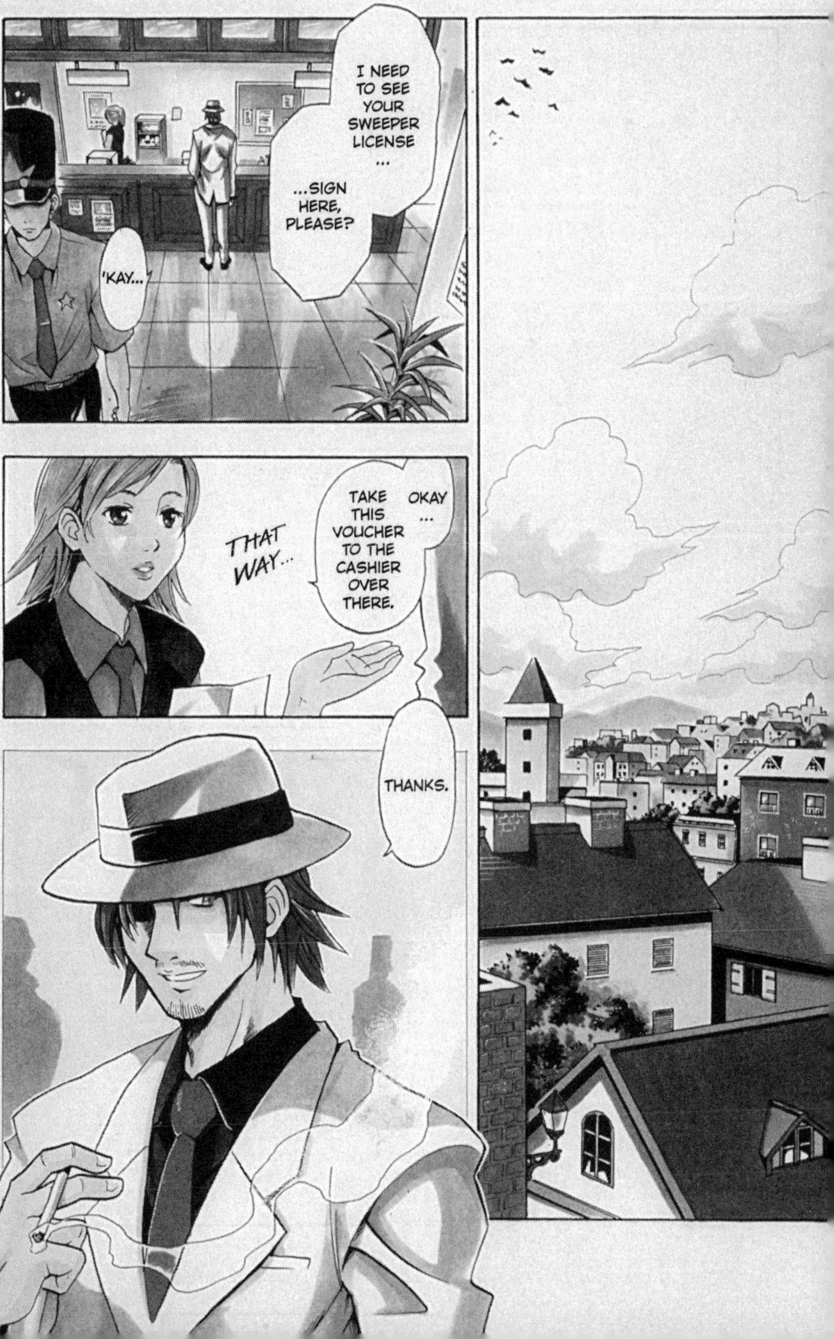
I NEED TO SEE YOUR SWEEPER LICENSE ...
...SIGN HERE, PLEASE?
'KAY...
OKAY ...
TAKE THIS VOUCHER TO THE CASHIER OVER THERE.
THAT WAY...
THANKS.

READ THIS WAY

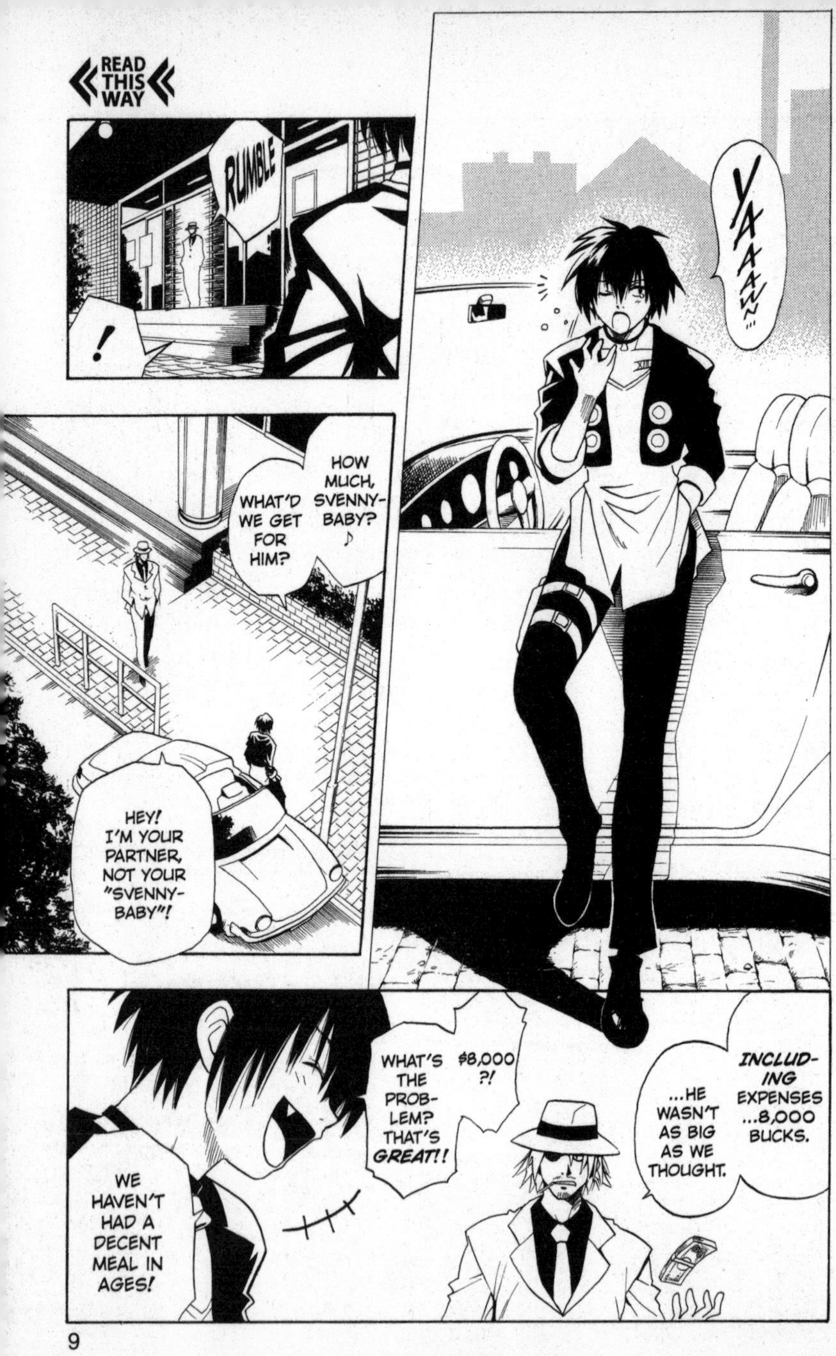
YAAAWN...
RUMBLE
!
HOW MUCH, SVENNY-BABY? ♪
WHAT'D WE GET FOR HIM?
HEY! I'M YOUR PARTNER, NOT YOUR "SVENNY-BABY"!
INCLUDING EXPENSES ...8,000 BUCKS.
...HE WASN'T AS BIG AS WE THOUGHT.
$8,000?!
WHAT'S THE PROBLEM? THAT'S GREAT!!
WE HAVEN'T HAD A DECENT MEAL IN AGES!

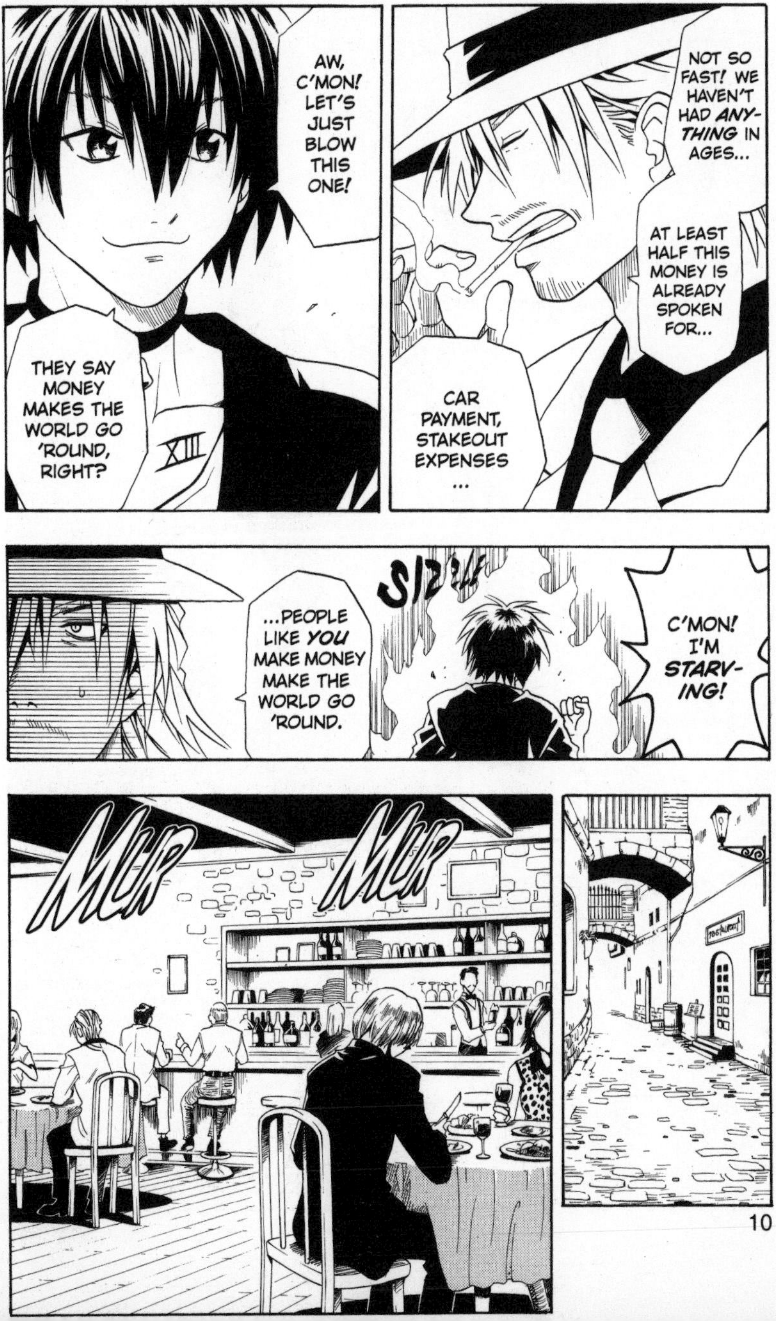
NOT SO FAST! WE HAVEN'T HAD *ANYTHING* IN AGES...
AT LEAST HALF THIS MONEY IS ALREADY SPOKEN FOR...
CAR PAYMENT, STAKEOUT EXPENSES ...
AW, C'MON! LET'S JUST BLOW THIS ONE!
THEY SAY MONEY MAKES THE WORLD GO 'ROUND, RIGHT?
C'MON! I'M *STARVING!*
...PEOPLE LIKE *YOU* MAKE MONEY MAKE THE WORLD GO 'ROUND.
MUR
MUR

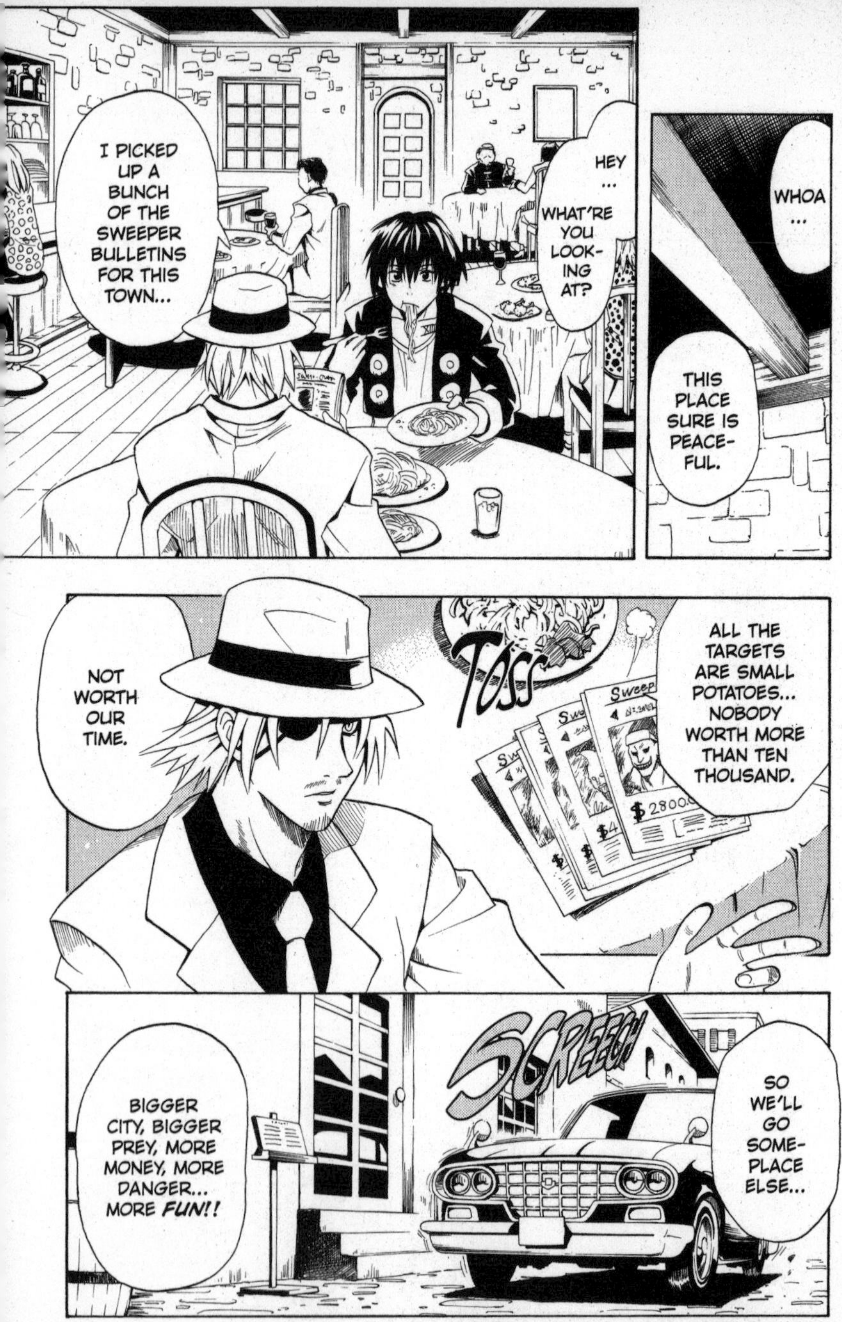
WHOA ...
THIS PLACE SURE IS PEACEFUL.
HEY ... WHAT'RE YOU LOOKING AT?
I PICKED UP A BUNCH OF THE SWEEPER BULLETINS FOR THIS TOWN...
ALL THE TARGETS ARE SMALL POTATOES... NOBODY WORTH MORE THAN TEN THOUSAND.
TOSS
NOT WORTH OUR TIME.
SCREECH
SO WE'LL GO SOMEPLACE ELSE...
BIGGER CITY, BIGGER PREY, MORE MONEY, MORE DANGER... MORE *FUN!!*

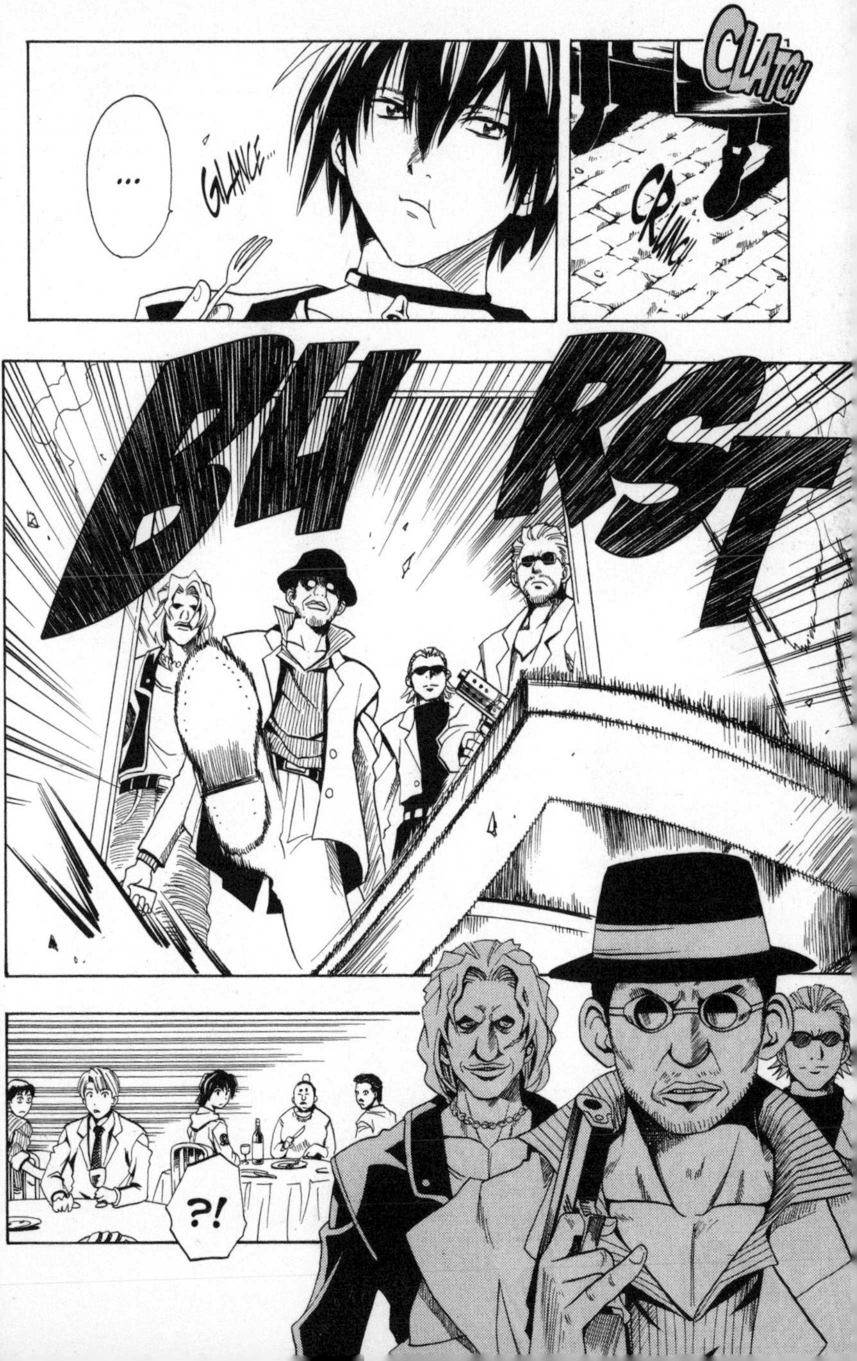
CLATCH
CRUNCH
GLANCE...
...
BURST
?!

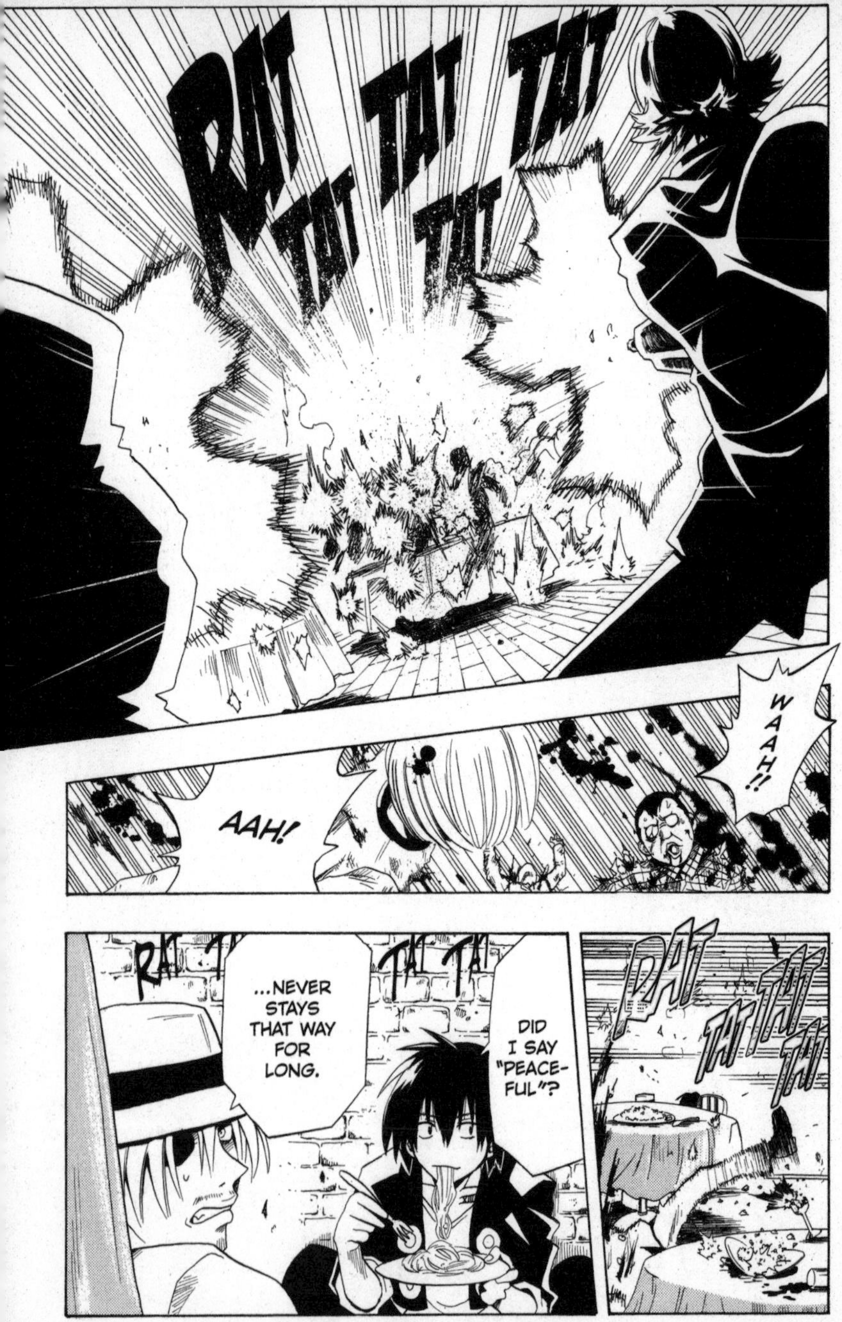
RAT TAT TAT TAT TAT TAT
WAAAH!!
AAH!
RAT TAT TAT TAT
DID I SAY "PEACE-FUL"?
...NEVER STAYS THAT WAY FOR LONG.

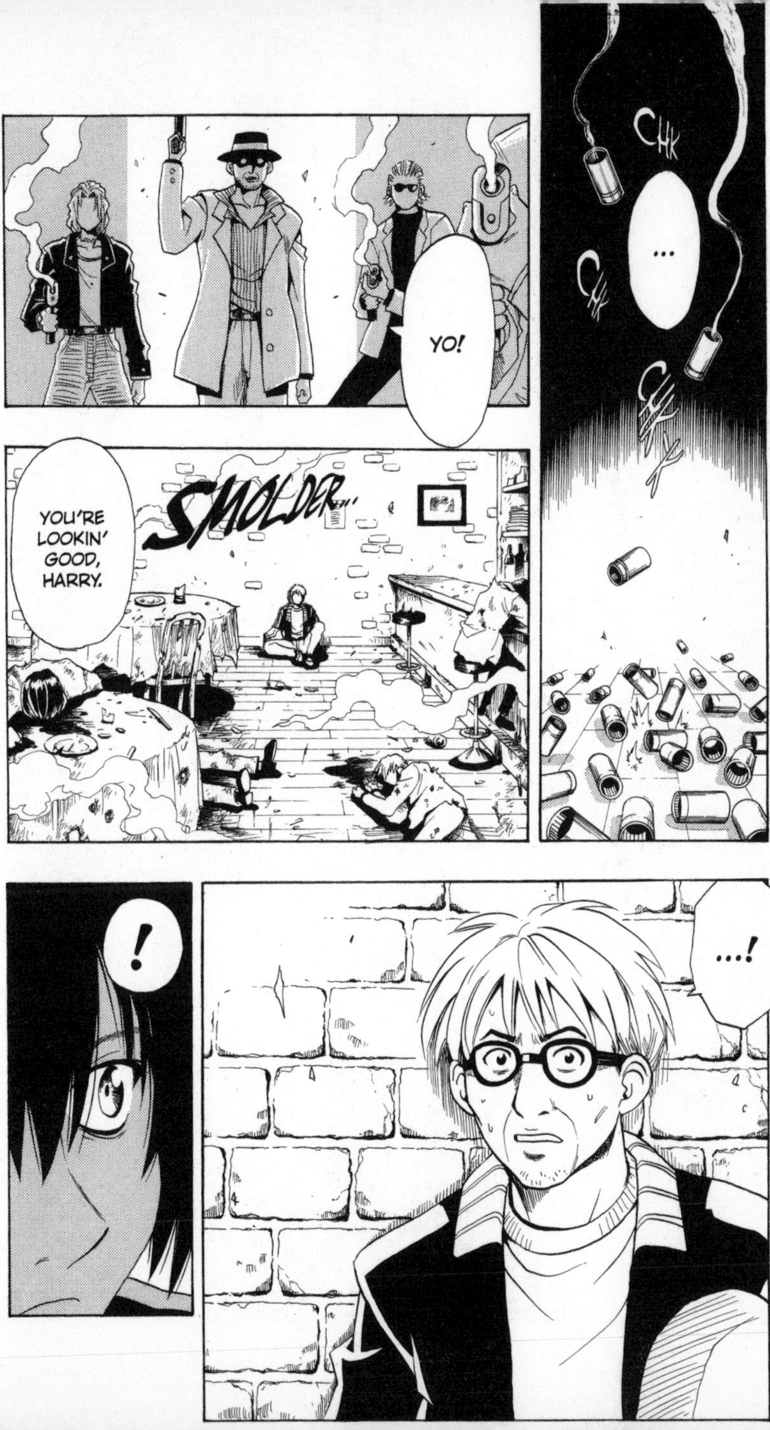
CHK
...
CHK
CHKKK
YO!
YOU'RE LOOKIN' GOOD, HARRY.
SMOLDER...
...!
!

READ THIS WAY

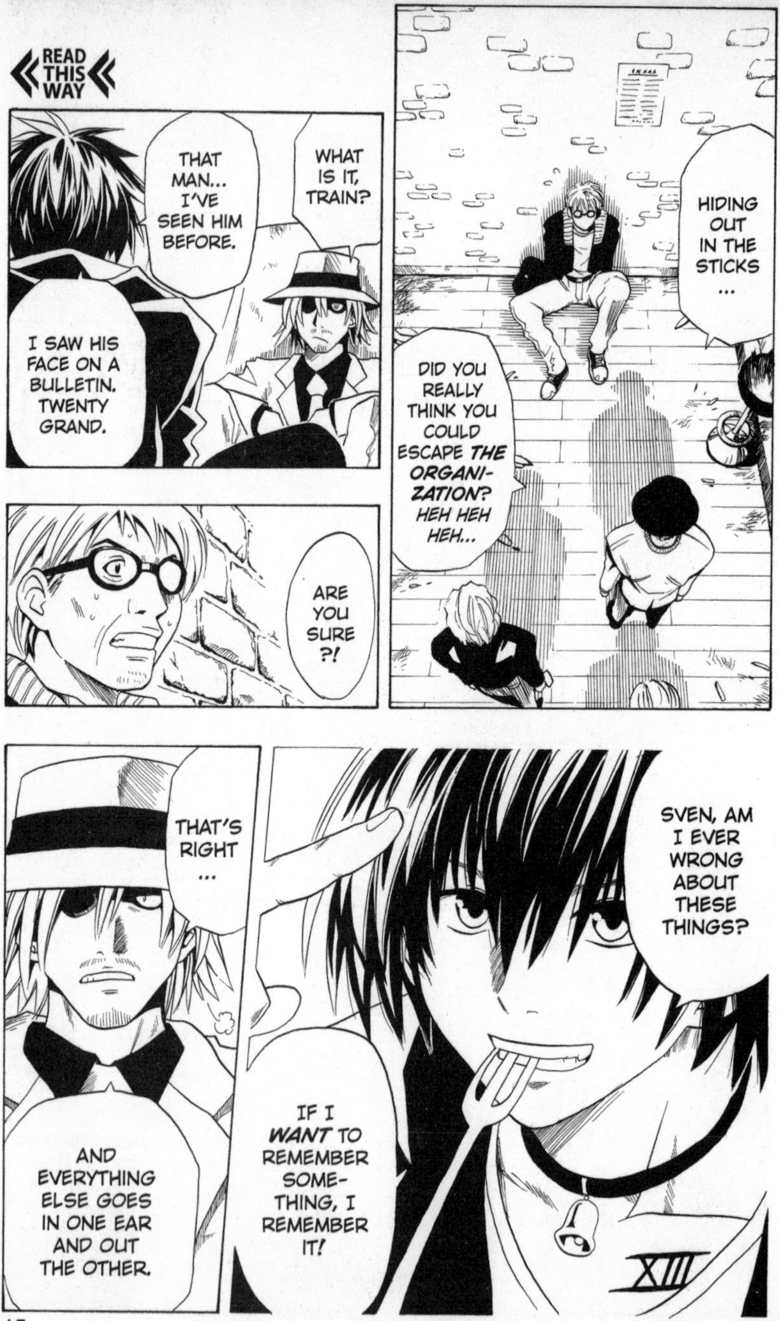
HIDING OUT IN THE STICKS...
DID YOU REALLY THINK YOU COULD ESCAPE *THE ORGANIZATION?* *HEH HEH HEH...*
WHAT IS IT, TRAIN?
THAT MAN... I'VE SEEN HIM BEFORE.
I SAW HIS FACE ON A BULLETIN. TWENTY GRAND.
ARE YOU SURE?!
SVEN, AM I EVER WRONG ABOUT THESE THINGS?
IF I *WANT* TO REMEMBER SOME-THING, I REMEMBER IT!
THAT'S RIGHT...
AND EVERYTHING ELSE GOES IN ONE EAR AND OUT THE OTHER.
XIII

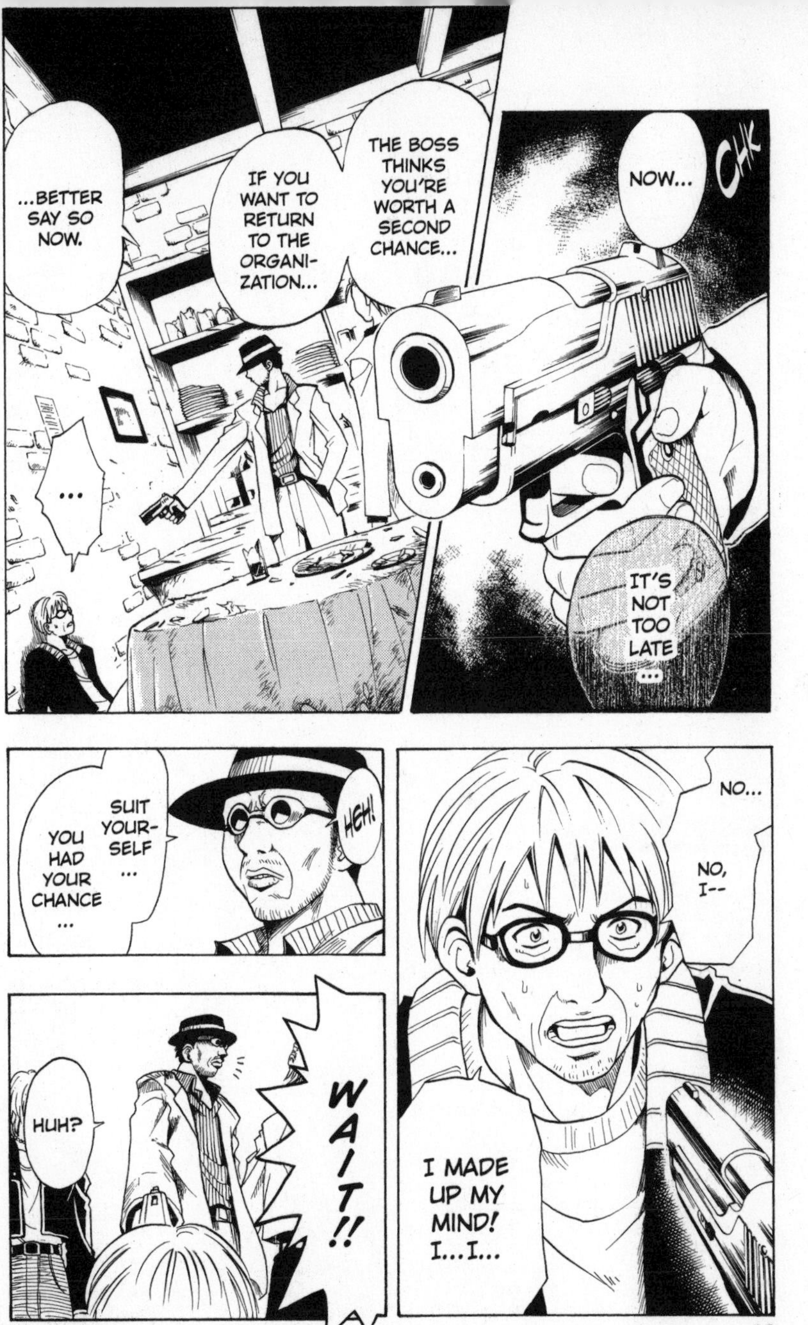
NOW...
CHK
IT'S NOT TOO LATE...
THE BOSS THINKS YOU'RE WORTH A SECOND CHANCE...
IF YOU WANT TO RETURN TO THE ORGANIZATION...
...BETTER SAY SO NOW.
...
NO...
NO, I--
I MADE UP MY MIND! I...I...
HEH!
SUIT YOURSELF...
YOU HAD YOUR CHANCE...
WAIT!!
HUH?

READ THIS WAY

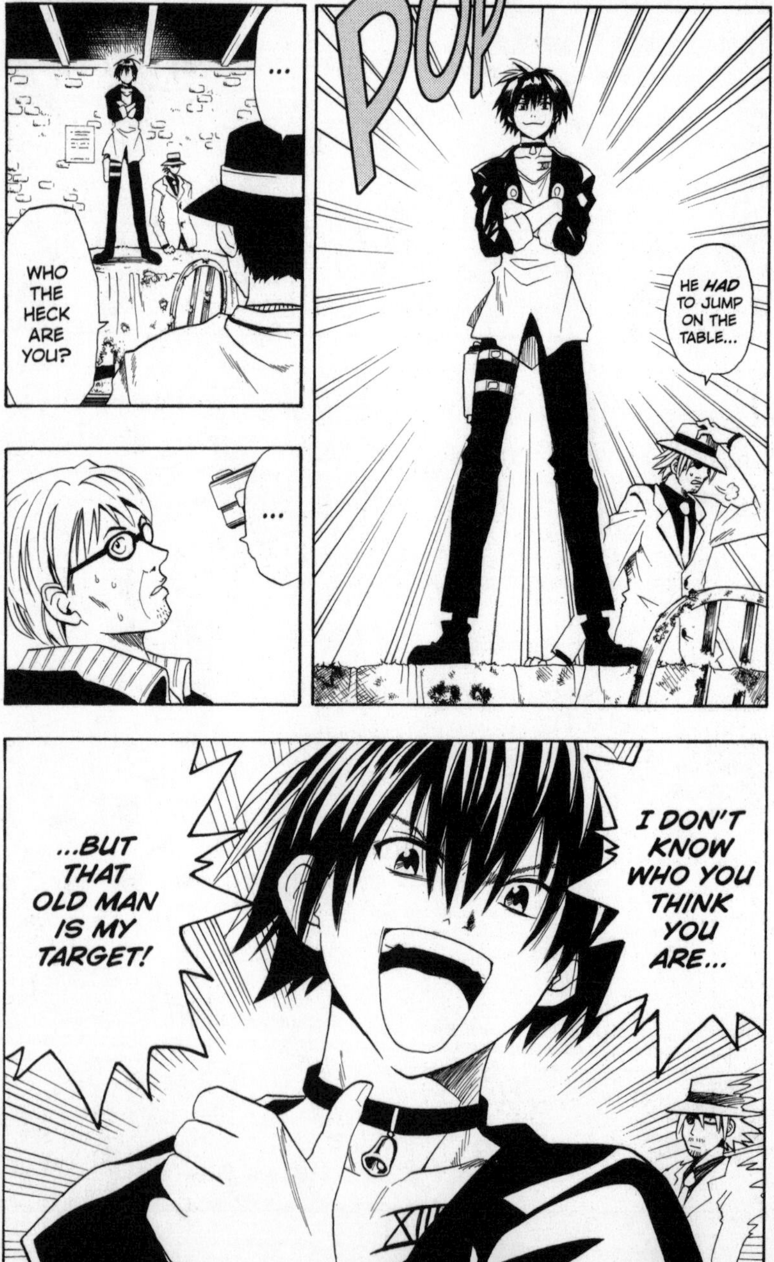
POP
HE *HAD* TO JUMP ON THE TABLE...
...
WHO THE HECK ARE YOU?
...
I DON'T KNOW WHO YOU THINK YOU ARE...
...BUT THAT OLD MAN IS MY TARGET!

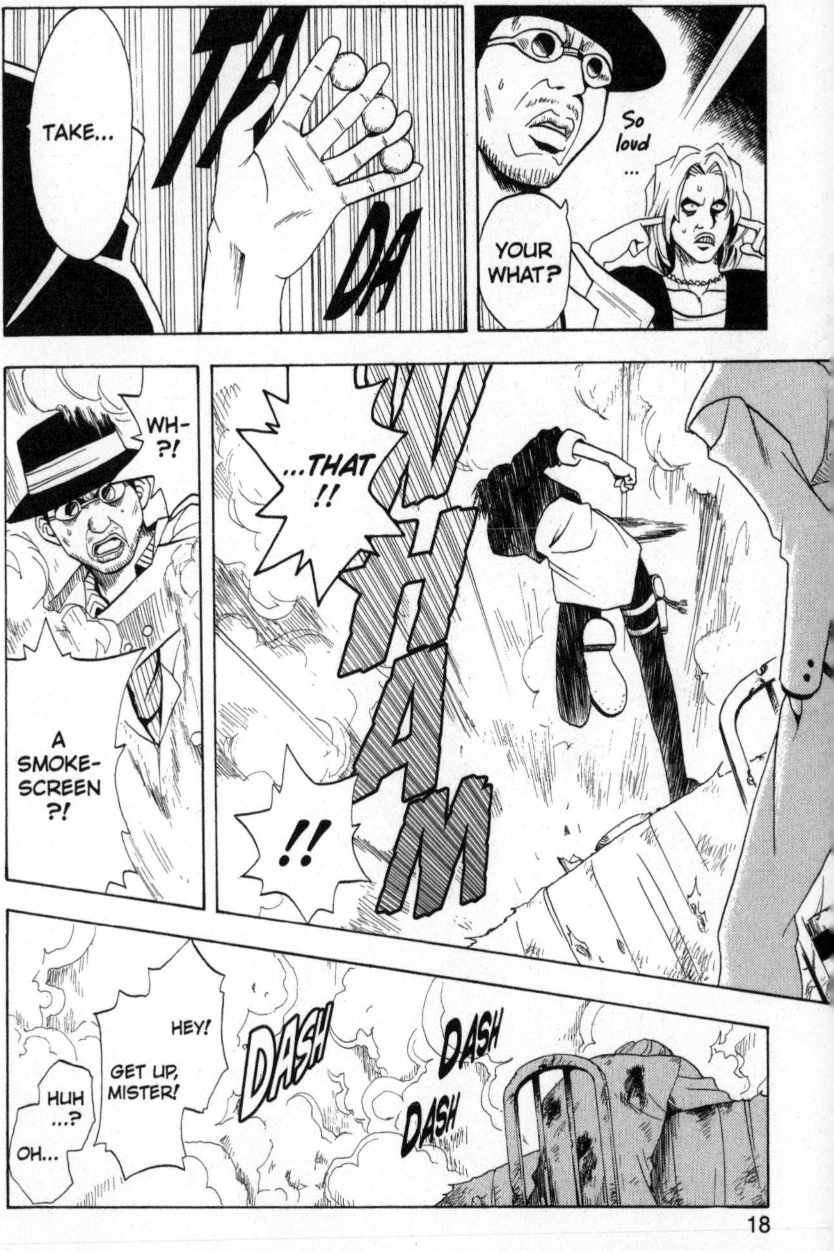
So loud ...
YOUR WHAT?
TA
TAKE...
DA
...THAT!!
WHAM
!!
WH-?!
A SMOKE-SCREEN?!
DASH
DASH
DASH
HEY!
GET UP, MISTER!
HUH ...?
OH...

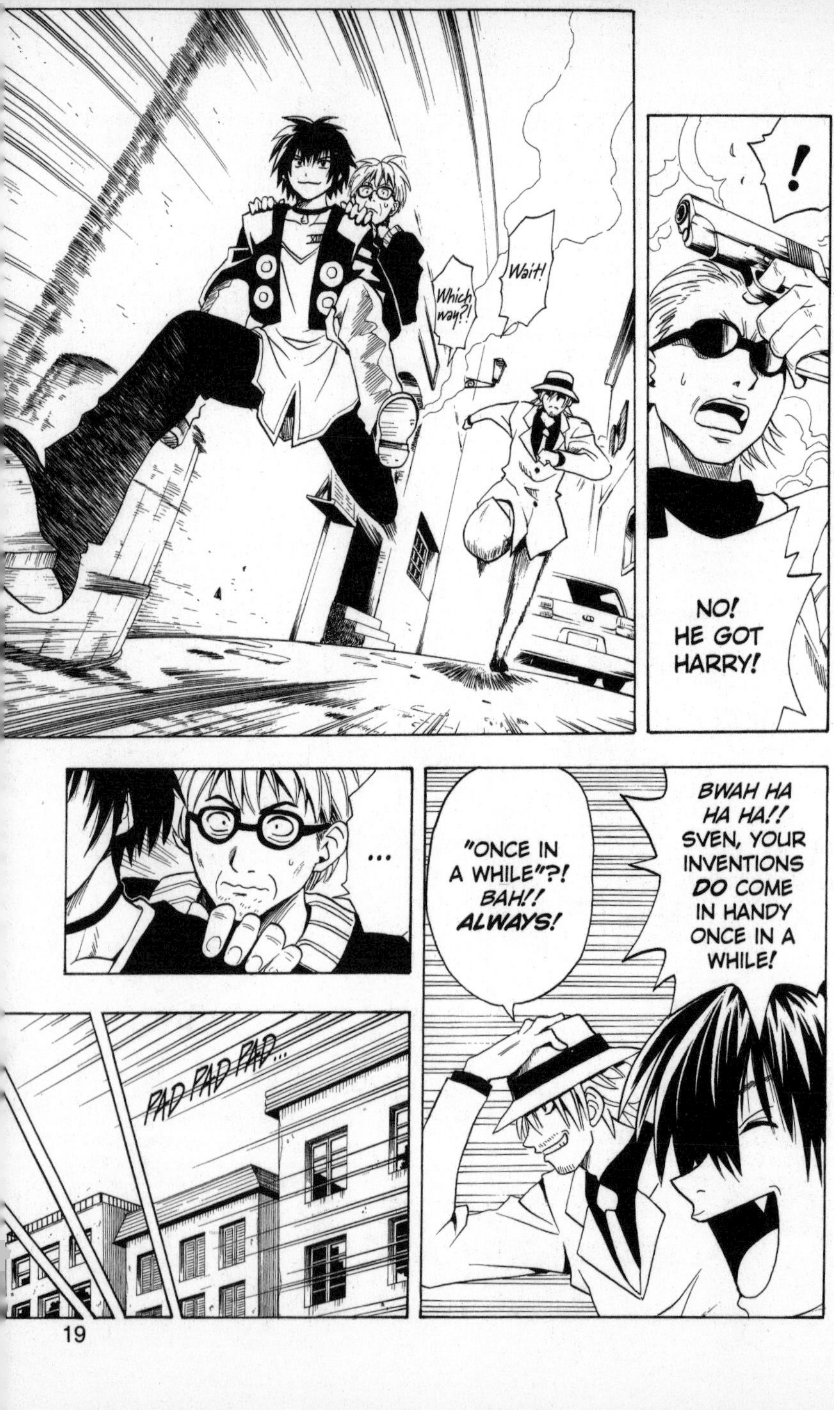
!
NO! HE GOT HARRY!
Wait!
Which way?!
BWAH HA HA HA!! SVEN, YOUR INVENTIONS DO COME IN HANDY ONCE IN A WHILE!
"ONCE IN A WHILE"?! BAH!! ALWAYS!
...
PAD PAD PAD...

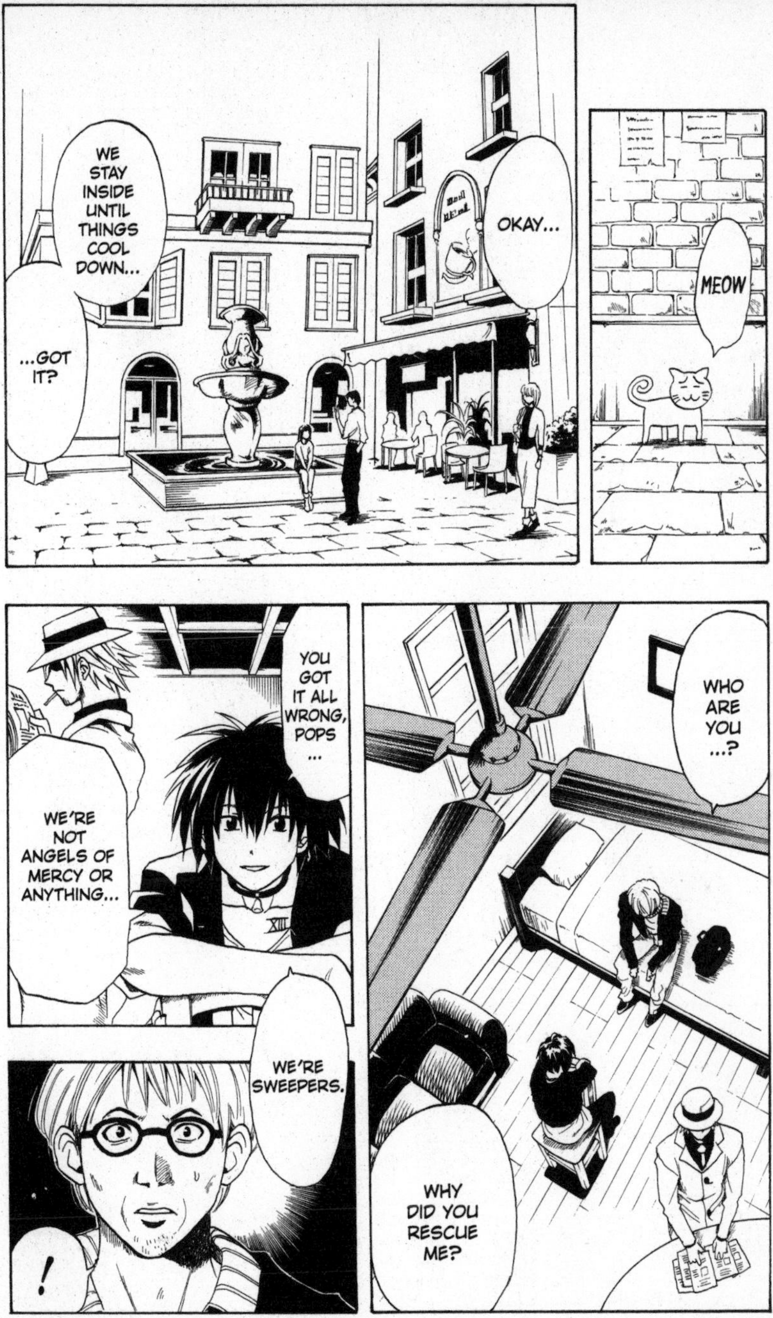
MEOW
OKAY...
WE STAY INSIDE UNTIL THINGS COOL DOWN...
...GOT IT?
WHO ARE YOU ...?
WHY DID YOU RESCUE ME?
YOU GOT IT ALL WRONG, POPS ...
WE'RE NOT ANGELS OF MERCY OR ANYTHING...
WE'RE SWEEPERS.
!

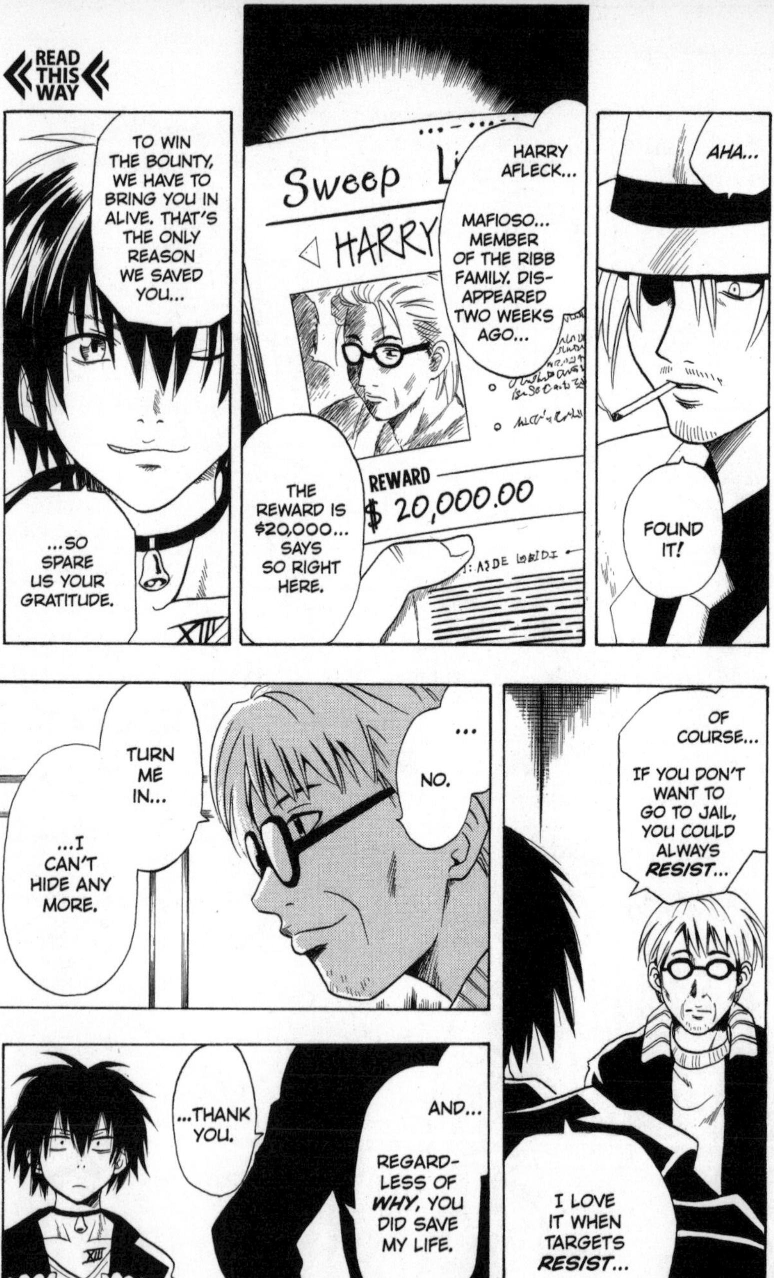
READ THIS WAY
AHA...
FOUND IT!
HARRY AFLECK...
MAFIOSO... MEMBER OF THE RIBB FAMILY. DIS-APPEARED TWO WEEKS AGO...
HARRY
REWARD
$ 20,000.00
THE REWARD IS $20,000... SAYS SO RIGHT HERE.
TO WIN THE BOUNTY, WE HAVE TO BRING YOU IN ALIVE. THAT'S THE ONLY REASON WE SAVED YOU...
...SO SPARE US YOUR GRATITUDE.
OF COURSE...
IF YOU DON'T WANT TO GO TO JAIL, YOU COULD ALWAYS *RESIST*...
I LOVE IT WHEN TARGETS *RESIST*...
...
NO.
TURN ME IN...
...I CAN'T HIDE ANY MORE.
AND...
REGARD-LESS OF *WHY*, YOU DID SAVE MY LIFE.
...THANK YOU.

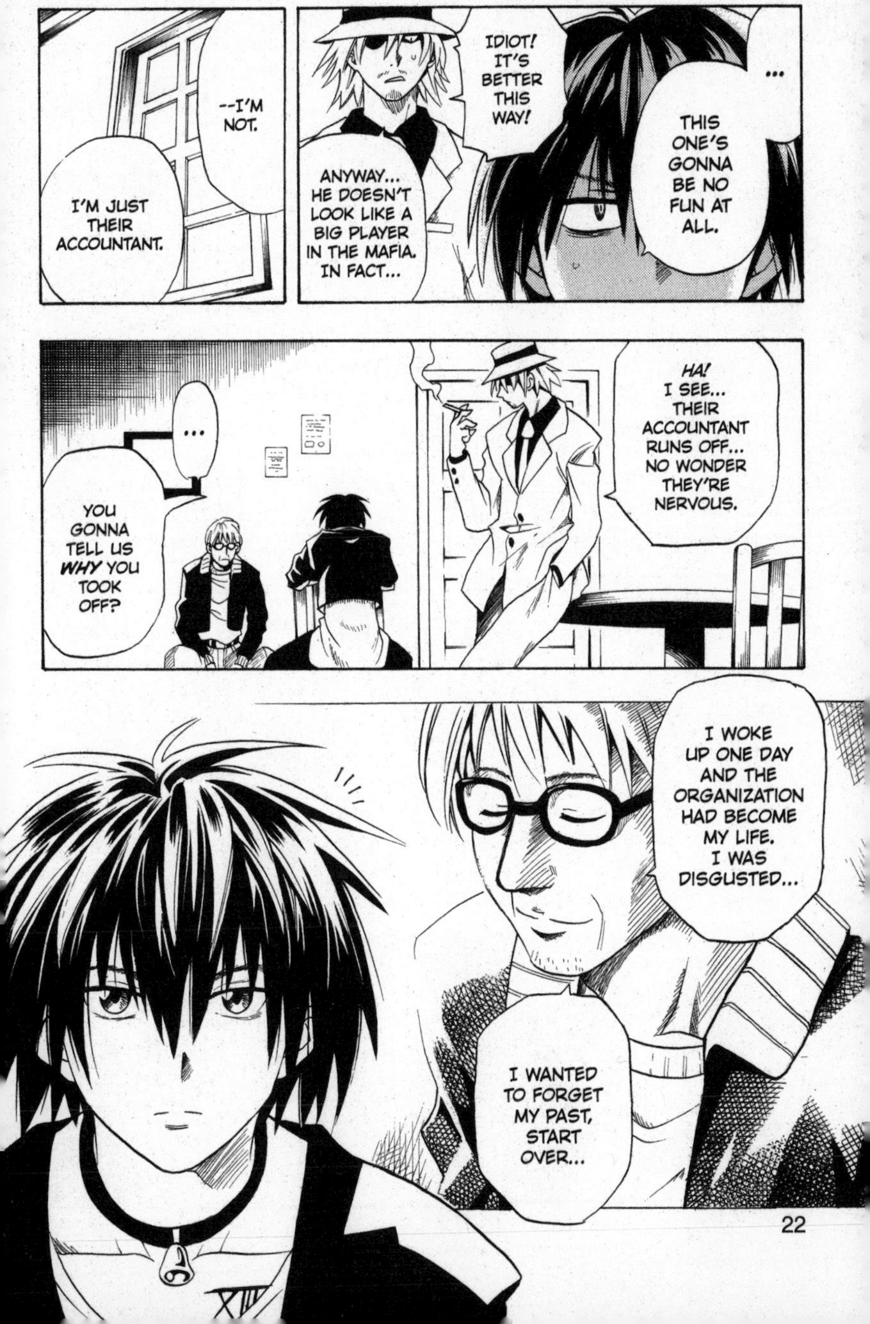
...
THIS ONE'S GONNA BE NO FUN AT ALL.
IDIOT! IT'S BETTER THIS WAY!
ANYWAY... HE DOESN'T LOOK LIKE A BIG PLAYER IN THE MAFIA. IN FACT...
--I'M NOT.
I'M JUST THEIR ACCOUNTANT.
HA! I SEE... THEIR ACCOUNTANT RUNS OFF... NO WONDER THEY'RE NERVOUS.
...
YOU GONNA TELL US *WHY* YOU TOOK OFF?
I WOKE UP ONE DAY AND THE ORGANIZATION HAD BECOME MY LIFE. I WAS DISGUSTED...
I WANTED TO FORGET MY PAST, START OVER...

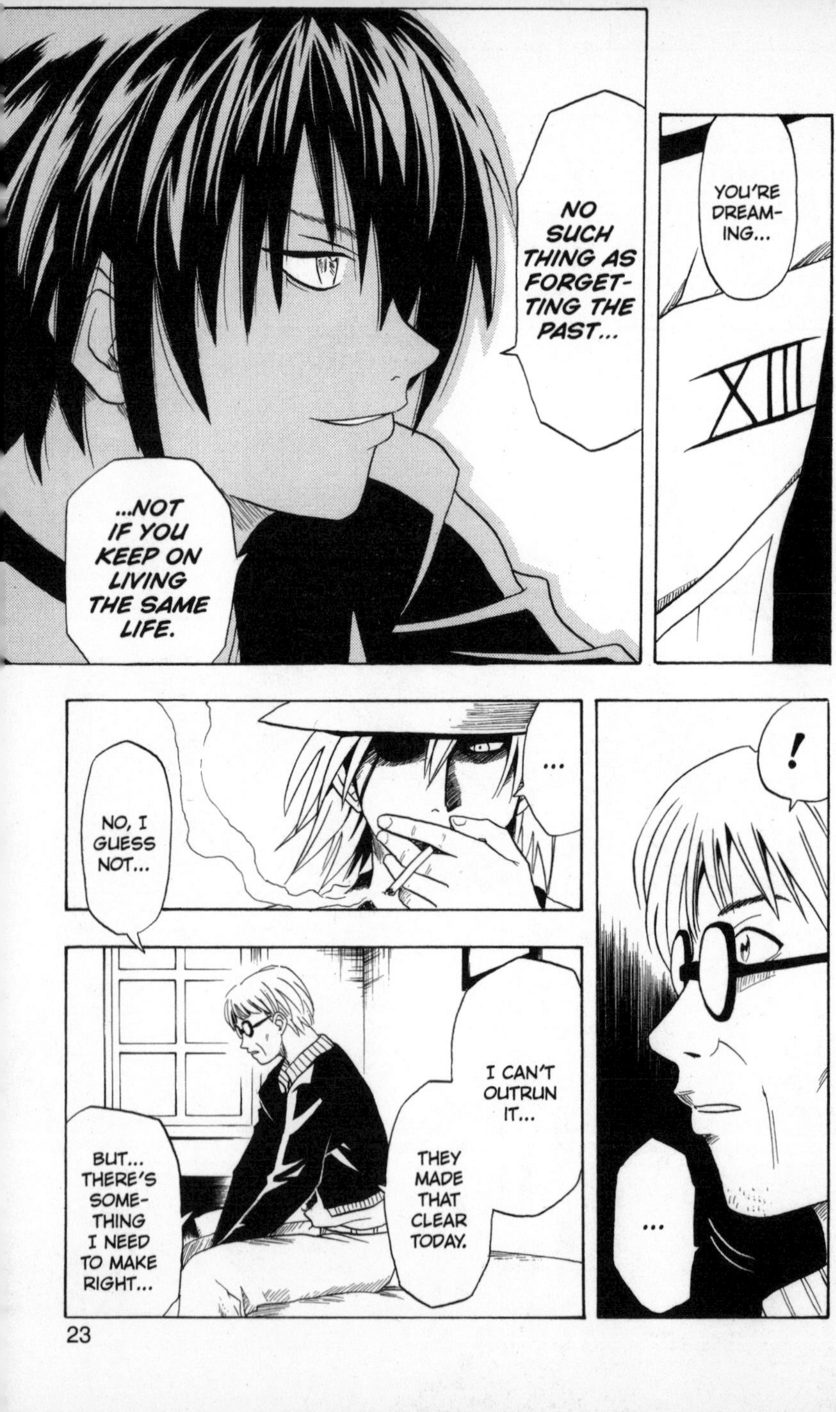
YOU'RE DREAMING...
NO SUCH THING AS FORGETTING THE PAST...
...NOT IF YOU KEEP ON LIVING THE SAME LIFE.
!
...
...
NO, I GUESS NOT...
I CAN'T OUTRUN IT...
THEY MADE THAT CLEAR TODAY.
BUT... THERE'S SOMETHING I NEED TO MAKE RIGHT...

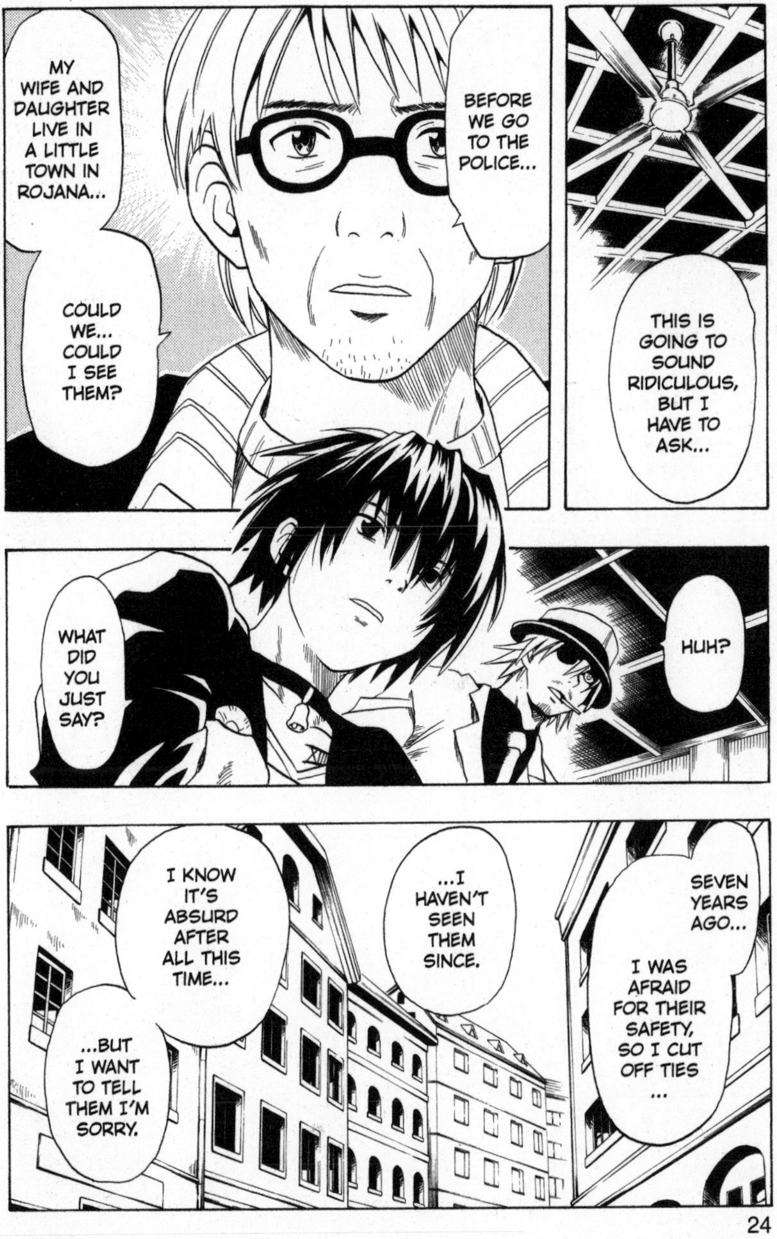
THIS IS GOING TO SOUND RIDICULOUS, BUT I HAVE TO ASK...
BEFORE WE GO TO THE POLICE...
MY WIFE AND DAUGHTER LIVE IN A LITTLE TOWN IN ROJANA...
COULD WE... COULD I SEE THEM?
HUH?
WHAT DID YOU JUST SAY?
SEVEN YEARS AGO...
I WAS AFRAID FOR THEIR SAFETY, SO I CUT OFF TIES ...
...I HAVEN'T SEEN THEM SINCE.
I KNOW IT'S ABSURD AFTER ALL THIS TIME...
...BUT I WANT TO TELL THEM I'M SORRY.

READ THIS WAY

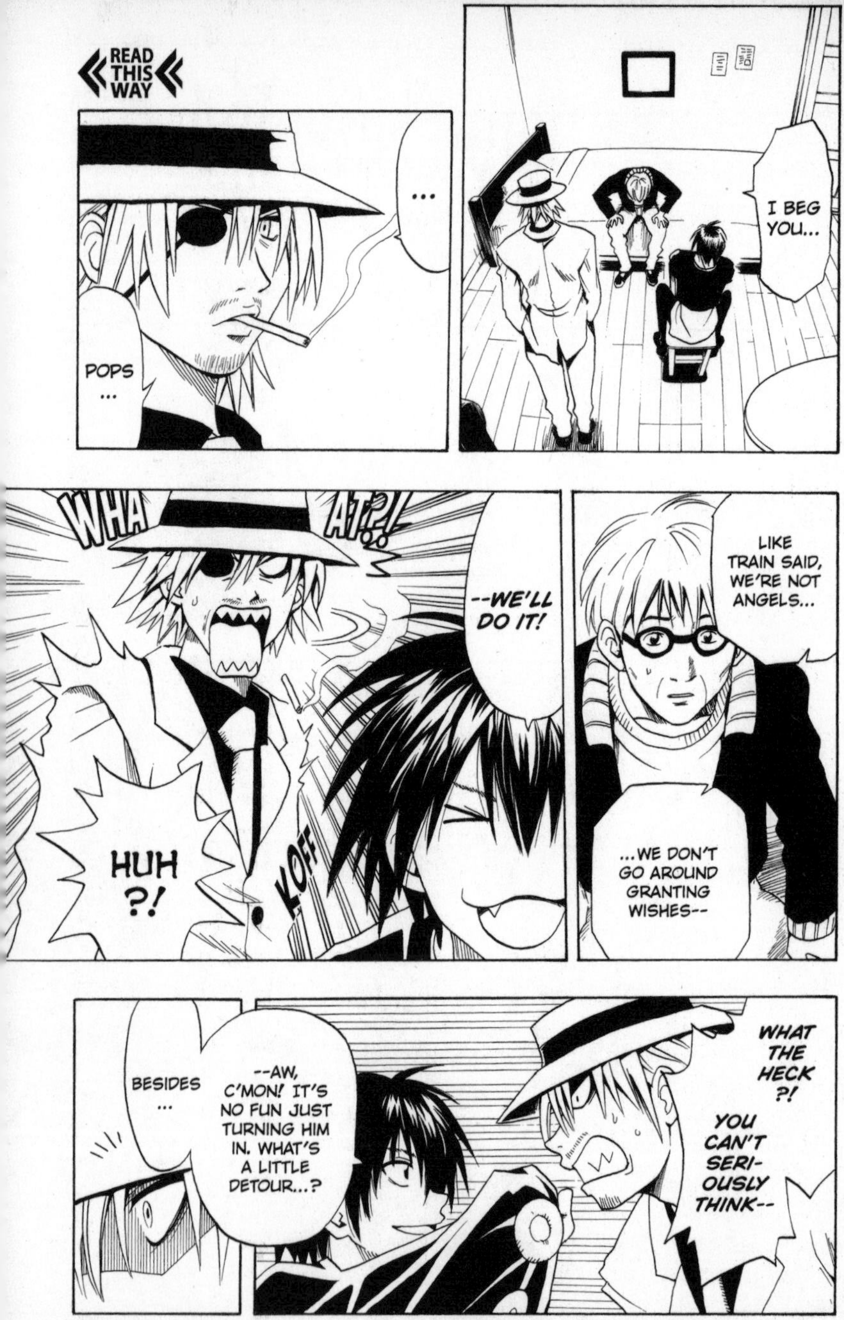
I BEG YOU...
...
POPS ...
LIKE TRAIN SAID, WE'RE NOT ANGELS...
...WE DON'T GO AROUND GRANTING WISHES--
--WE'LL DO IT!
WHA AT?!
KOFF
HUH ?!
WHAT THE HECK ?!
YOU CAN'T SERI-OUSLY THINK--
--AW, C'MON! IT'S NO FUN JUST TURNING HIM IN. WHAT'S A LITTLE DETOUR...?
BESIDES ...

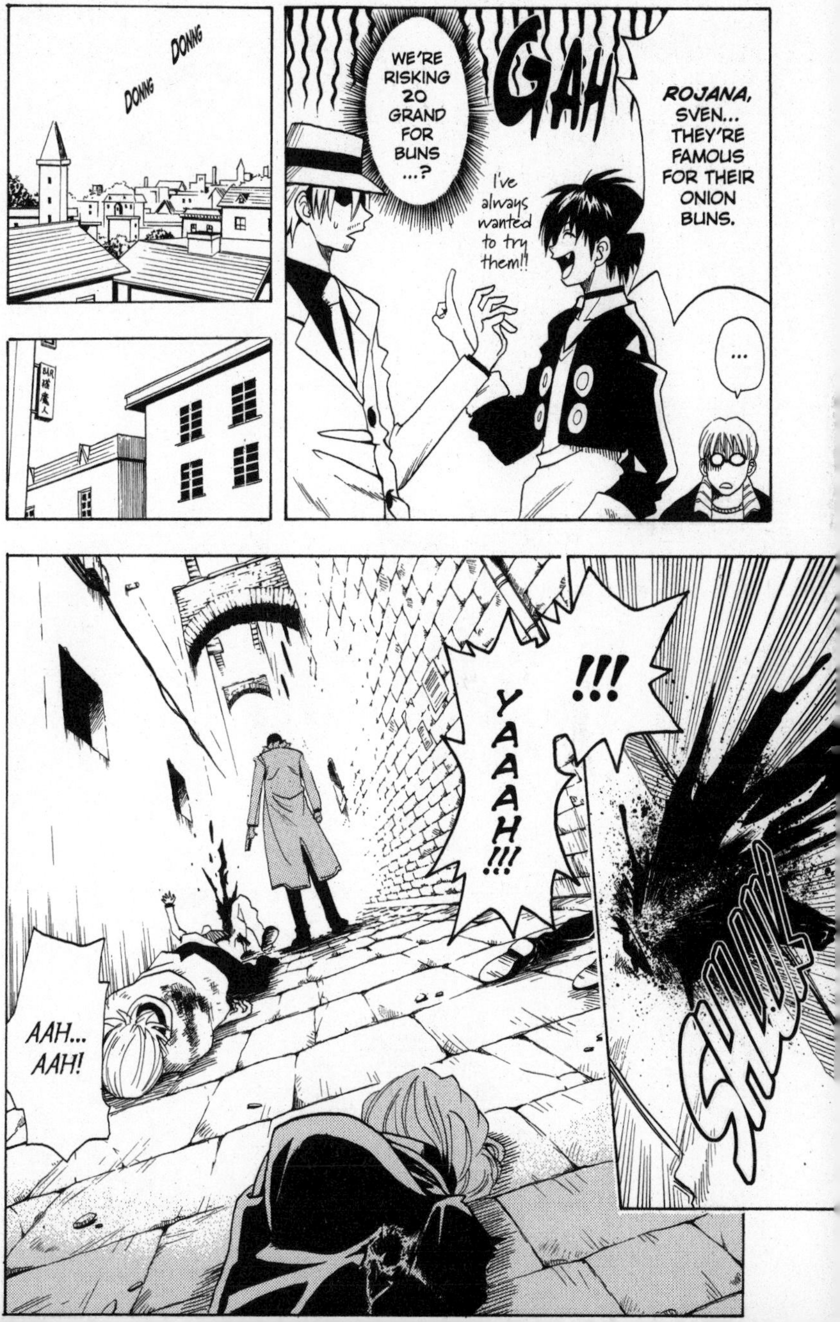
ROJANA, SVEN... THEY'RE FAMOUS FOR THEIR ONION BUNS.
GAH
WE'RE RISKING 20 GRAND FOR BUNS ...?
I've always wanted to try them!!
...
DONNG
DONNG
SHUNK
!!!
YAAAAH!!!
AAH... AAH!

READ THIS WAY

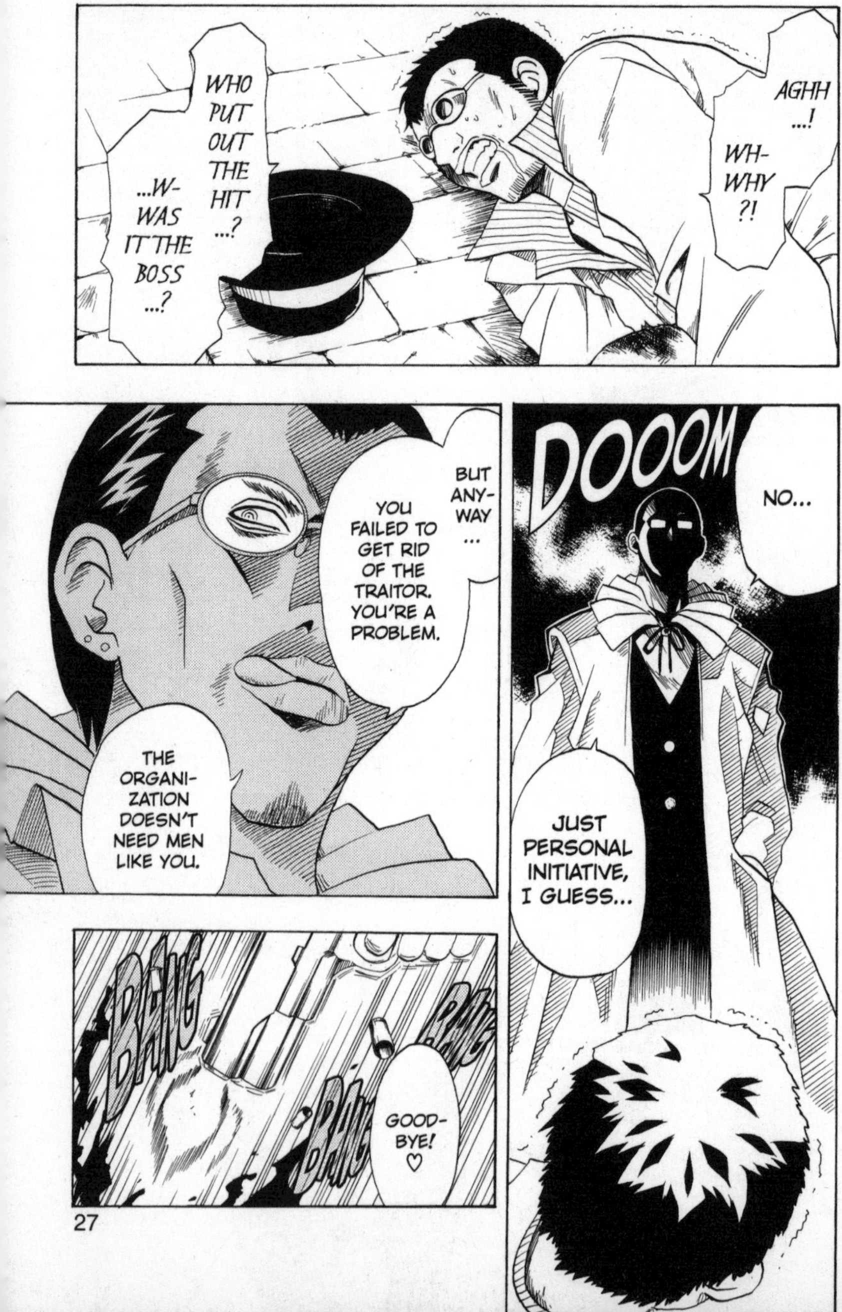
AGHH ...!
WH-WHY ?!
WHO PUT OUT THE HIT ...?
...W-WAS IT THE BOSS ...?
DOOOM
NO...
JUST PERSONAL INITIATIVE, I GUESS...
BUT ANYWAY ...
YOU FAILED TO GET RID OF THE TRAITOR. YOU'RE A PROBLEM.
THE ORGANIZATION DOESN'T NEED MEN LIKE YOU.
BANG
BANG
BANG
BANG
GOOD-BYE! ♡

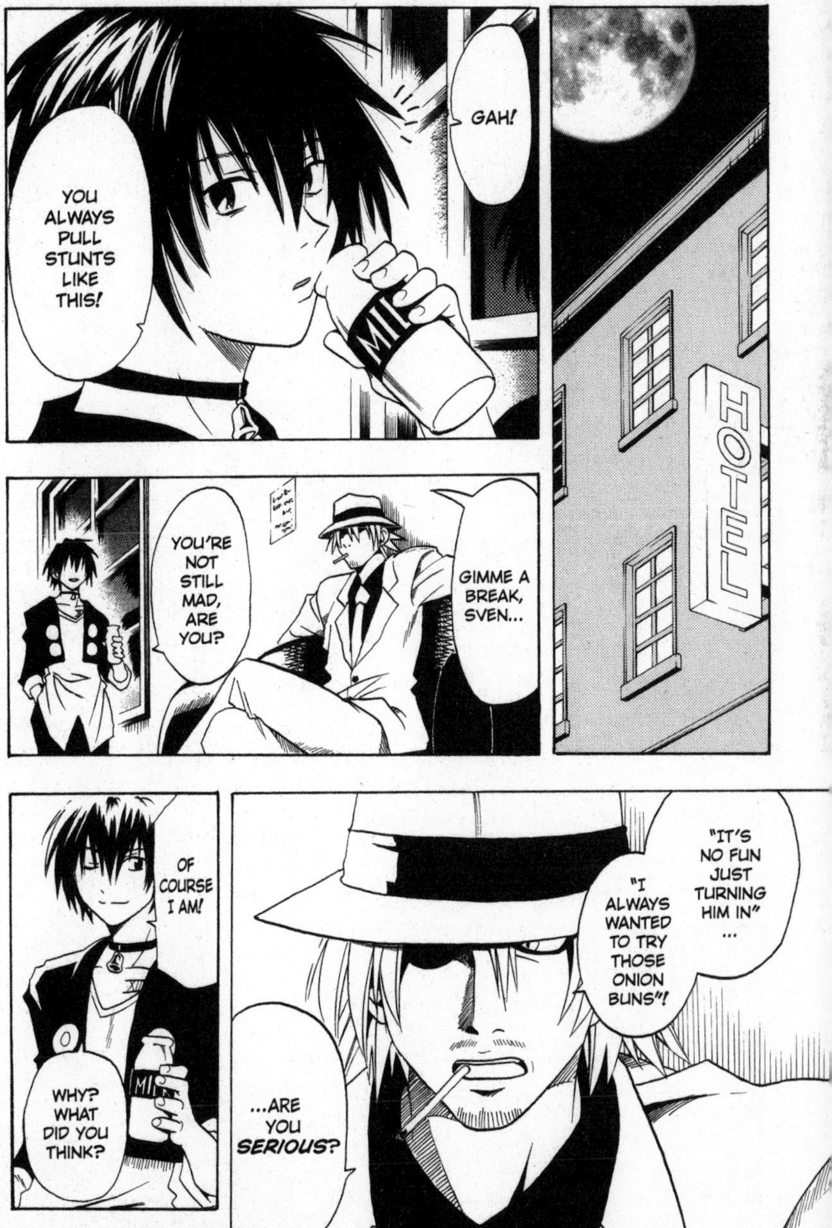
HOTEL
GAH!
YOU ALWAYS PULL STUNTS LIKE THIS!
GIMME A BREAK, SVEN...
YOU'RE NOT STILL MAD, ARE YOU?
"IT'S NO FUN JUST TURNING HIM IN"...
"I ALWAYS WANTED TO TRY THOSE ONION BUNS"!
...ARE YOU *SERIOUS?*
OF COURSE I AM!
WHY? WHAT DID YOU THINK?

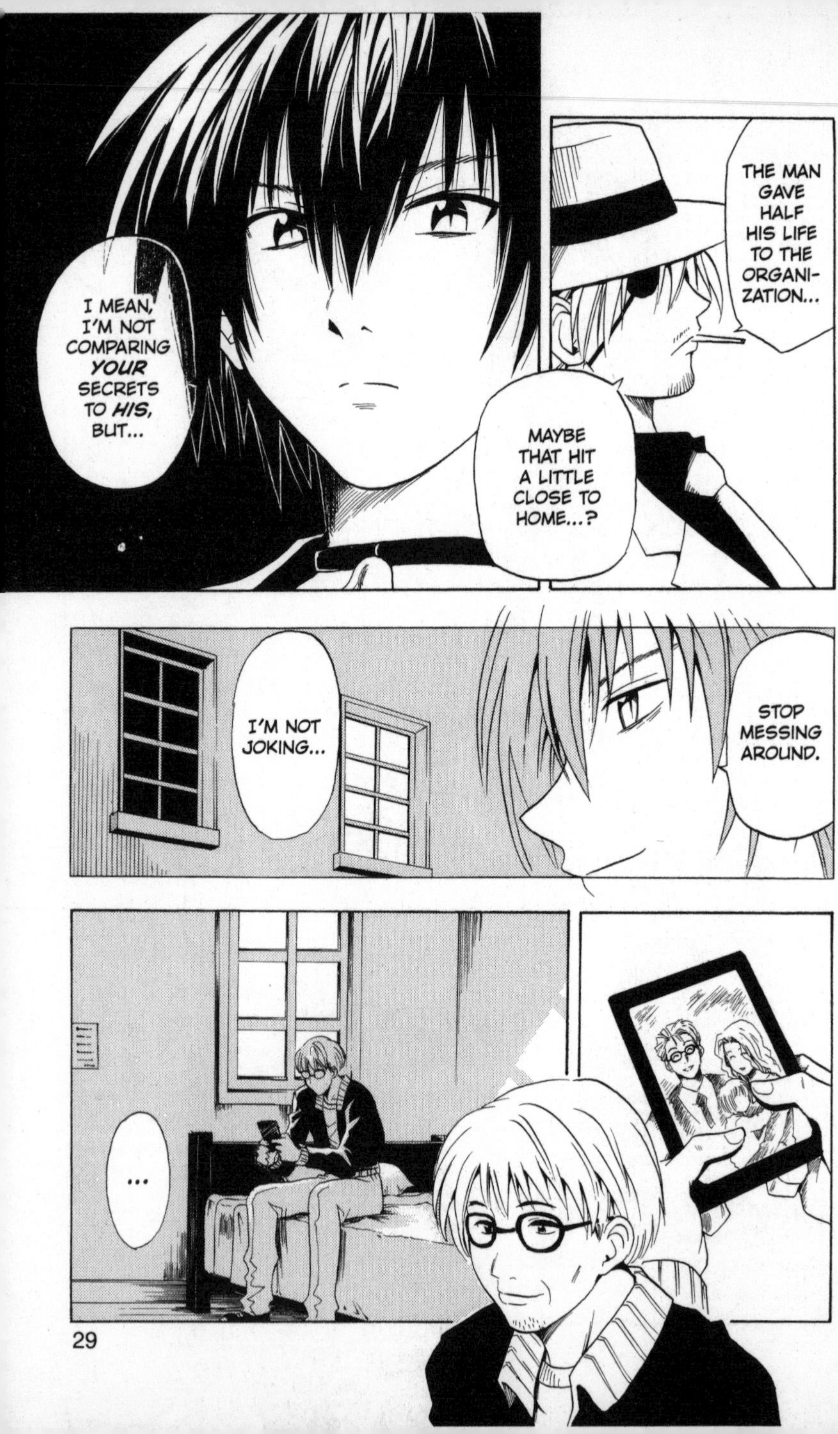
THE MAN GAVE HALF HIS LIFE TO THE ORGANIZATION...
MAYBE THAT HIT A LITTLE CLOSE TO HOME...?
I MEAN, I'M NOT COMPARING *YOUR* SECRETS TO *HIS*, BUT...
STOP MESSING AROUND.
I'M NOT JOKING...
...

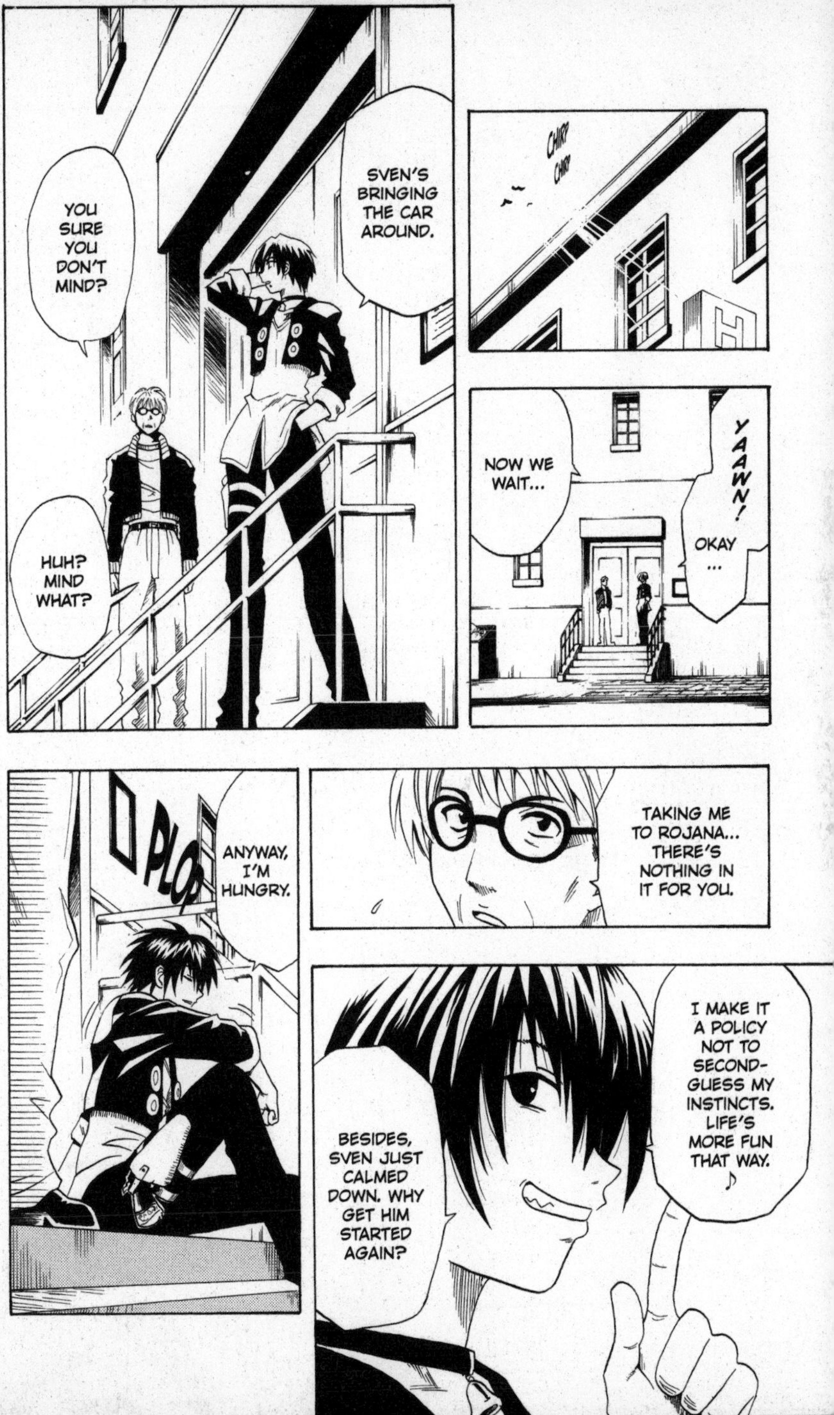
CHIRP
CHIRP
YAAWN!
NOW WE WAIT...
OKAY ...
SVEN'S BRINGING THE CAR AROUND.
YOU SURE YOU DON'T MIND?
HUH? MIND WHAT?
TAKING ME TO ROJANA... THERE'S NOTHING IN IT FOR YOU.
I MAKE IT A POLICY NOT TO SECOND-GUESS MY INSTINCTS. LIFE'S MORE FUN THAT WAY. ♪
BESIDES, SVEN JUST CALMED DOWN. WHY GET HIM STARTED AGAIN?
PLOP
ANYWAY, I'M HUNGRY.

READ THIS WAY

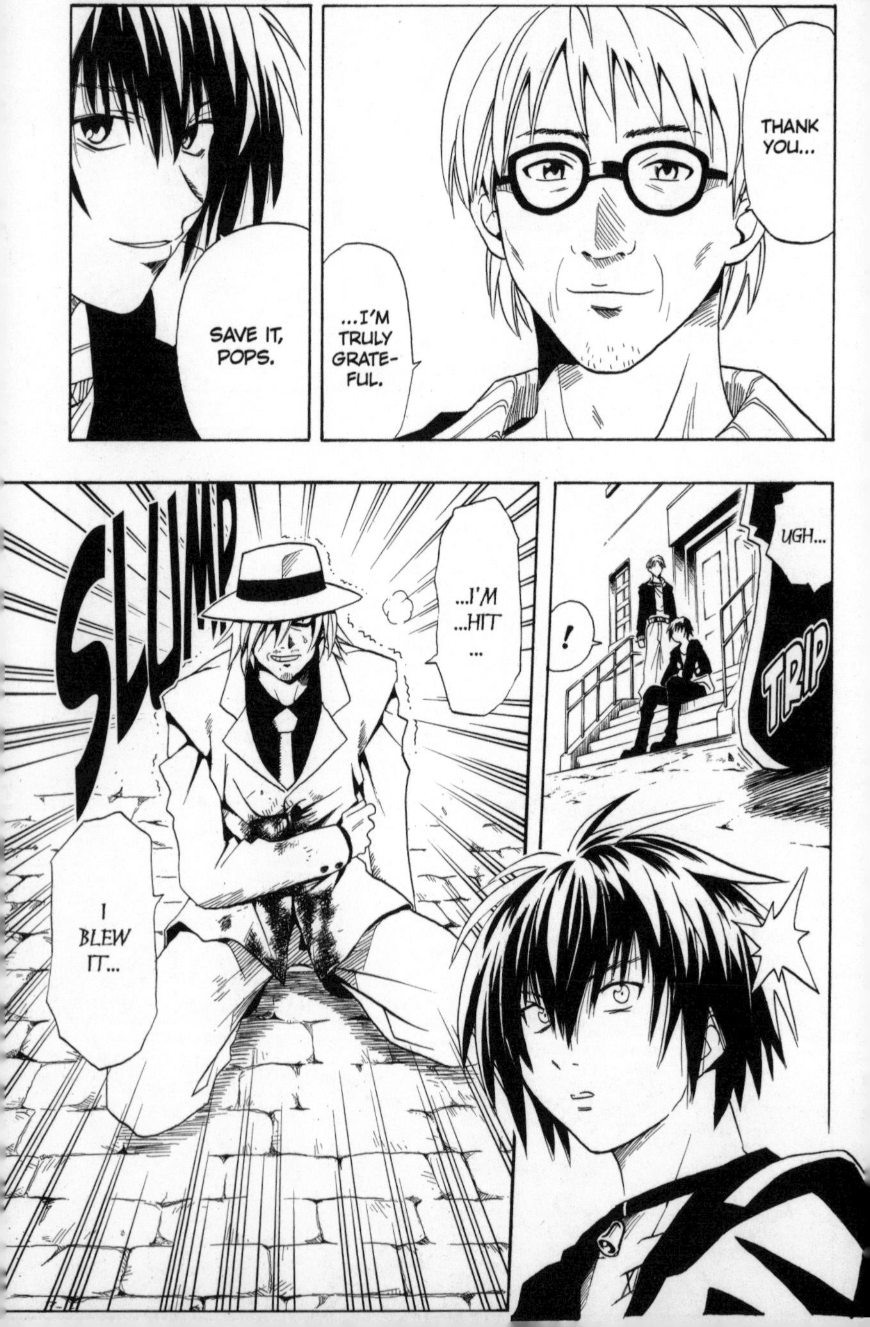
THANK YOU...
...I'M TRULY GRATEFUL.
SAVE IT, POPS.
UGH...
TRIP
!
SLUMP
...I'M ...HIT ...
I BLEW IT...

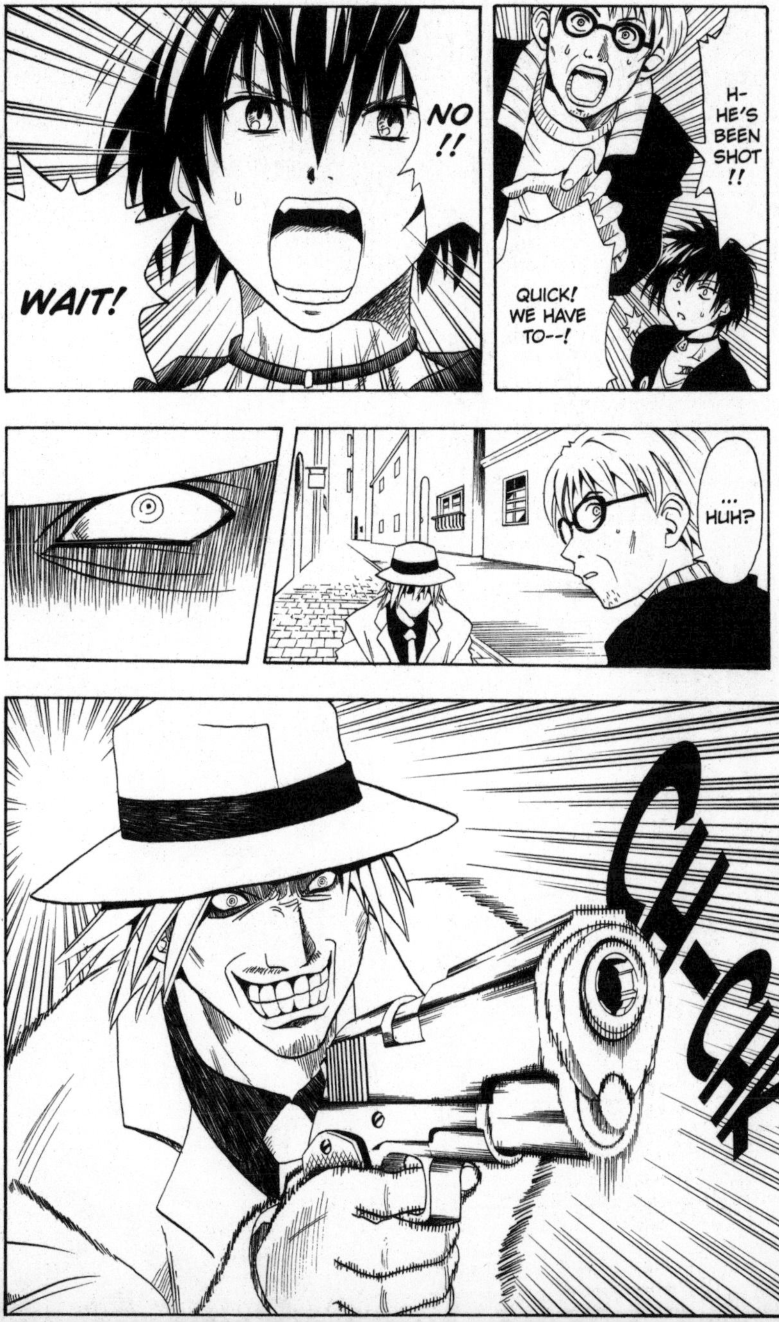
H- HE'S BEEN SHOT !!
QUICK! WE HAVE TO--!
NO !!
WAIT!
... HUH?
CH-CHK

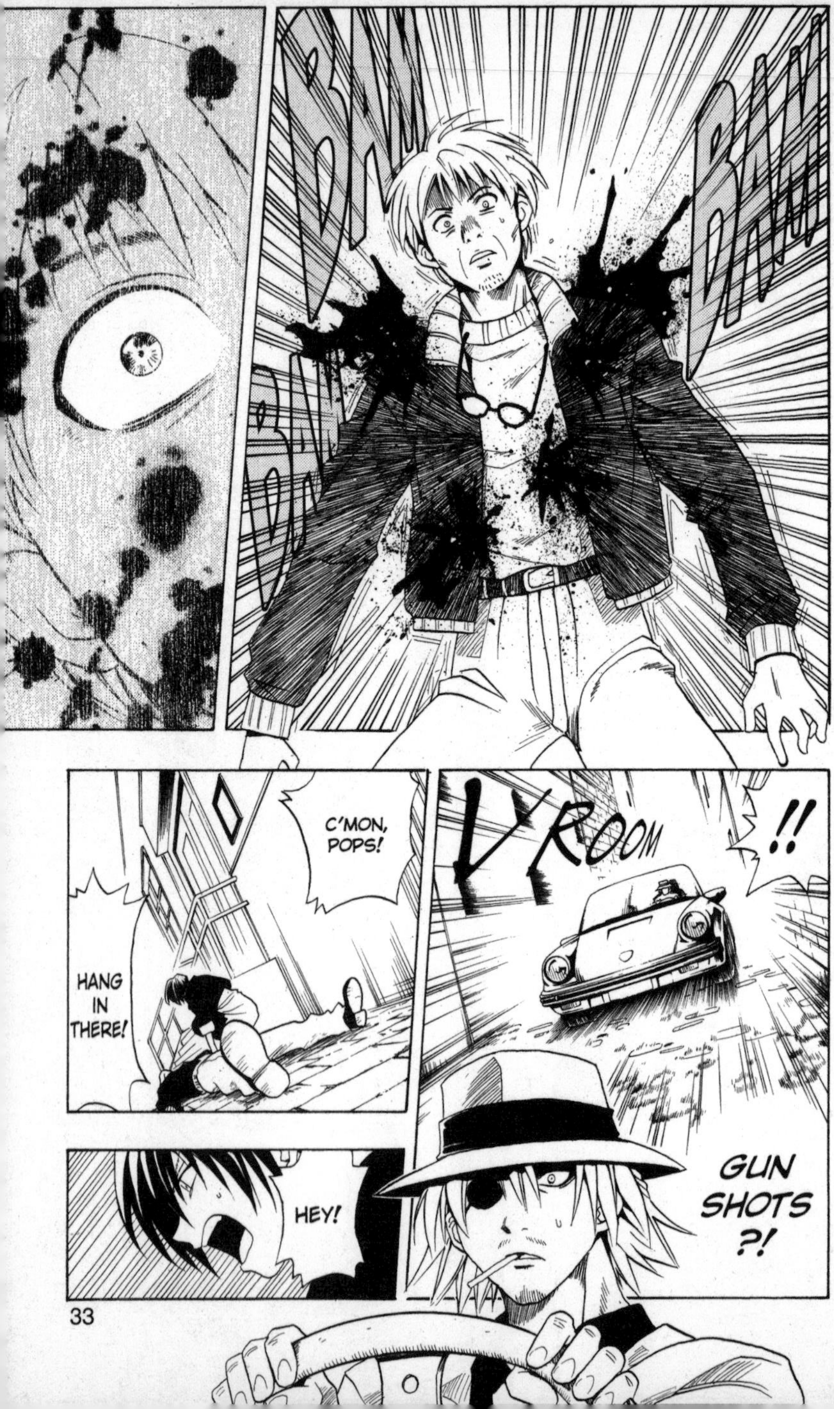
BAM
BAM
BAM
VROOM
!!
GUN SHOTS ?!
C'MON, POPS!
HANG IN THERE!
HEY!

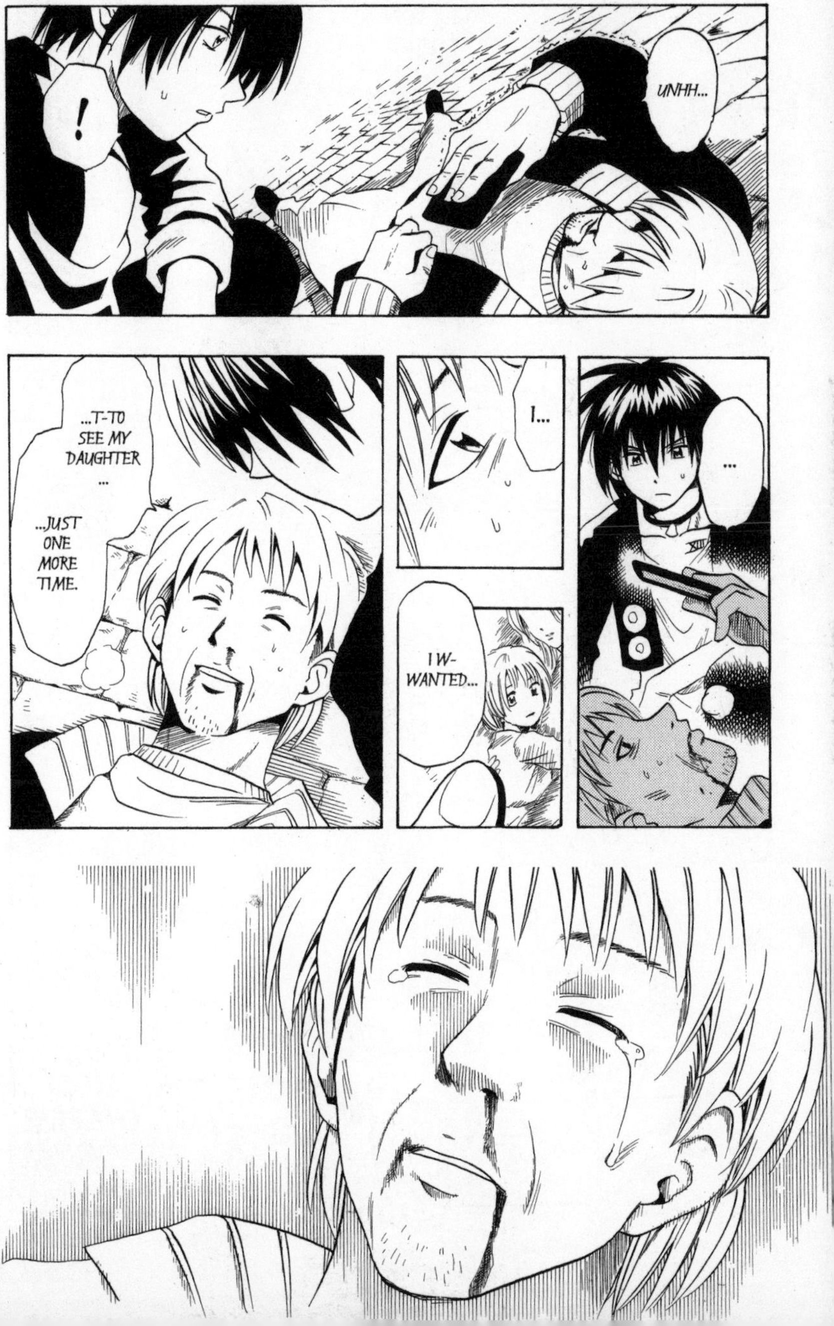
UNHH...
!
...
I...
I W-WANTED...
...T-TO SEE MY DAUGHTER ...
...JUST ONE MORE TIME.

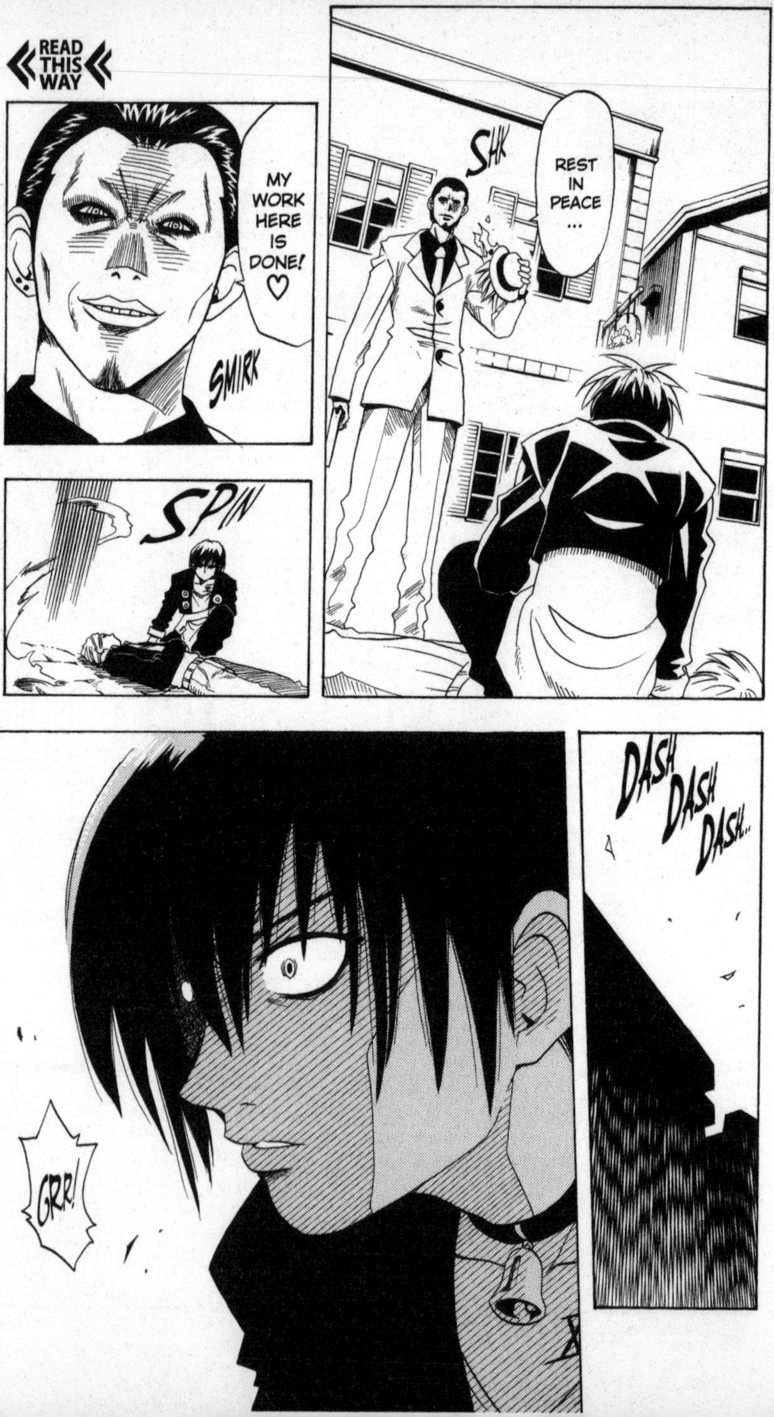
READ THIS WAY
SHK
REST IN PEACE ...
MY WORK HERE IS DONE! ♡
SMIRK
SPIN
DASH DASH DASH...
GRR!

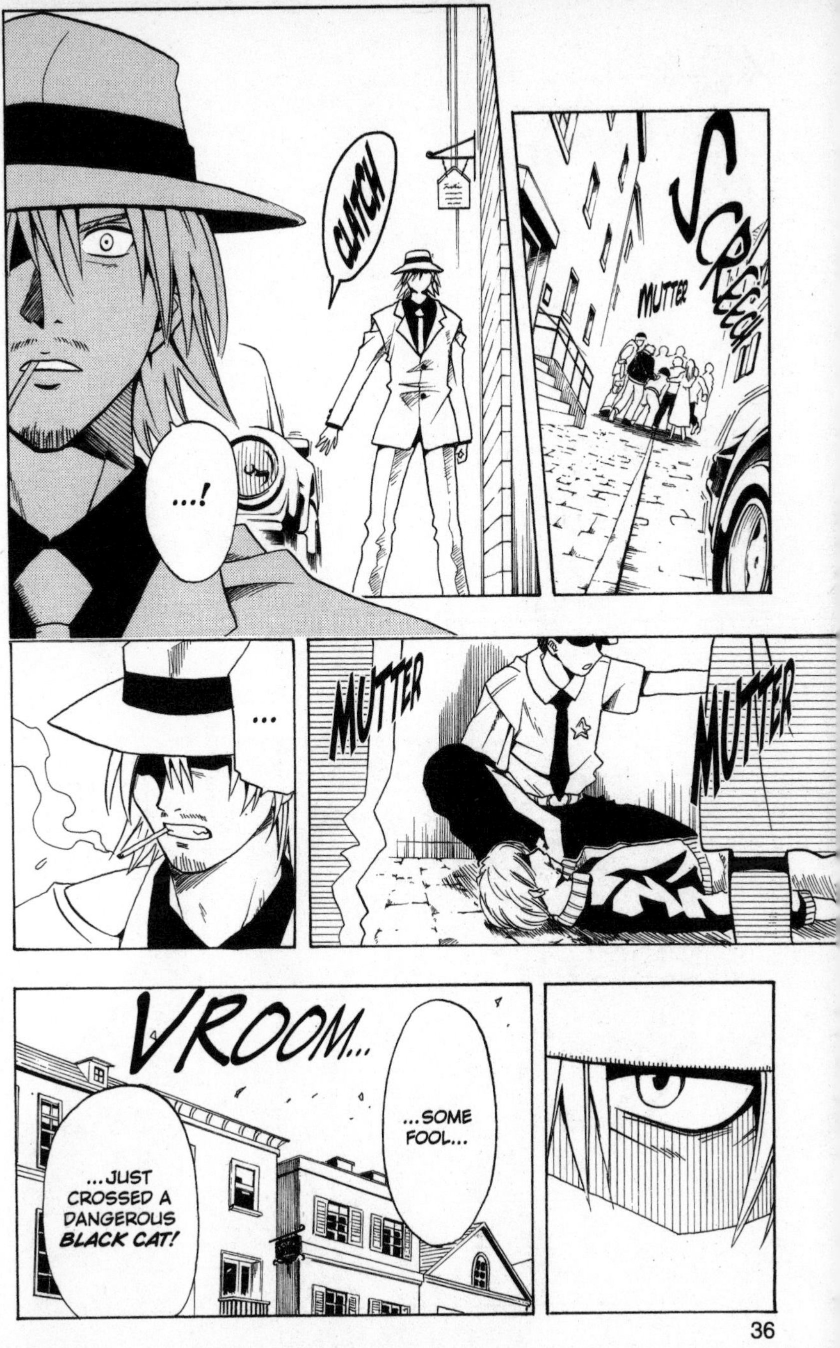
SCREECH
MUTTER
CLATCH
...!
MUTTER
MUTTER
...
VROOM...
...SOME FOOL...
...JUST CROSSED A DANGEROUS BLACK CAT!

READ THIS WAY

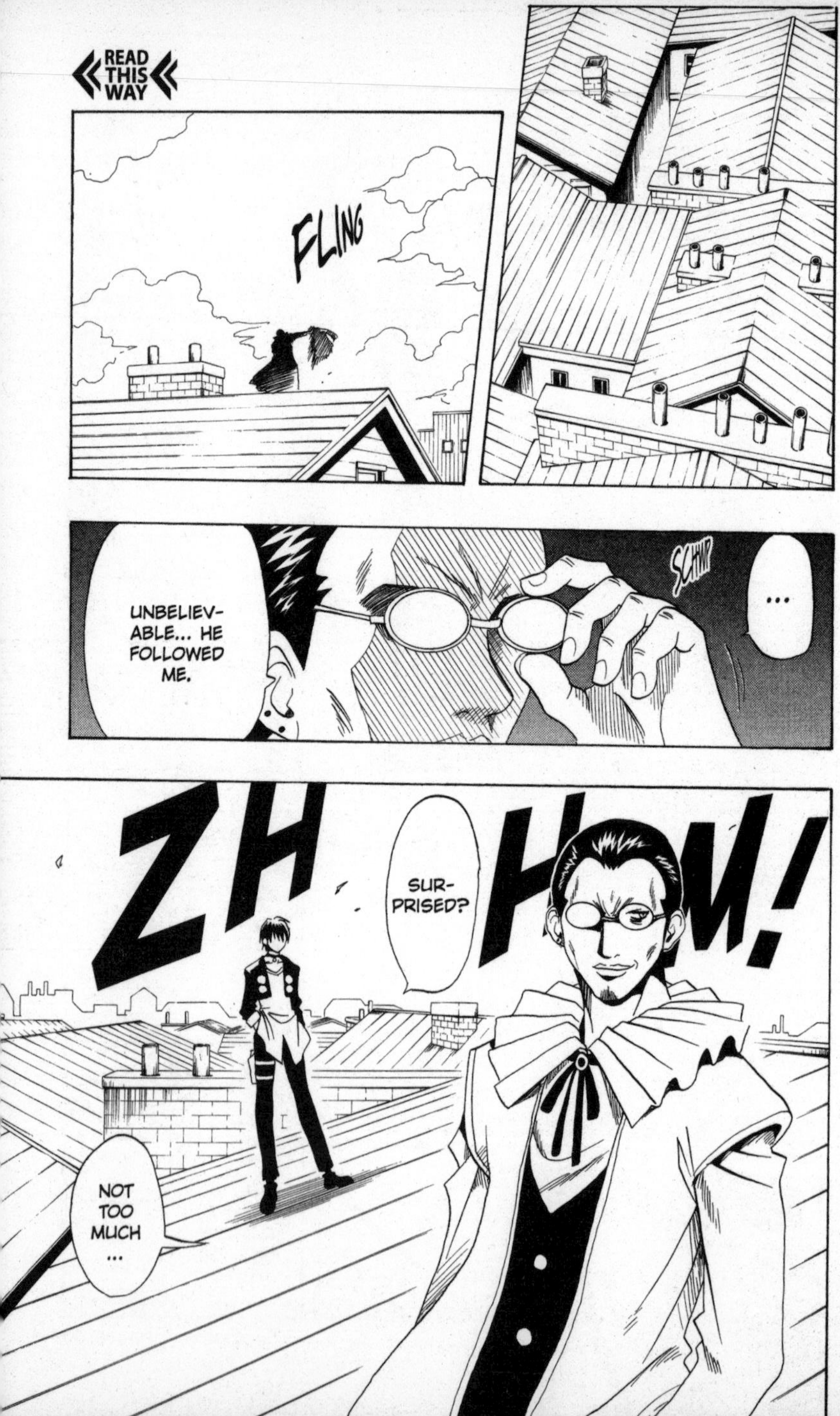
FLING
SCHMP
...
UNBELIEVABLE... HE FOLLOWED ME.
ZH M!
SURPRISED?
NOT TOO MUCH...

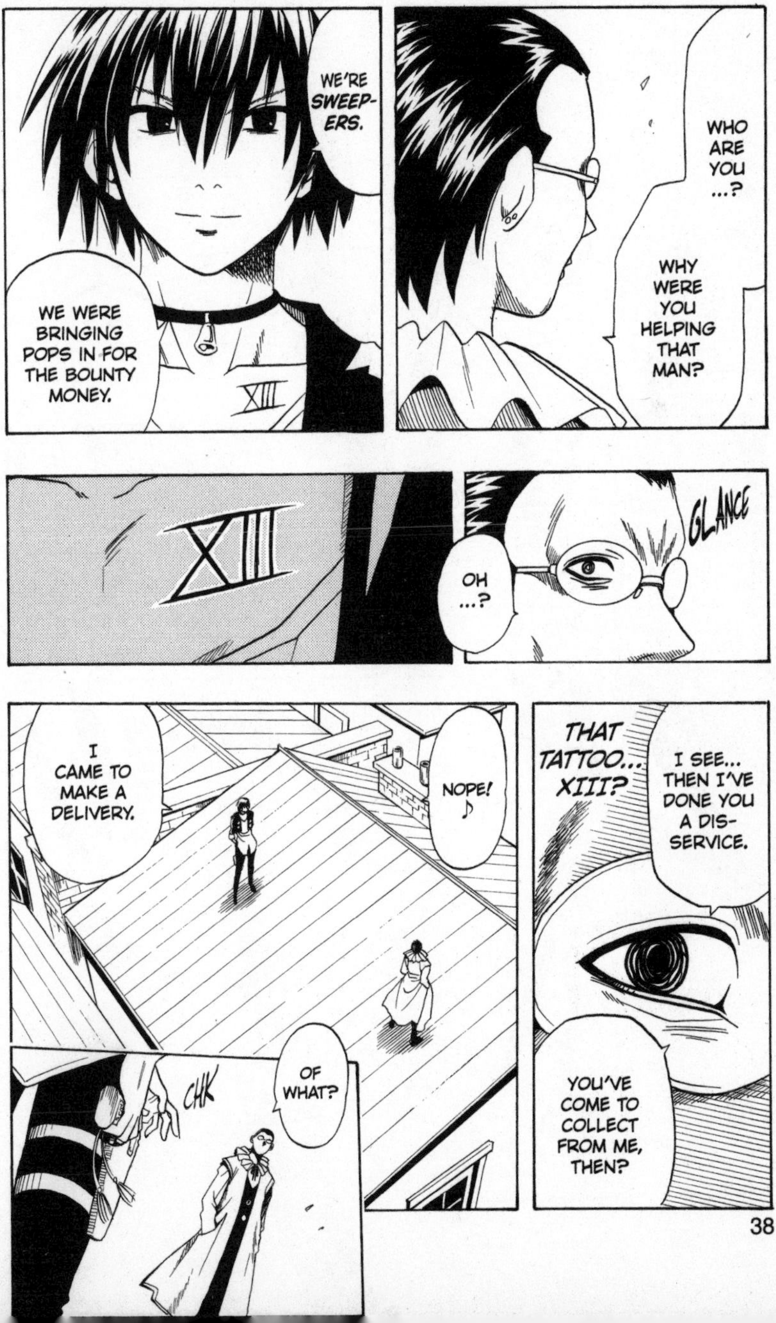
WHO ARE YOU ...?
WHY WERE YOU HELPING THAT MAN?
WE'RE SWEEPERS.
WE WERE BRINGING POPS IN FOR THE BOUNTY MONEY.
GLANCE
OH ...?
THAT TATTOO... XIII?
I SEE... THEN I'VE DONE YOU A DIS-SERVICE.
YOU'VE COME TO COLLECT FROM ME, THEN?
NOPE! ♪
I CAME TO MAKE A DELIVERY.
OF WHAT?
CHK

READ THIS WAY

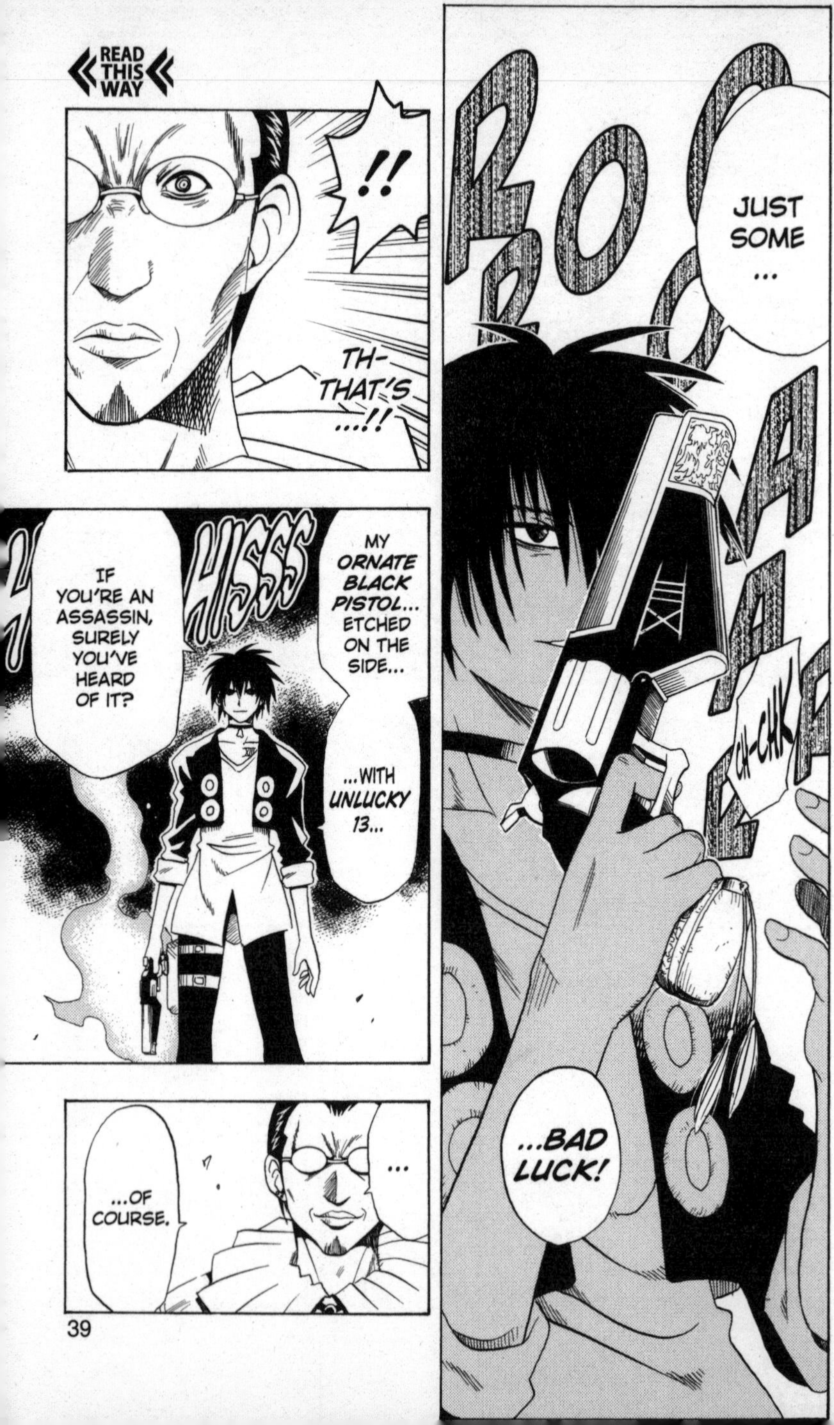
JUST SOME ...
CH-CHK
...BAD LUCK!
!!
TH- THAT'S ...!!
HISSS
MY ORNATE BLACK PISTOL... ETCHED ON THE SIDE...
...WITH UNLUCKY 13...
IF YOU'RE AN ASSASSIN, SURELY YOU'VE HEARD OF IT?
...
...OF COURSE.

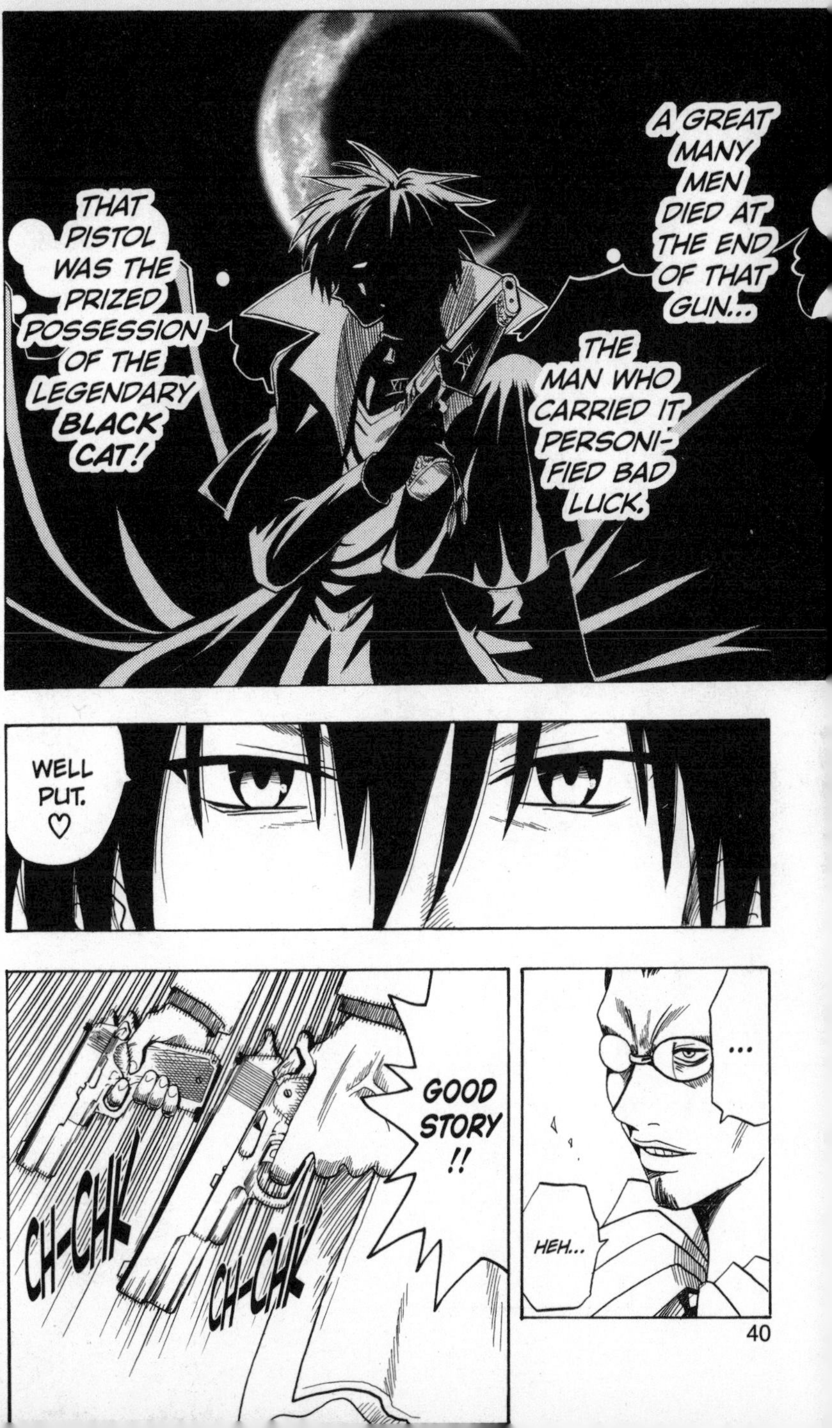
A GREAT MANY MEN DIED AT THE END OF THAT GUN...
THE MAN WHO CARRIED IT PERSONIFIED BAD LUCK.
THAT PISTOL WAS THE PRIZED POSSESSION OF THE LEGENDARY BLACK CAT!
WELL PUT. ♡
...
HEH...
GOOD STORY !!
CH-CHK
CH-CHK

READ THIS WAY

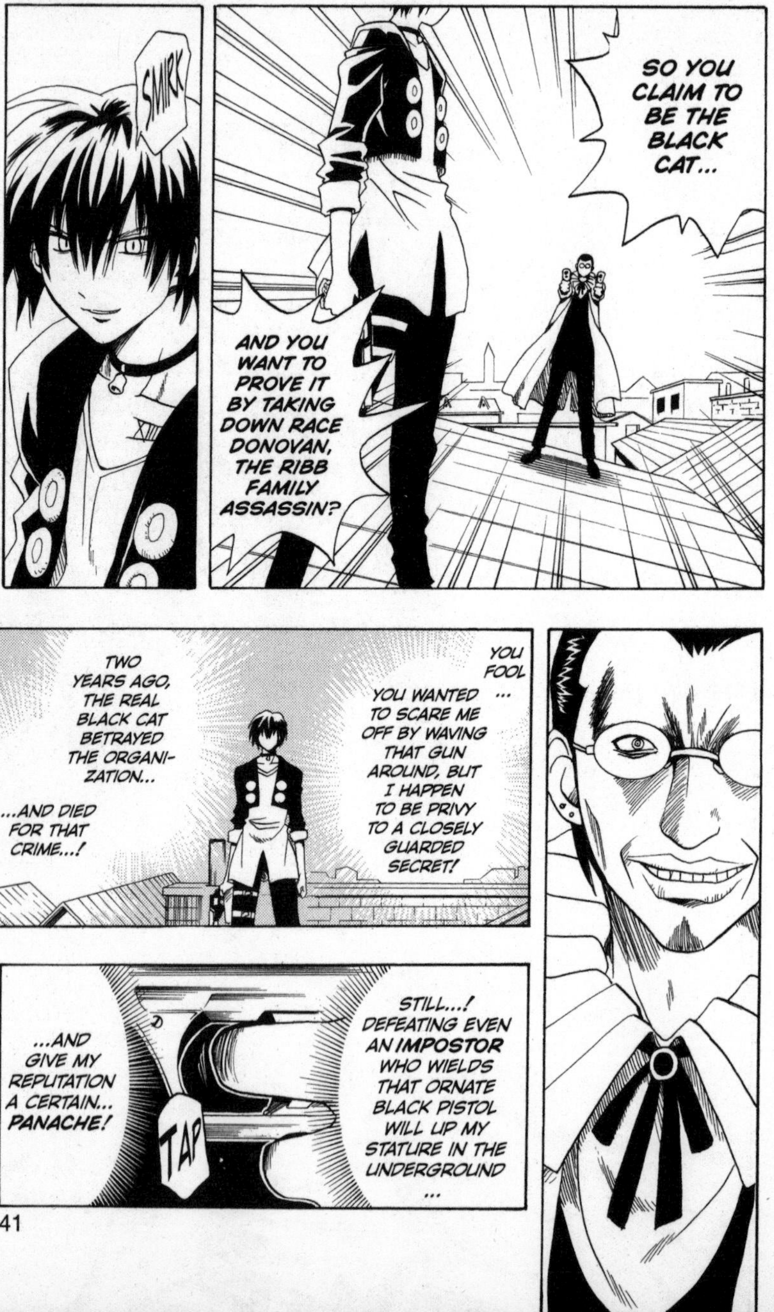
SO YOU CLAIM TO BE THE BLACK CAT...
AND YOU WANT TO PROVE IT BY TAKING DOWN RACE DONOVAN, THE RIBB FAMILY ASSASSIN?
SMIRK
YOU FOOL ...
YOU WANTED TO SCARE ME OFF BY WAVING THAT GUN AROUND, BUT I HAPPEN TO BE PRIVY TO A CLOSELY GUARDED SECRET!
TWO YEARS AGO, THE REAL BLACK CAT BETRAYED THE ORGANI-ZATION...
...AND DIED FOR THAT CRIME...!
STILL...! DEFEATING EVEN AN **IMPOSTOR** WHO WIELDS THAT ORNATE BLACK PISTOL WILL UP MY STATURE IN THE UNDERGROUND ...
...AND GIVE MY REPUTATION A CERTAIN... **PANACHE!**
TAP

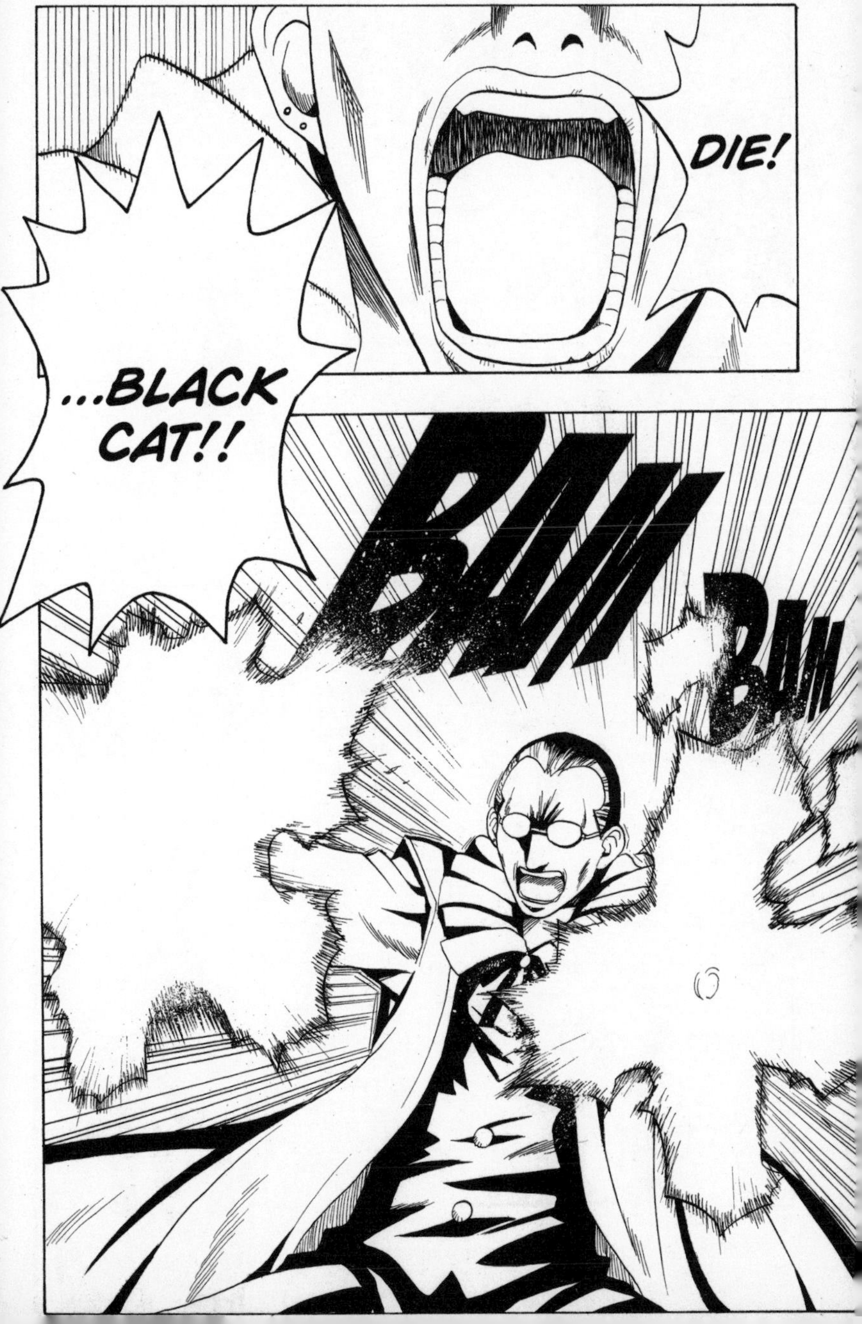
DIE!
...BLACK CAT!!
BAM
BAM

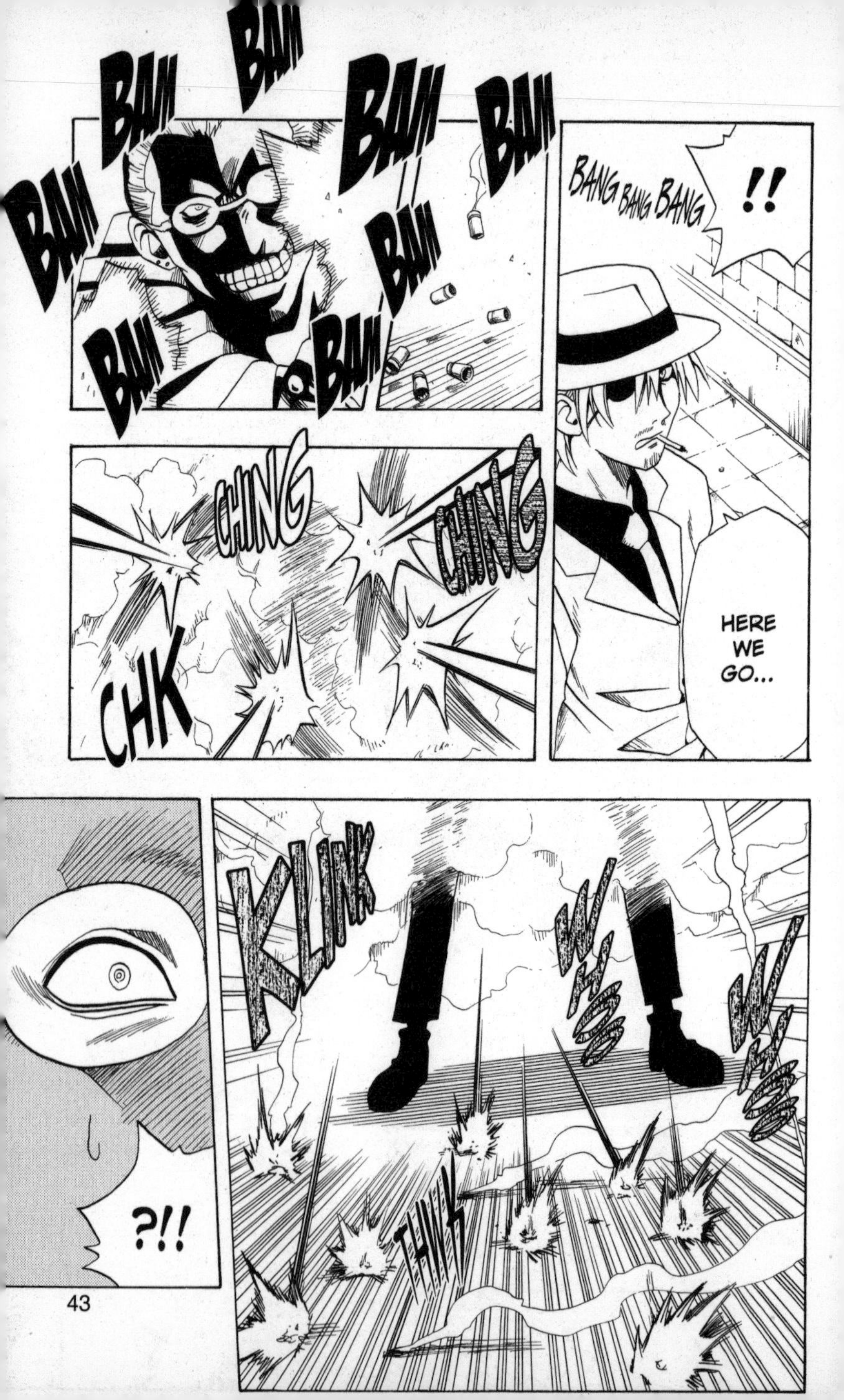
BANG BANG BANG
!!
HERE WE GO...
BAM
BAM
BAM
BAM
BAM
BAM
BAM
BAM
CHING
CHING
CHK
KLINK
WHOOSH
WHOOSH
THWK
?!!

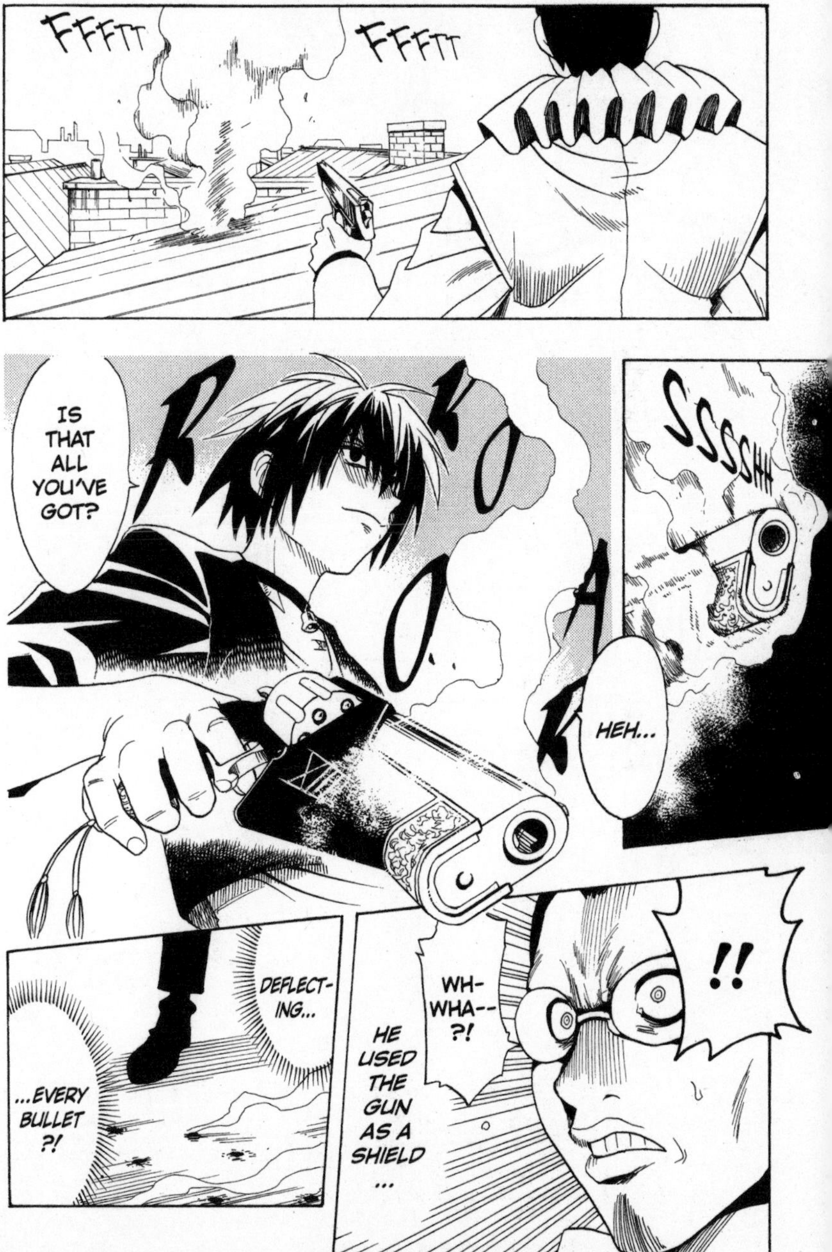
FFFTT
FFFTT
SSSSHH
HEH...
IS THAT ALL YOU'VE GOT?
!!
WH- WHA-- ?!
HE USED THE GUN AS A SHIELD ...
DEFLECTING...
...EVERY BULLET ?!

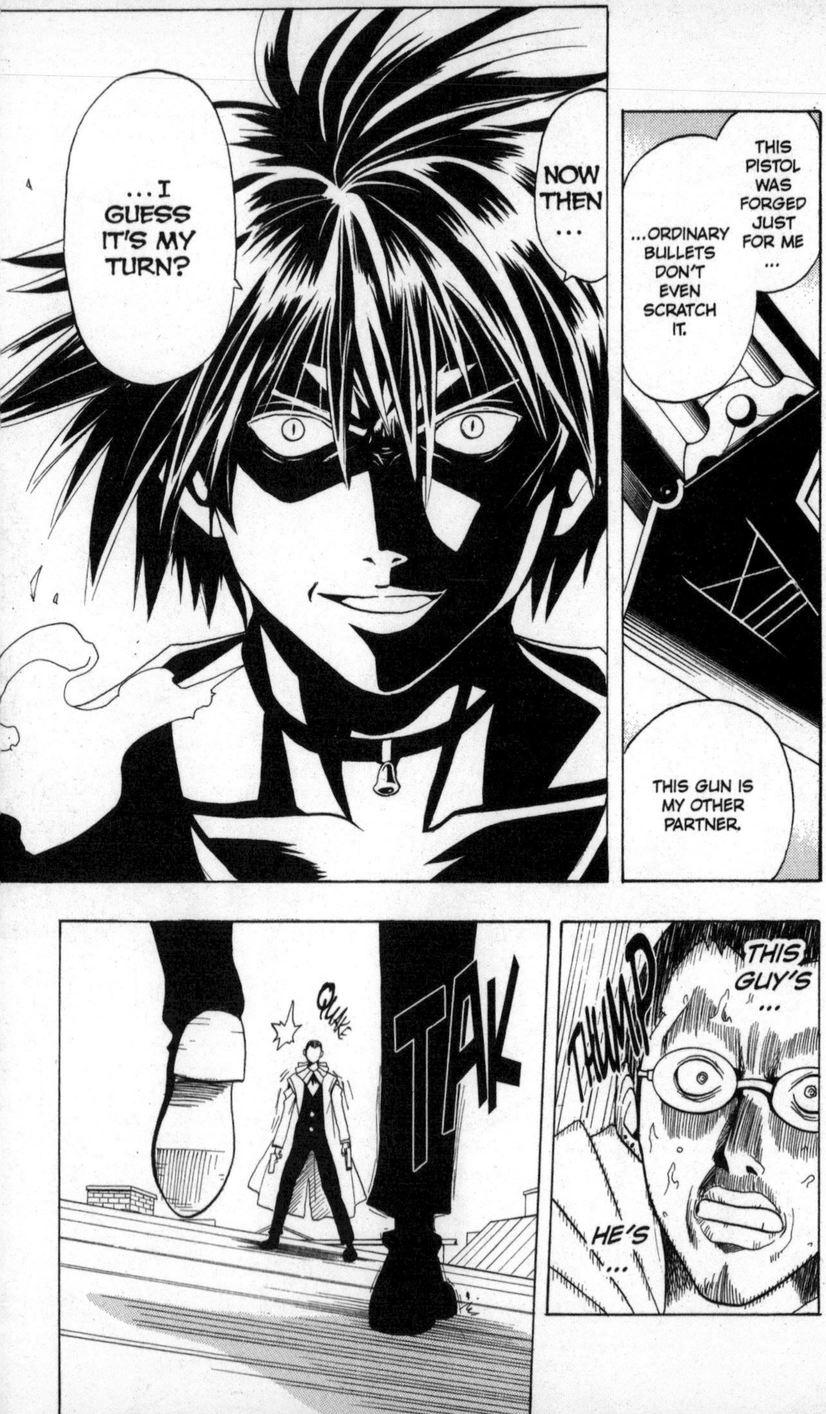
THIS PISTOL WAS FORGED JUST FOR ME ...
...ORDINARY BULLETS DON'T EVEN SCRATCH IT.
THIS GUN IS MY OTHER PARTNER.
NOW THEN ...
...I GUESS IT'S MY TURN?
THIS GUY'S ...
THUMP
HE'S ...
TAK
QUAKE

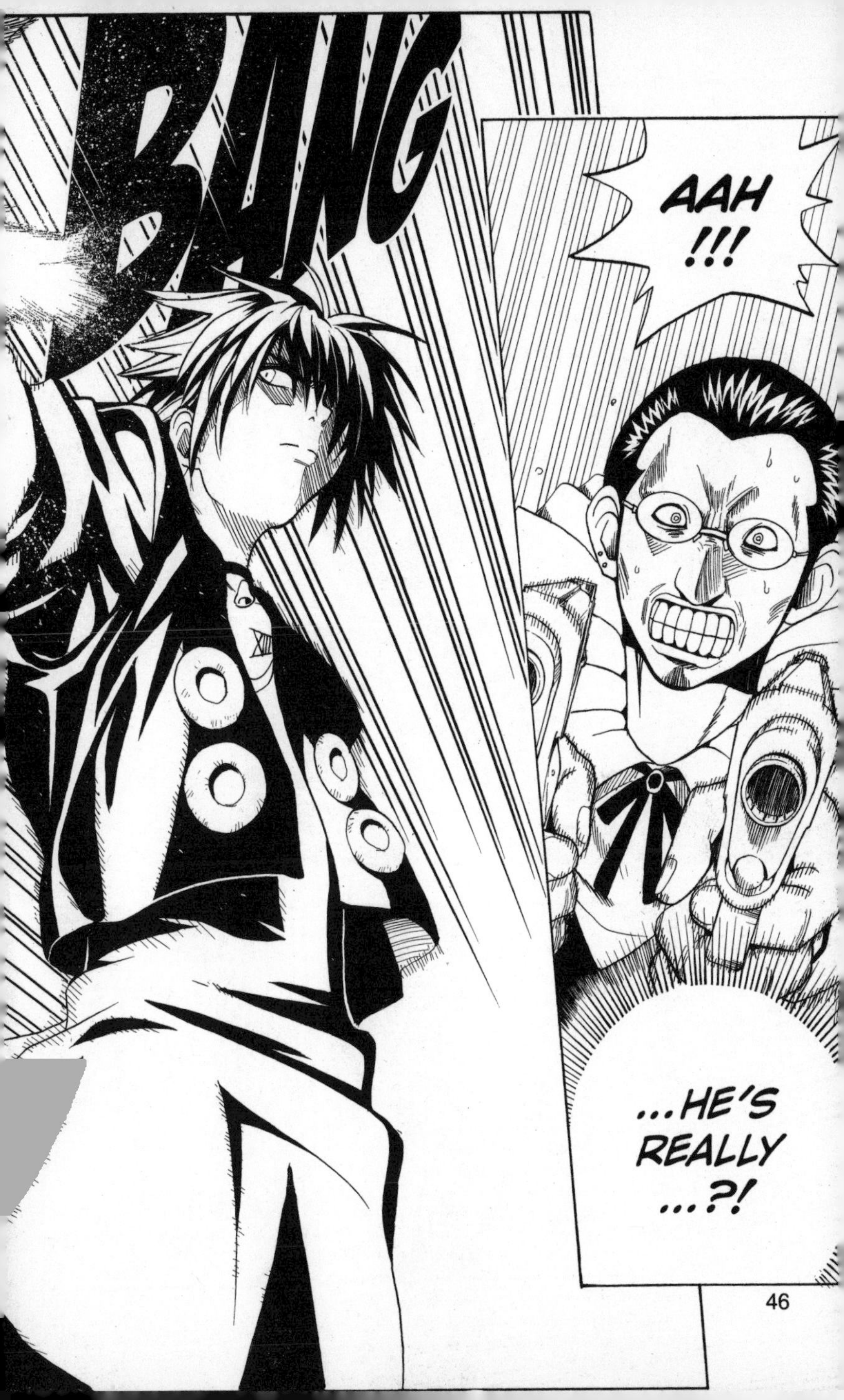
AAH !!!
...HE'S REALLY ...?!
BANG

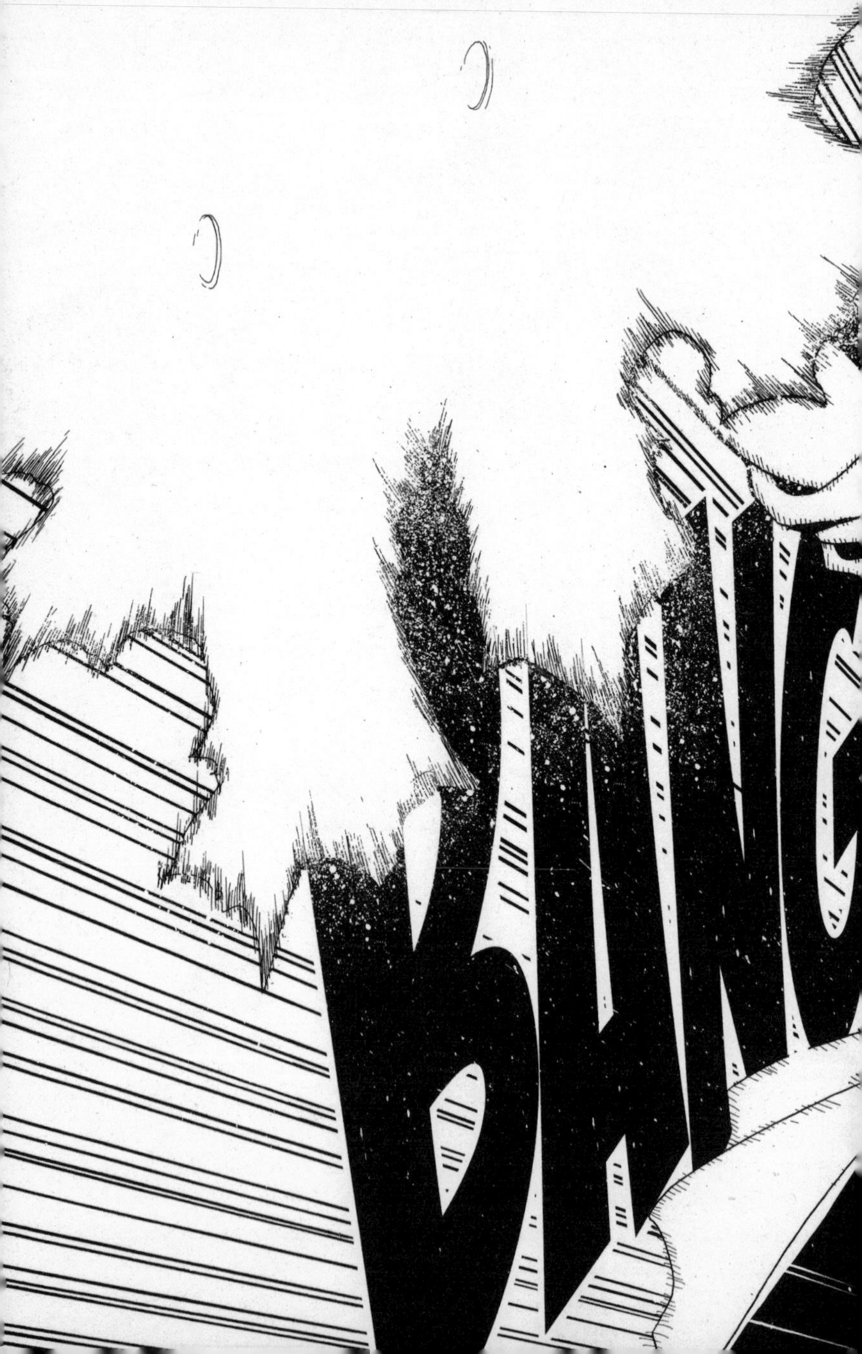
SHING

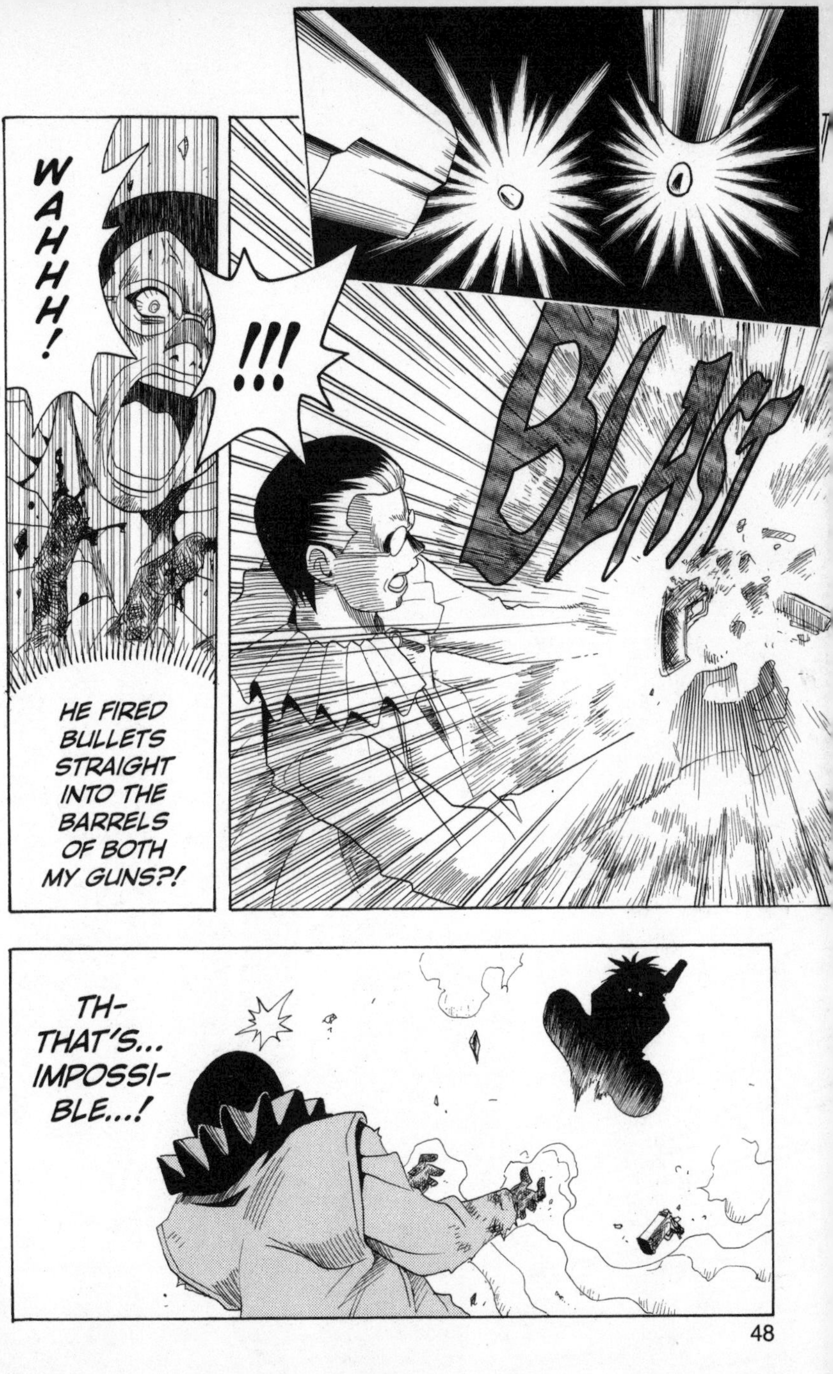
!!!
BLAST
WAHHHH!
HE FIRED BULLETS STRAIGHT INTO THE BARRELS OF BOTH MY GUNS?!
TH-THAT'S... IMPOSSI-BLE...!

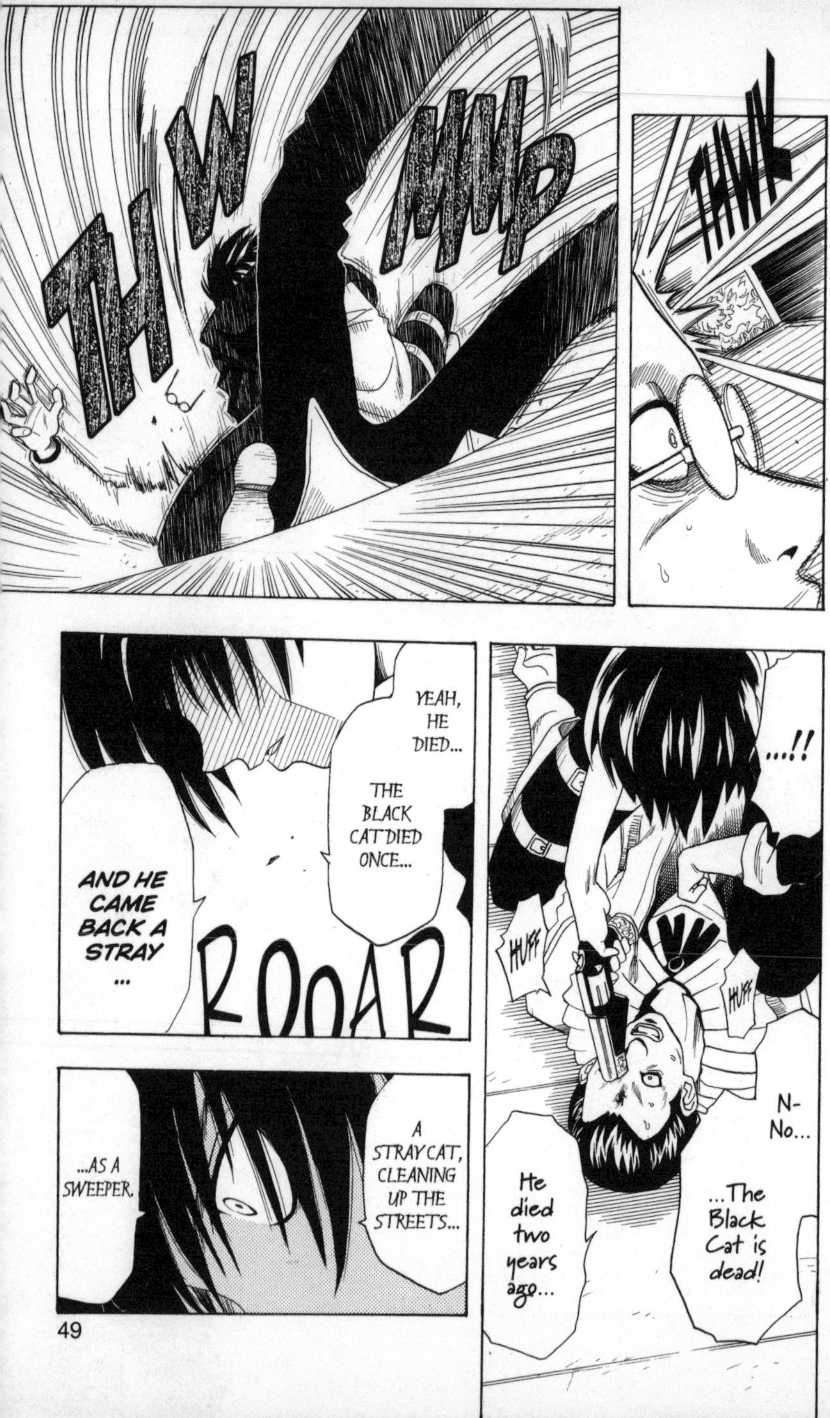
THWAK
THWMMP
...!!
HUFF
N- No...
...The Black Cat is dead!
He died two years ago...
HUFF
YEAH, HE DIED...
THE BLACK CAT DIED ONCE...
AND HE CAME BACK A STRAY ...
ROOAR
A STRAY CAT, CLEANING UP THE STREETS...
...AS A SWEEPER.

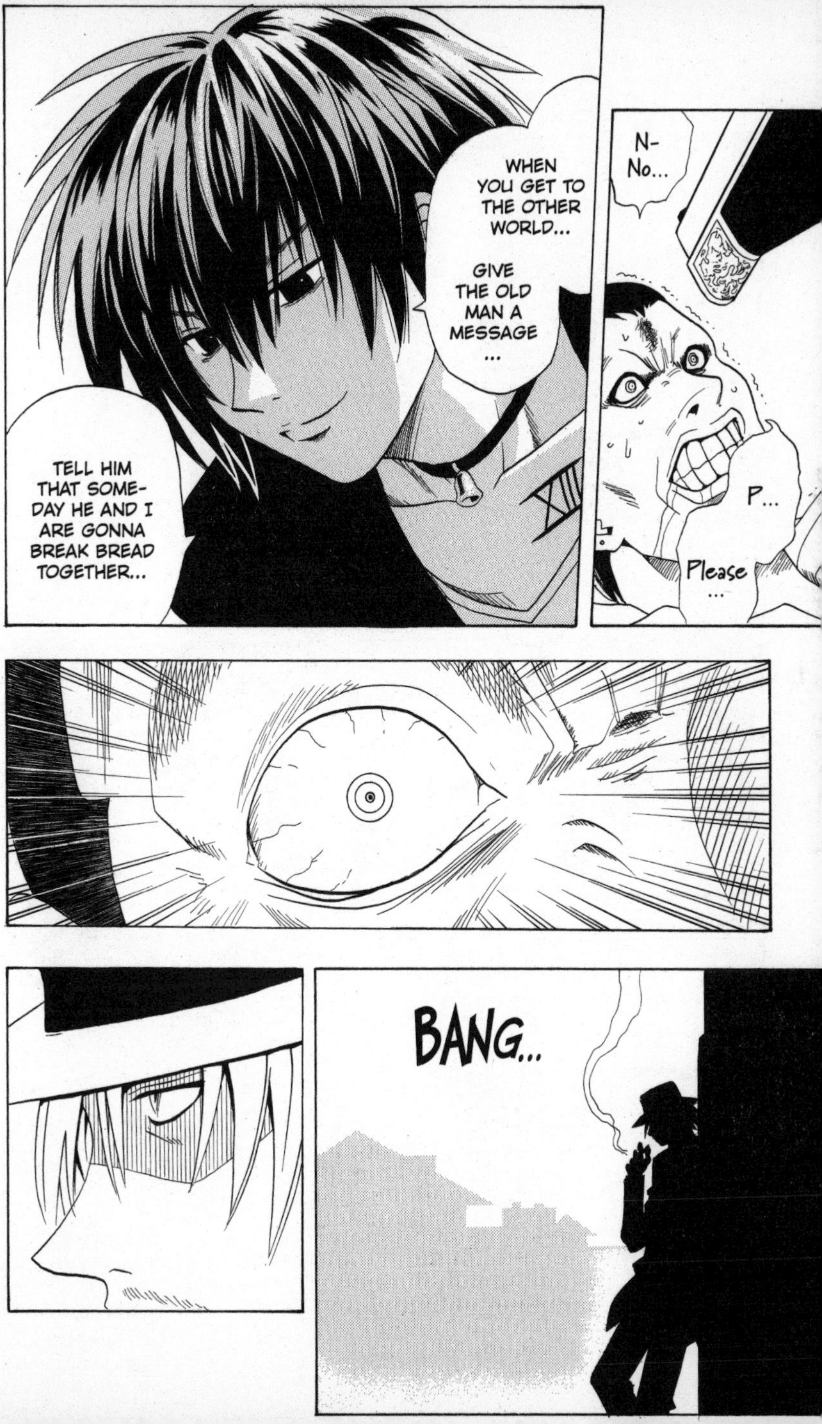
N- No...
P... Please...
WHEN YOU GET TO THE OTHER WORLD...
GIVE THE OLD MAN A MESSAGE ...
TELL HIM THAT SOME-DAY HE AND I ARE GONNA BREAK BREAD TOGETHER...
BANG...

READ THIS WAY

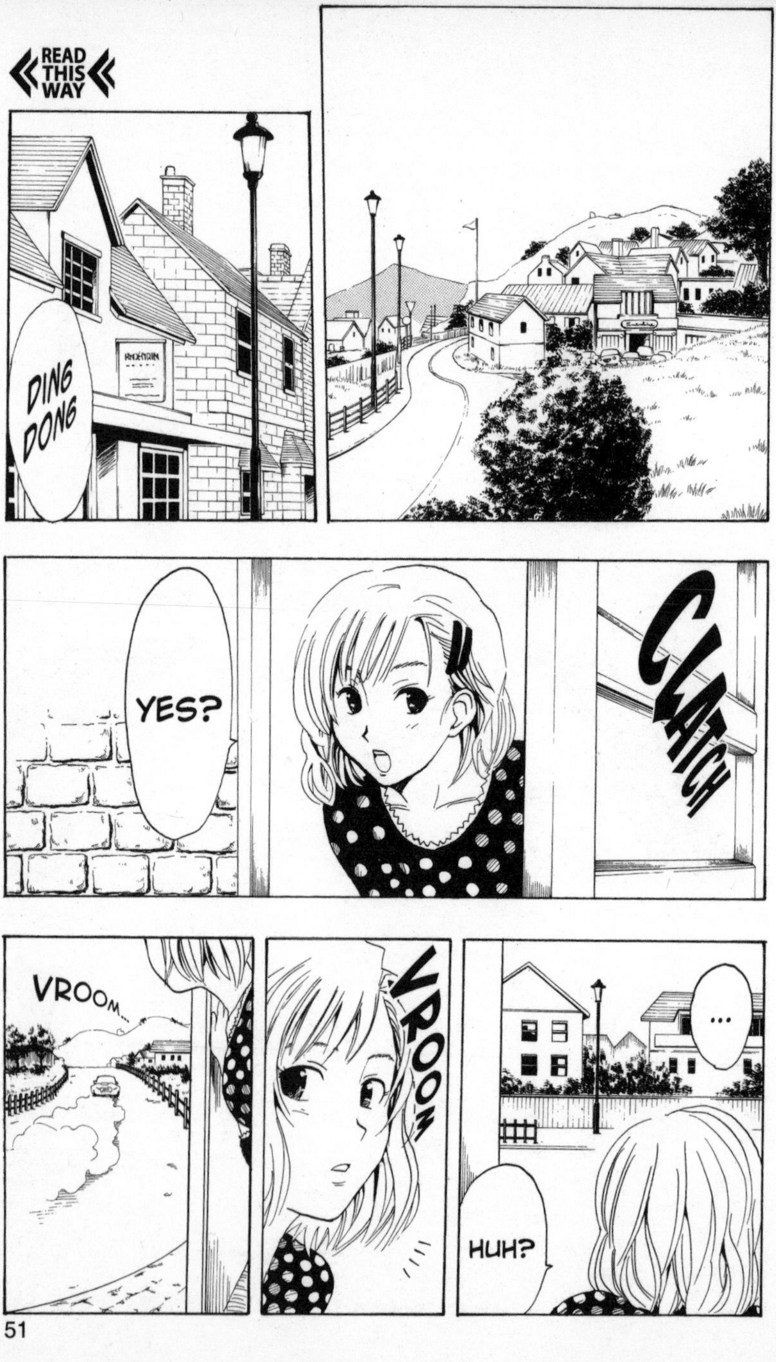

DING DONG
CLATCH
YES?
...
HUH?
VROOM
VROOM...

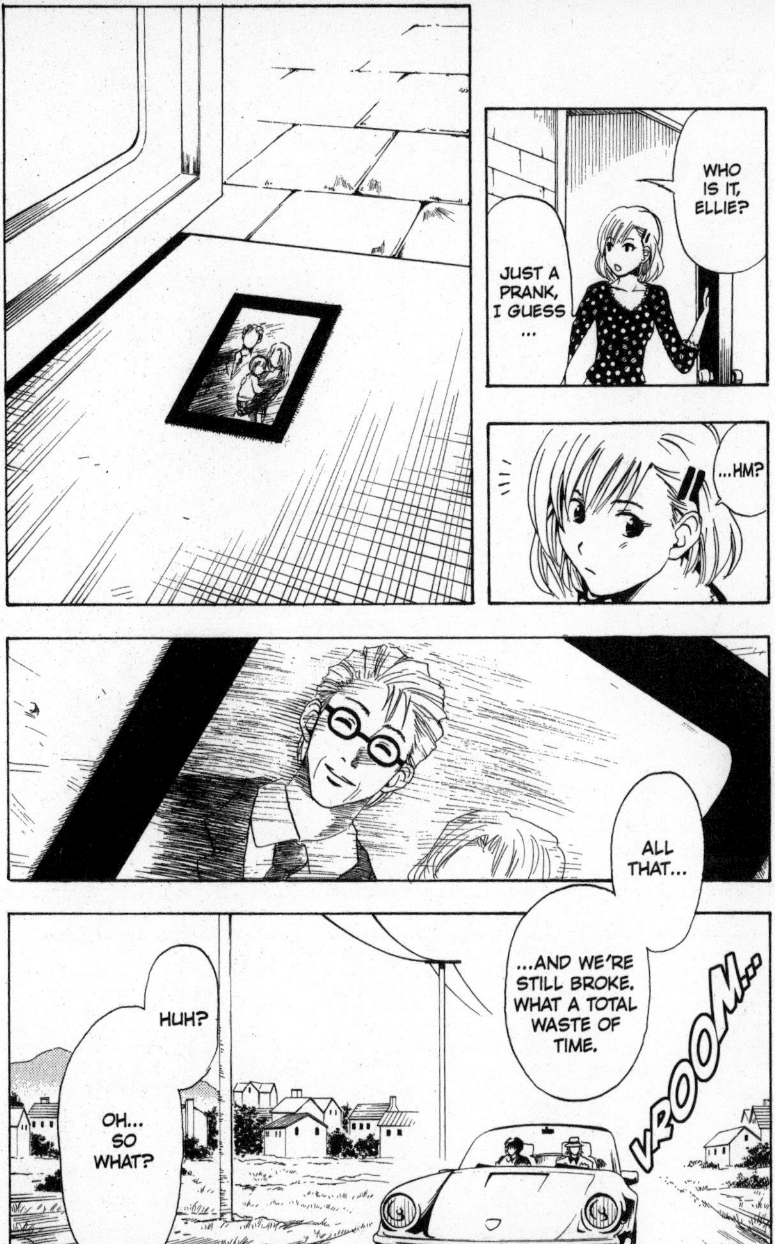

WHO IS IT, ELLIE?
JUST A PRANK, I GUESS ...
...HM?
ALL THAT...
...AND WE'RE STILL BROKE. WHAT A TOTAL WASTE OF TIME.
VROOM...
HUH?
OH... SO WHAT?

READ THIS WAY

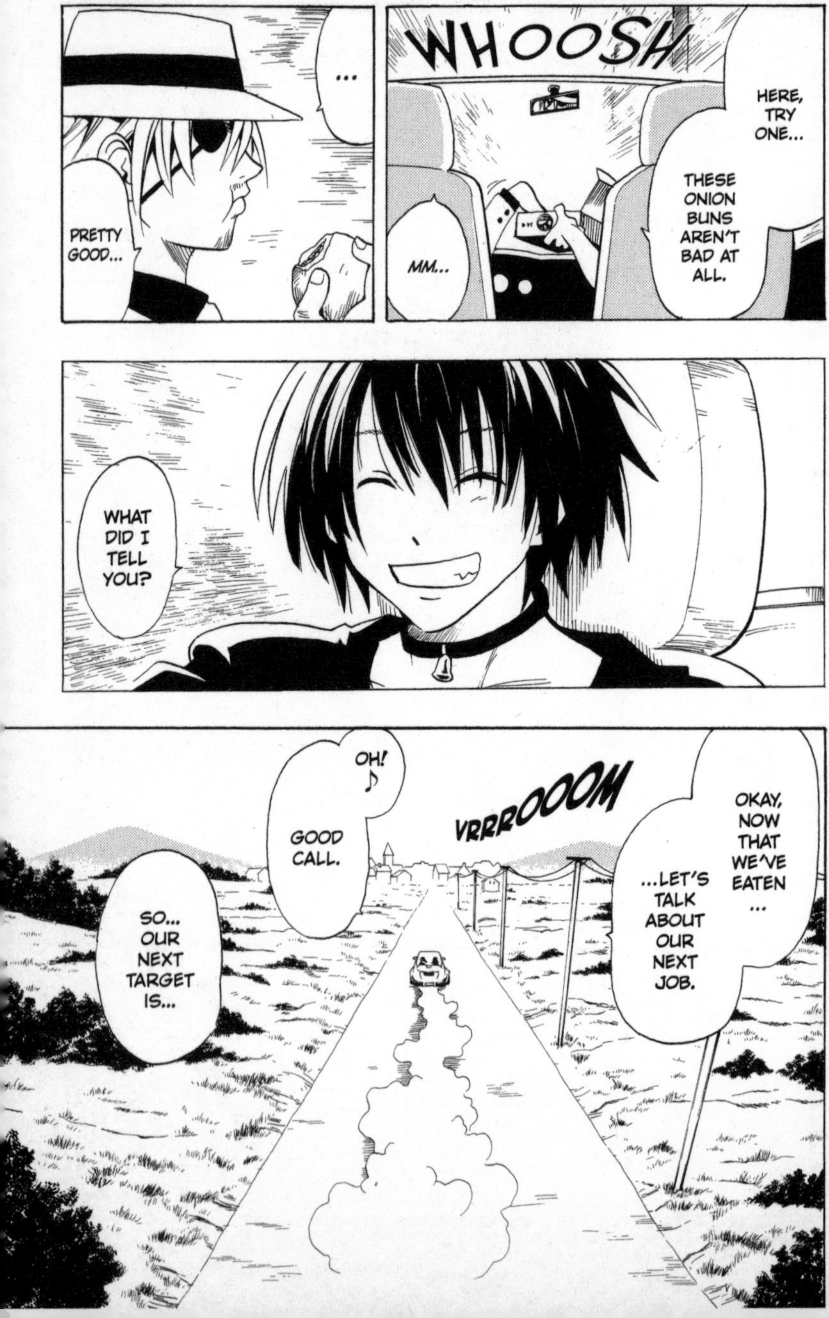
WHOOSH
HERE, TRY ONE...
THESE ONION BUNS AREN'T BAD AT ALL.
MM...
...
PRETTY GOOD...
WHAT DID I TELL YOU?
OKAY, NOW THAT WE'VE EATEN...
...LET'S TALK ABOUT OUR NEXT JOB.
VRRROOOM
OH! ♪
GOOD CALL.
SO... OUR NEXT TARGET IS...

☆ About Chapter Two ☆

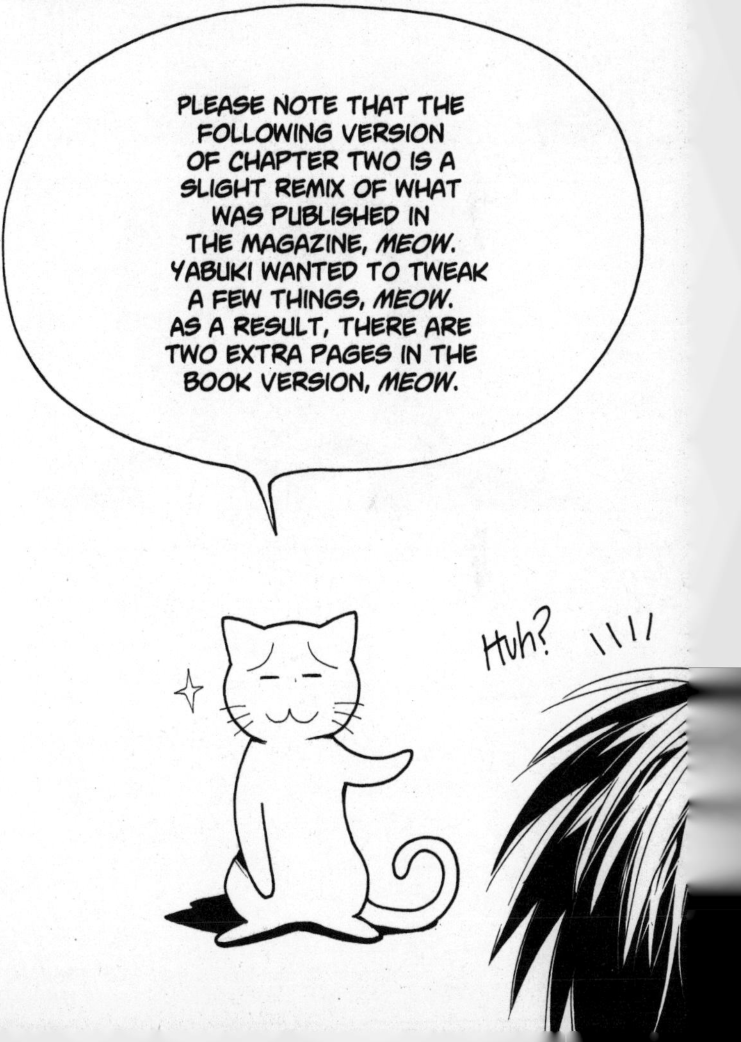
PLEASE NOTE THAT THE FOLLOWING VERSION OF CHAPTER TWO IS A SLIGHT REMIX OF WHAT WAS PUBLISHED IN THE MAGAZINE, *MEOW*. YABUKI WANTED TO TWEAK A FEW THINGS, *MEOW*. AS A RESULT, THERE ARE TWO EXTRA PAGES IN THE BOOK VERSION, *MEOW*.
Huh?

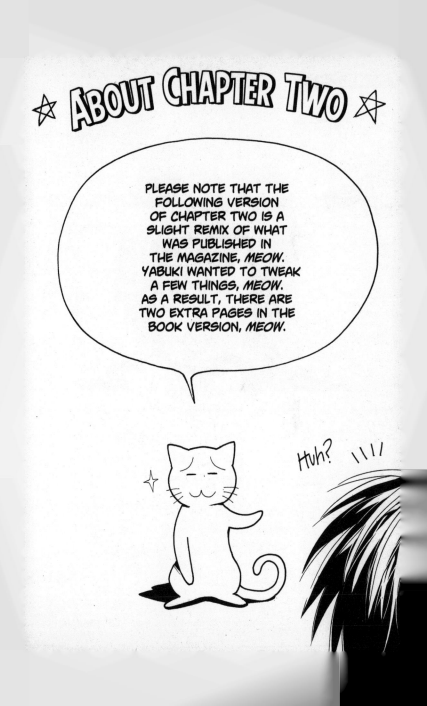

Chapter Two: The Messenger from Chronos

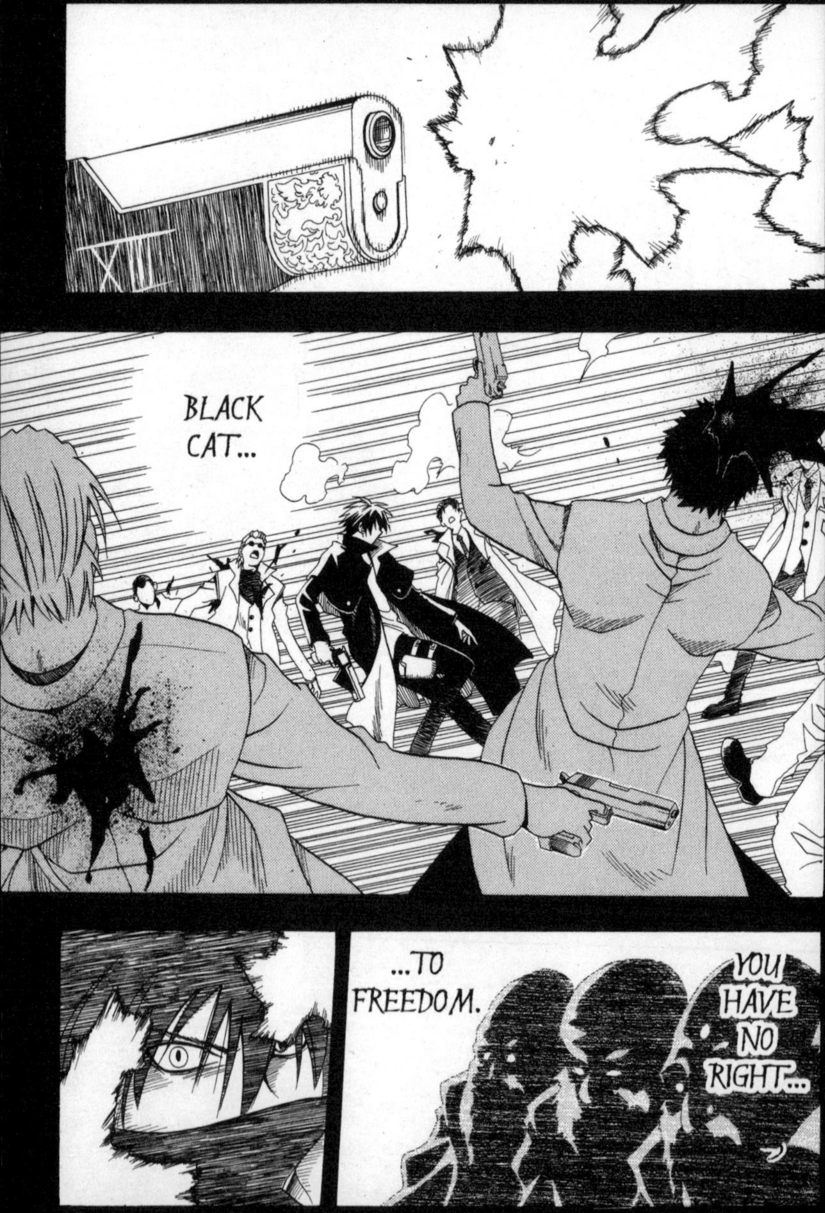
BLACK CAT...
YOU HAVE NO RIGHT...
...TO FREEDOM.

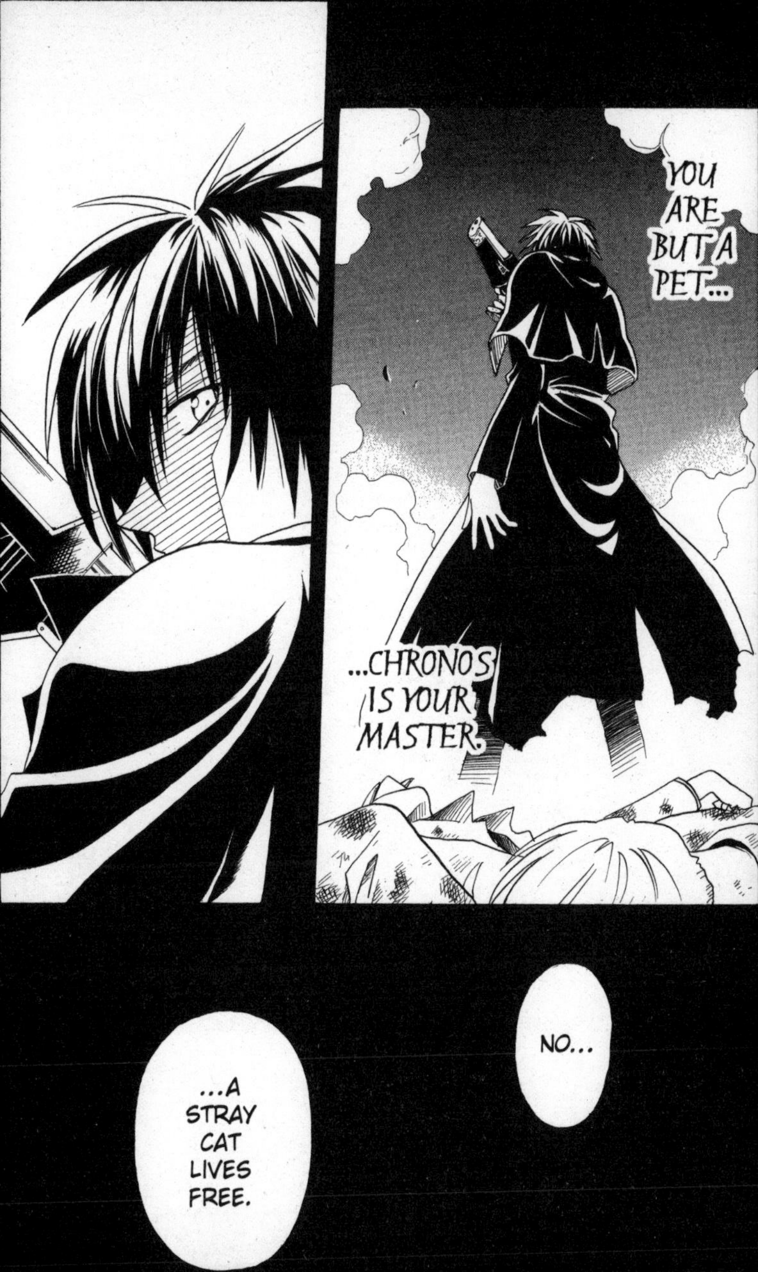
YOU ARE BUT A PET...
...CHRONOS IS YOUR MASTER.
NO...
...A STRAY CAT LIVES FREE.

Chapter Two:
The Messenger from Chronos

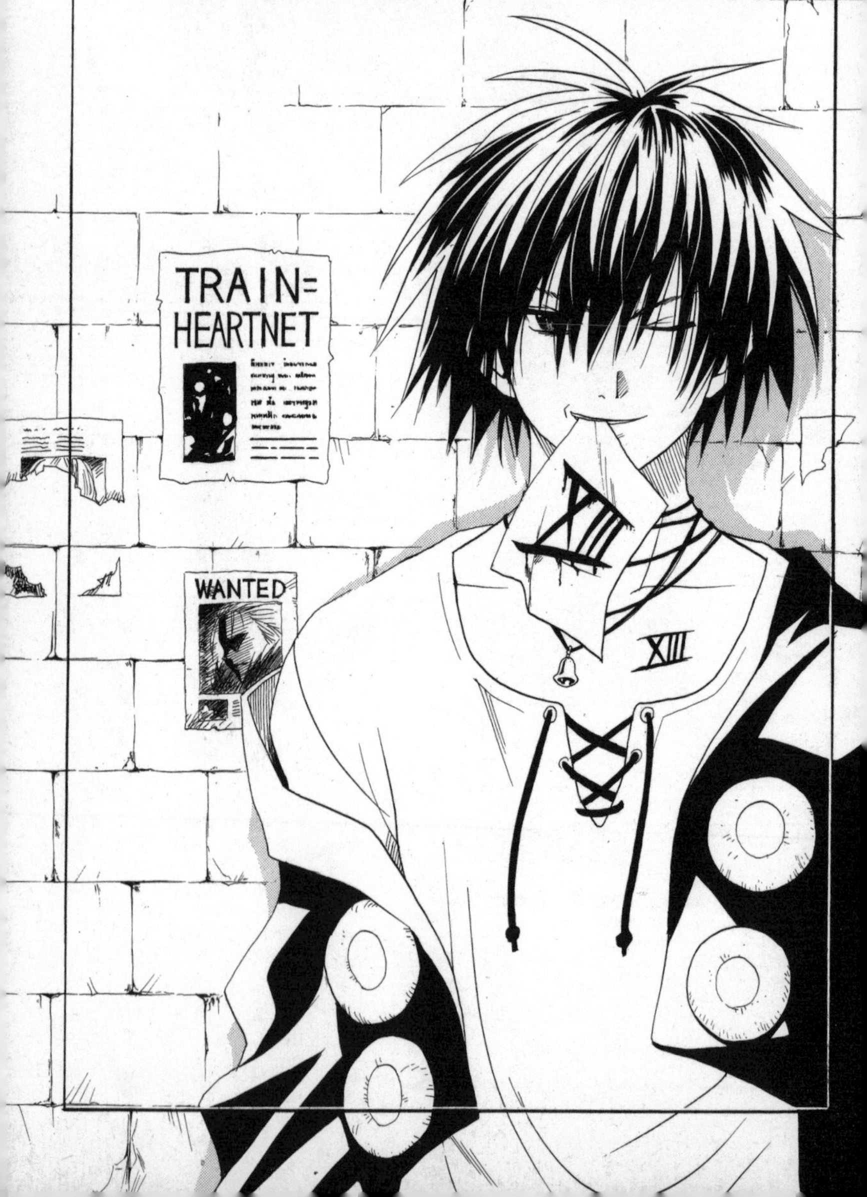
TRAIN=
HEARTNET
WANTED
XIII

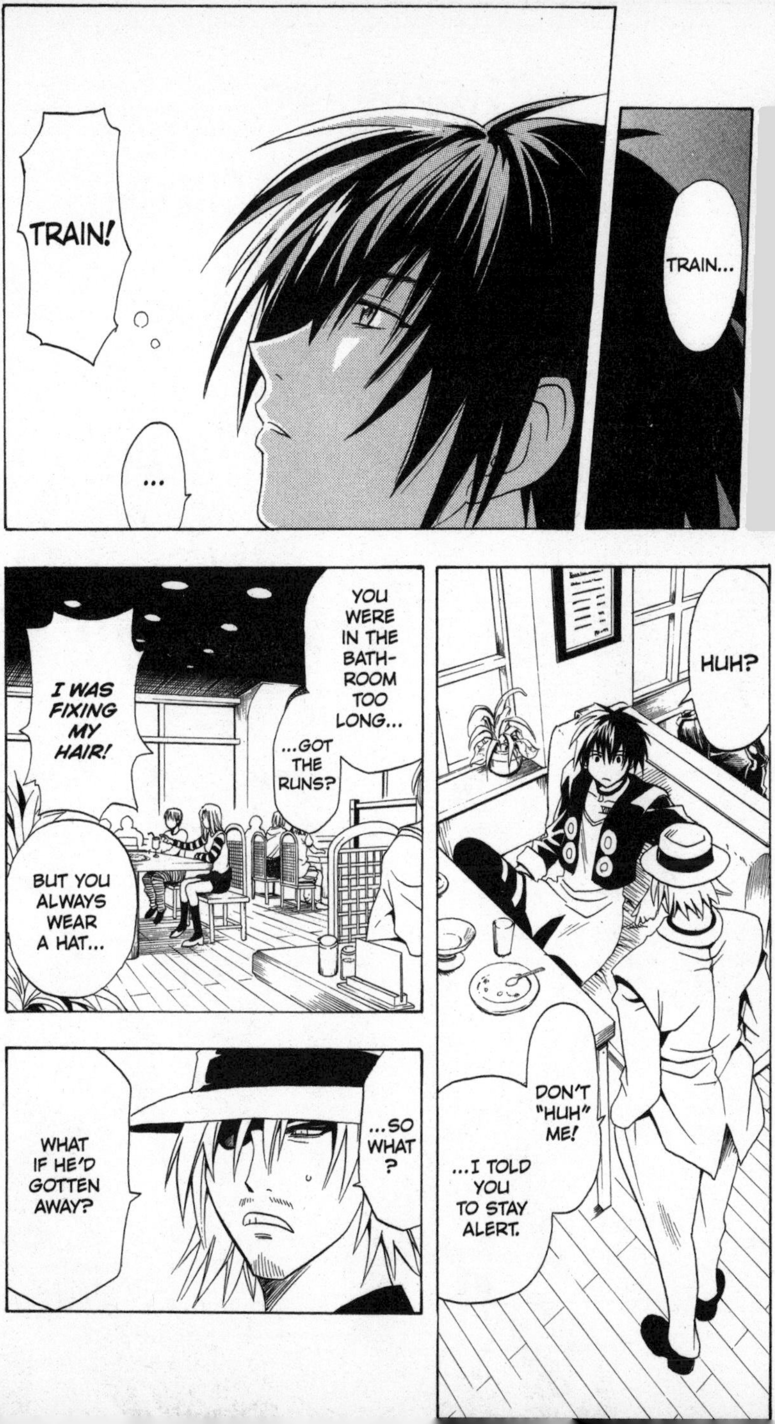
TRAIN...
TRAIN!
...
HUH?
DON'T "HUH" ME!
...I TOLD YOU TO STAY ALERT.
YOU WERE IN THE BATH-ROOM TOO LONG...
...GOT THE RUNS?
I WAS FIXING MY HAIR!
BUT YOU ALWAYS WEAR A HAT...
...SO WHAT?
WHAT IF HE'D GOTTEN AWAY?

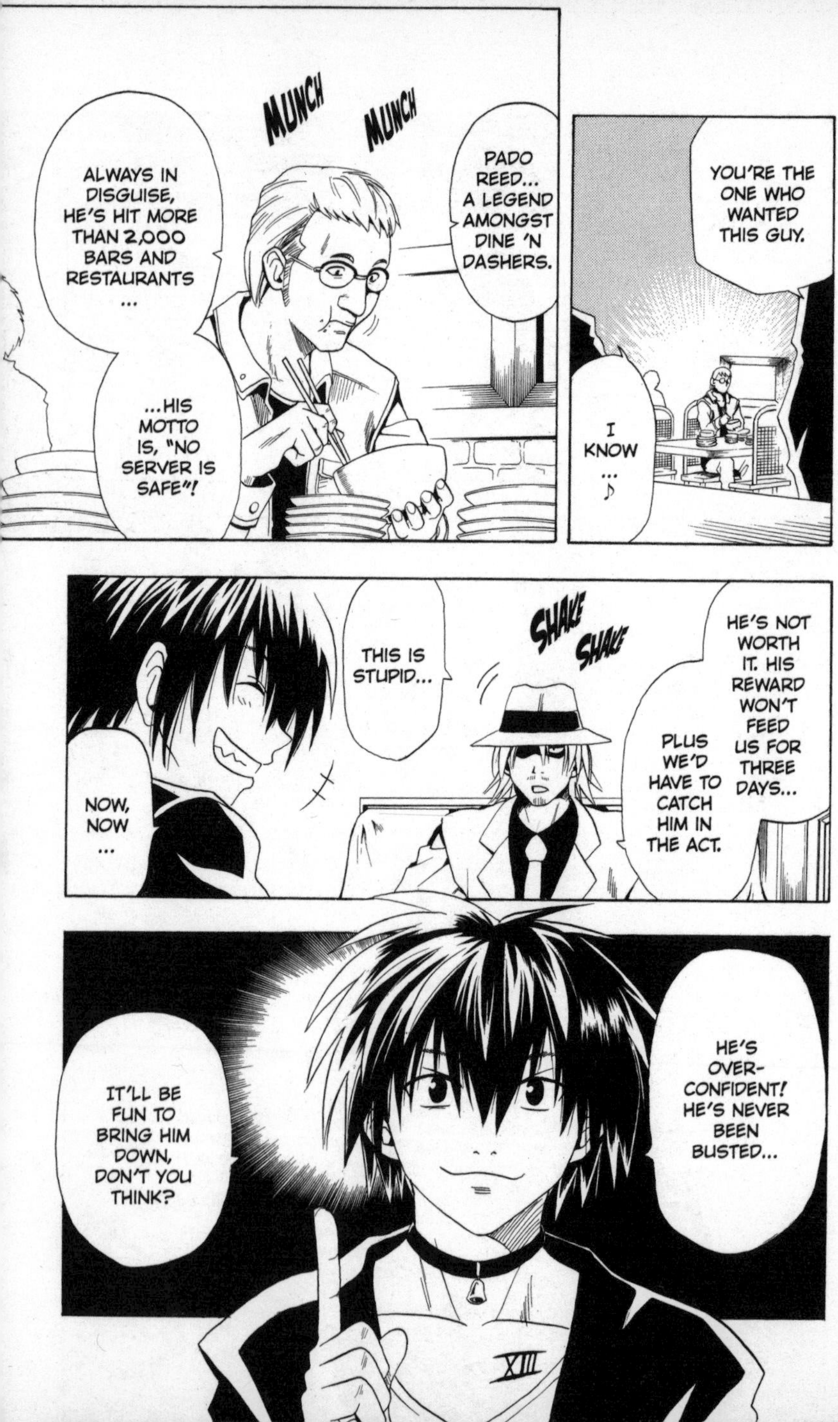
YOU'RE THE ONE WHO WANTED THIS GUY.
I KNOW ... ♪
MUNCH MUNCH
PADO REED... A LEGEND AMONGST DINE 'N DASHERS.
ALWAYS IN DISGUISE, HE'S HIT MORE THAN 2,000 BARS AND RESTAURANTS ...
...HIS MOTTO IS, "NO SERVER IS SAFE"!
HE'S NOT WORTH IT. HIS REWARD WON'T FEED US FOR THREE DAYS...
PLUS WE'D HAVE TO CATCH HIM IN THE ACT.
SHAKE SHAKE
THIS IS STUPID...
NOW, NOW ...
HE'S OVER-CONFIDENT! HE'S NEVER BEEN BUSTED...
IT'LL BE FUN TO BRING HIM DOWN, DON'T YOU THINK?
XIII

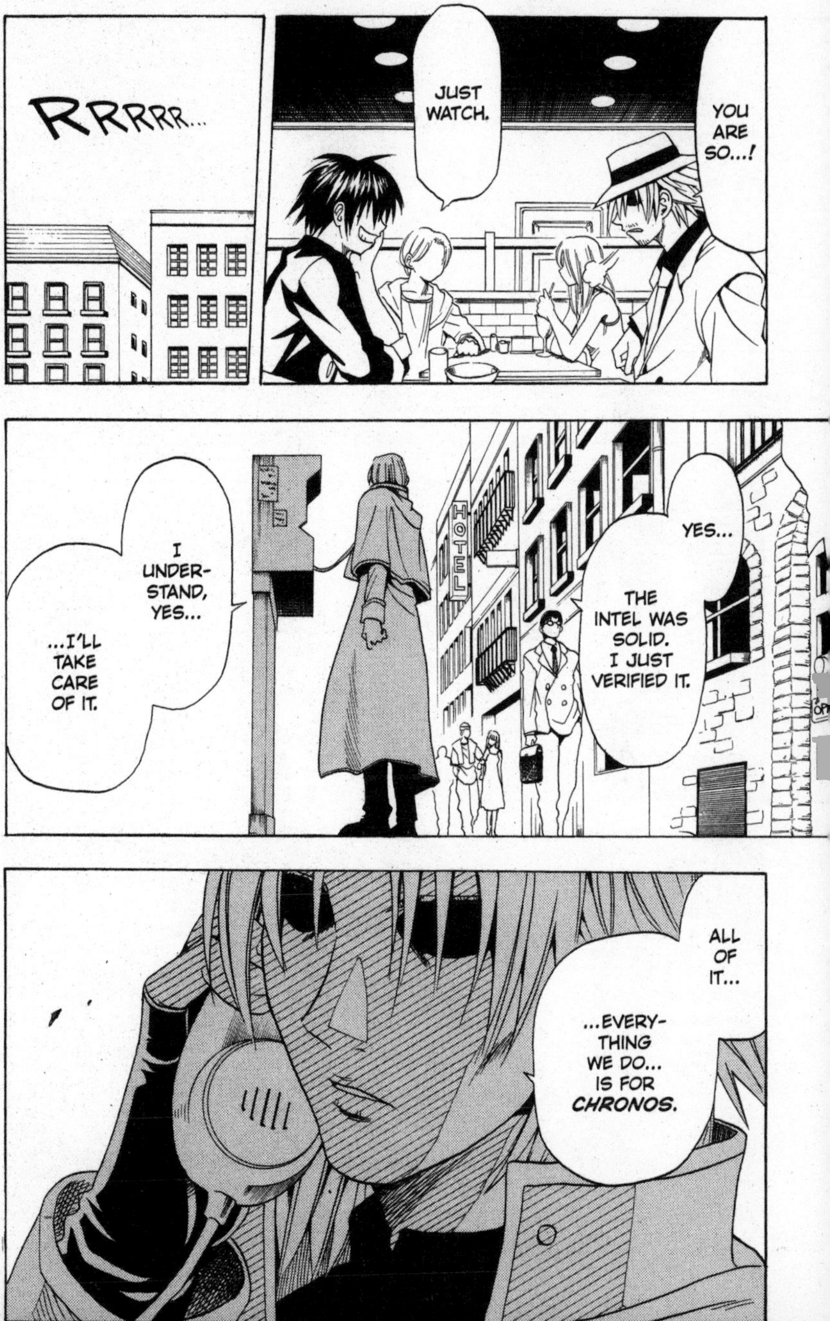
YOU ARE SO...!
JUST WATCH.
RRRRR...
YES...
THE INTEL WAS SOLID. I JUST VERIFIED IT.
I UNDER-STAND, YES...
...I'LL TAKE CARE OF IT.
ALL OF IT...
...EVERY-THING WE DO... IS FOR *CHRONOS.*

READ THIS WAY

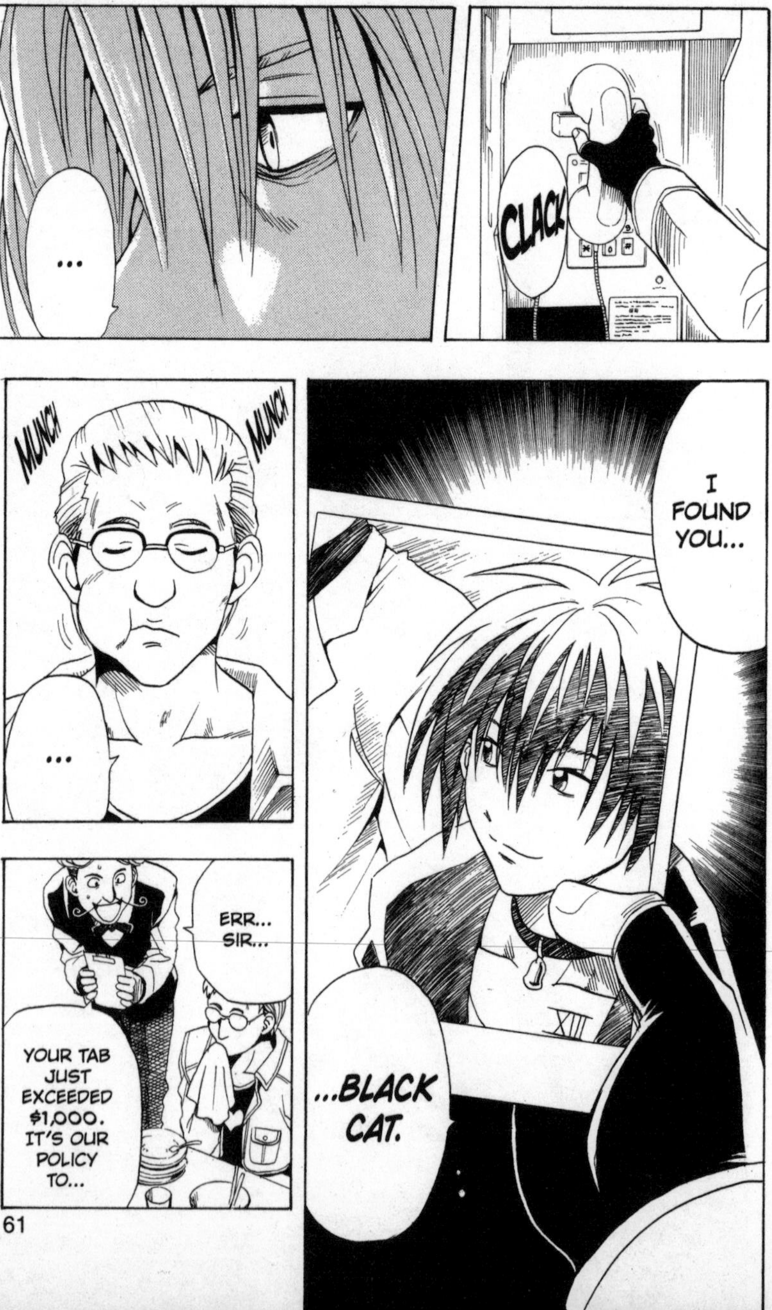
CLACK
...
I FOUND YOU...
...BLACK CAT.
MUNCH
MUNCH
...
ERR... SIR...
YOUR TAB JUST EXCEEDED $1,000. IT'S OUR POLICY TO...

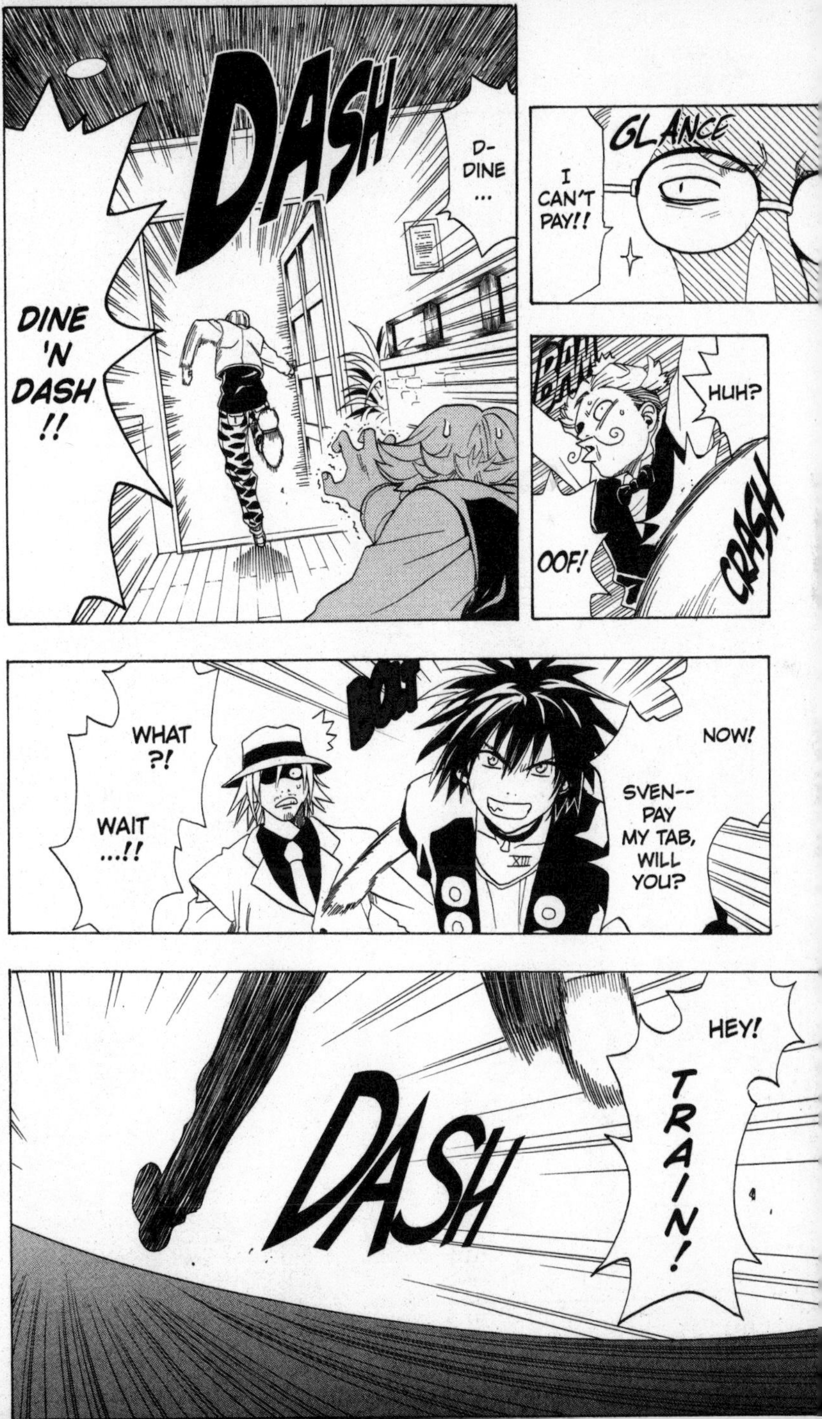
GLANCE
I CAN'T PAY!!
HUH?
CRASH
OOF!
D-DINE...
DASH
DINE 'N DASH!!
NOW!
SVEN--PAY MY TAB, WILL YOU?
BOLT
WHAT?!
WAIT...!!
HEY!
TRAIN!
DASH

READ THIS WAY

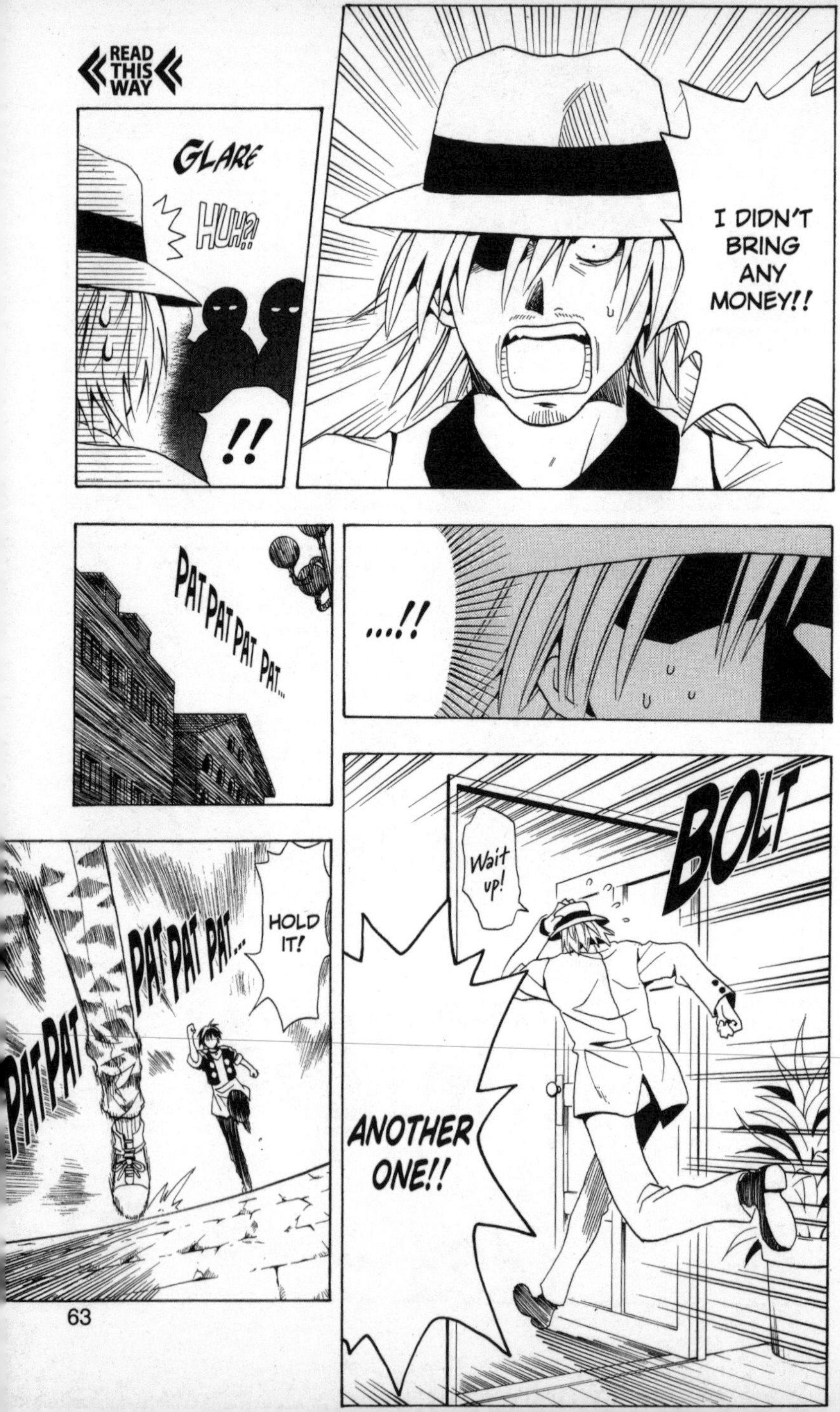
I DIDN'T BRING ANY MONEY!!
GLARE
HUH?!
!!
...!!
PAT PAT PAT PAT PAT...
BOLT
Wait up!
ANOTHER ONE!!
HOLD IT!
PAT PAT PAT...
PAT PAT

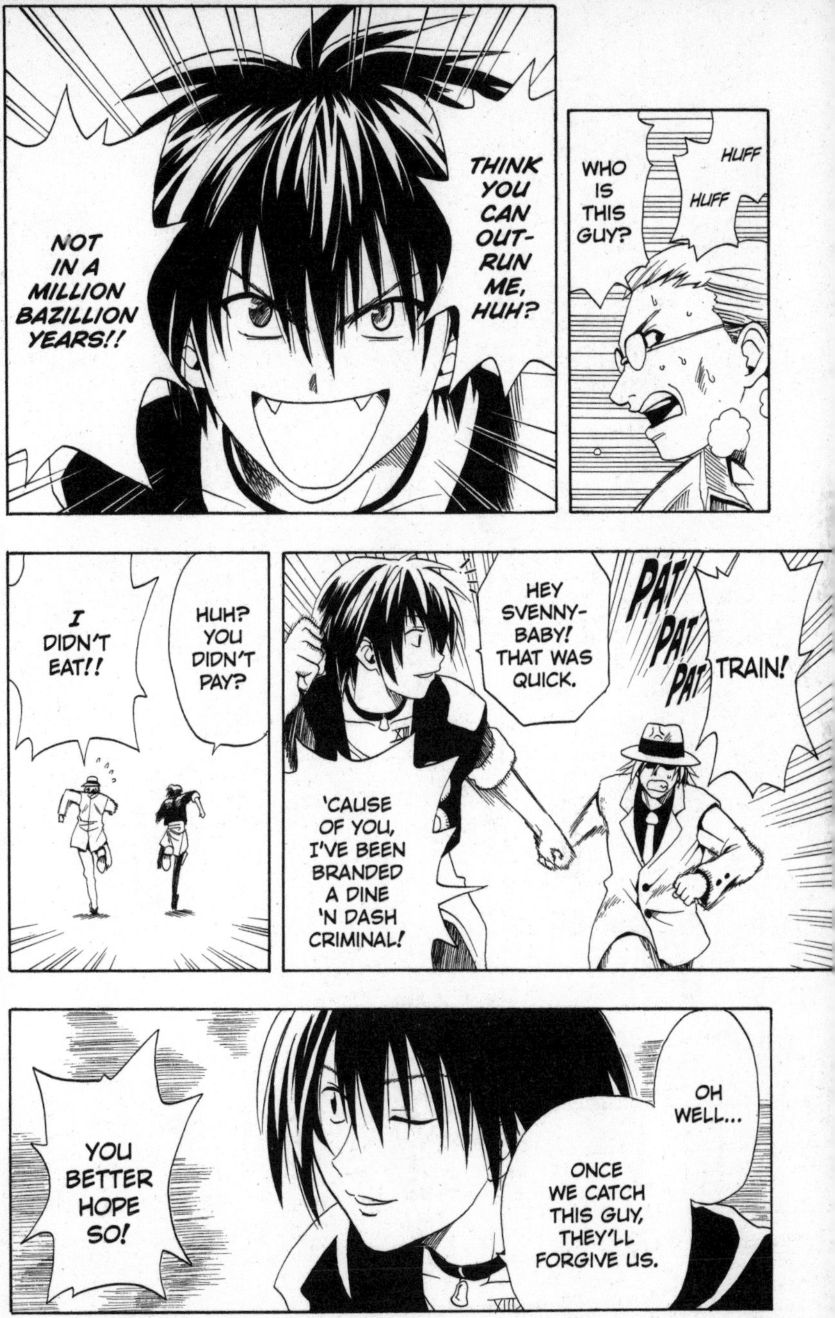
HUFF
HUFF
WHO IS THIS GUY?
THINK YOU CAN OUT-RUN ME, HUH?
NOT IN A MILLION BAZILLION YEARS!!
PAT PAT PAT
TRAIN!
HEY SVENNY-BABY! THAT WAS QUICK.
'CAUSE OF YOU, I'VE BEEN BRANDED A DINE 'N DASH CRIMINAL!
HUH? YOU DIDN'T PAY?
I DIDN'T EAT!!
OH WELL...
ONCE WE CATCH THIS GUY, THEY'LL FORGIVE US.
YOU BETTER HOPE SO!

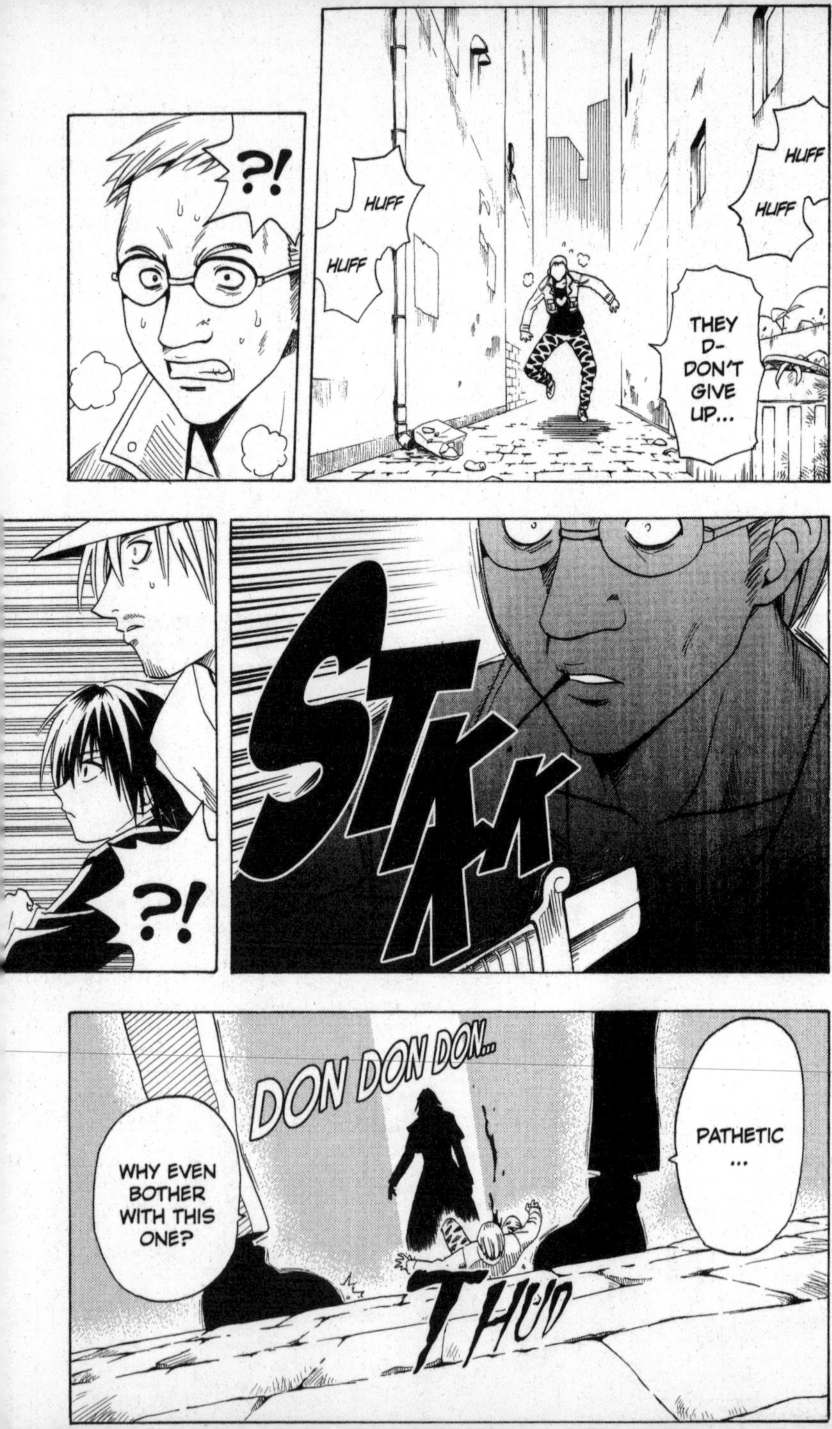
HUFF
HUFF
HUFF
HUFF
THEY D-DON'T GIVE UP...
?!
STKK
?!
DON DON DON...
PATHETIC...
WHY EVEN BOTHER WITH THIS ONE?
THUD

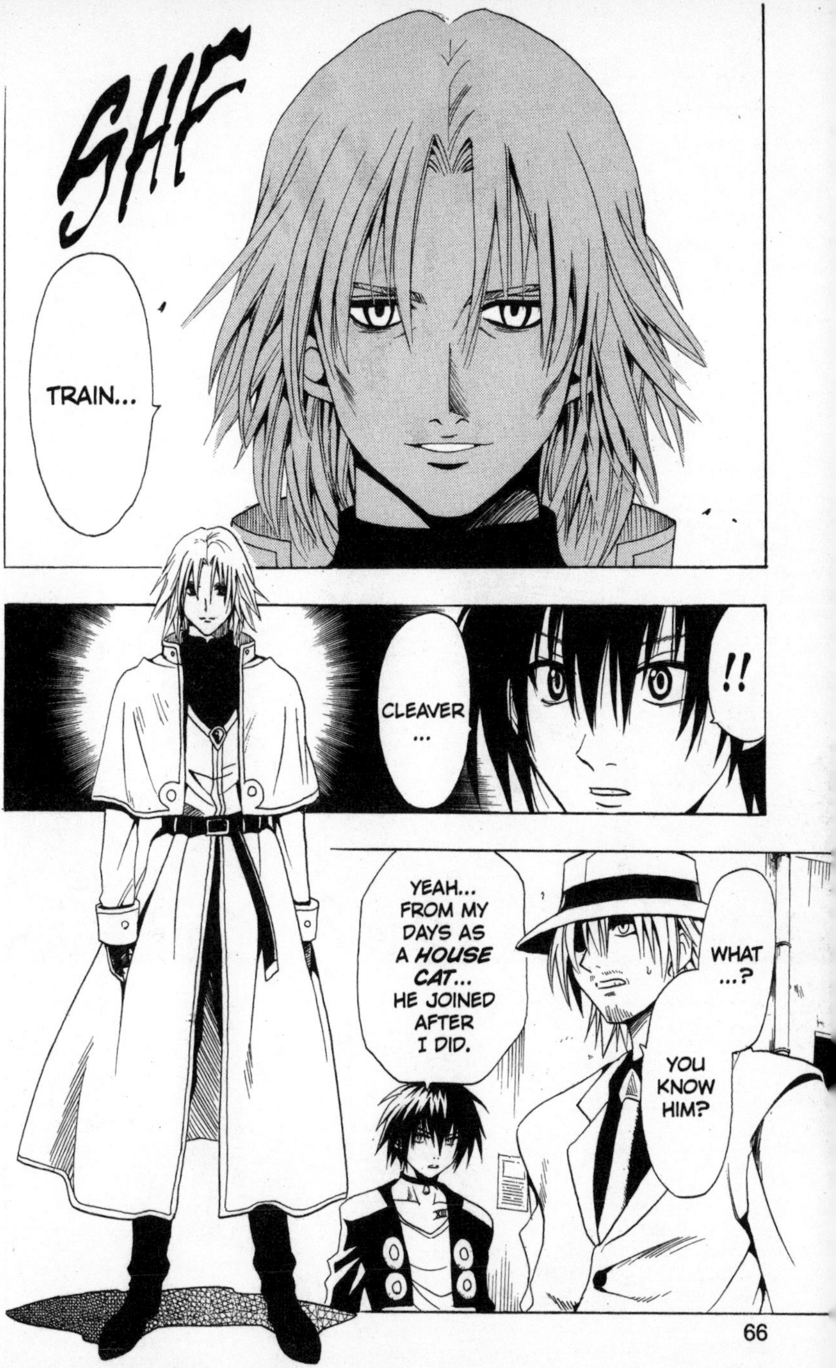
SHF
TRAIN...
!!
CLEAVER ...
WHAT ...?
YOU KNOW HIM?
YEAH... FROM MY DAYS AS A *HOUSE CAT*... HE JOINED AFTER I DID.

READ THIS WAY

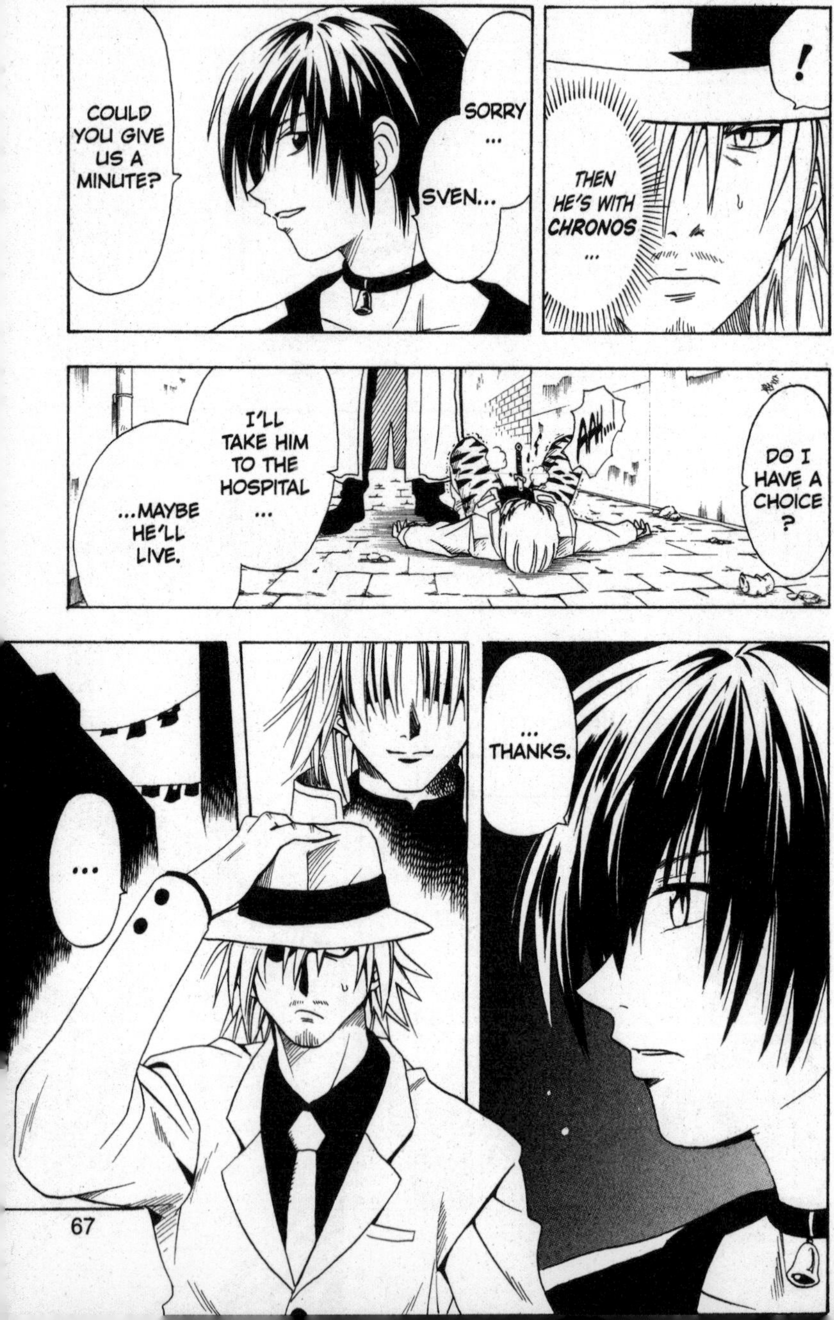
!
THEN HE'S WITH CHRONOS ...
SORRY ...
SVEN...
COULD YOU GIVE US A MINUTE?
DO I HAVE A CHOICE ?
AAH...!
I'LL TAKE HIM TO THE HOSPITAL ...
...MAYBE HE'LL LIVE.
... THANKS.
...

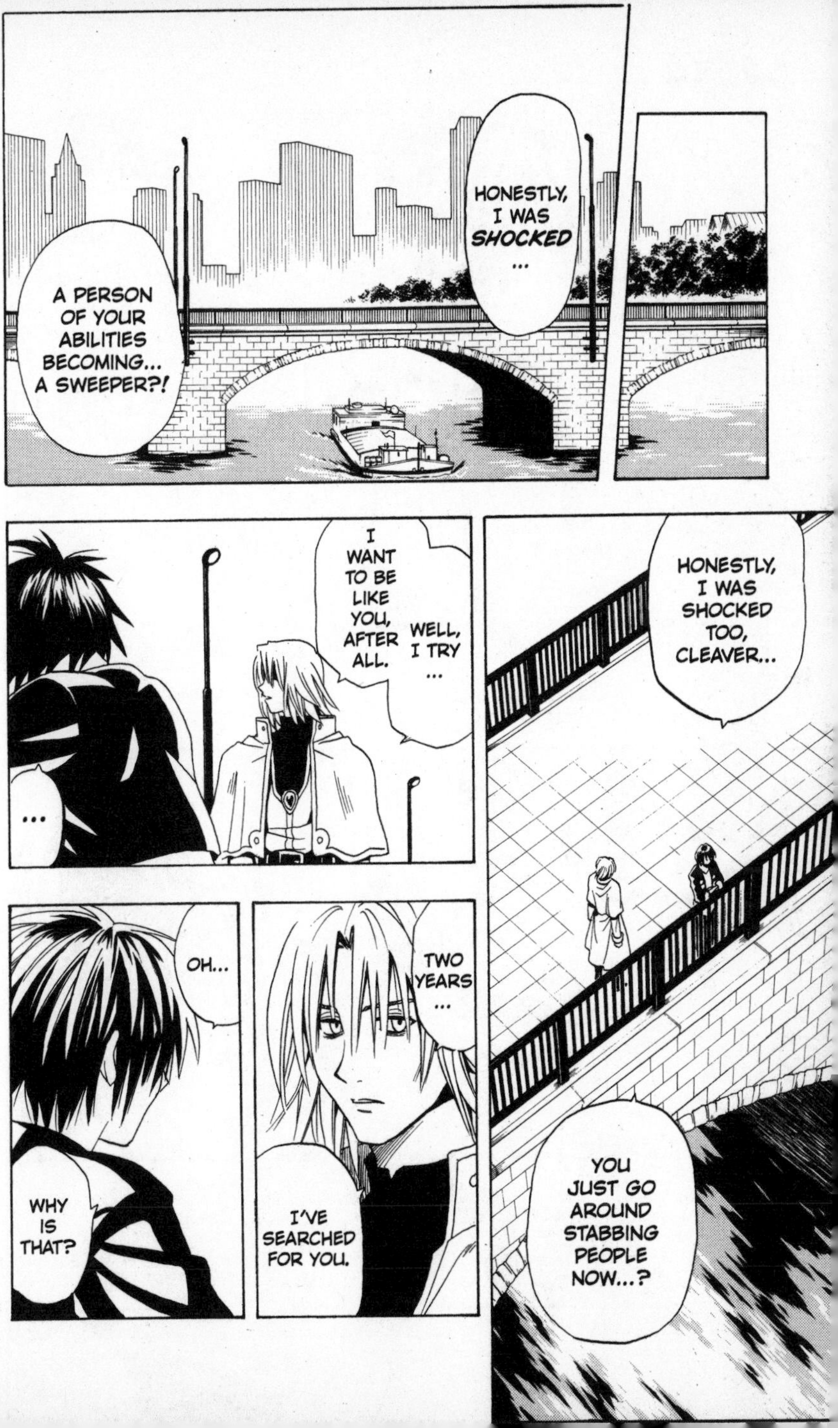
HONESTLY, I WAS SHOCKED ...
A PERSON OF YOUR ABILITIES BECOMING... A SWEEPER?!
HONESTLY, I WAS SHOCKED TOO, CLEAVER...
YOU JUST GO AROUND STABBING PEOPLE NOW...?
WELL, I TRY ...
I WANT TO BE LIKE YOU, AFTER ALL.
...
TWO YEARS ...
I'VE SEARCHED FOR YOU.
OH...
WHY IS THAT?

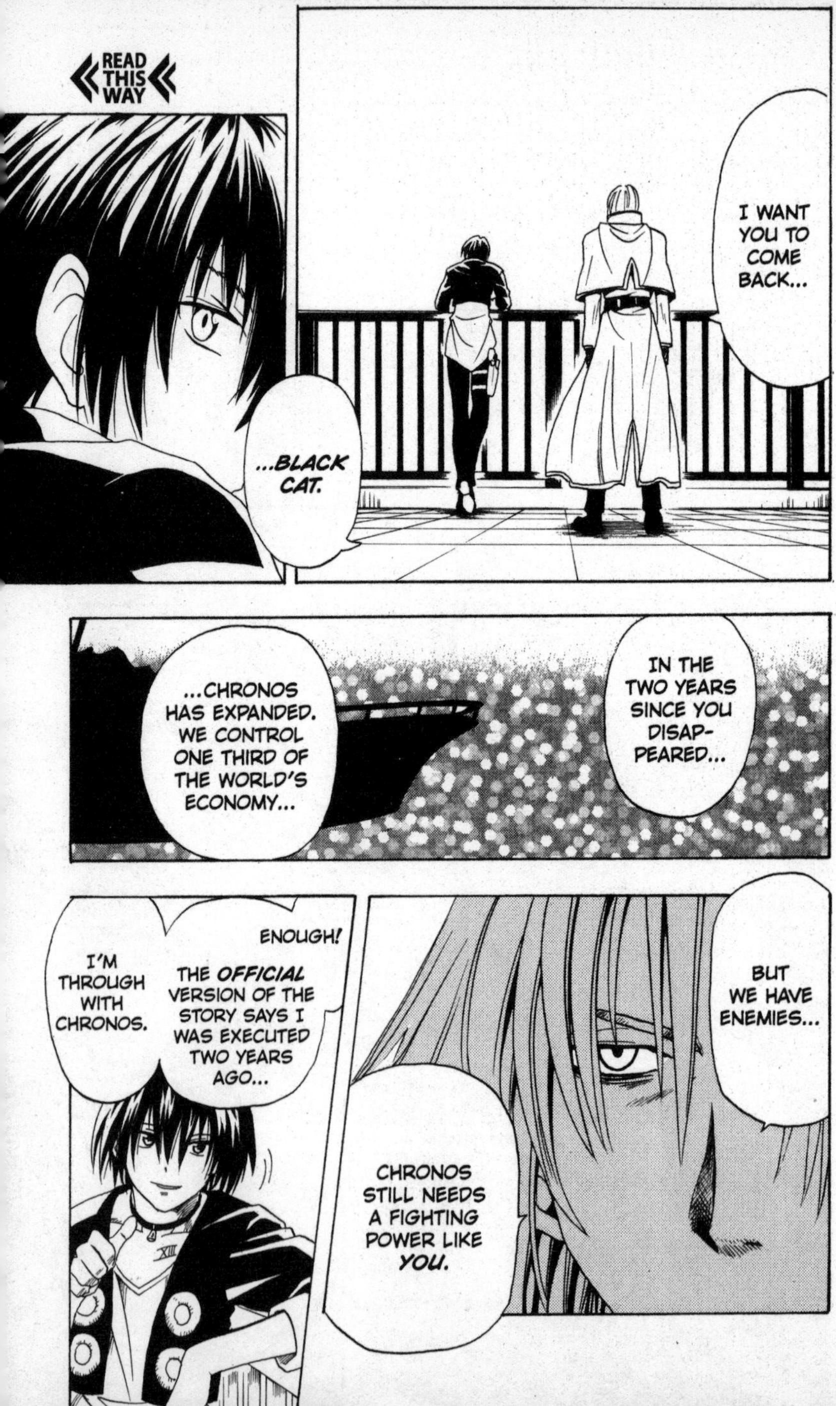
READ THIS WAY
I WANT YOU TO COME BACK...
...BLACK CAT.
IN THE TWO YEARS SINCE YOU DISAPPEARED...
...CHRONOS HAS EXPANDED. WE CONTROL ONE THIRD OF THE WORLD'S ECONOMY...
BUT WE HAVE ENEMIES...
CHRONOS STILL NEEDS A FIGHTING POWER LIKE YOU.
ENOUGH!
THE OFFICIAL VERSION OF THE STORY SAYS I WAS EXECUTED TWO YEARS AGO...
I'M THROUGH WITH CHRONOS.

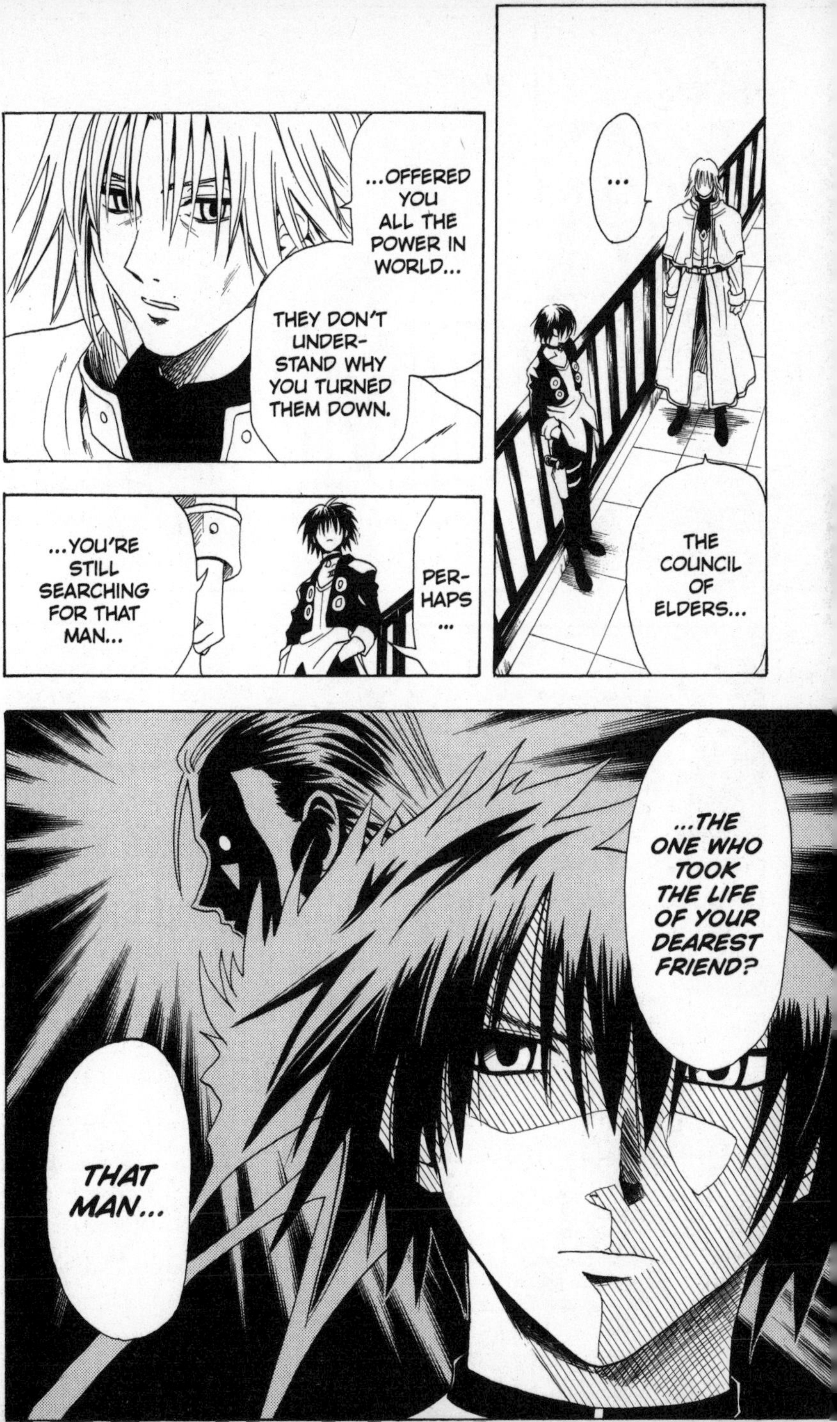
...
THE COUNCIL OF ELDERS...
...OFFERED YOU ALL THE POWER IN WORLD...
THEY DON'T UNDER-STAND WHY YOU TURNED THEM DOWN.
PER-HAPS...
...YOU'RE STILL SEARCHING FOR THAT MAN...
...THE ONE WHO TOOK THE LIFE OF YOUR DEAREST FRIEND?
THAT MAN...

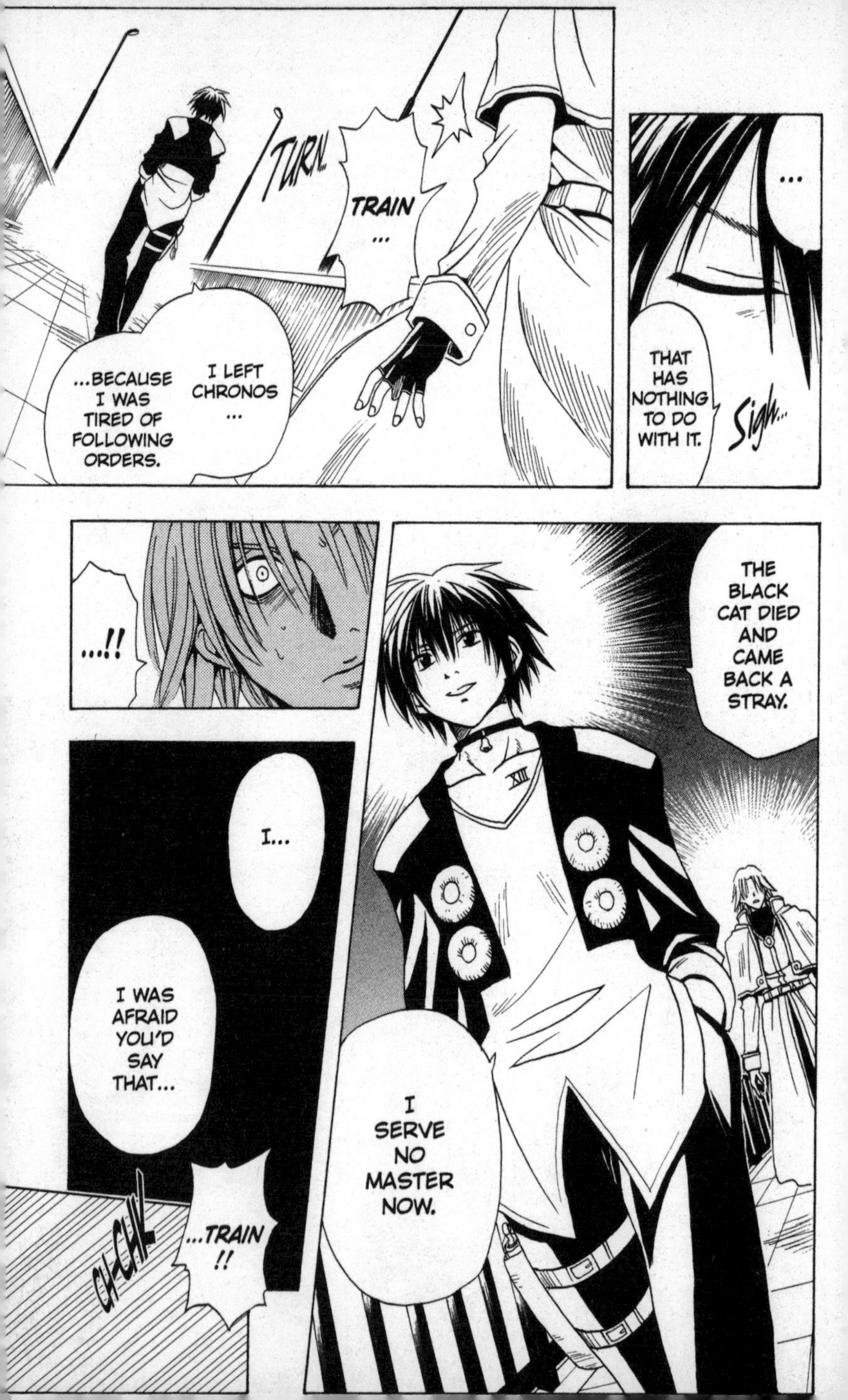
...
THAT HAS NOTHING TO DO WITH IT.
Sigh...
TRAIN ...
TURN
I LEFT CHRONOS ...
...BECAUSE I WAS TIRED OF FOLLOWING ORDERS.
THE BLACK CAT DIED AND CAME BACK A STRAY.
I SERVE NO MASTER NOW.
...!!
I...
I WAS AFRAID YOU'D SAY THAT...
...TRAIN !!
CH-CHK

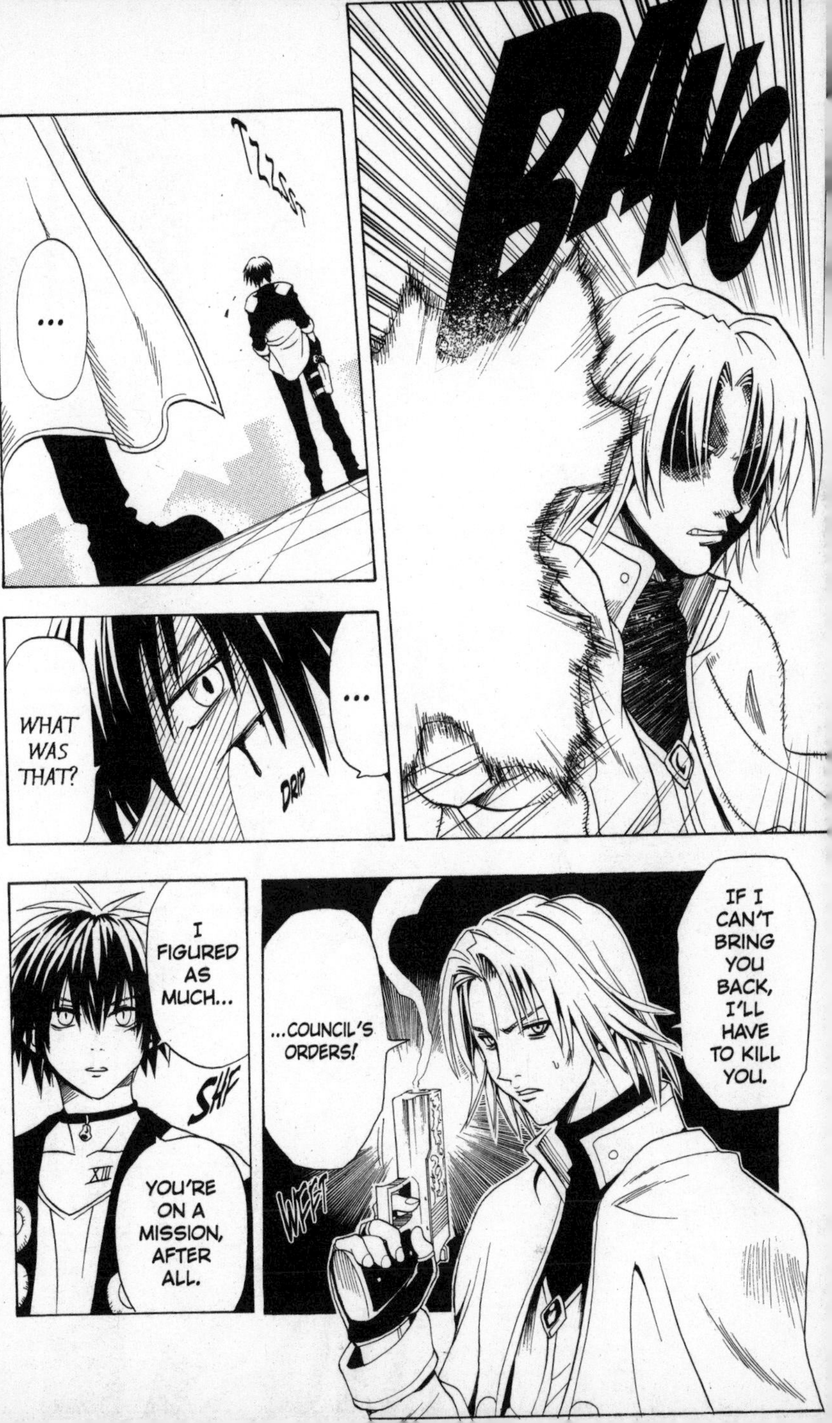
BANG
TZZZSST
...
...
DRIP
WHAT WAS THAT?
IF I CAN'T BRING YOU BACK, I'LL HAVE TO KILL YOU.
...COUNCIL'S ORDERS!
WFFT
I FIGURED AS MUCH...
SHF
YOU'RE ON A MISSION, AFTER ALL.

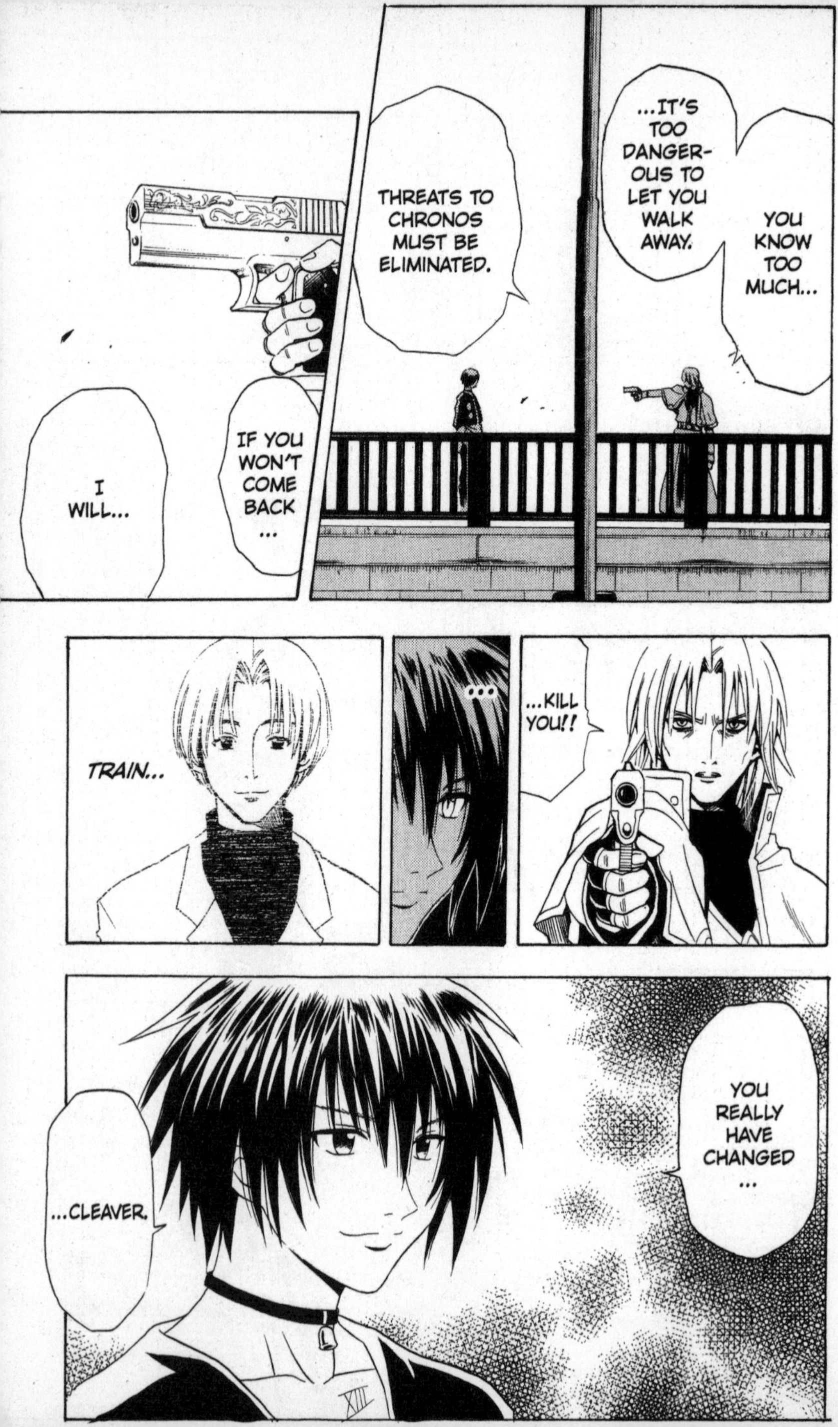
YOU KNOW TOO MUCH...
...IT'S TOO DANGER-OUS TO LET YOU WALK AWAY.
THREATS TO CHRONOS MUST BE ELIMINATED.
IF YOU WON'T COME BACK ...
I WILL...
...KILL YOU!!
...
TRAIN...
YOU REALLY HAVE CHANGED ...
...CLEAVER.

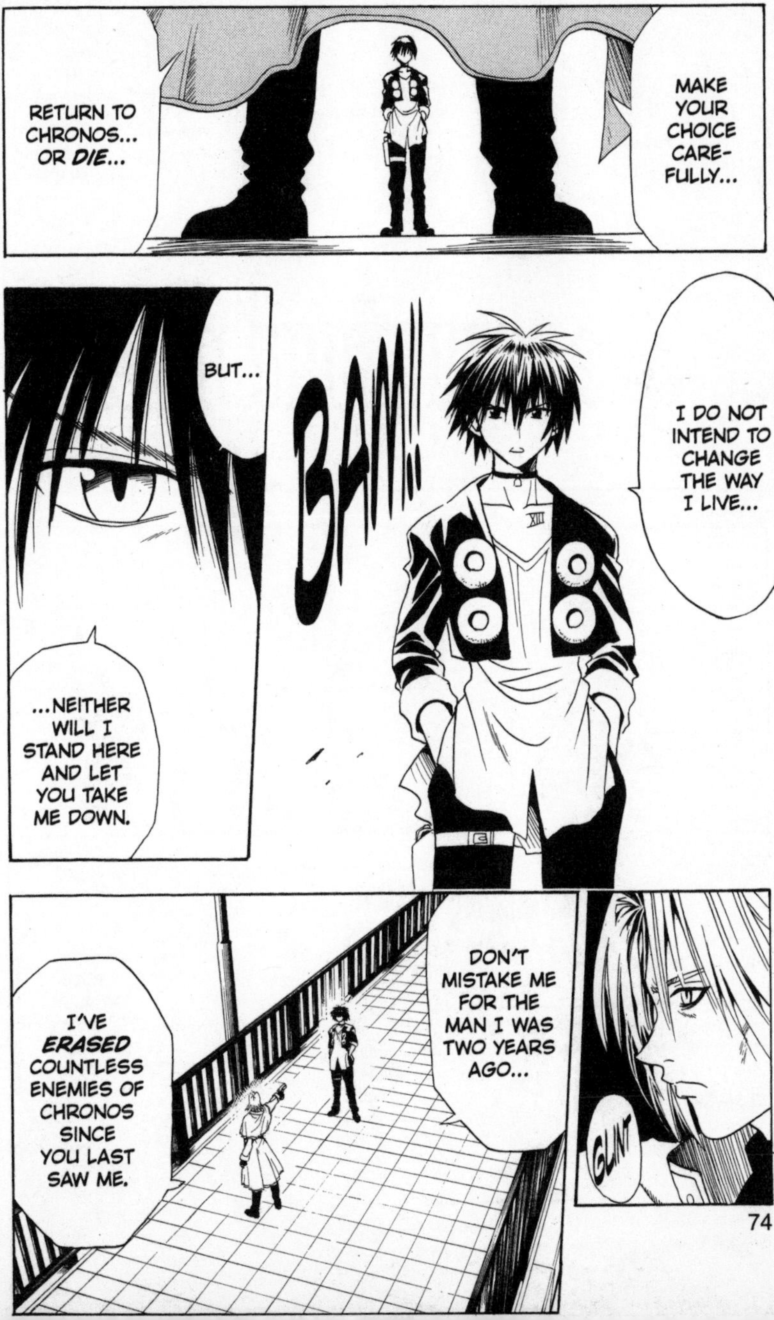
MAKE YOUR CHOICE CARE-FULLY...
RETURN TO CHRONOS... OR *DIE*...
I DO NOT INTEND TO CHANGE THE WAY I LIVE...
BAM!!
BUT...
...NEITHER WILL I STAND HERE AND LET YOU TAKE ME DOWN.
GLINT
DON'T MISTAKE ME FOR THE MAN I WAS TWO YEARS AGO...
I'VE ***ERASED*** COUNTLESS ENEMIES OF CHRONOS SINCE YOU LAST SAW ME.

READ THIS WAY

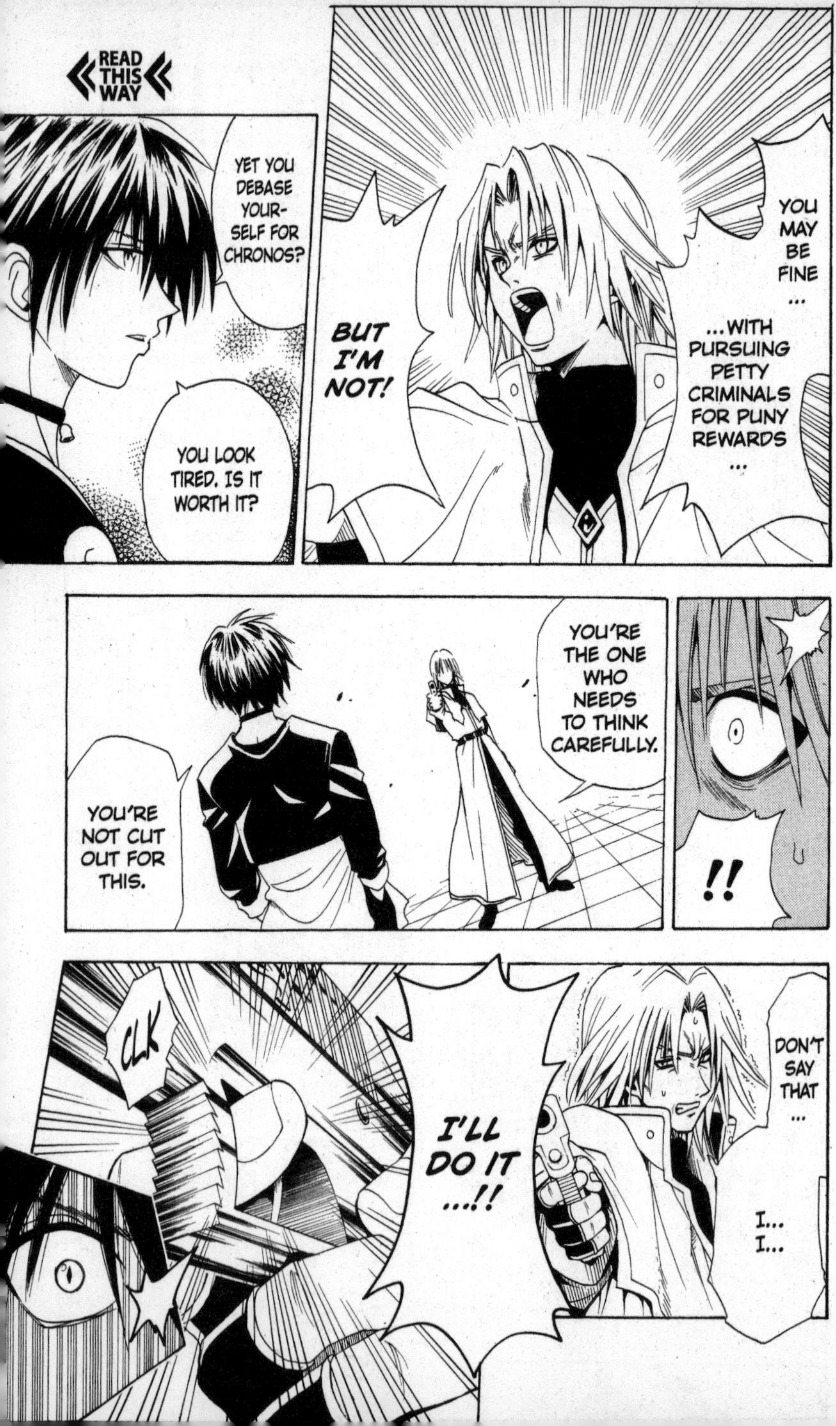
YOU MAY BE FINE ...
...WITH PURSUING PETTY CRIMINALS FOR PUNY REWARDS ...
BUT I'M NOT!
YET YOU DEBASE YOUR-SELF FOR CHRONOS?
YOU LOOK TIRED. IS IT WORTH IT?
!!
YOU'RE THE ONE WHO NEEDS TO THINK CAREFULLY.
YOU'RE NOT CUT OUT FOR THIS.
DON'T SAY THAT ...
I... I...
I'LL DO IT ...!!
CLK

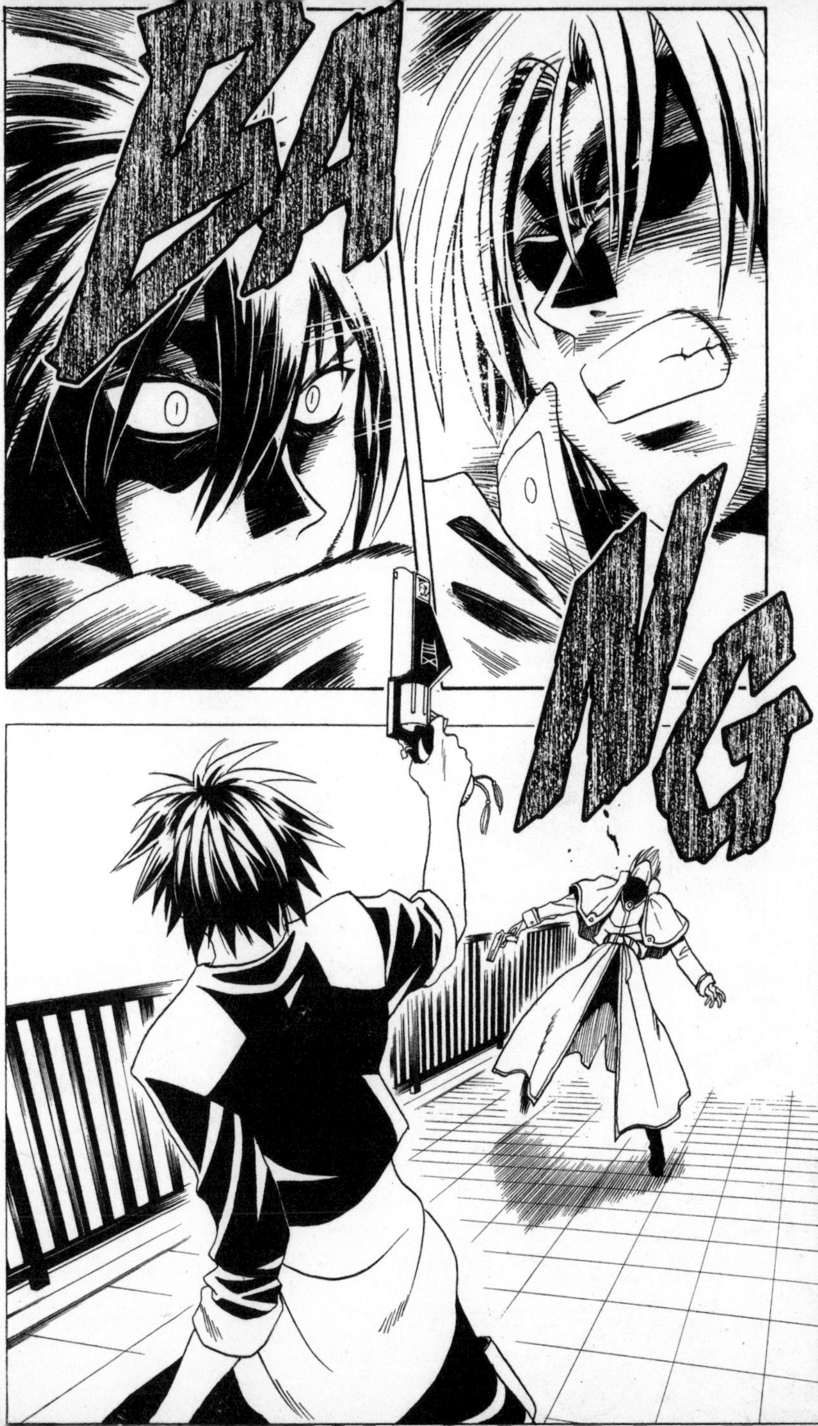
BANG

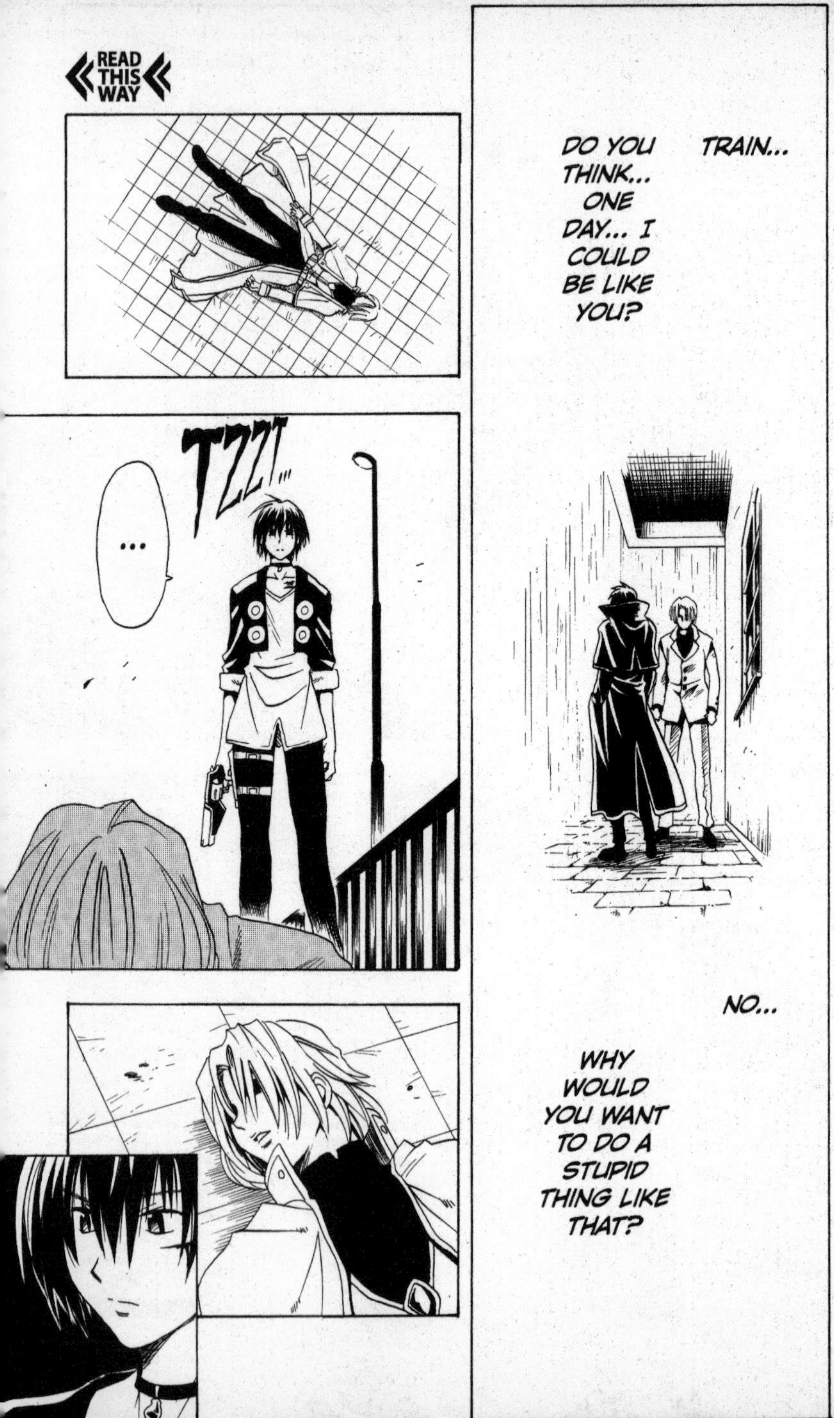
READ THIS WAY
TRAIN...
DO YOU THINK... ONE DAY... I COULD BE LIKE YOU?
NO...
WHY WOULD YOU WANT TO DO A STUPID THING LIKE THAT?
TZZT...
...

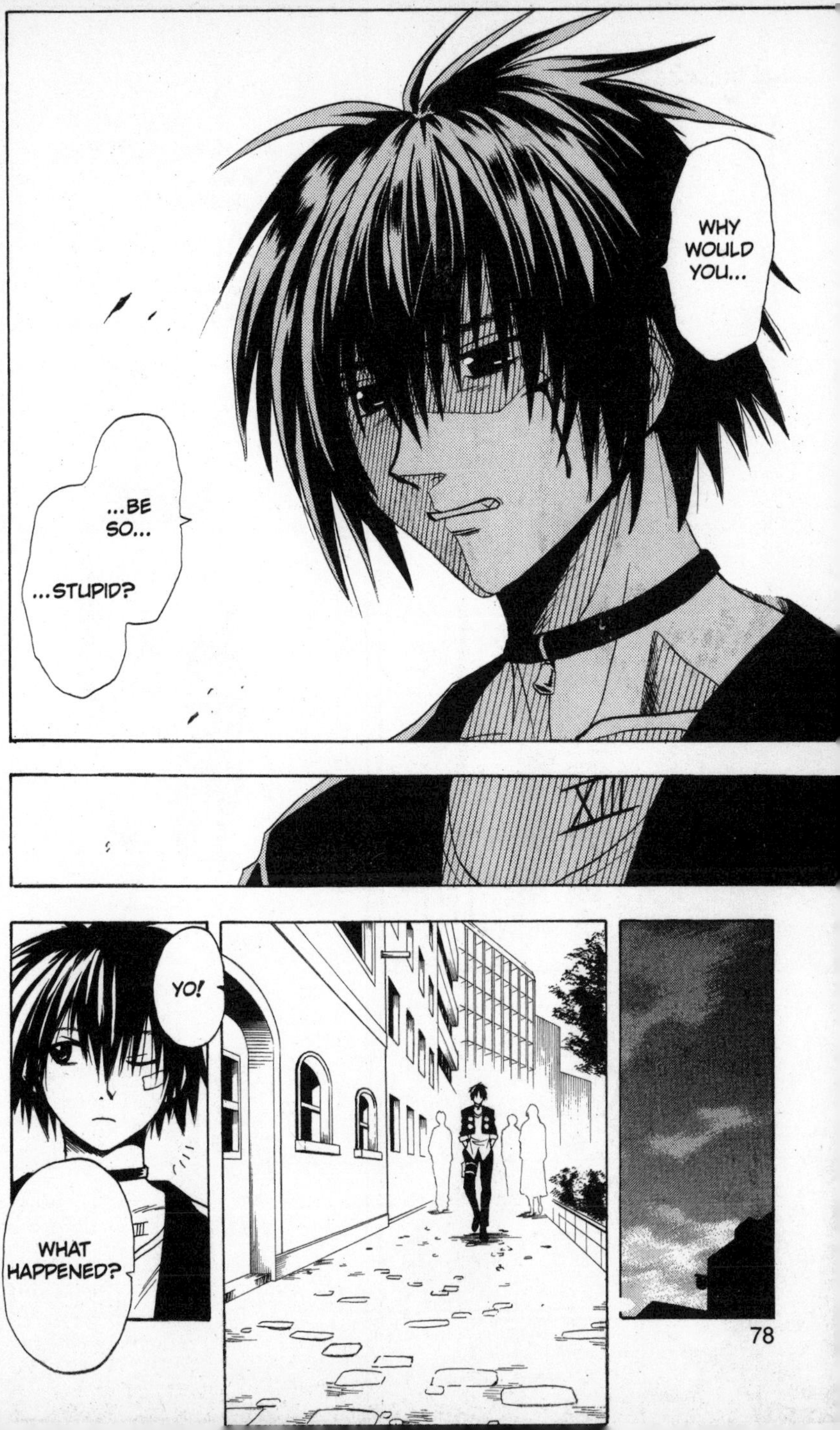
WHY WOULD YOU...
...BE SO...
...STUPID?
YO!
WHAT HAPPENED?

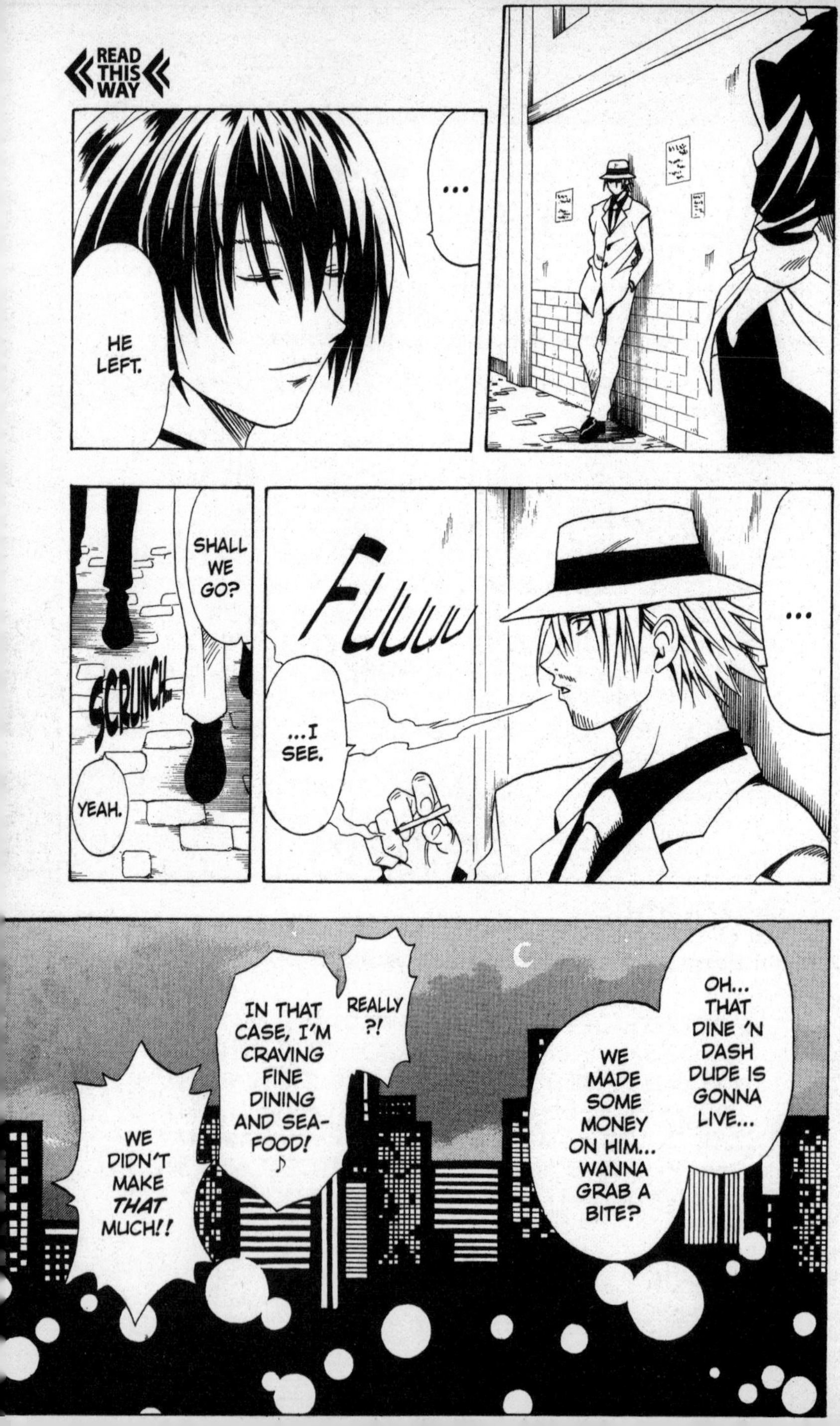
READ THIS WAY
...
HE LEFT.
...
FUUUU
...I SEE.
SHALL WE GO?
SCRUNCH...
YEAH.
OH... THAT DINE 'N DASH DUDE IS GONNA LIVE...
WE MADE SOME MONEY ON HIM... WANNA GRAB A BITE?
REALLY?!
IN THAT CASE, I'M CRAVING FINE DINING AND SEA-FOOD! ♪
WE DIDN'T MAKE *THAT* MUCH!!

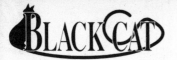 **FACTOIDS**

SWEEPER (ONE WHO CLEANS UP)

A SLANG TERM FOR "BOUNTY HUNTER." THOUGH SPECIFICS MAY VARY FROM PERSON TO PERSON, IT CAN BASICALLY BE SAID THAT A SWEEPER PURSUES FUGITIVES FOR WHOM A REWARD HAS BEEN OFFERED.

IN ORDER TO WORK AS A SWEEPER, ONE MUST BE LICENSED BY THE IBI (INTERNATIONAL BUREAU OF INVESTIGATIONS). OBTAINING A LICENSE IS FAIRLY EASY AND IS CONTINGENT UPON A PRACTICAL SKILLS TEST. (A TESTING OFFICIAL ACTING AS A FUGITIVE MUST BE APPREHENDED WITHIN A SPECIFIED TIME PERIOD.)

THERE ARE ROUGHLY 1,000 LICENSED SWEEPERS WORLDWIDE. IT SHOULD BE NOTED THAT THIS PARTICULAR VOCATION ATTRACTS AN INORDINATE NUMBER OF ECCENTRICS AND INDIVIDUALS WITH AXES TO GRIND.

REWARDS

THE BOUNTY OFFERED FOR A PARTICULAR FUGITIVE IS USUALLY LISTED ON A POLICE BULLETIN. IN SOME CASES (E.G., WHEN THE CRIMINAL HAS NOT YET BEEN PLACED ON A WANTED LIST), THE BOUNTY AMOUNT IS DETERMINED AFTER THE FUGITIVE IS IN POLICE CUSTODY AND AN INVESTIGATION HAS BEEN CONDUCTED.

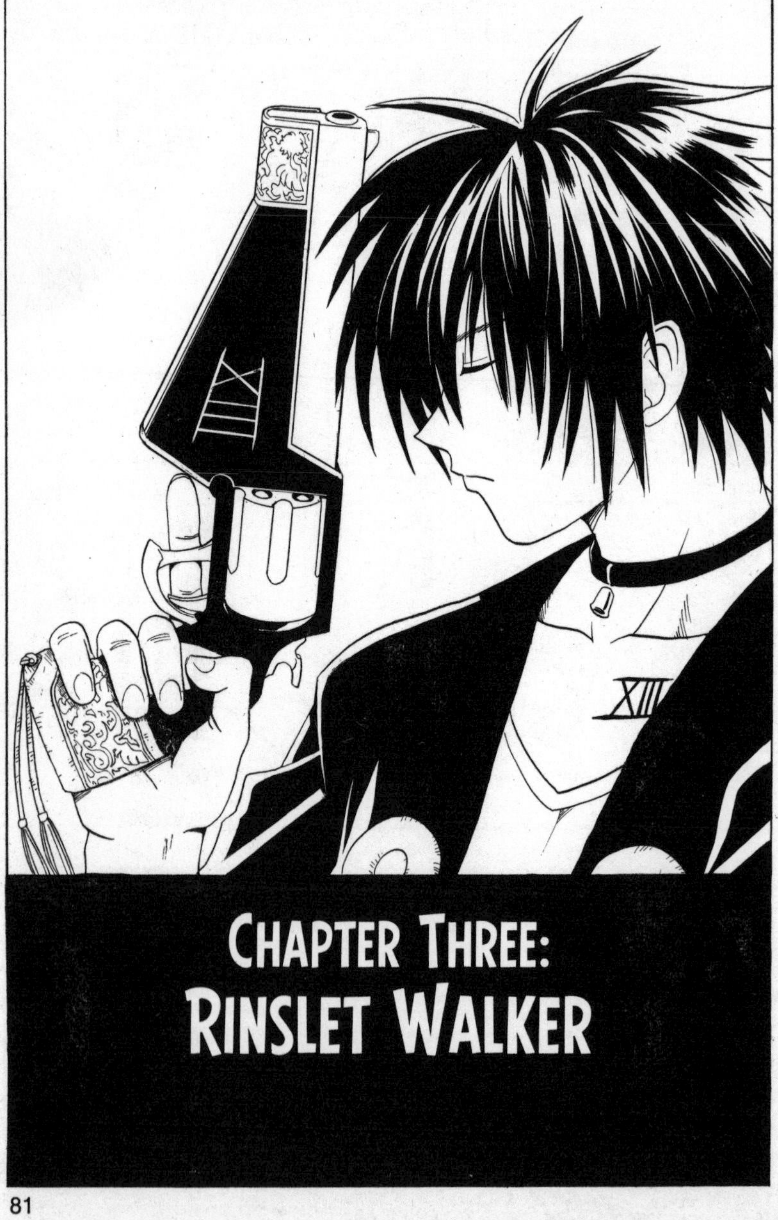

Chapter Three: Rinslet Walker

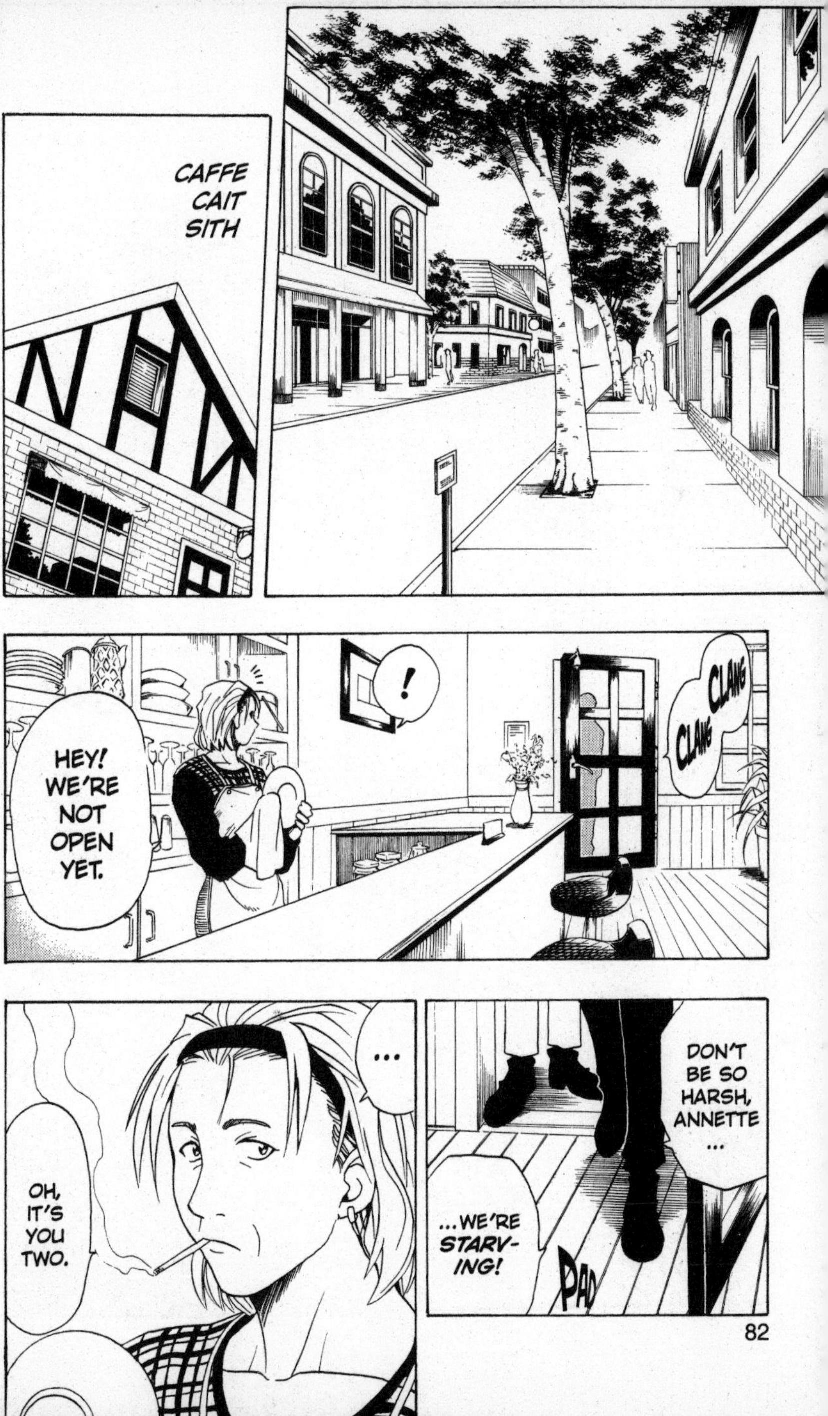

CAFFE CAIT SITH
CLANG CLANG
!
HEY! WE'RE NOT OPEN YET.
DON'T BE SO HARSH, ANNETTE...
...WE'RE STARVING!
PAD
...
OH, IT'S YOU TWO.

READ THIS WAY

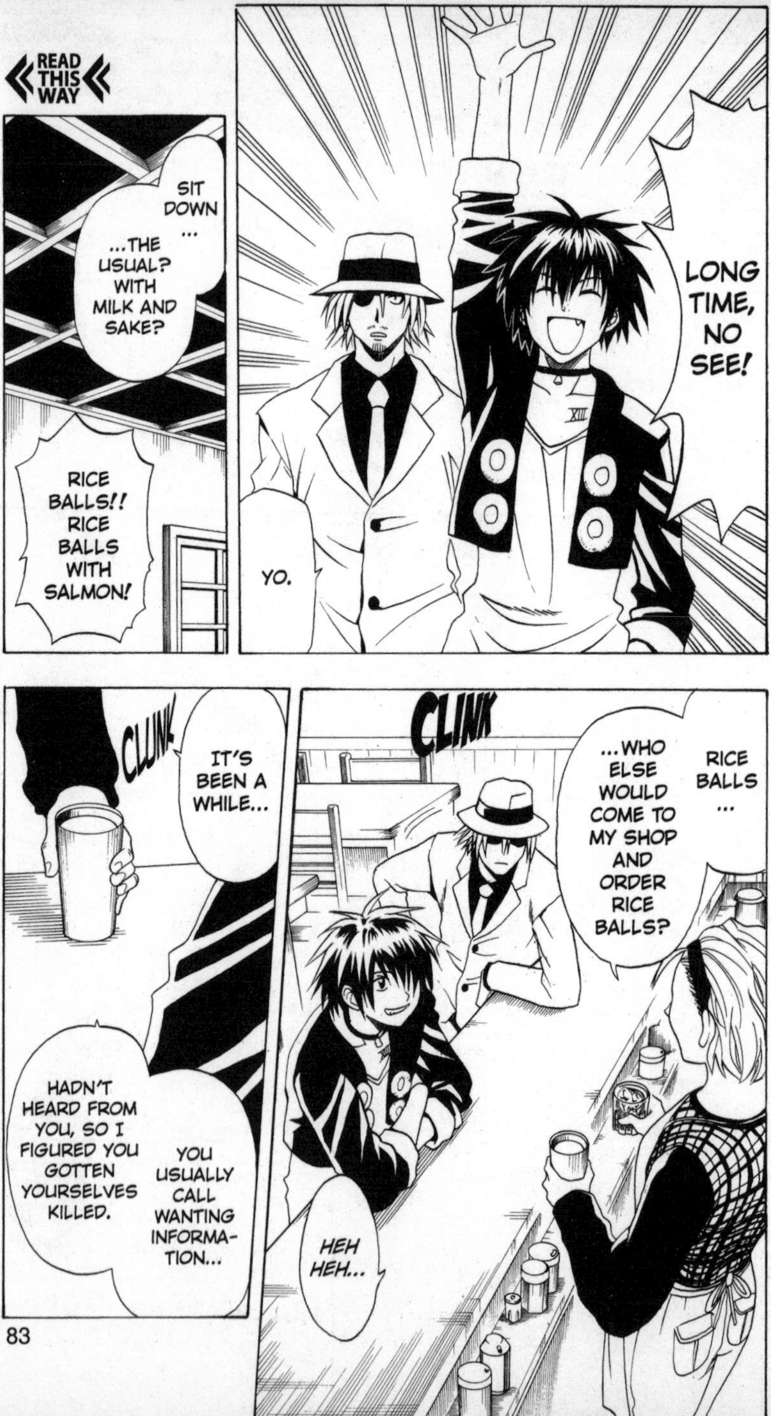
LONG TIME, NO SEE!
YO.
SIT DOWN ...
...THE USUAL? WITH MILK AND SAKE?
RICE BALLS!! RICE BALLS WITH SALMON!
CLINK
RICE BALLS ...
...WHO ELSE WOULD COME TO MY SHOP AND ORDER RICE BALLS?
HEH HEH...
CLINK
IT'S BEEN A WHILE...
YOU USUALLY CALL WANTING INFORMATION...
HADN'T HEARD FROM YOU, SO I FIGURED YOU GOTTEN YOURSELVES KILLED.

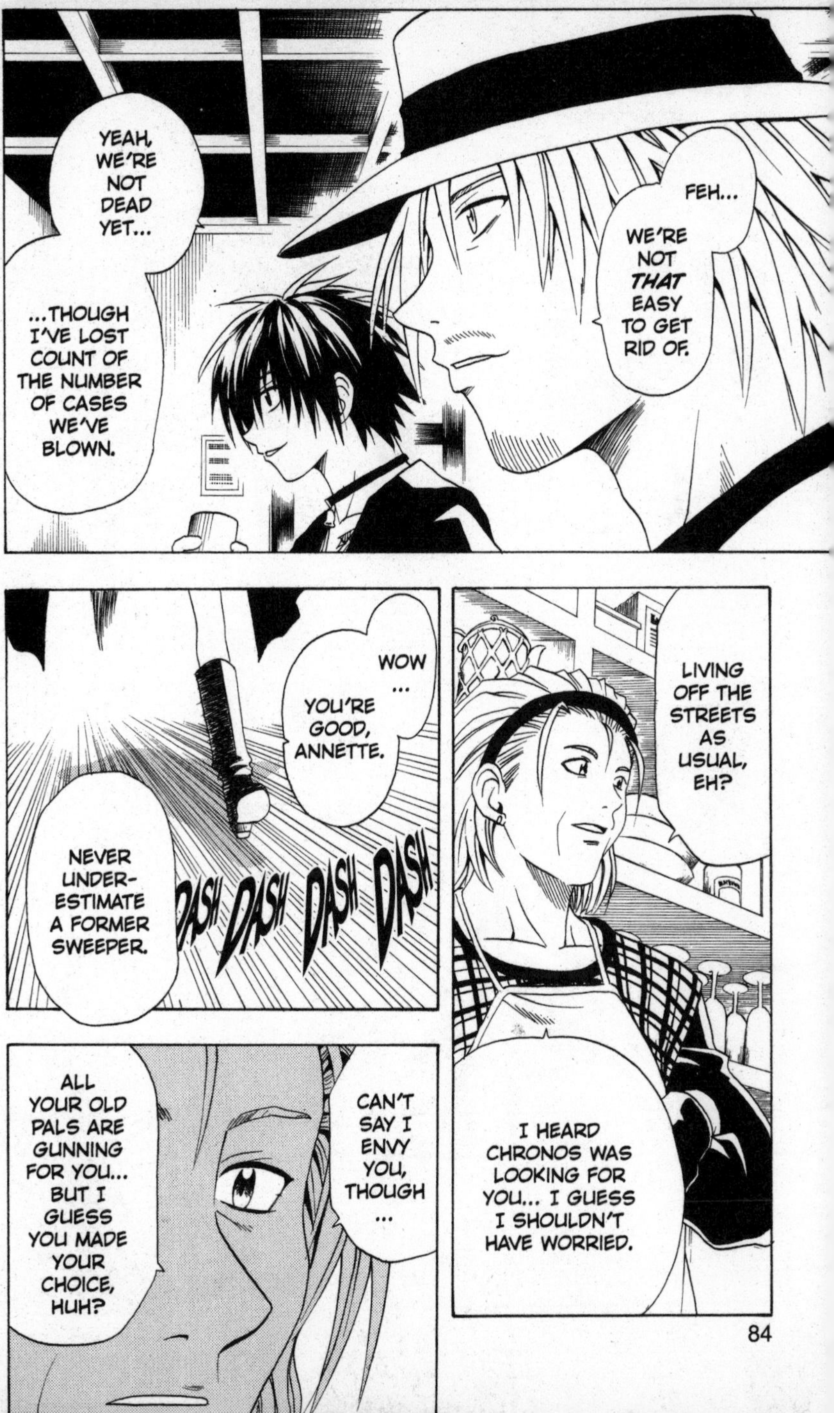
FEH... WE'RE NOT *THAT* EASY TO GET RID OF.
YEAH, WE'RE NOT DEAD YET...
...THOUGH I'VE LOST COUNT OF THE NUMBER OF CASES WE'VE BLOWN.
LIVING OFF THE STREETS AS USUAL, EH?
I HEARD CHRONOS WAS LOOKING FOR YOU... I GUESS I SHOULDN'T HAVE WORRIED.
WOW... YOU'RE GOOD, ANNETTE.
NEVER UNDER-ESTIMATE A FORMER SWEEPER.
DASH DASH DASH DASH
CAN'T SAY I ENVY YOU, THOUGH...
ALL YOUR OLD PALS ARE GUNNING FOR YOU... BUT I GUESS YOU MADE YOUR CHOICE, HUH?

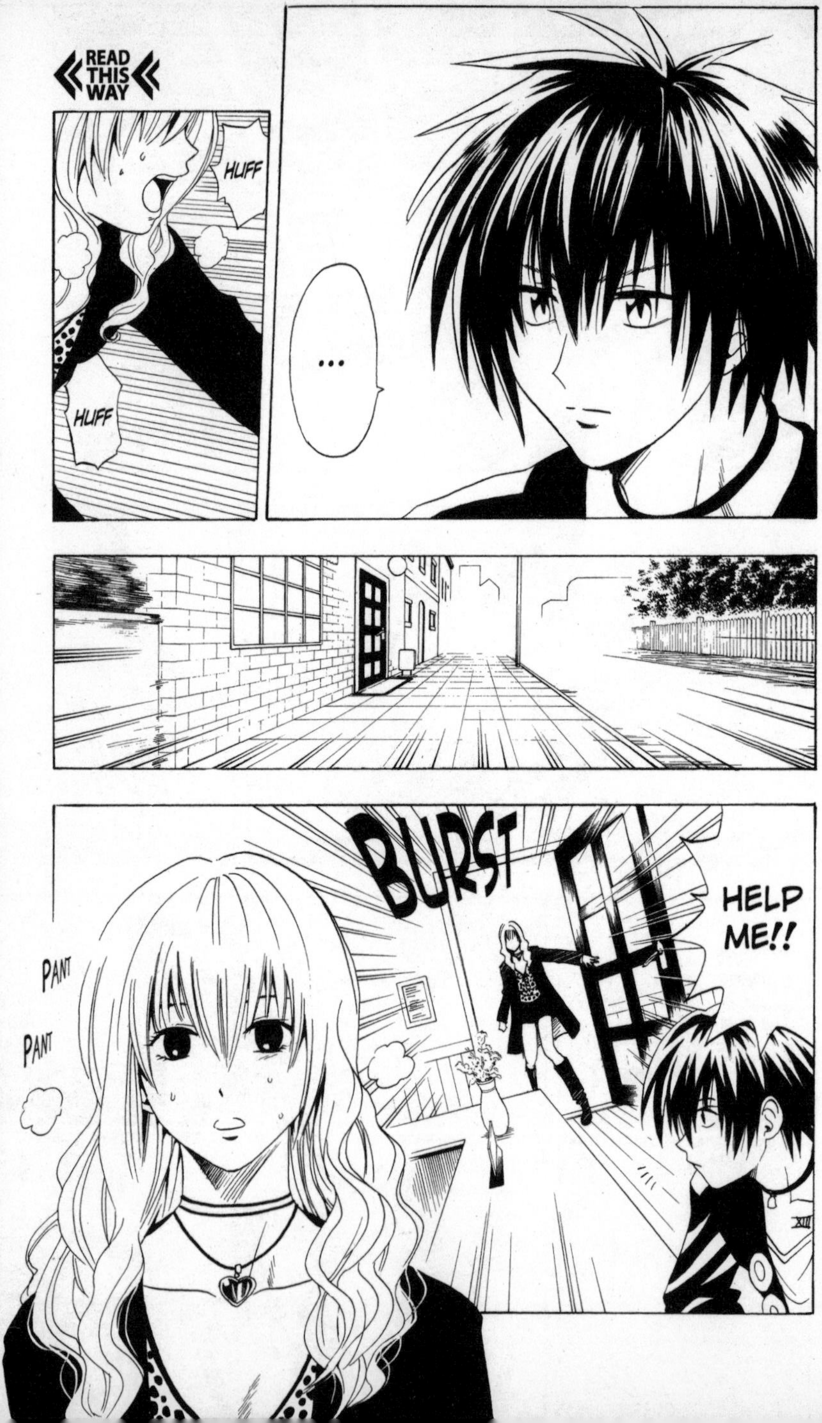
READ THIS WAY
...
HUFF
HUFF
BURST
HELP ME!!
PANT
PANT

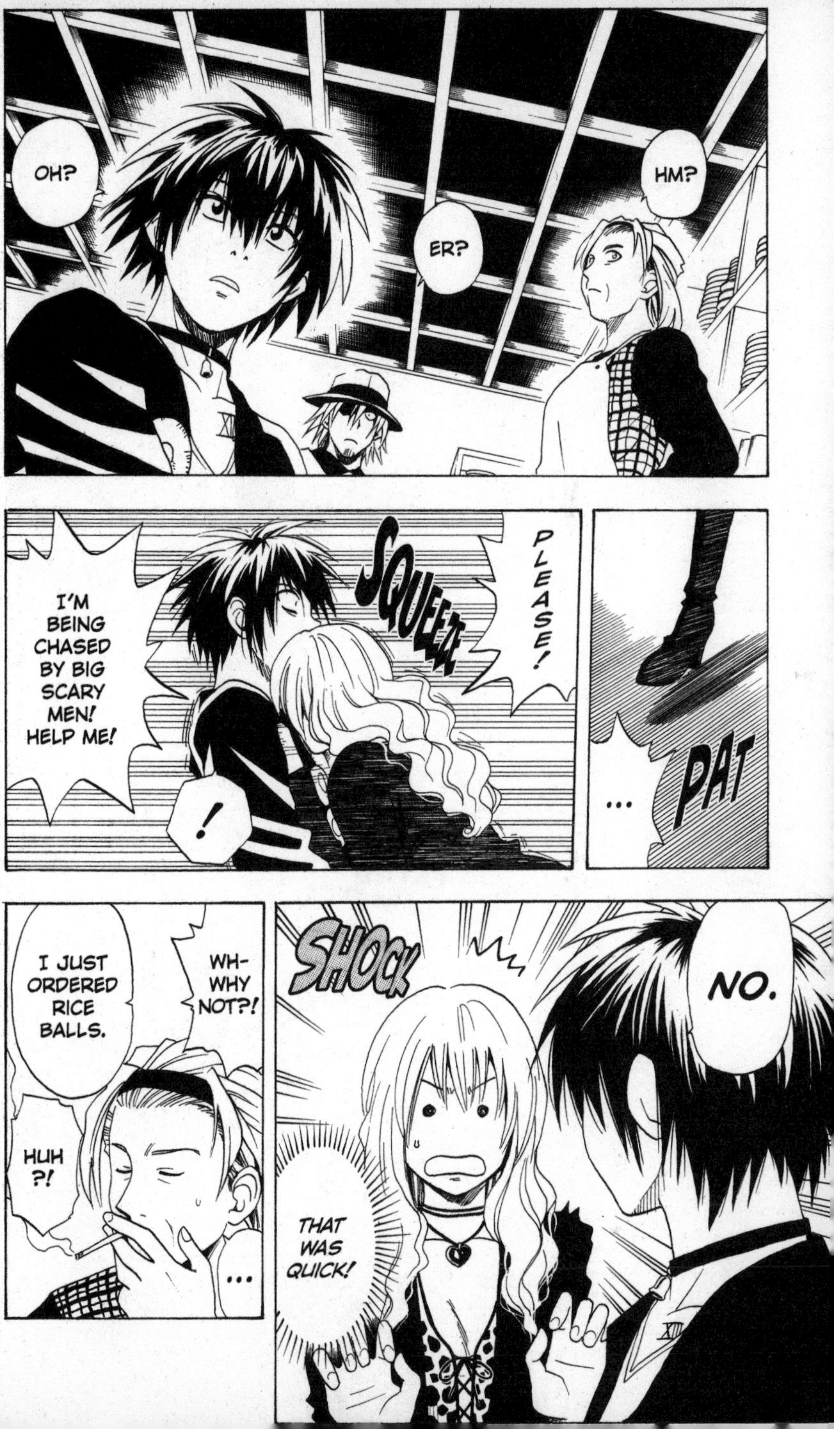
HM?
ER?
OH?
...
PAT
PLEASE!
SQUEEEZE
I'M BEING CHASED BY BIG SCARY MEN! HELP ME!
!
NO.
SHOCK
THAT WAS QUICK!
WH-WHY NOT?!
I JUST ORDERED RICE BALLS.
HUH?!
...

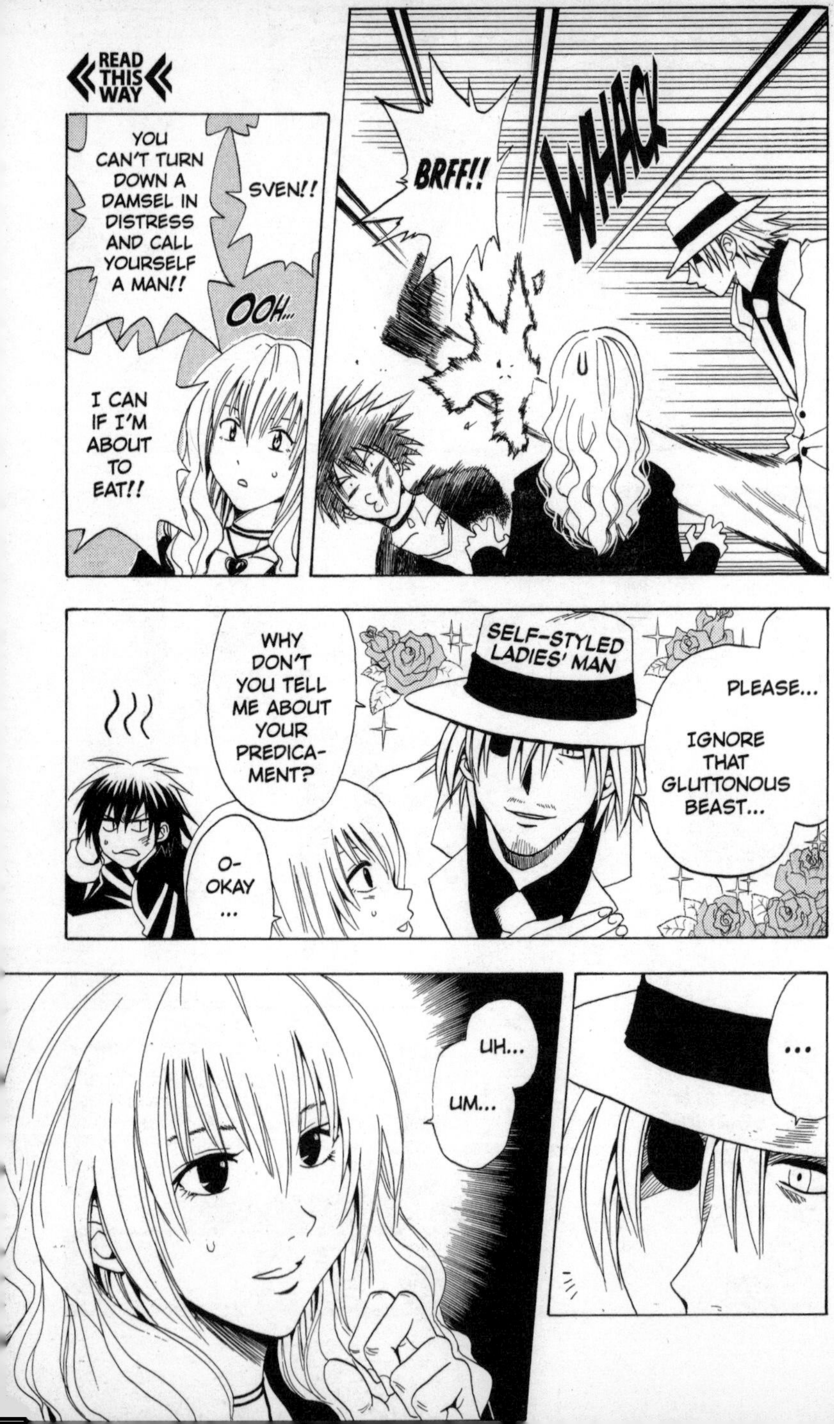

READ THIS WAY
WHACK
BRFF!!
SVEN!!
YOU CAN'T TURN DOWN A DAMSEL IN DISTRESS AND CALL YOURSELF A MAN!!
OOH...
I CAN IF I'M ABOUT TO EAT!!
PLEASE...
IGNORE THAT GLUTTONOUS BEAST...
SELF-STYLED LADIES' MAN
WHY DON'T YOU TELL ME ABOUT YOUR PREDICA-MENT?
O-OKAY ...
...
UH...
UM...

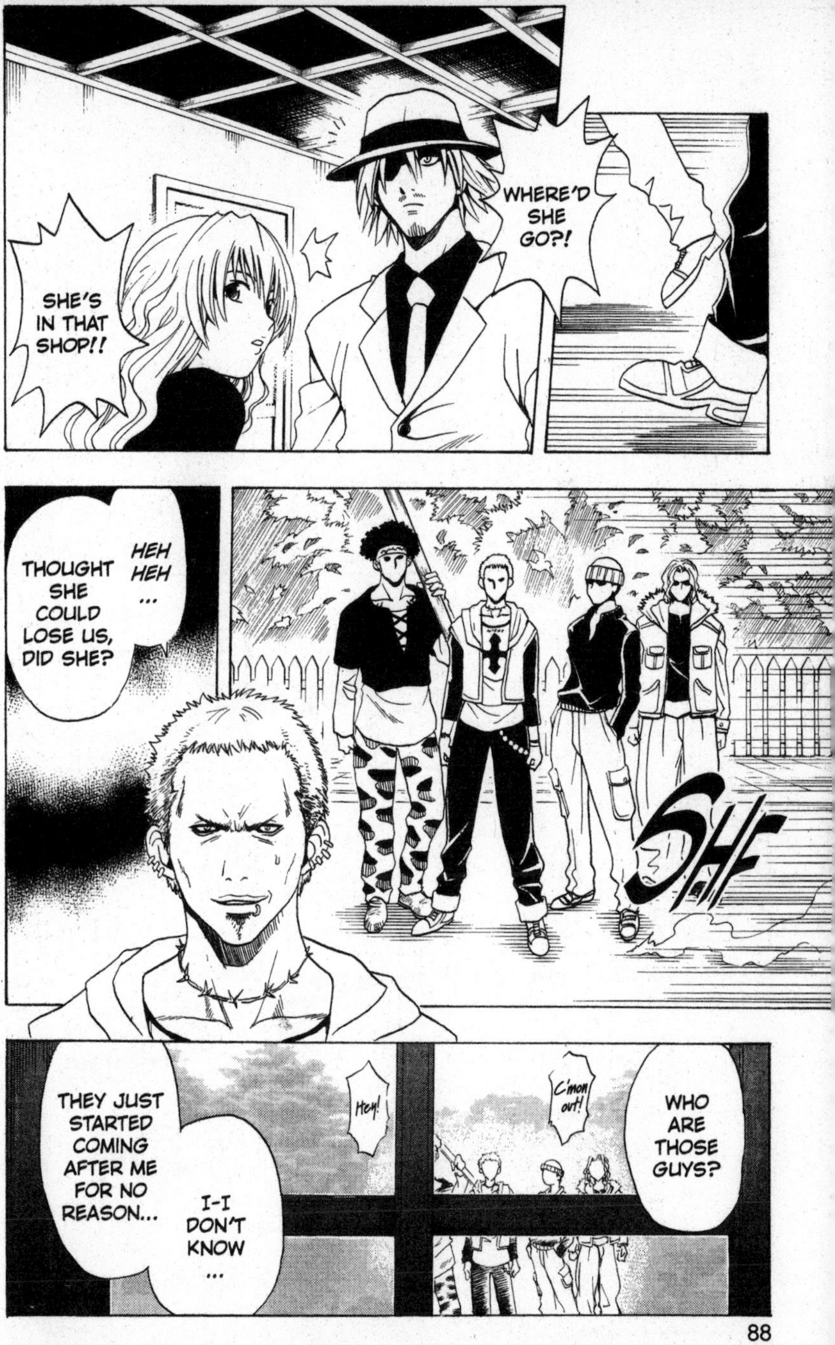
WHERE'D SHE GO?!
SHE'S IN THAT SHOP!!
SH
HEH HEH ...
THOUGHT SHE COULD LOSE US, DID SHE?
WHO ARE THOSE GUYS?
C'mon out!
Hey!
I-I DON'T KNOW ...
THEY JUST STARTED COMING AFTER ME FOR NO REASON...

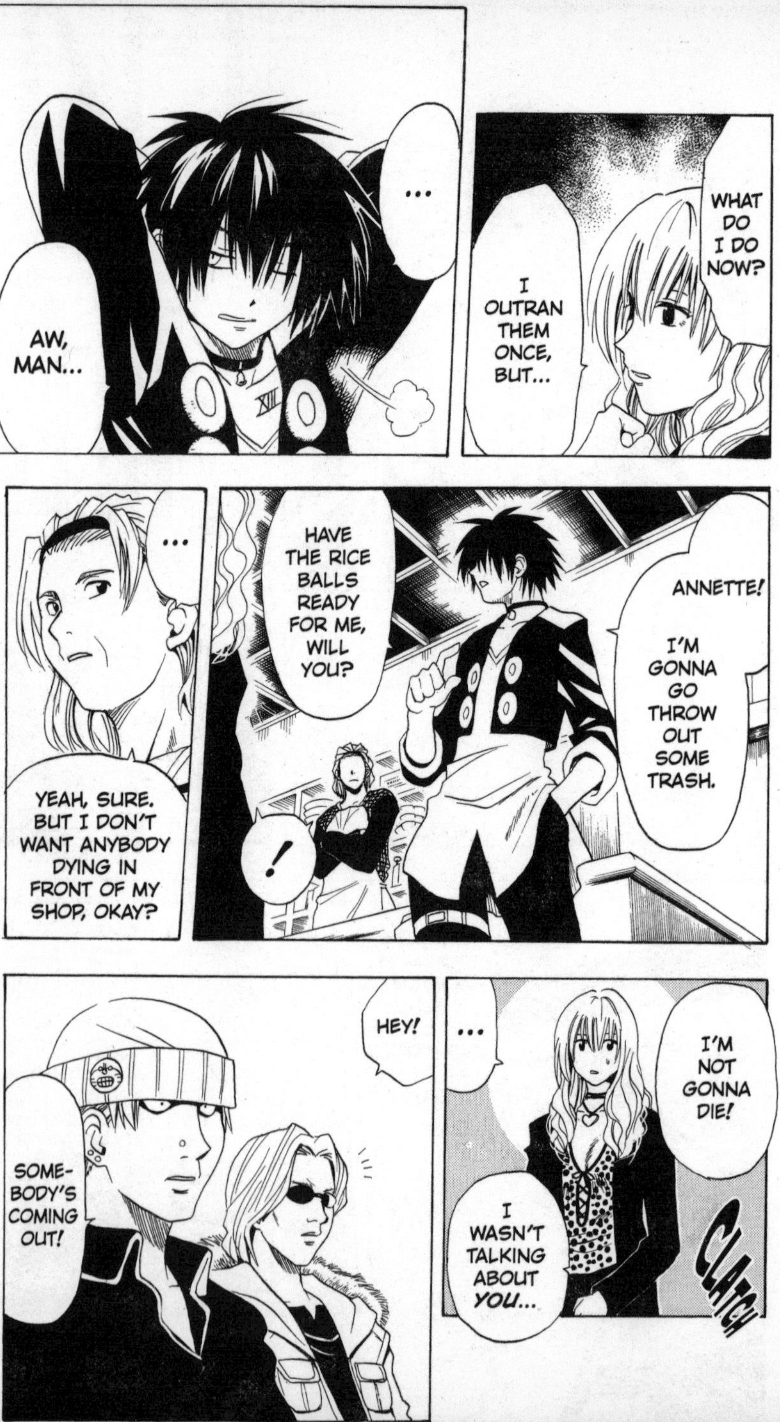
WHAT DO I DO NOW?
I OUTRAN THEM ONCE, BUT...
...
AW, MAN...
ANNETTE!
I'M GONNA GO THROW OUT SOME TRASH.
HAVE THE RICE BALLS READY FOR ME, WILL YOU?
!
...
YEAH, SURE. BUT I DON'T WANT ANYBODY DYING IN FRONT OF MY SHOP, OKAY?
I'M NOT GONNA DIE!
...
I WASN'T TALKING ABOUT *YOU*...
CLATCH
HEY!
SOME-BODY'S COMING OUT!

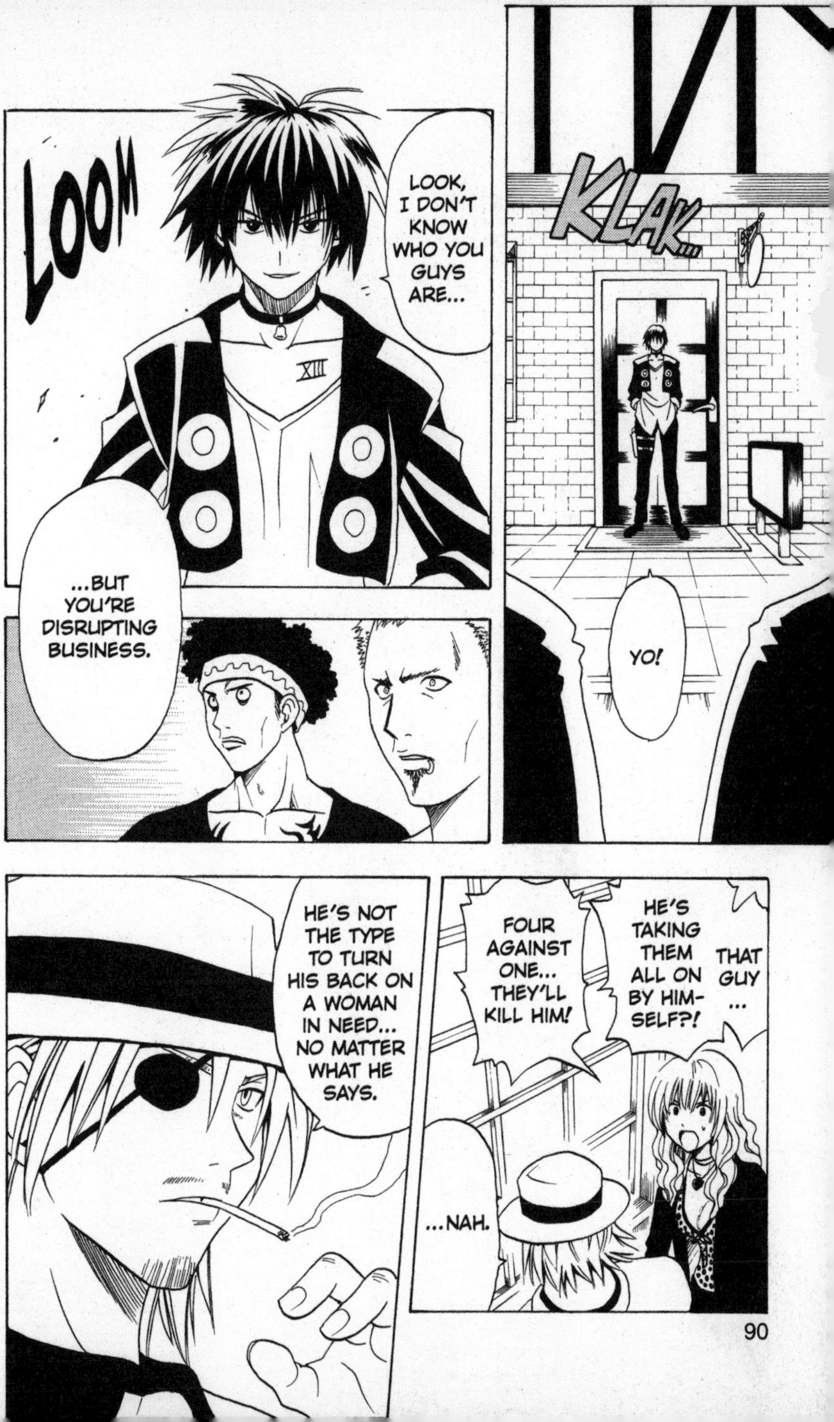
KLAK...
YO!
LOOM
LOOK, I DON'T KNOW WHO YOU GUYS ARE...
...BUT YOU'RE DISRUPTING BUSINESS.
THAT GUY...
HE'S TAKING THEM ALL ON BY HIM-SELF?!
FOUR AGAINST ONE... THEY'LL KILL HIM!
...NAH.
HE'S NOT THE TYPE TO TURN HIS BACK ON A WOMAN IN NEED... NO MATTER WHAT HE SAYS.

READ THIS WAY

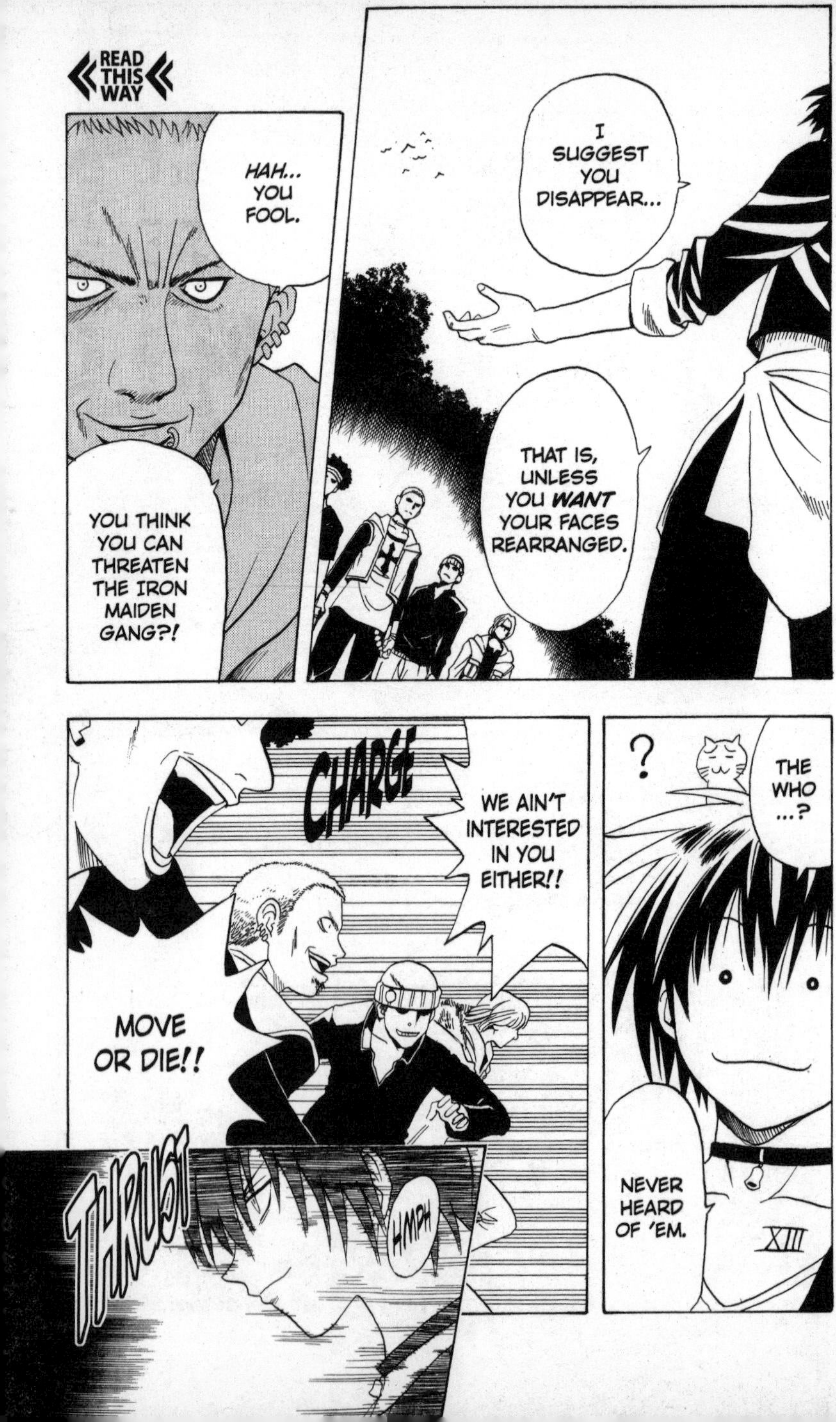

I SUGGEST YOU DISAPPEAR...
THAT IS, UNLESS YOU *WANT* YOUR FACES REARRANGED.
HAH... YOU FOOL.
YOU THINK YOU CAN THREATEN THE IRON MAIDEN GANG?!
THE WHO ...?
?
NEVER HEARD OF 'EM.
XIII
CHARGE
WE AIN'T INTERESTED IN YOU EITHER!!
MOVE OR DIE!!
THRUST
HMPH

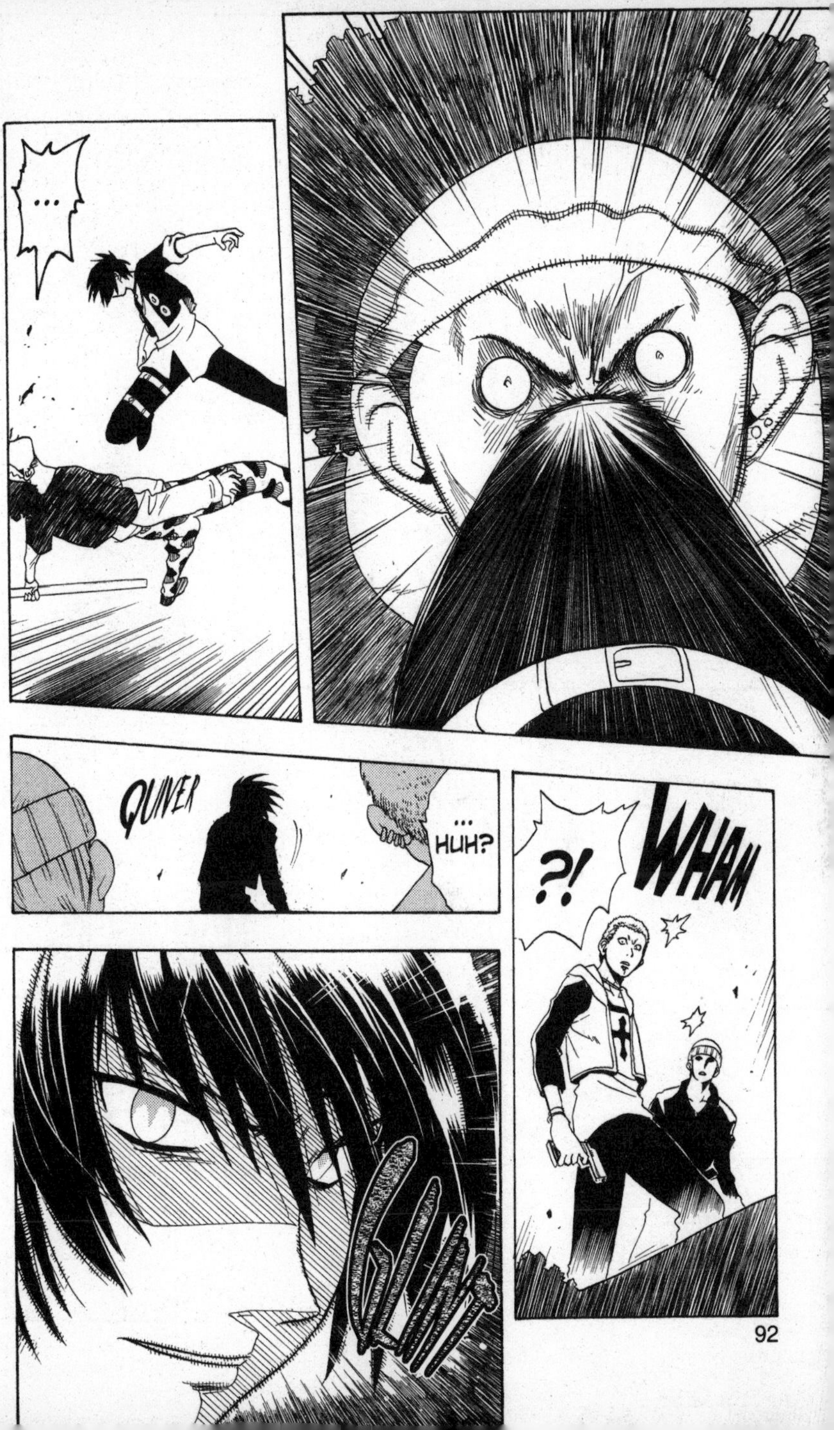
...
?!
WHAM
QUIVER
... HUH?

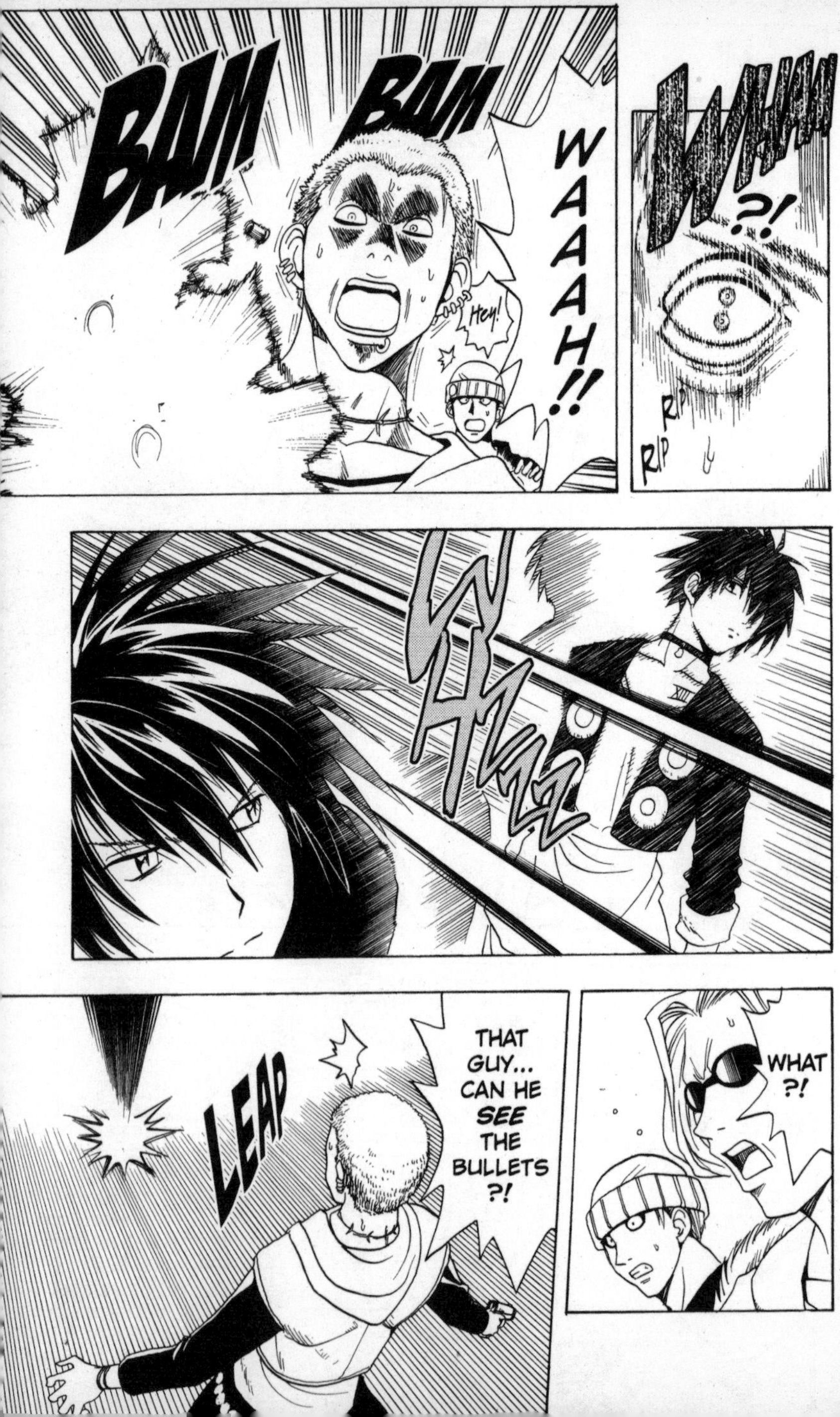
?!
RIP
RIP
BAM
BAM
WAAAAH!!
Hey!
WHAT ?!
THAT GUY... CAN HE SEE THE BULLETS ?!
LEAP

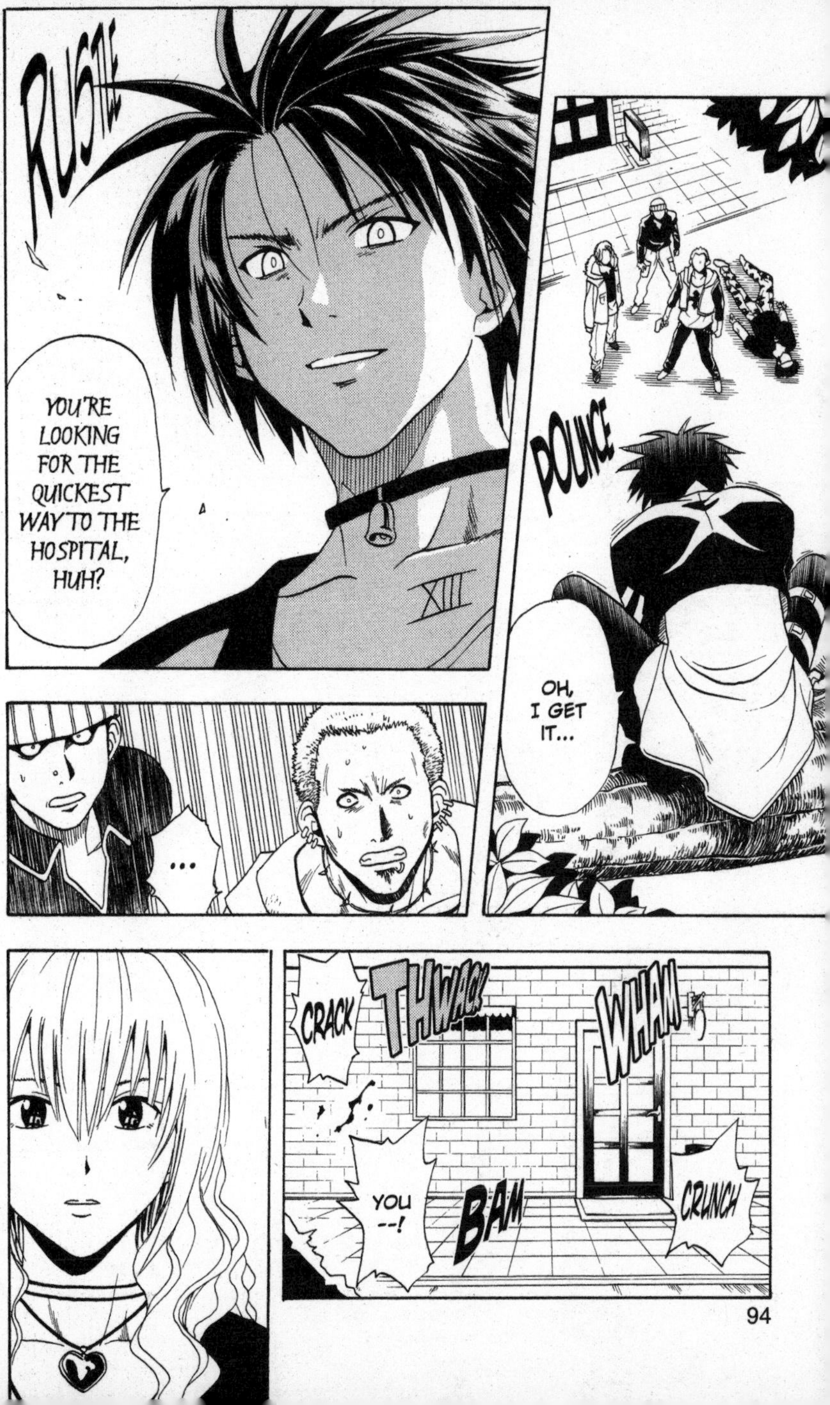
POUNCE
OH, I GET IT...
RUSTLE
YOU'RE LOOKING FOR THE QUICKEST WAY TO THE HOSPITAL, HUH?
...
CRACK
THWACK
WHAM
YOU --!
BAM
CRUNCH

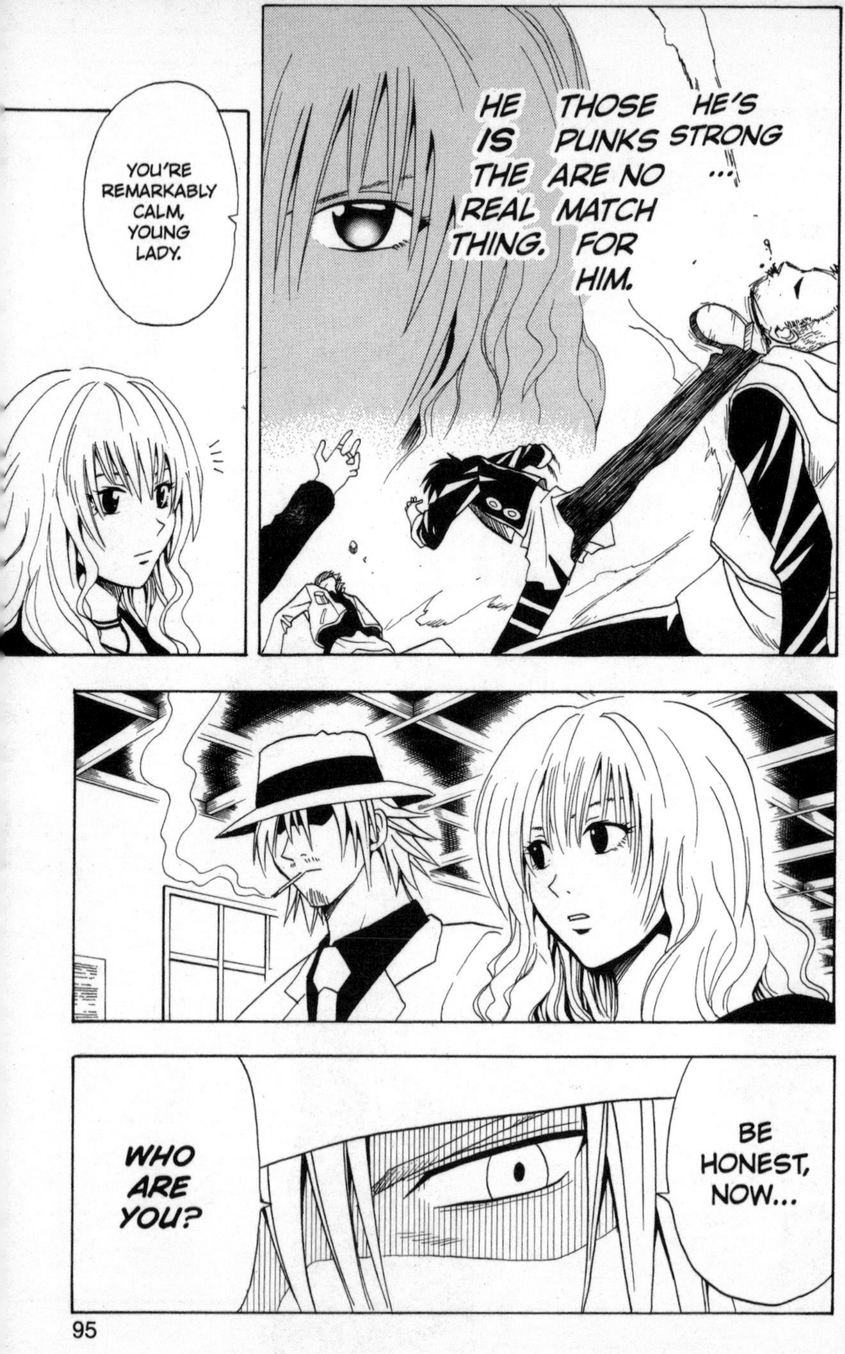
HE'S STRONG ...
THOSE PUNKS ARE NO MATCH FOR HIM.
HE IS THE REAL THING.
YOU'RE REMARKABLY CALM, YOUNG LADY.
BE HONEST, NOW...
WHO ARE YOU?

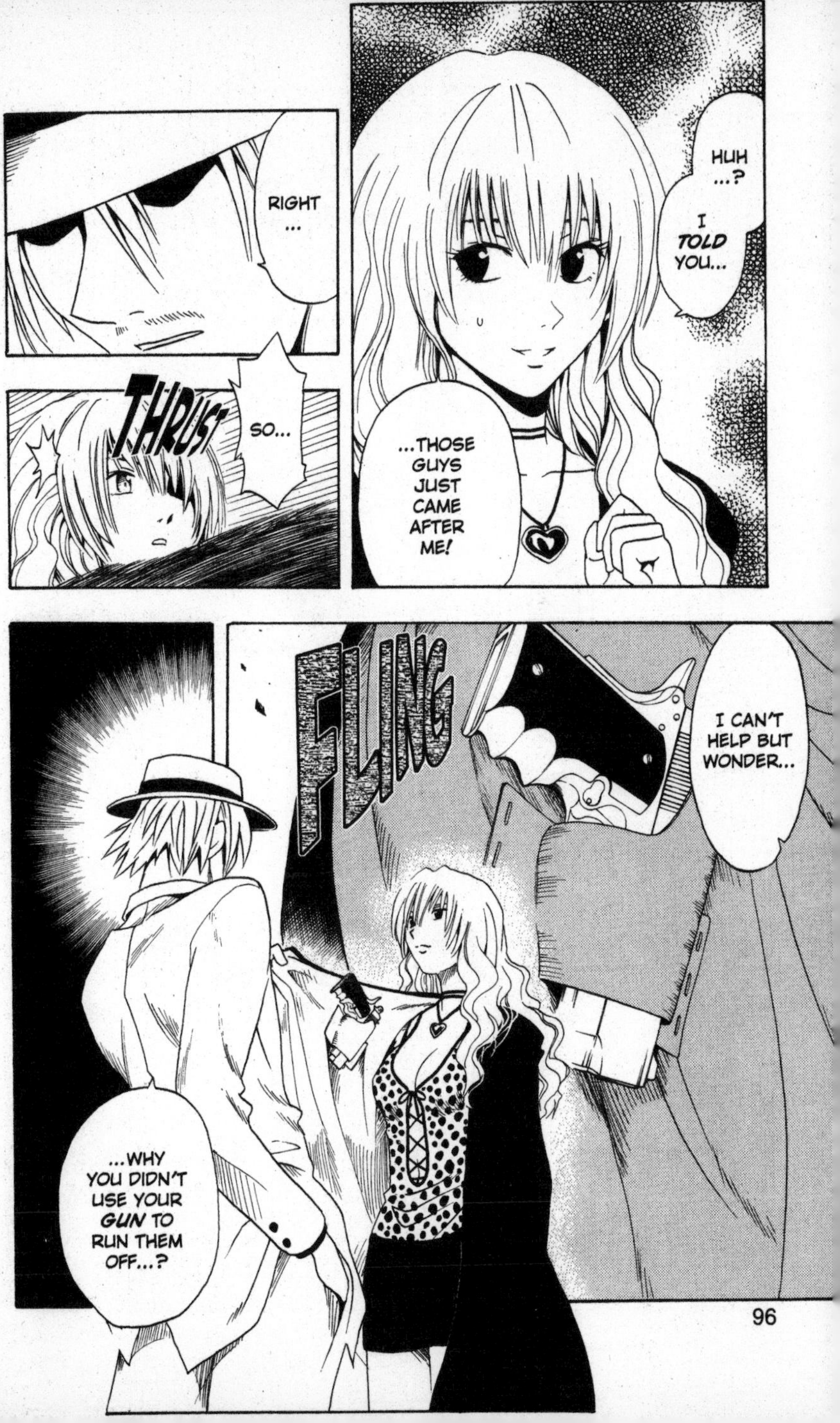
HUH ...?
I *TOLD* YOU...
...THOSE GUYS JUST CAME AFTER ME!
RIGHT ...
THRUST
SO...
I CAN'T HELP BUT WONDER...
FLING
...WHY YOU DIDN'T USE YOUR *GUN* TO RUN THEM OFF...?

READ THIS WAY

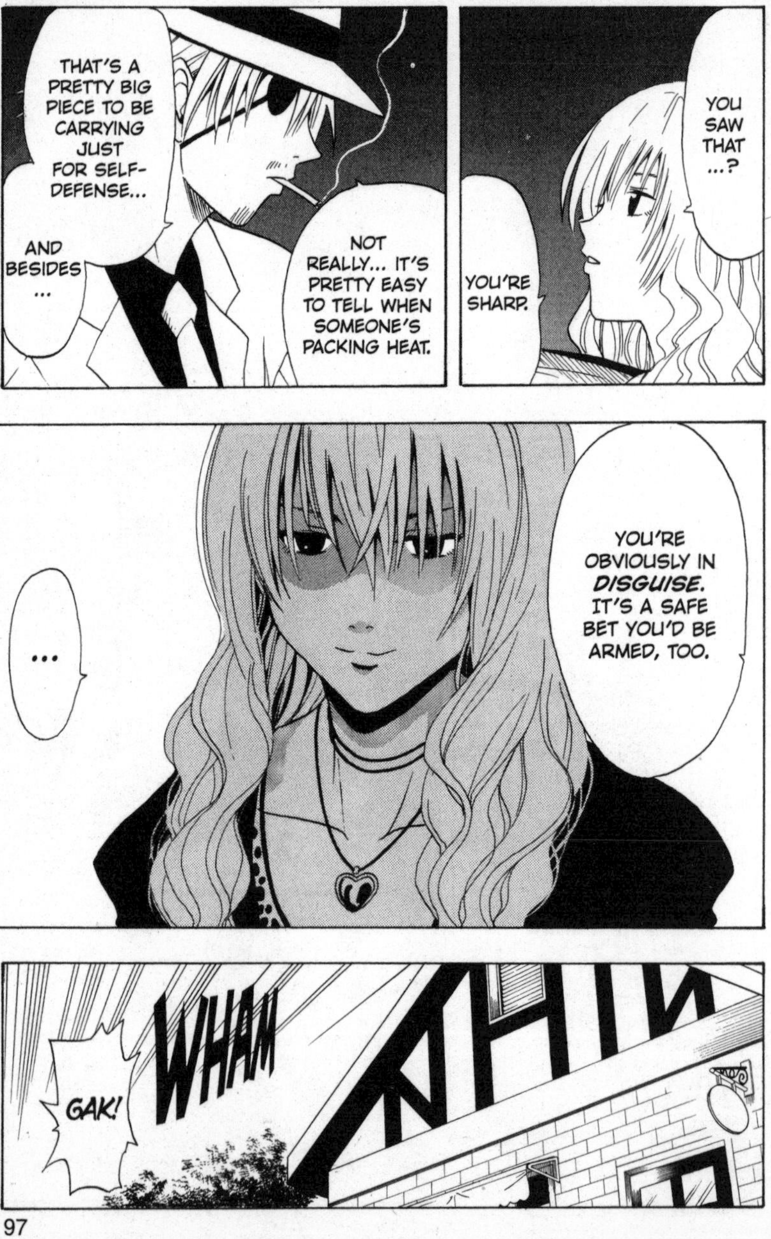

YOU SAW THAT ...?
YOU'RE SHARP.
NOT REALLY... IT'S PRETTY EASY TO TELL WHEN SOMEONE'S PACKING HEAT.
THAT'S A PRETTY BIG PIECE TO BE CARRYING JUST FOR SELF-DEFENSE...
AND BESIDES ...
YOU'RE OBVIOUSLY IN ***DISGUISE***. IT'S A SAFE BET YOU'D BE ARMED, TOO.
...
WHAM
GAK!

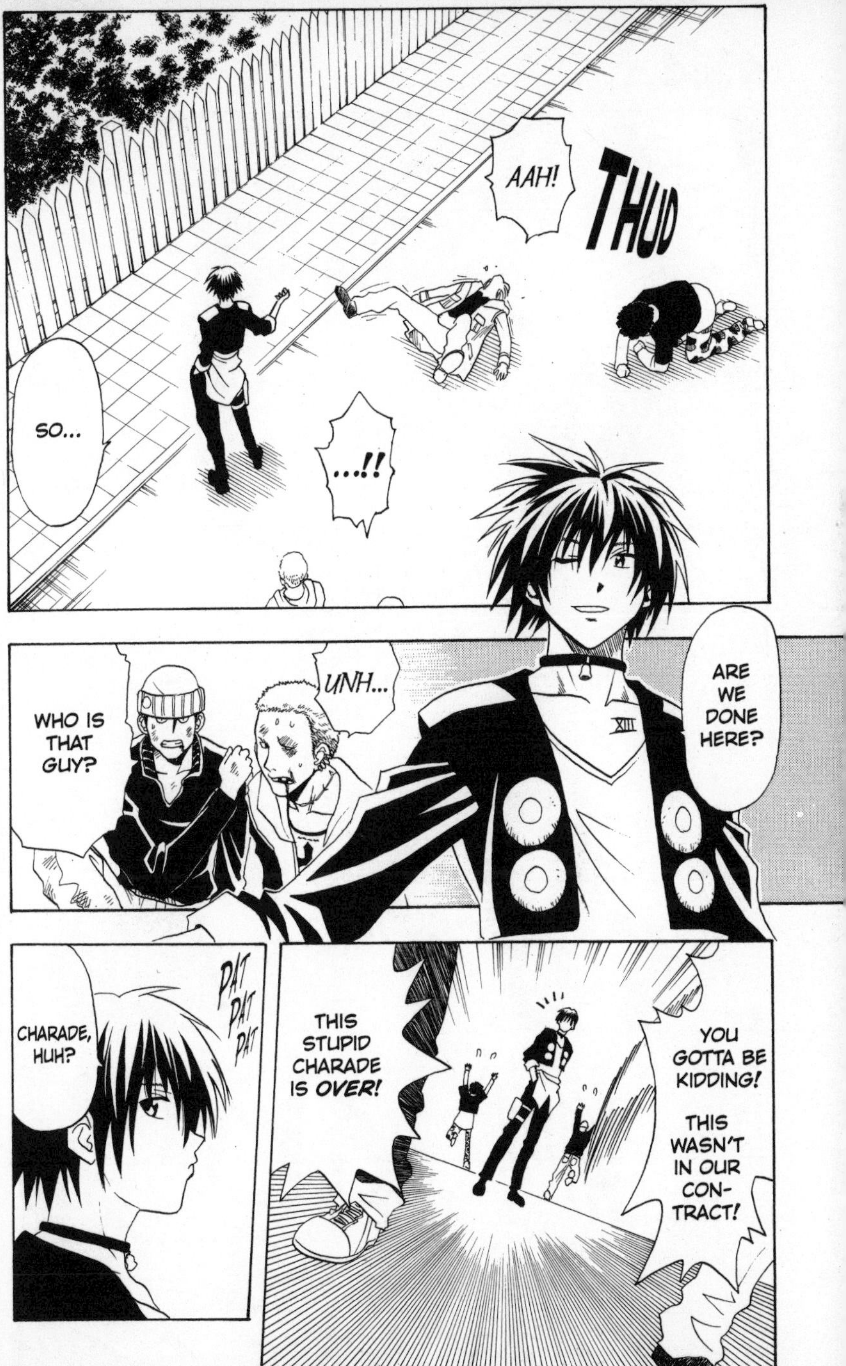
THUD
AAH!
...!!
SO...
ARE WE DONE HERE?
UNH...
WHO IS THAT GUY?
YOU GOTTA BE KIDDING!
THIS WASN'T IN OUR CONTRACT!
THIS STUPID CHARADE IS OVER!
PAT PAT PAT
CHARADE, HUH?

READ THIS WAY

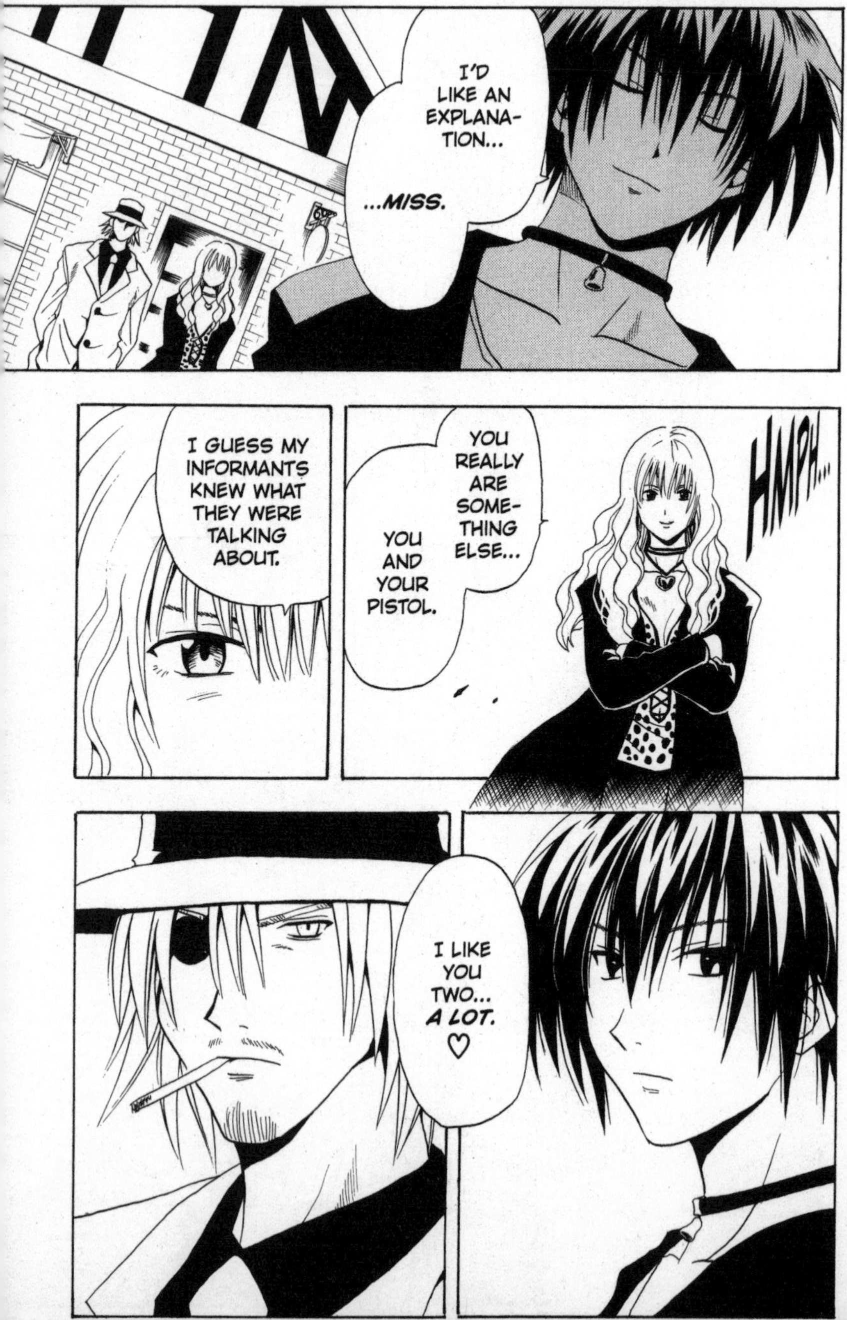
I'D LIKE AN EXPLANATION...
...MISS.
HMPH...
YOU REALLY ARE SOMETHING ELSE...
YOU AND YOUR PISTOL.
I GUESS MY INFORMANTS KNEW WHAT THEY WERE TALKING ABOUT.
I LIKE YOU TWO... A LOT. ♡

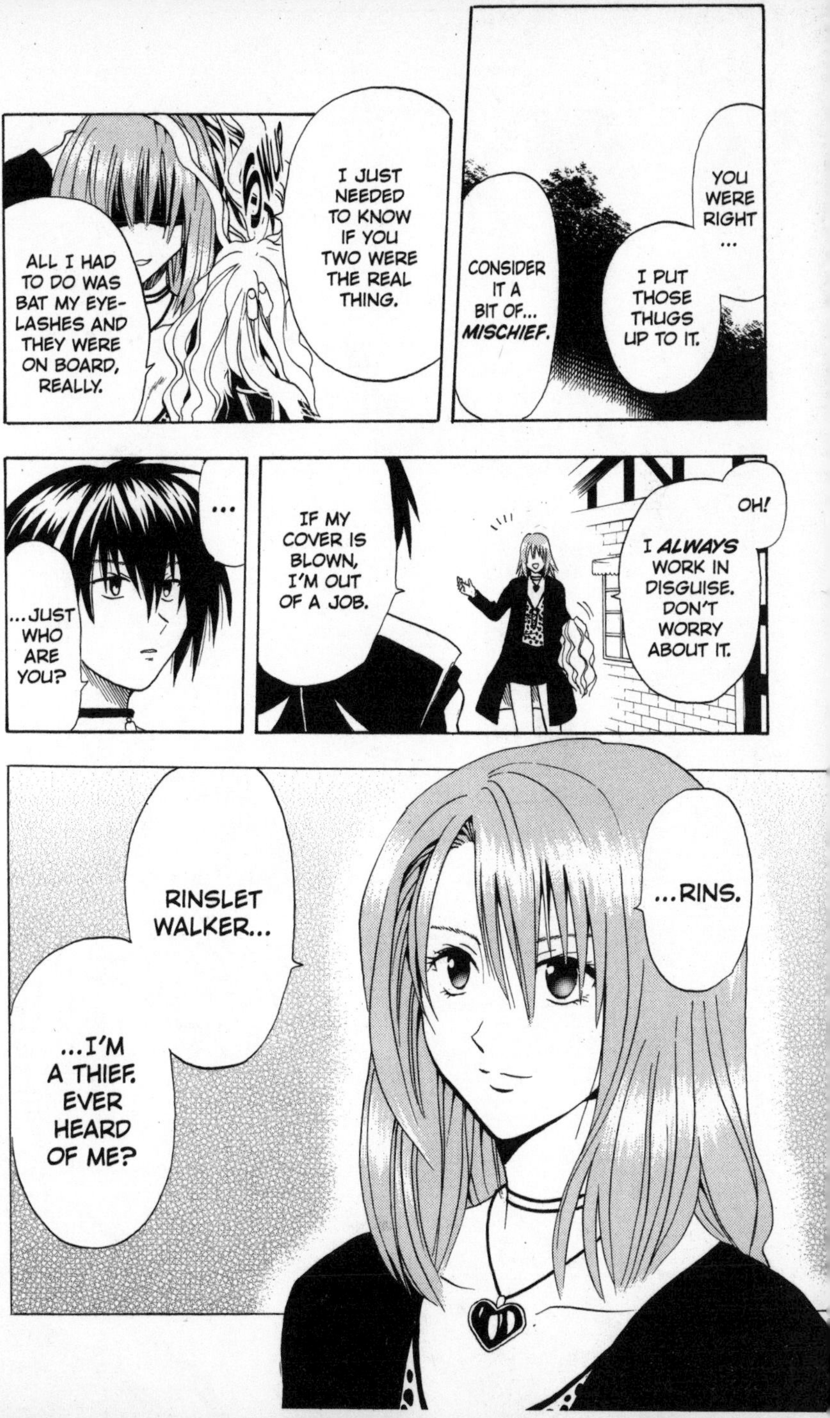
YOU WERE RIGHT...
I PUT THOSE THUGS UP TO IT.
CONSIDER IT A BIT OF... *MISCHIEF.*
I JUST NEEDED TO KNOW IF YOU TWO WERE THE REAL THING.
ALL I HAD TO DO WAS BAT MY EYE-LASHES AND THEY WERE ON BOARD, REALLY.
OH!
I *ALWAYS* WORK IN DISGUISE. DON'T WORRY ABOUT IT.
IF MY COVER IS BLOWN, I'M OUT OF A JOB.
...
...JUST WHO ARE YOU?
...RINS.
RINSLET WALKER...
...I'M A THIEF. EVER HEARD OF ME?

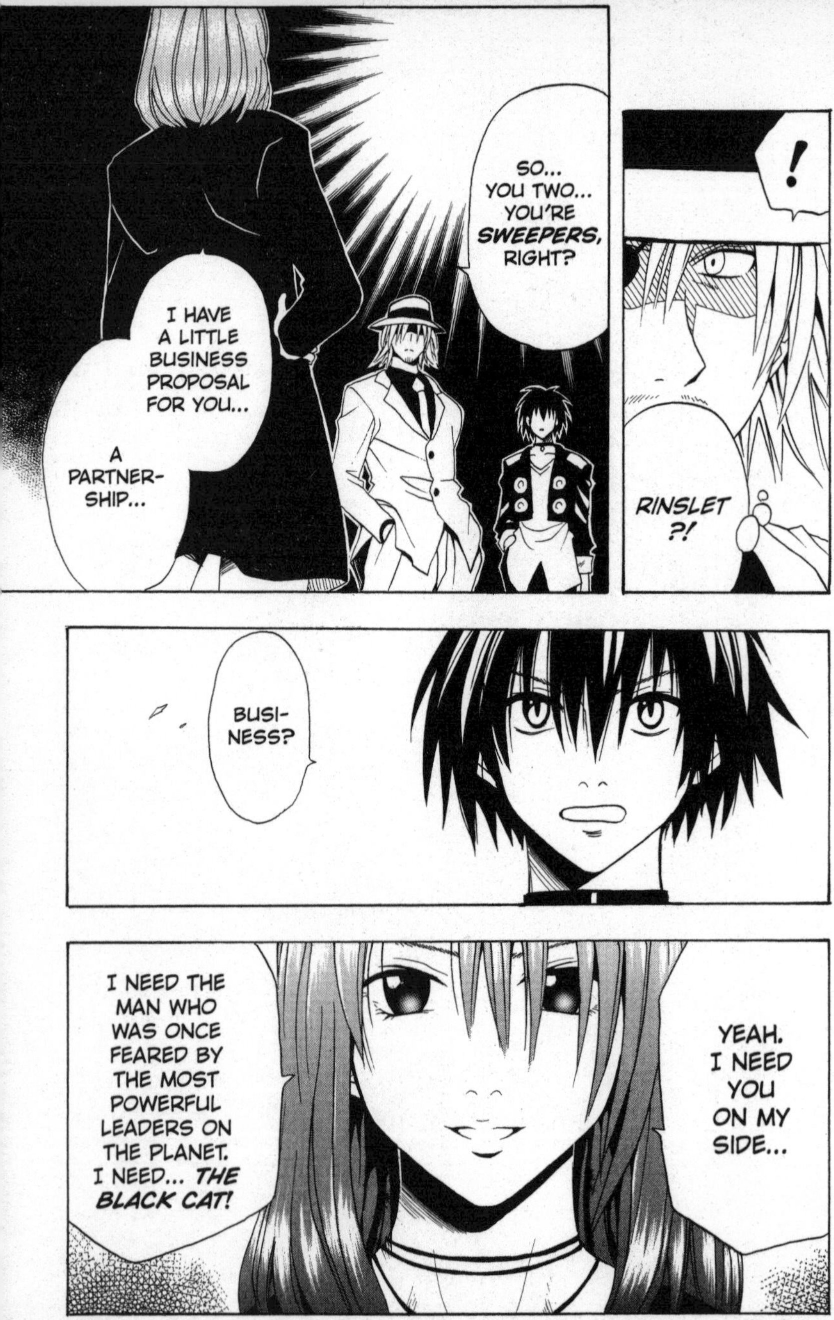
!
RINSLET ?!
SO... YOU TWO... YOU'RE **SWEEPERS,** RIGHT?
I HAVE A LITTLE BUSINESS PROPOSAL FOR YOU...
A PARTNER-SHIP...
BUSI-NESS?
YEAH. I NEED YOU ON MY SIDE...
I NEED THE MAN WHO WAS ONCE FEARED BY THE MOST POWERFUL LEADERS ON THE PLANET. I NEED... ***THE BLACK CAT!***

BLACK CAT

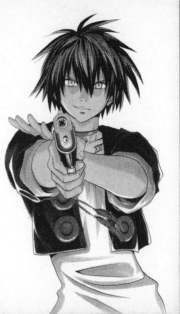

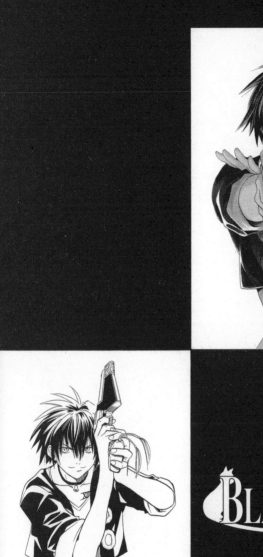

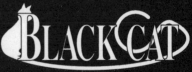

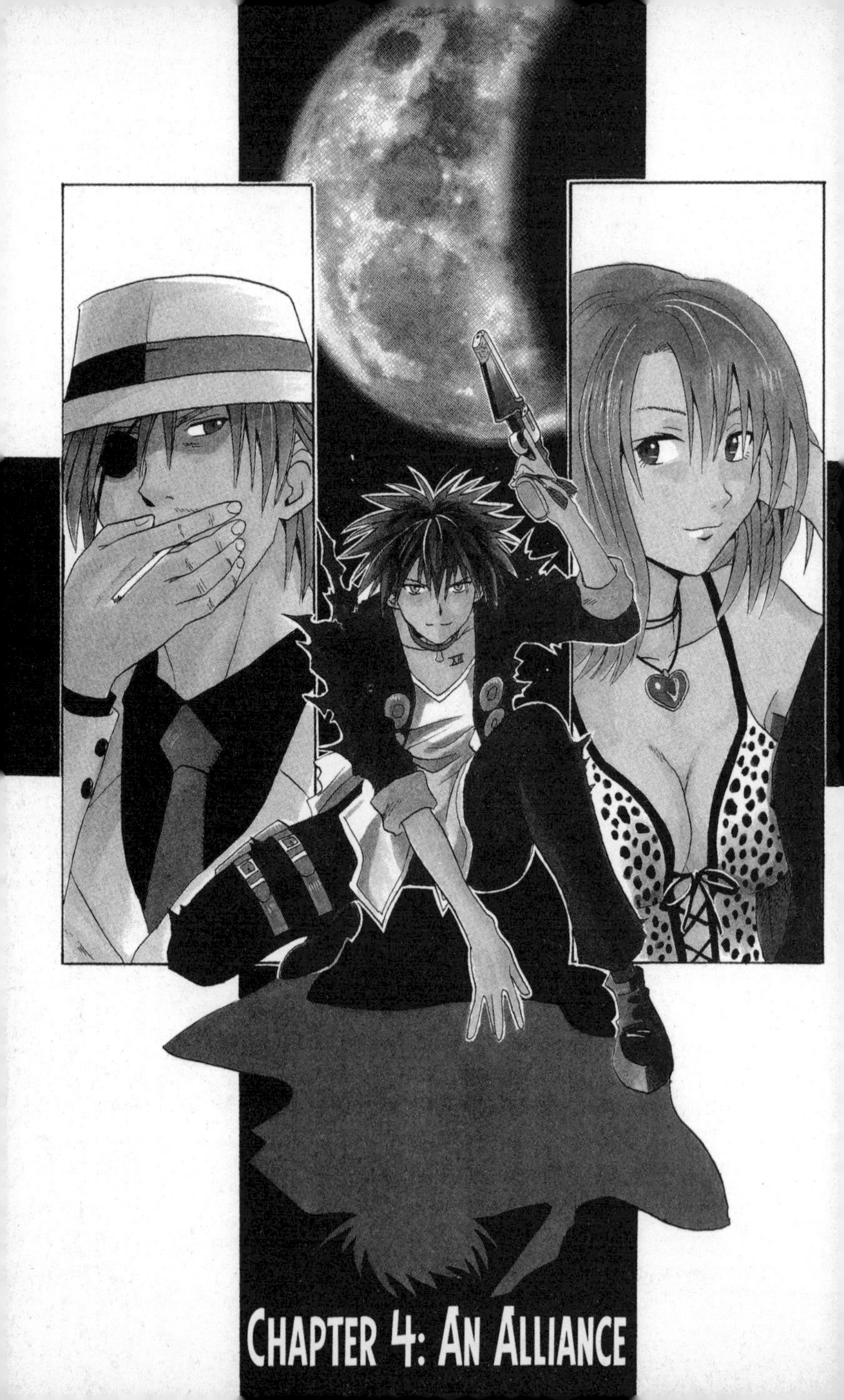
CHAPTER 4: AN ALLIANCE

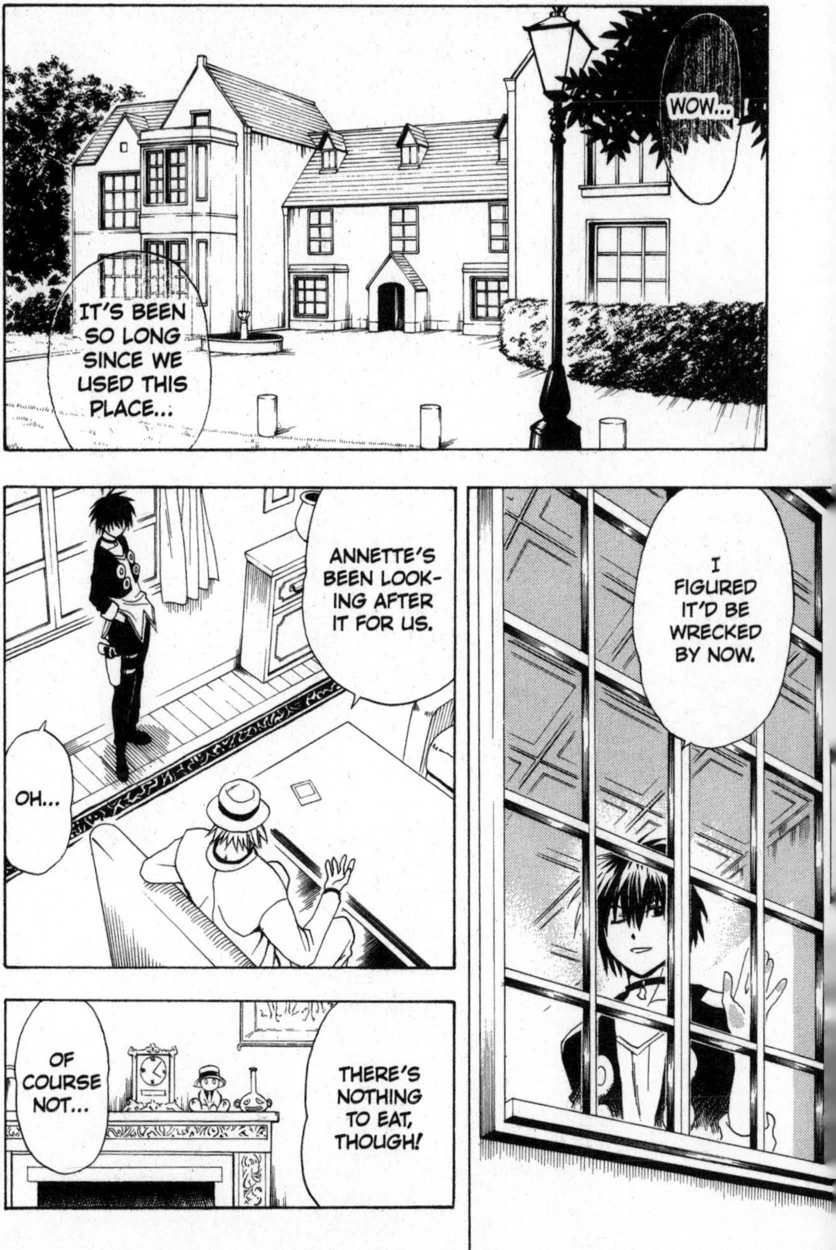
WOW...
IT'S BEEN SO LONG SINCE WE USED THIS PLACE...
I FIGURED IT'D BE WRECKED BY NOW.
ANNETTE'S BEEN LOOK-ING AFTER IT FOR US.
OH...
THERE'S NOTHING TO EAT, THOUGH!
OF COURSE NOT...

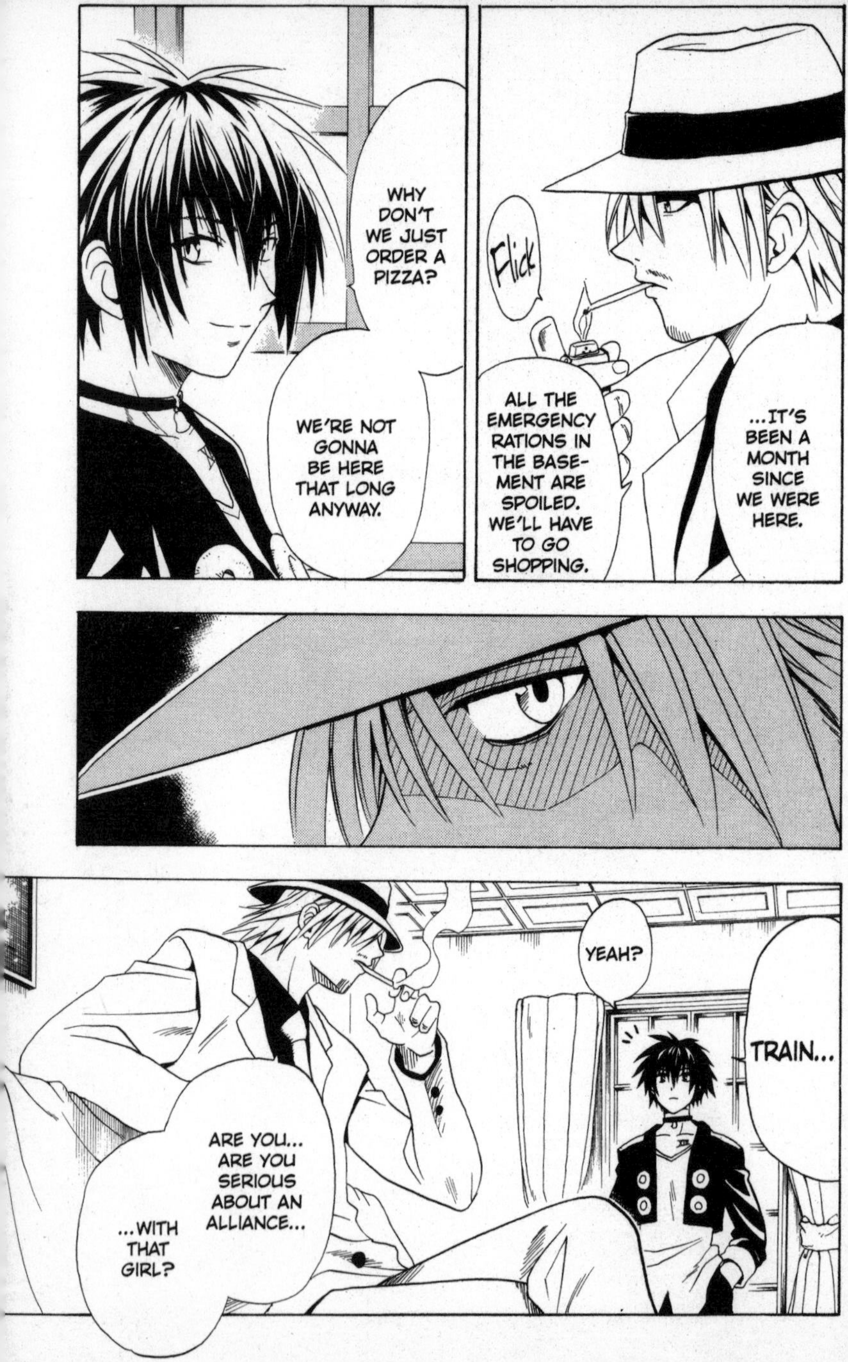
...IT'S BEEN A MONTH SINCE WE WERE HERE.
Flick
ALL THE EMERGENCY RATIONS IN THE BASEMENT ARE SPOILED. WE'LL HAVE TO GO SHOPPING.
WHY DON'T WE JUST ORDER A PIZZA?
WE'RE NOT GONNA BE HERE THAT LONG ANYWAY.
TRAIN...
YEAH?
ARE YOU... ARE YOU SERIOUS ABOUT AN ALLIANCE...
...WITH THAT GIRL?

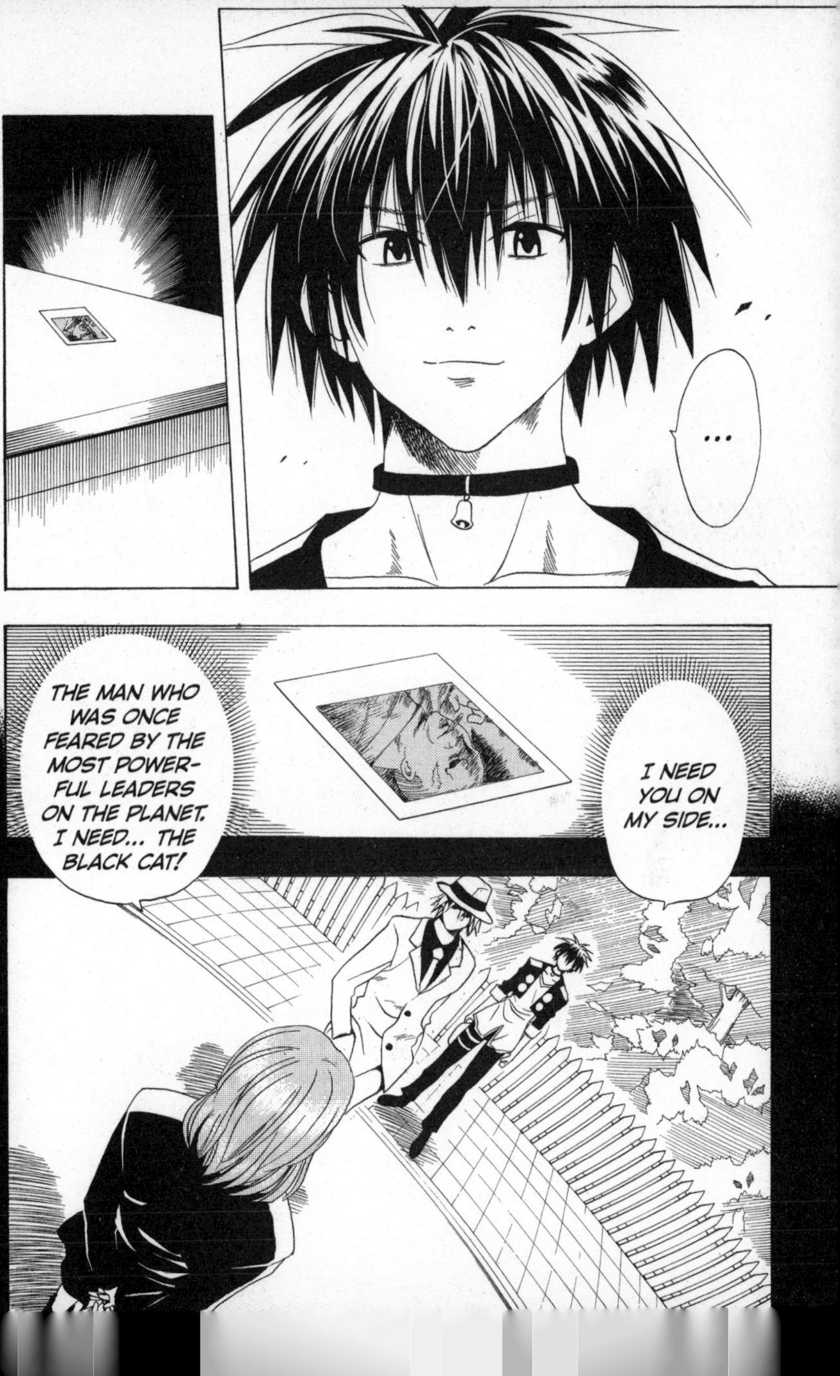
...
I NEED YOU ON MY SIDE...
THE MAN WHO WAS ONCE FEARED BY THE MOST POWER-FUL LEADERS ON THE PLANET. I NEED... THE BLACK CAT!

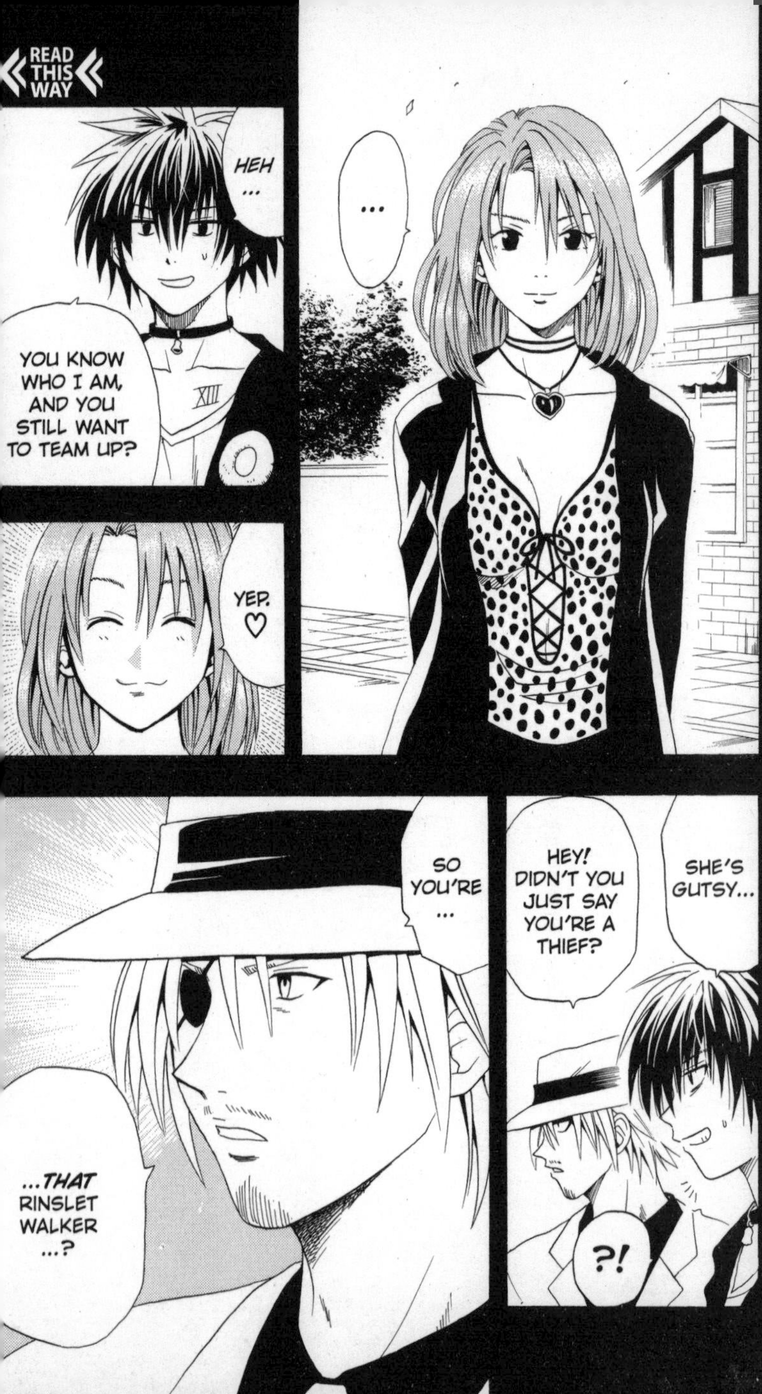
READ THIS WAY
...
HEH ...
YOU KNOW WHO I AM, AND YOU STILL WANT TO TEAM UP?
YEP. ♡
SHE'S GUTSY...
HEY! DIDN'T YOU JUST SAY YOU'RE A THIEF?
?!
SO YOU'RE ...
...THAT RINSLET WALKER ...?

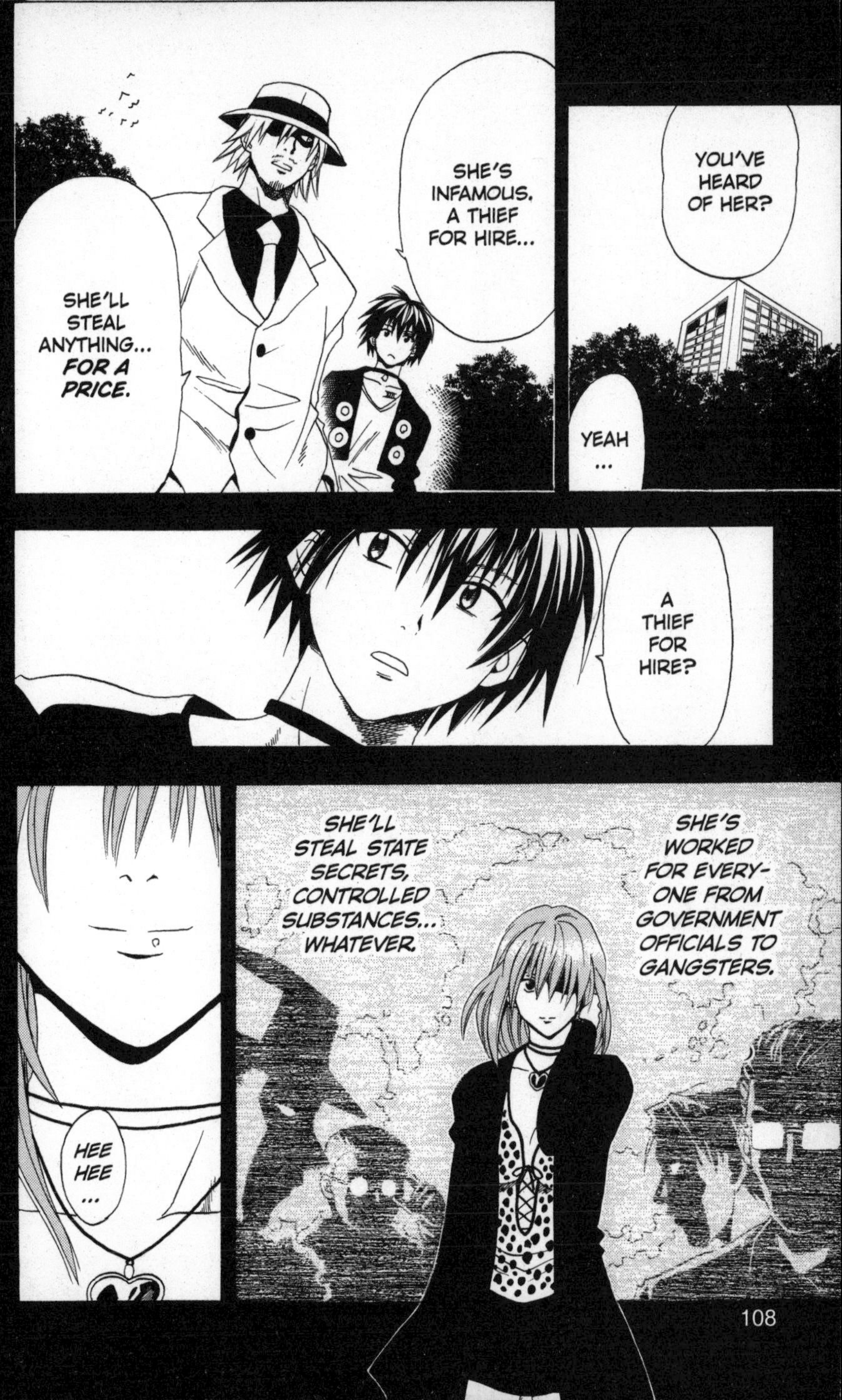
YOU'VE HEARD OF HER?
YEAH ...
SHE'S INFAMOUS. A THIEF FOR HIRE...
SHE'LL STEAL ANYTHING... FOR A PRICE.
A THIEF FOR HIRE?
SHE'S WORKED FOR EVERY-ONE FROM GOVERNMENT OFFICIALS TO GANGSTERS.
SHE'LL STEAL STATE SECRETS, CONTROLLED SUBSTANCES... WHATEVER.
HEE HEE ...

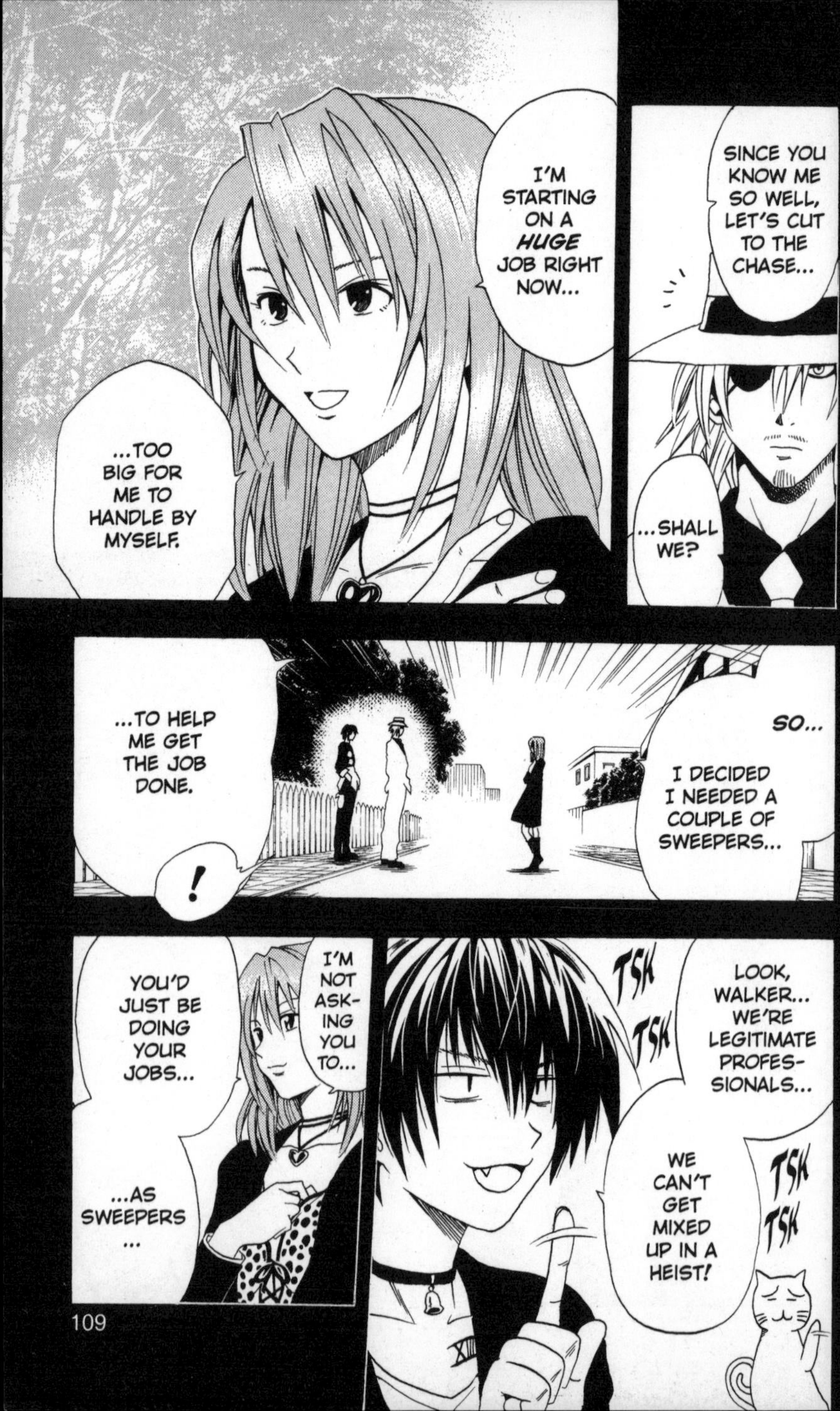
SINCE YOU KNOW ME SO WELL, LET'S CUT TO THE CHASE...
...SHALL WE?
I'M STARTING ON A *HUGE* JOB RIGHT NOW...
...TOO BIG FOR ME TO HANDLE BY MYSELF.
SO...
I DECIDED I NEEDED A COUPLE OF SWEEPERS...
...TO HELP ME GET THE JOB DONE.
!
TSK TSK
LOOK, WALKER... WE'RE LEGITIMATE PROFES-SIONALS...
WE CAN'T GET MIXED UP IN A HEIST!
TSK TSK
I'M NOT ASK-ING YOU TO...
YOU'D JUST BE DOING YOUR JOBS...
...AS SWEEPERS ...

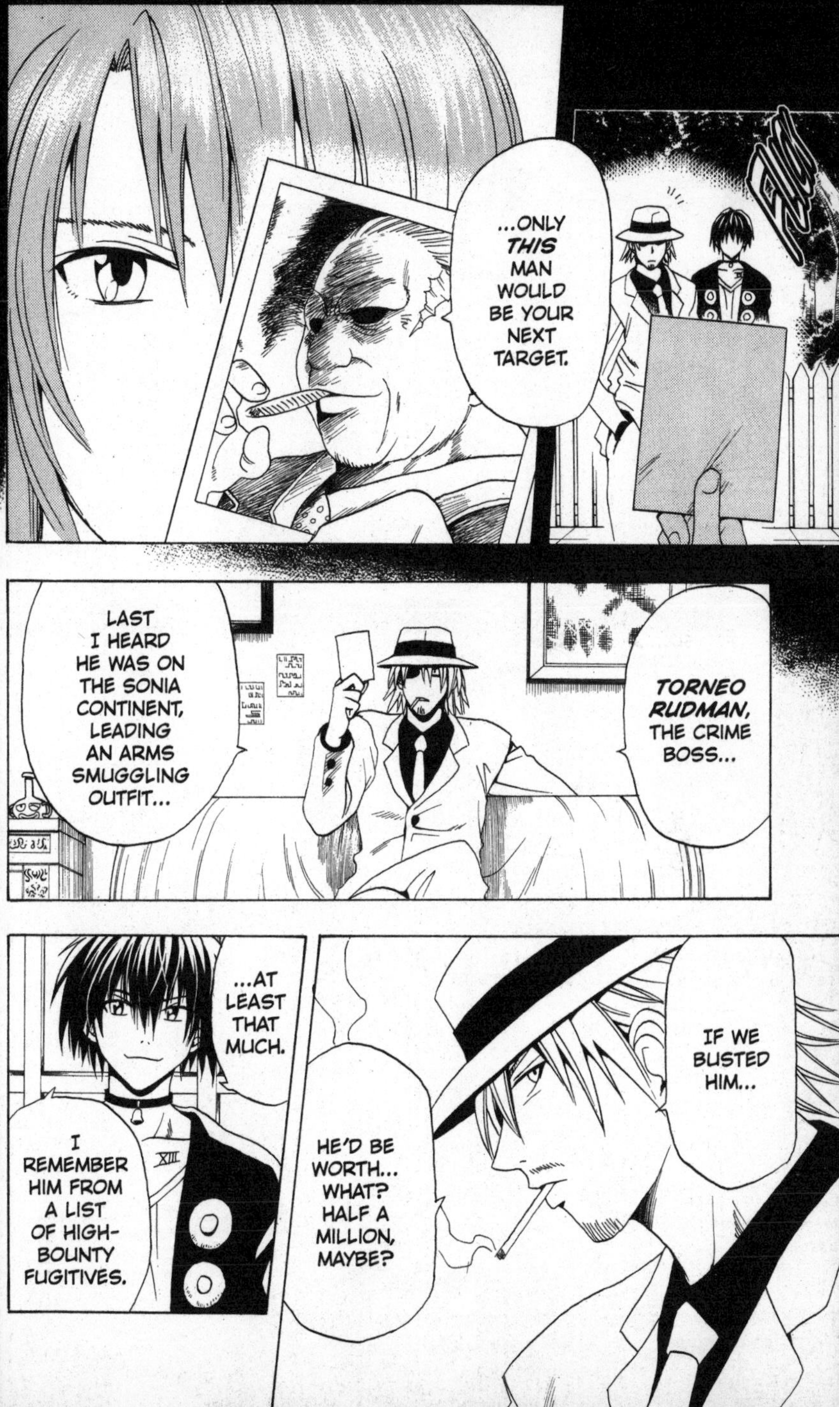
...ONLY *THIS* MAN WOULD BE YOUR NEXT TARGET.
TORNEO RUDMAN, THE CRIME BOSS...
LAST I HEARD HE WAS ON THE SONIA CONTINENT, LEADING AN ARMS SMUGGLING OUTFIT...
IF WE BUSTED HIM...
HE'D BE WORTH... WHAT? HALF A MILLION, MAYBE?
...AT LEAST THAT MUCH.
I REMEMBER HIM FROM A LIST OF HIGH-BOUNTY FUGITIVES.

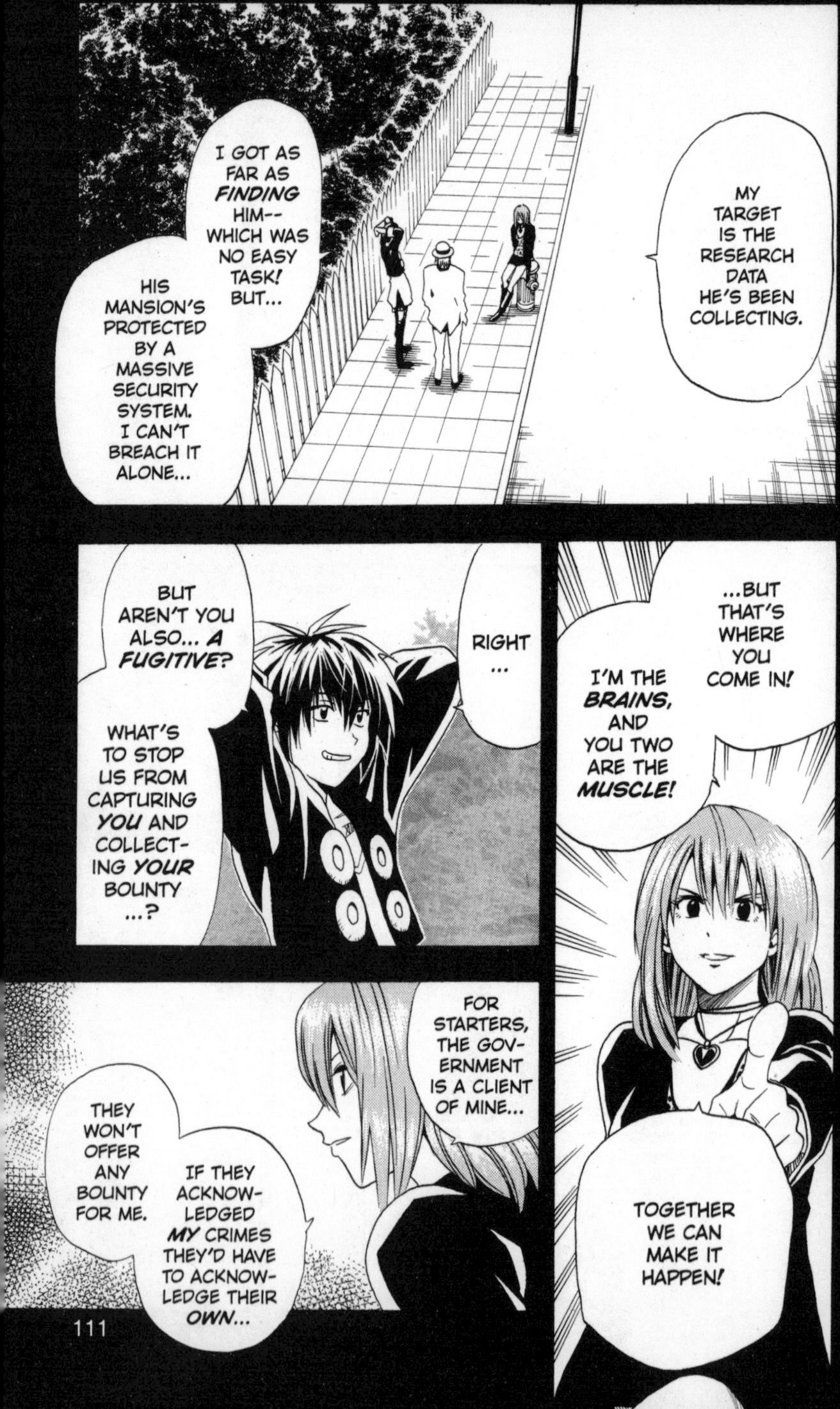
MY TARGET IS THE RESEARCH DATA HE'S BEEN COLLECTING.
I GOT AS FAR AS *FINDING* HIM-- WHICH WAS NO EASY TASK! BUT...
HIS MANSION'S PROTECTED BY A MASSIVE SECURITY SYSTEM. I CAN'T BREACH IT ALONE...
...BUT THAT'S WHERE YOU COME IN!
I'M THE *BRAINS,* AND YOU TWO ARE THE *MUSCLE!*
TOGETHER WE CAN MAKE IT HAPPEN!
RIGHT...
BUT AREN'T YOU ALSO... *A FUGITIVE?*
WHAT'S TO STOP US FROM CAPTURING *YOU* AND COLLECT-ING *YOUR* BOUNTY...?
FOR STARTERS, THE GOV-ERNMENT IS A CLIENT OF MINE...
THEY WON'T OFFER ANY BOUNTY FOR ME.
IF THEY ACKNOW-LEDGED *MY* CRIMES THEY'D HAVE TO ACKNOW-LEDGE THEIR *OWN*...

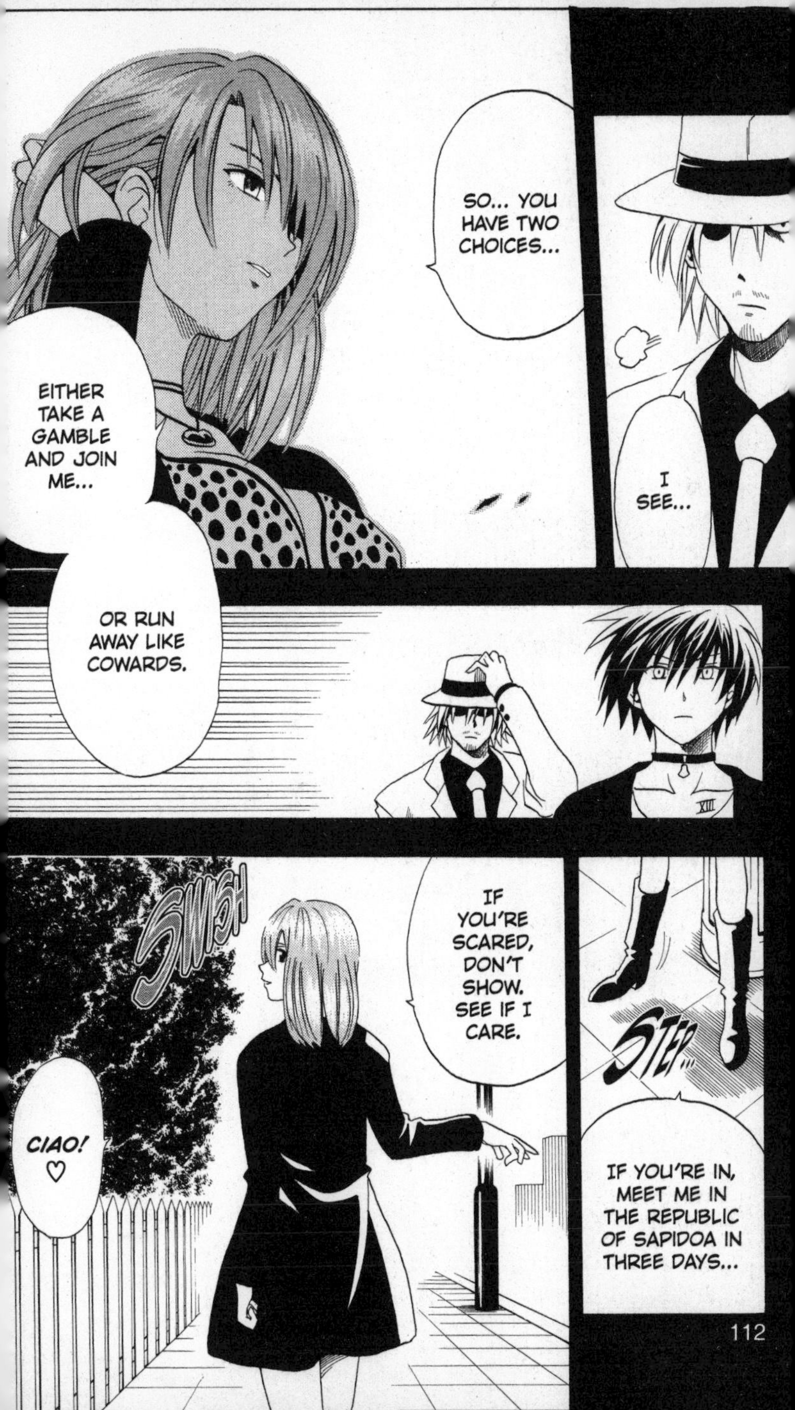
I SEE...
SO... YOU HAVE TWO CHOICES...
EITHER TAKE A GAMBLE AND JOIN ME...
OR RUN AWAY LIKE COWARDS.
STEP...
IF YOU'RE IN, MEET ME IN THE REPUBLIC OF SAPIDOA IN THREE DAYS...
IF YOU'RE SCARED, DON'T SHOW. SEE IF I CARE.
SWISH
CIAO! ♡

READ THIS WAY

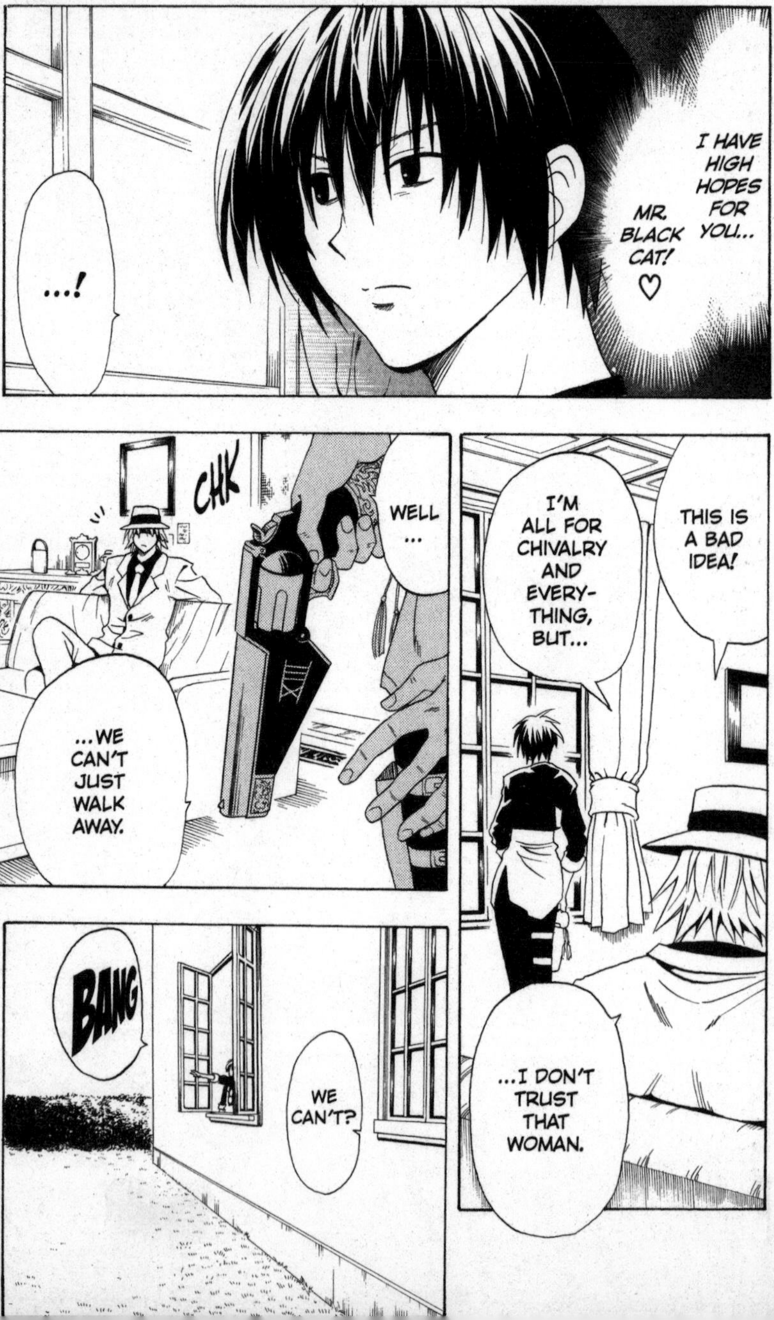

I HAVE HIGH HOPES FOR YOU...
MR. BLACK CAT! ♡
...!
THIS IS A BAD IDEA!
I'M ALL FOR CHIVALRY AND EVERY-THING, BUT...
...I DON'T TRUST THAT WOMAN.
WELL ...
CHK
...WE CAN'T JUST WALK AWAY.
WE CAN'T?
BANG

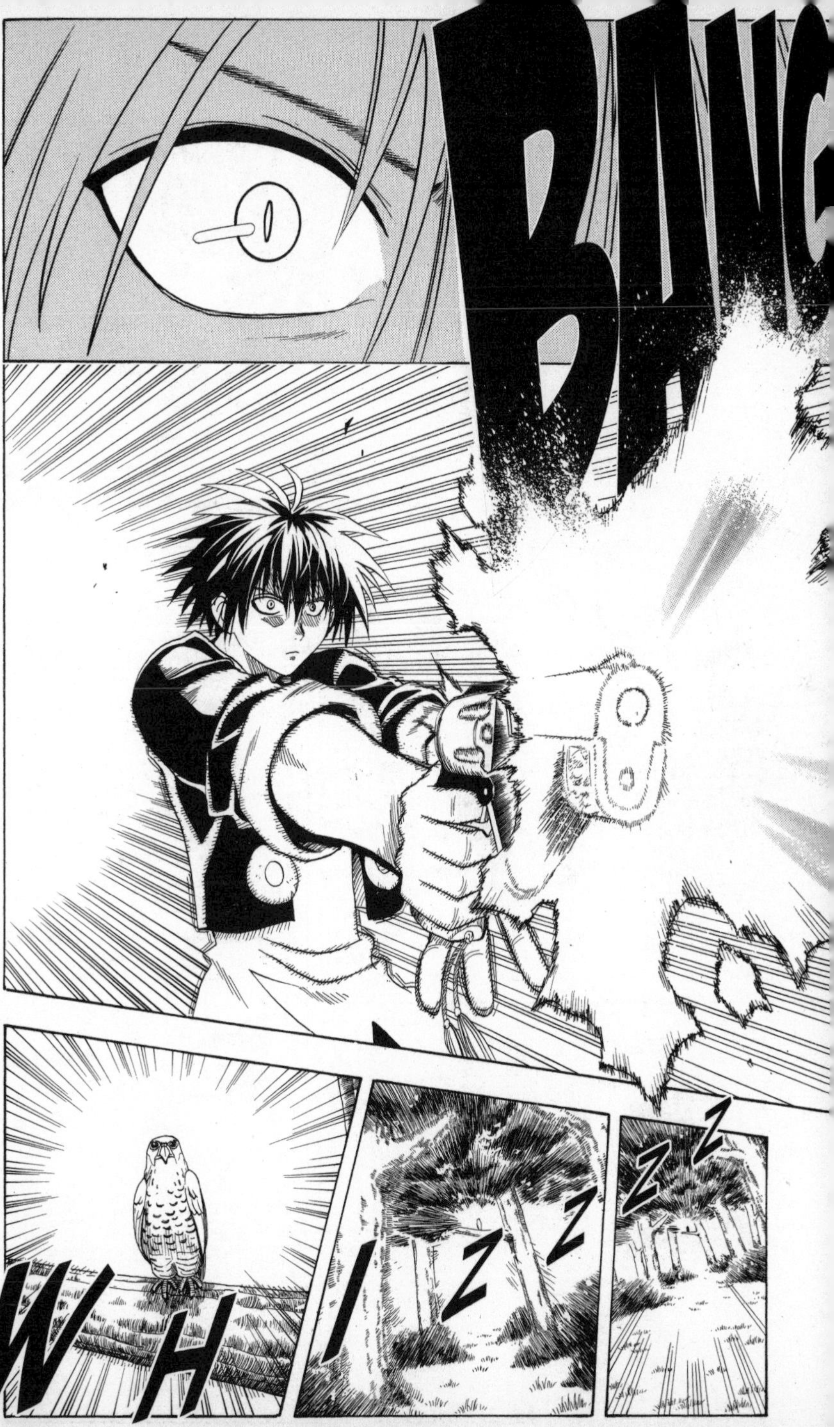
BANG
WHIZZZZ

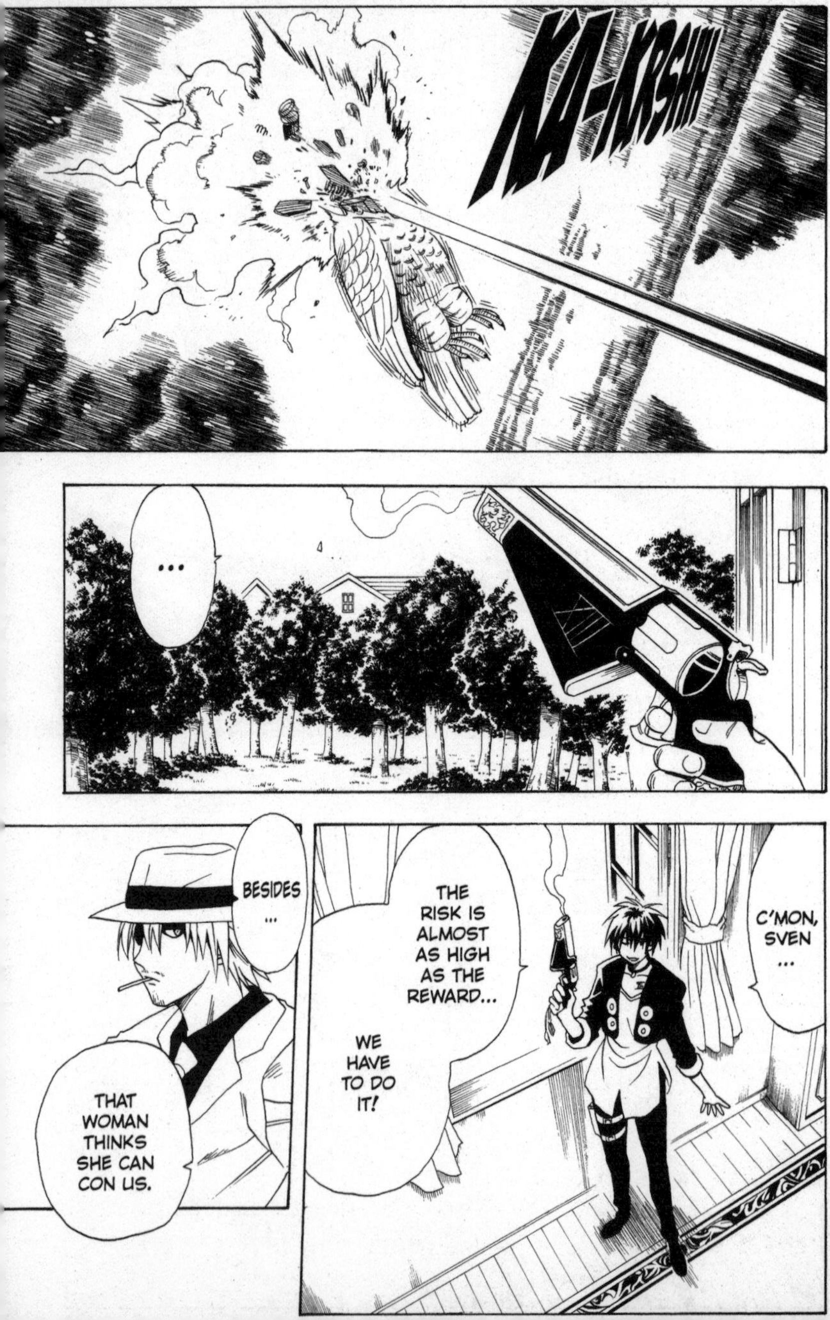
KA-KRSHH
...
C'MON, SVEN ...
THE RISK IS ALMOST AS HIGH AS THE REWARD...
WE HAVE TO DO IT!
BESIDES ...
THAT WOMAN THINKS SHE CAN CON US.

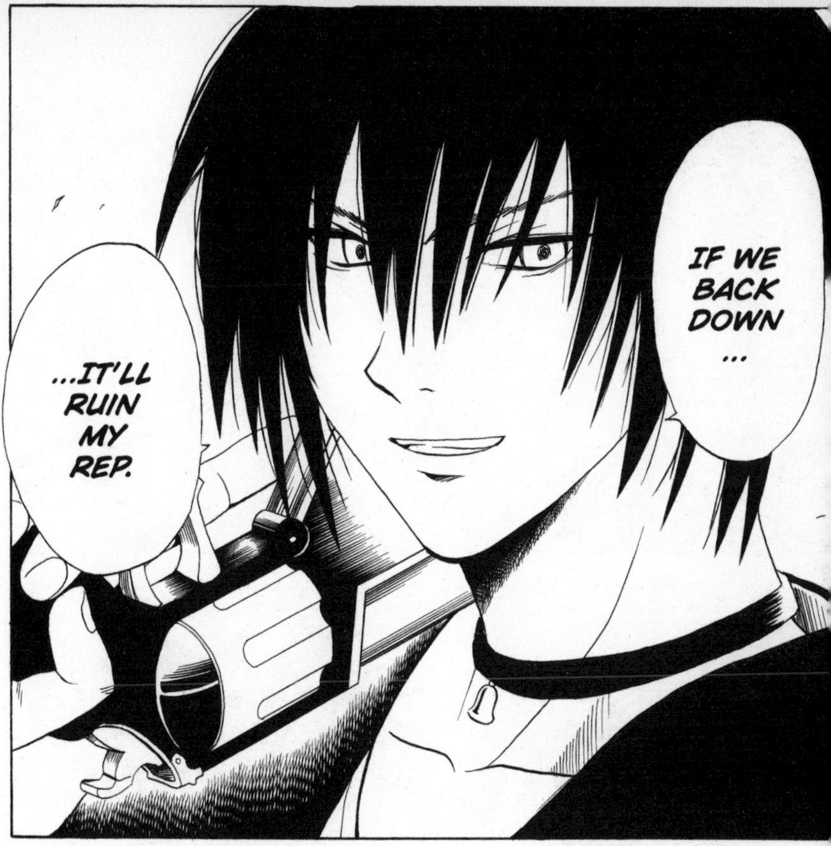
IF WE BACK DOWN ...
...IT'LL RUIN MY REP.

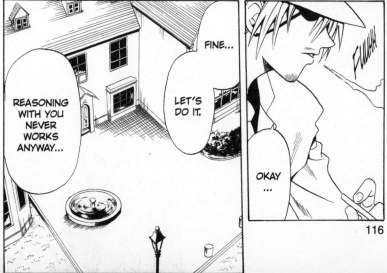

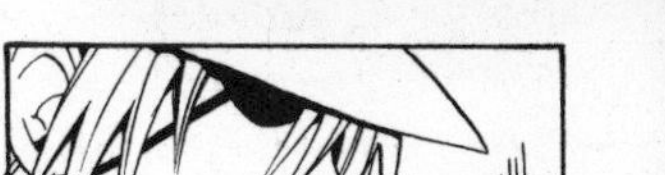
FUUHH
OKAY ...

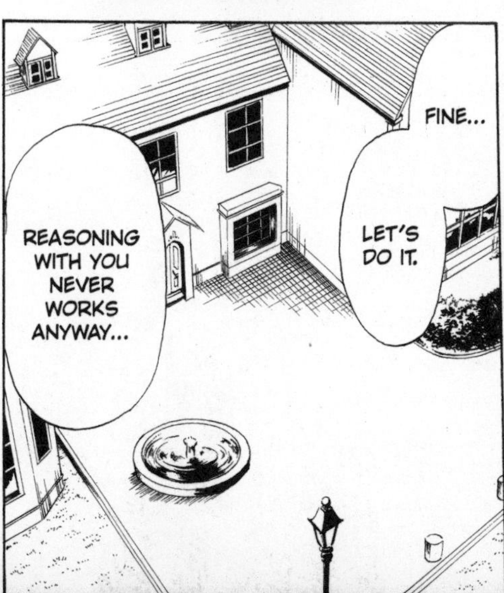
FINE...
LET'S DO IT.
REASONING WITH YOU NEVER WORKS ANYWAY...

READ THIS WAY

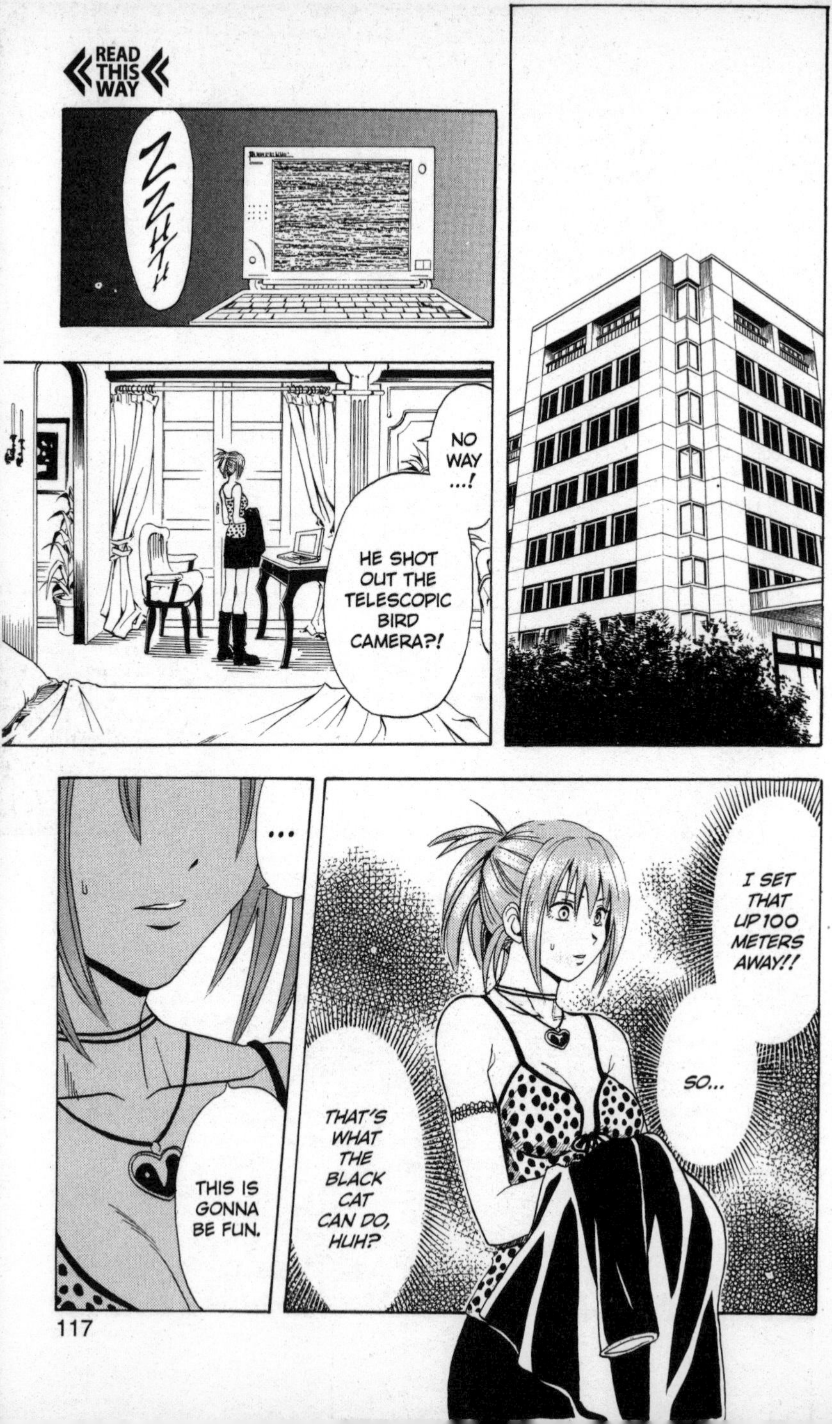

ZZHTT
NO WAY ...!
HE SHOT OUT THE TELESCOPIC BIRD CAMERA?!
I SET THAT UP 100 METERS AWAY!!
SO...
THAT'S WHAT THE BLACK CAT CAN DO, HUH?
...
THIS IS GONNA BE FUN.

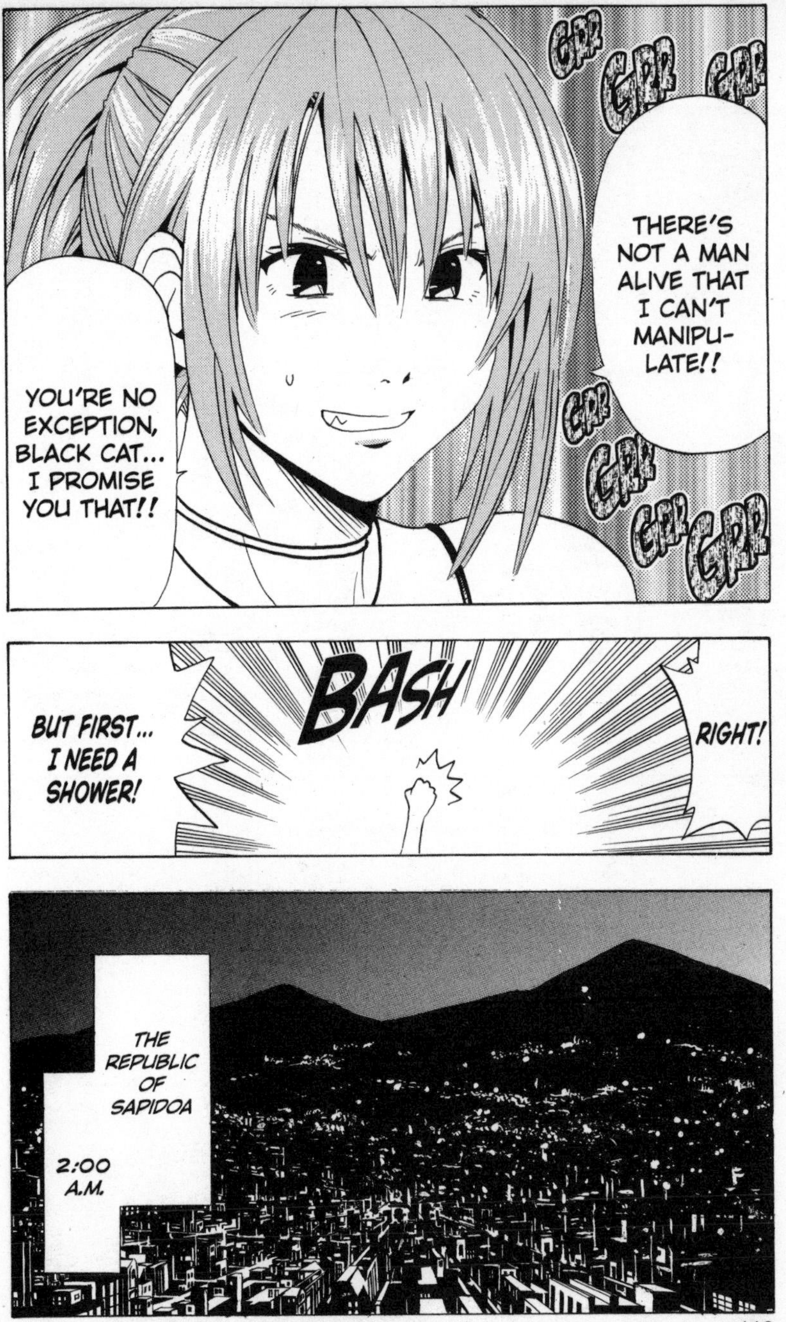
GRR GRR GRR
THERE'S NOT A MAN ALIVE THAT I CAN'T MANIPU-LATE!!
YOU'RE NO EXCEPTION, BLACK CAT... I PROMISE YOU THAT!!
GRR GRR GRR GRR
RIGHT!
BASH
BUT FIRST... I NEED A SHOWER!
THE REPUBLIC OF SAPIDOA
2:00 A.M.

READ THIS WAY

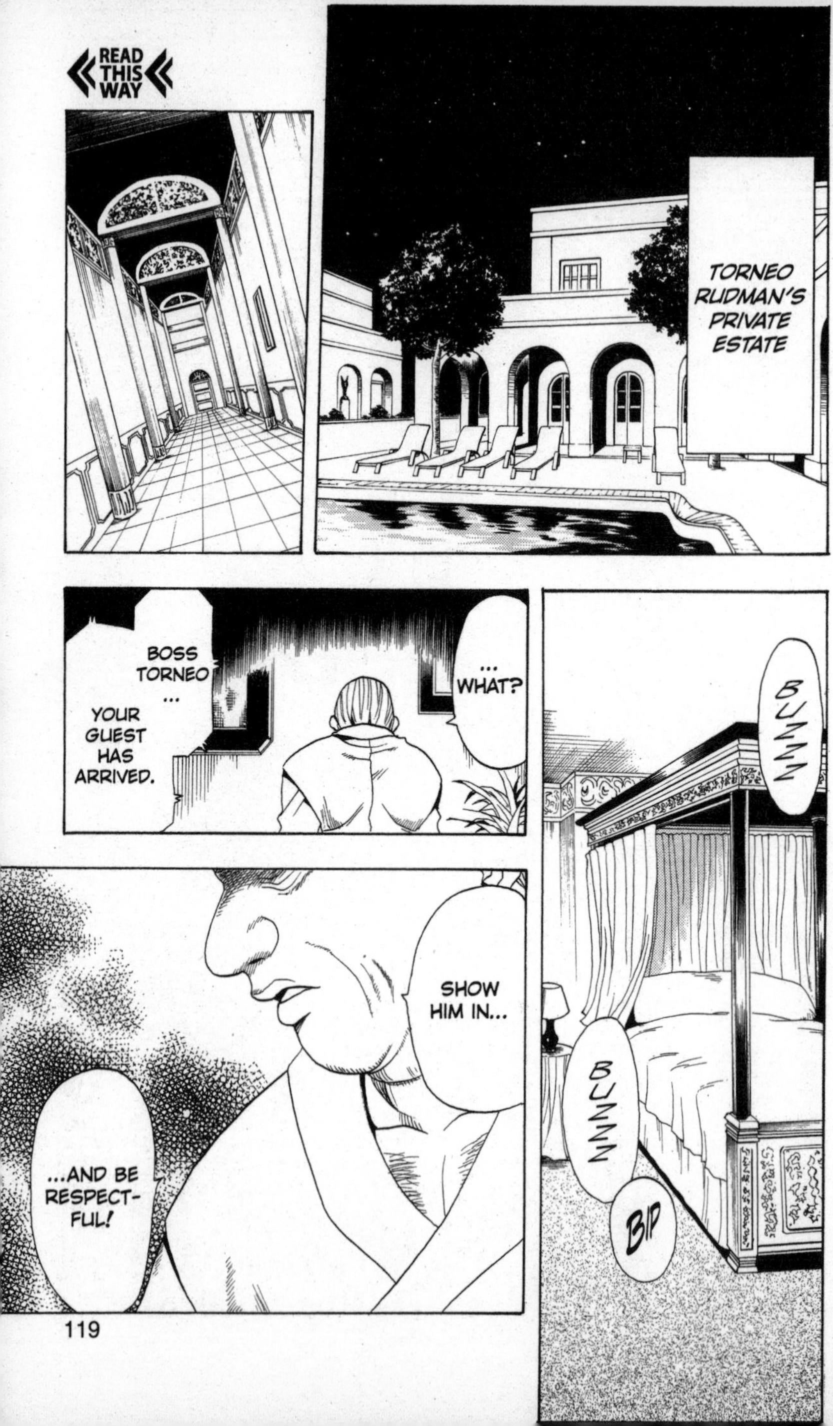
TORNEO RUDMAN'S PRIVATE ESTATE
BUZZZ
BUZZZ
BIP
... WHAT?
BOSS TORNEO ... YOUR GUEST HAS ARRIVED.
SHOW HIM IN...
...AND BE RESPECT-FUL!

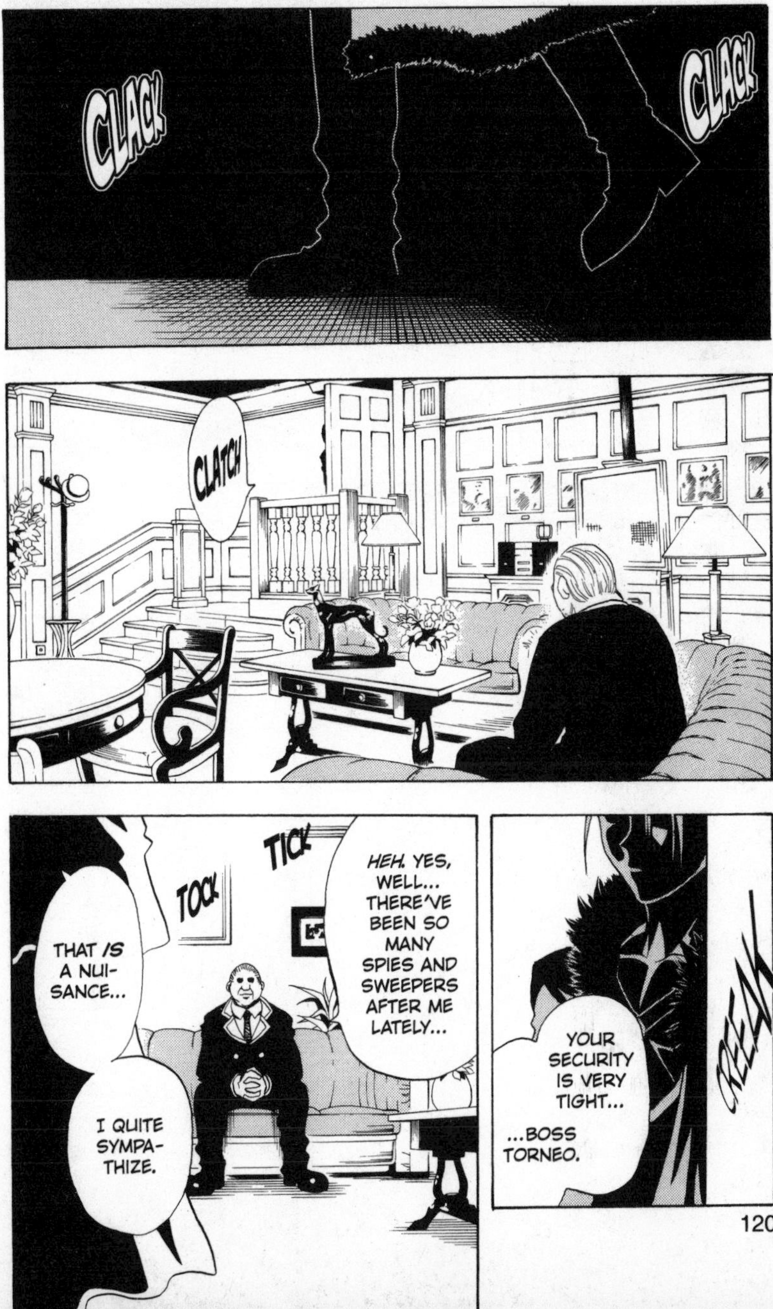
CLACK
CLACK
CLATCH
CREEAK
YOUR SECURITY IS VERY TIGHT...
...BOSS TORNEO.
TICK
TOCK
HEH. YES, WELL... THERE'VE BEEN SO MANY SPIES AND SWEEPERS AFTER ME LATELY...
THAT *IS* A NUISANCE...
I QUITE SYMPATHIZE.

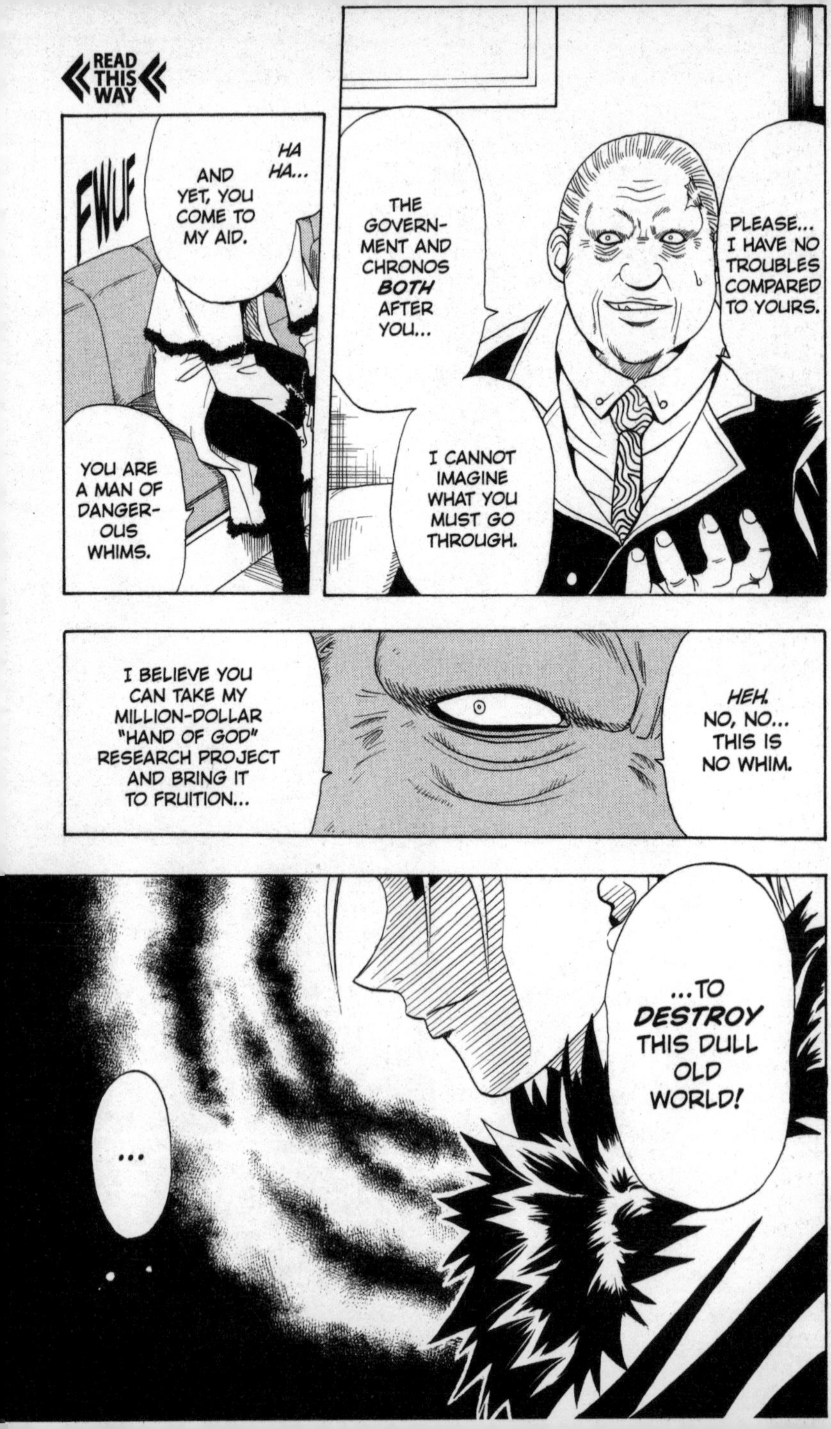
READ THIS WAY
PLEASE... I HAVE NO TROUBLES COMPARED TO YOURS.
THE GOVERNMENT AND CHRONOS BOTH AFTER YOU...
I CANNOT IMAGINE WHAT YOU MUST GO THROUGH.
HA HA... AND YET, YOU COME TO MY AID.
FWUF
YOU ARE A MAN OF DANGEROUS WHIMS.
HEH. NO, NO... THIS IS NO WHIM.
I BELIEVE YOU CAN TAKE MY MILLION-DOLLAR "HAND OF GOD" RESEARCH PROJECT AND BRING IT TO FRUITION...
...TO DESTROY THIS DULL OLD WORLD!
...

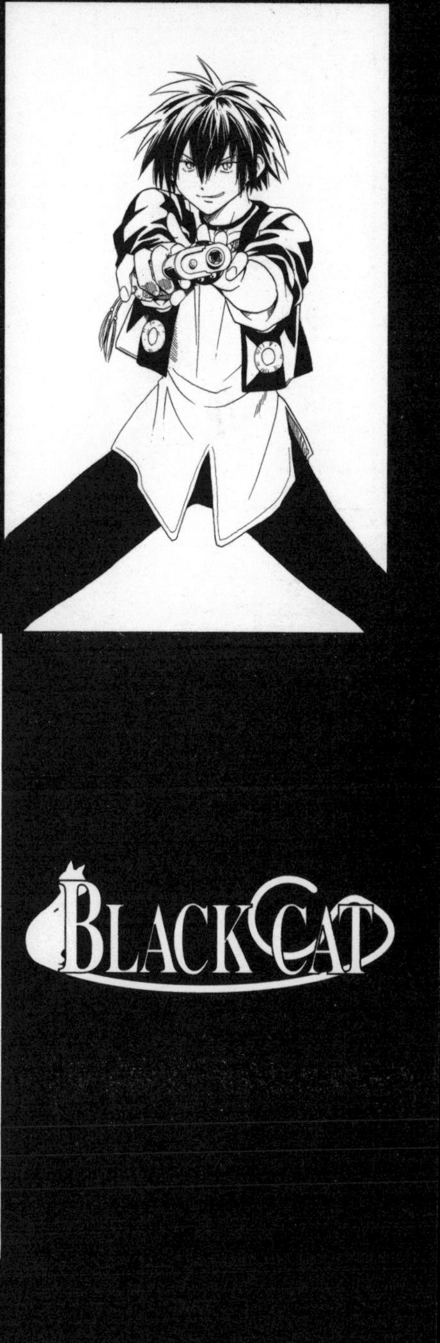

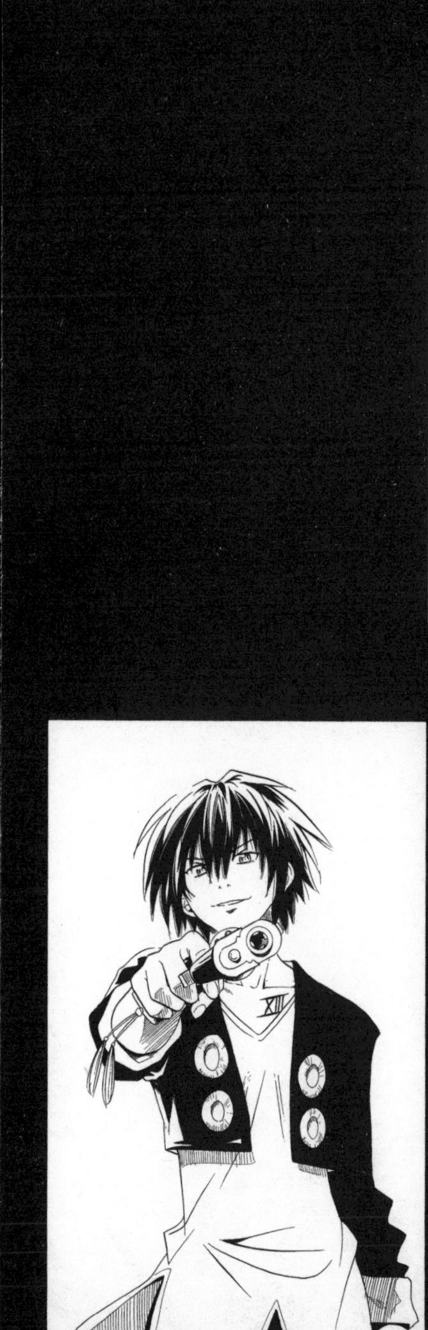

BLACK CAT

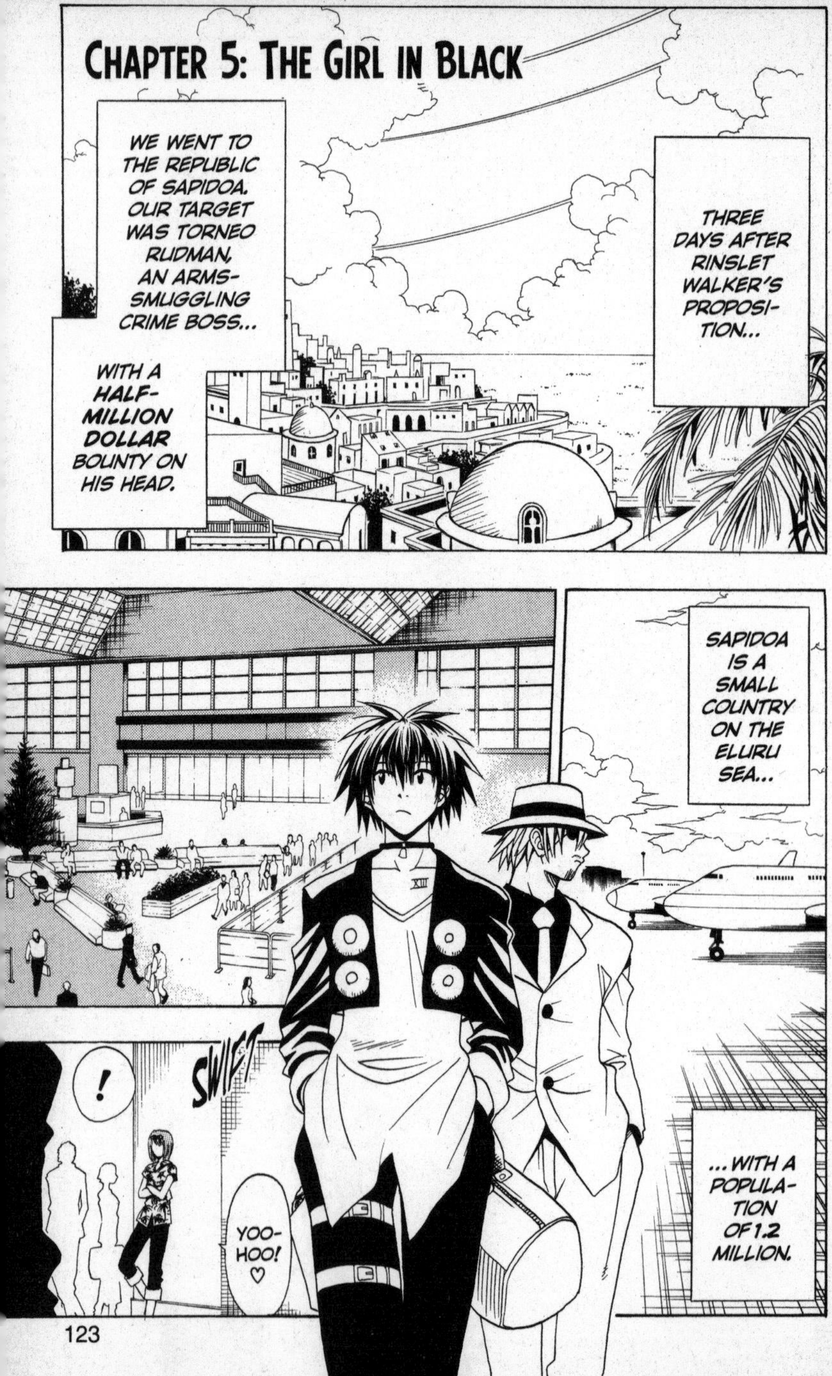
CHAPTER 5: THE GIRL IN BLACK
THREE DAYS AFTER RINSLET WALKER'S PROPOSITION...
WE WENT TO THE REPUBLIC OF SAPIDOA. OUR TARGET WAS TORNEO RUDMAN, AN ARMS-SMUGGLING CRIME BOSS...
WITH A HALF-MILLION DOLLAR BOUNTY ON HIS HEAD.
SAPIDOA IS A SMALL COUNTRY ON THE ELURU SEA...
...WITH A POPULATION OF 1.2 MILLION.
SWIFT
!
YOO-HOO! ♥

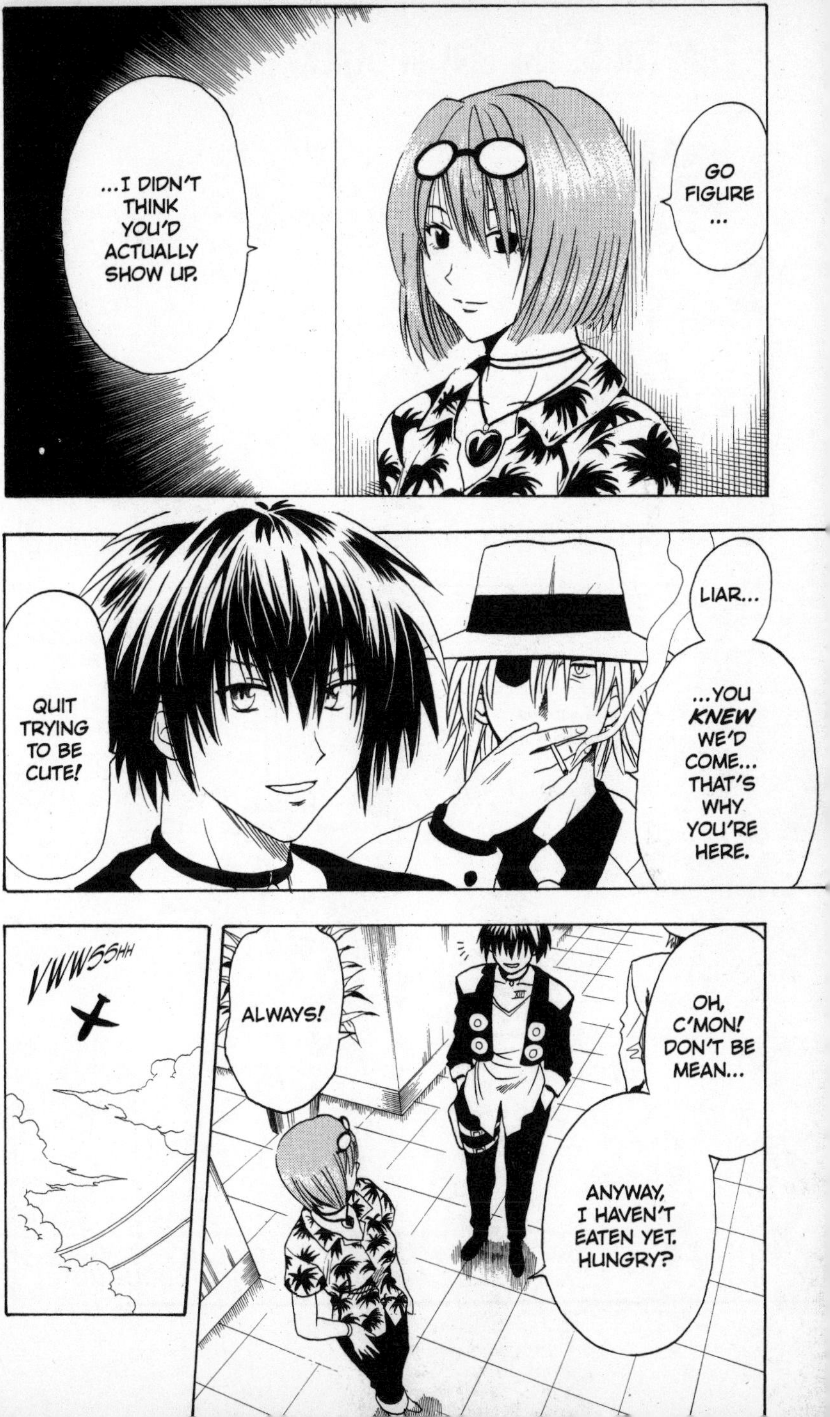
GO FIGURE ...
...I DIDN'T THINK YOU'D ACTUALLY SHOW UP.
LIAR...
...YOU *KNEW* WE'D COME... THAT'S WHY YOU'RE HERE.
QUIT TRYING TO BE CUTE!
OH, C'MON! DON'T BE MEAN...
ALWAYS!
ANYWAY, I HAVEN'T EATEN YET. HUNGRY?
VWWSSHH

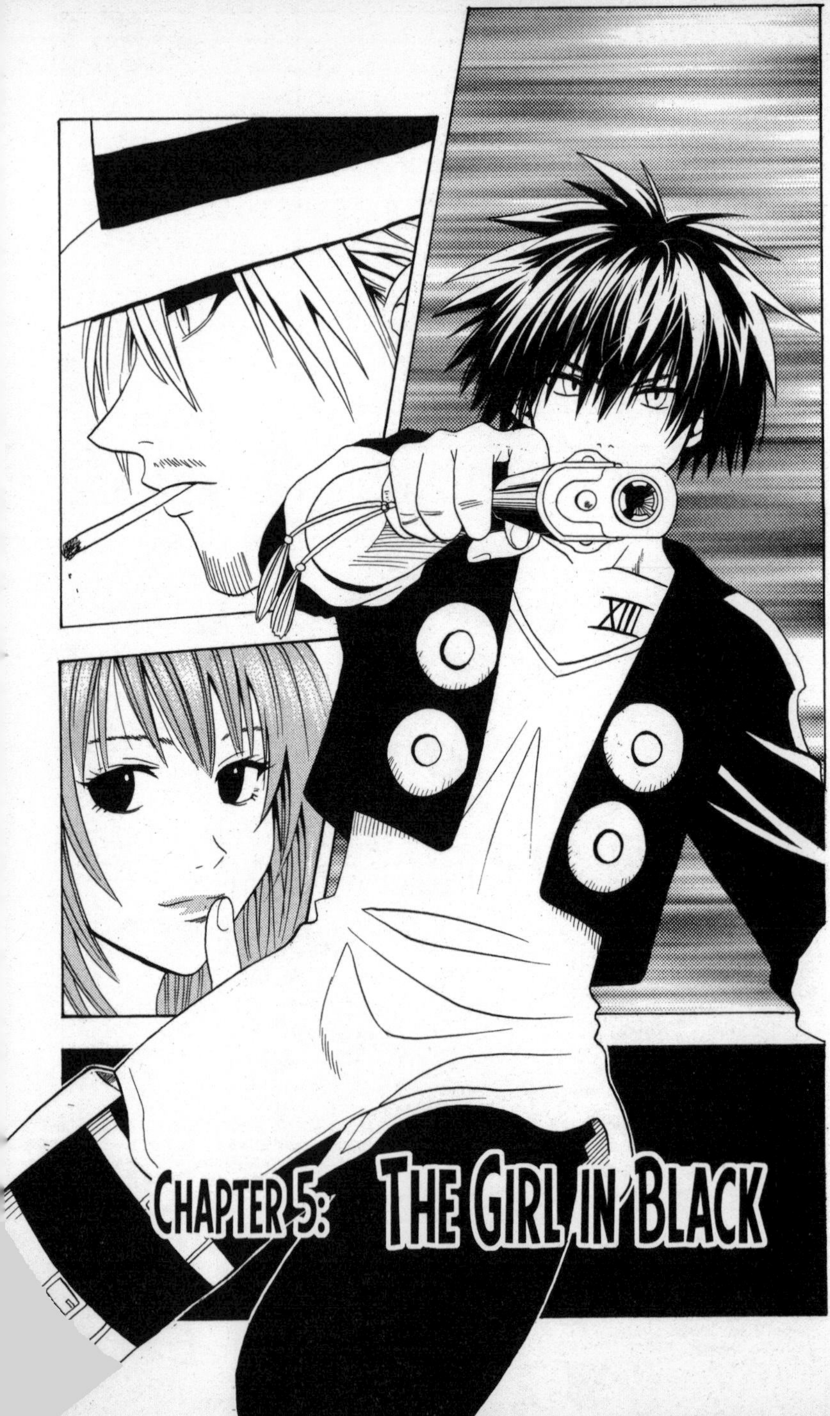
Chapter 5: The Girl in Black

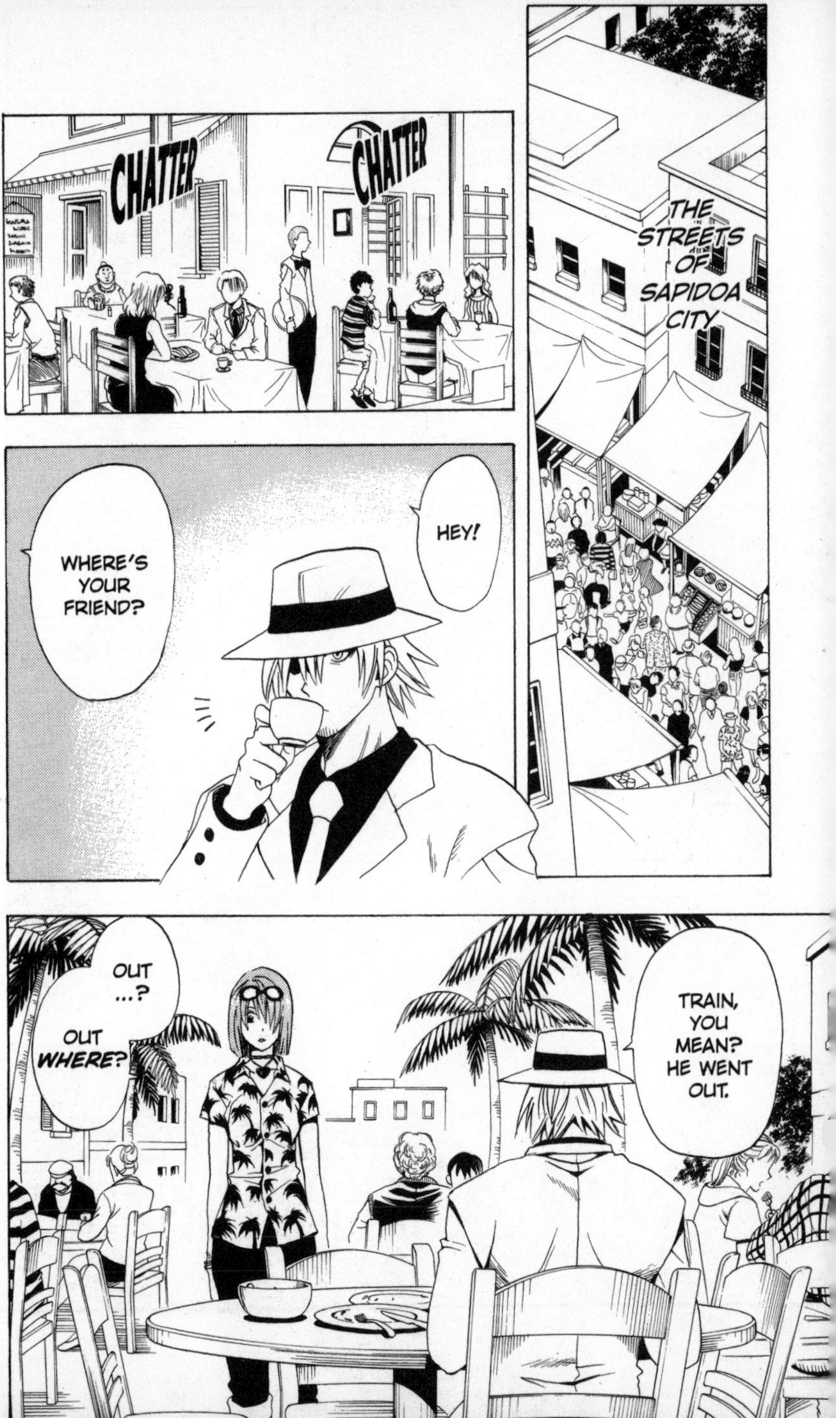
THE STREETS OF SAPIDOA CITY
CHATTER
CHATTER
HEY!
WHERE'S YOUR FRIEND?
TRAIN, YOU MEAN? HE WENT OUT.
OUT ...?
OUT WHERE?

READ THIS WAY

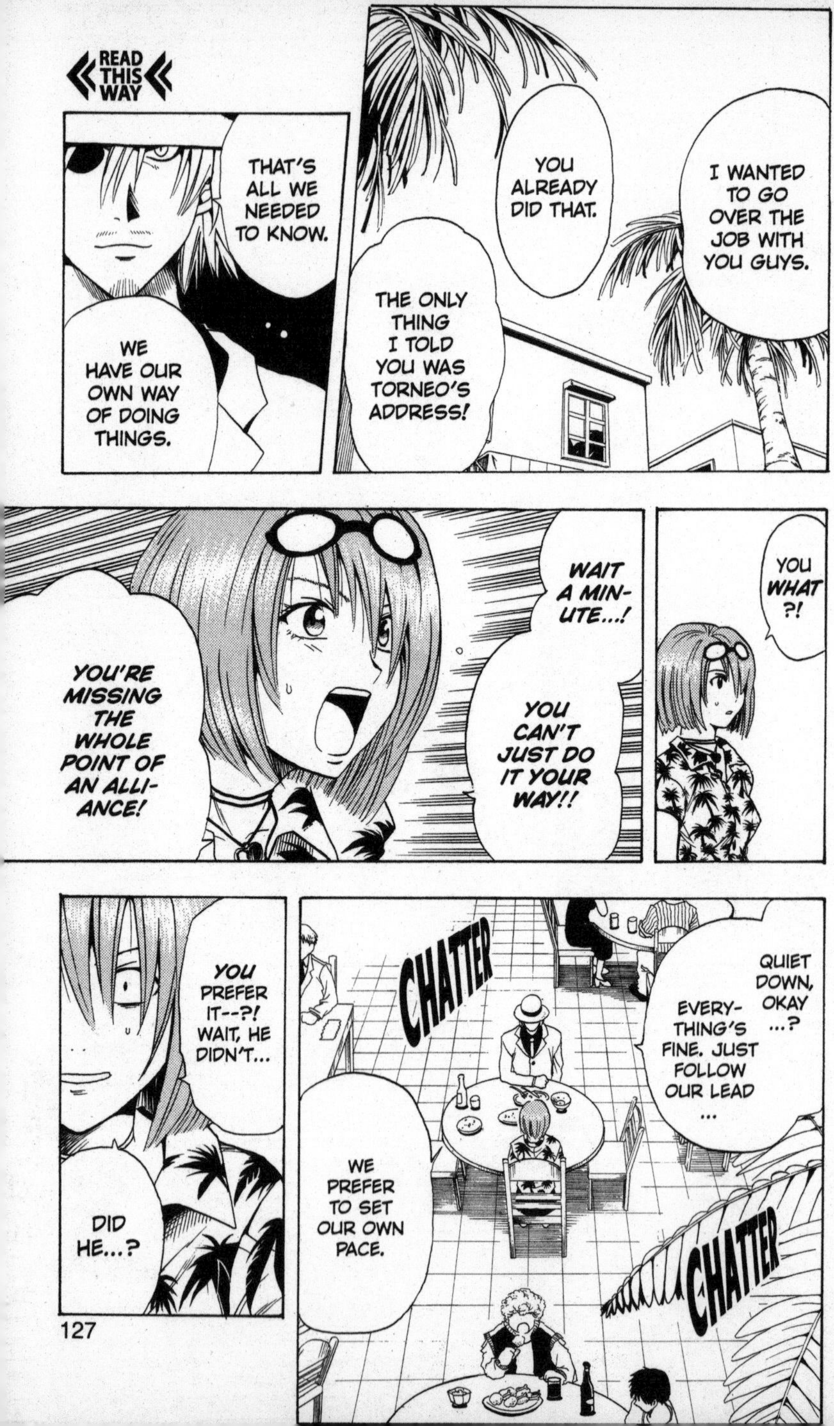
I WANTED TO GO OVER THE JOB WITH YOU GUYS.
YOU ALREADY DID THAT.
THE ONLY THING I TOLD YOU WAS TORNEO'S ADDRESS!
THAT'S ALL WE NEEDED TO KNOW.
WE HAVE OUR OWN WAY OF DOING THINGS.
YOU *WHAT* ?!
WAIT A MIN-UTE...!
YOU CAN'T JUST DO IT YOUR WAY!!
YOU'RE MISSING THE WHOLE POINT OF AN ALLI-ANCE!
CHATTER
QUIET DOWN, OKAY ...?
EVERY-THING'S FINE. JUST FOLLOW OUR LEAD ...
WE PREFER TO SET OUR OWN PACE.
CHATTER
YOU PREFER IT--?! WAIT, HE DIDN'T...
DID HE...?

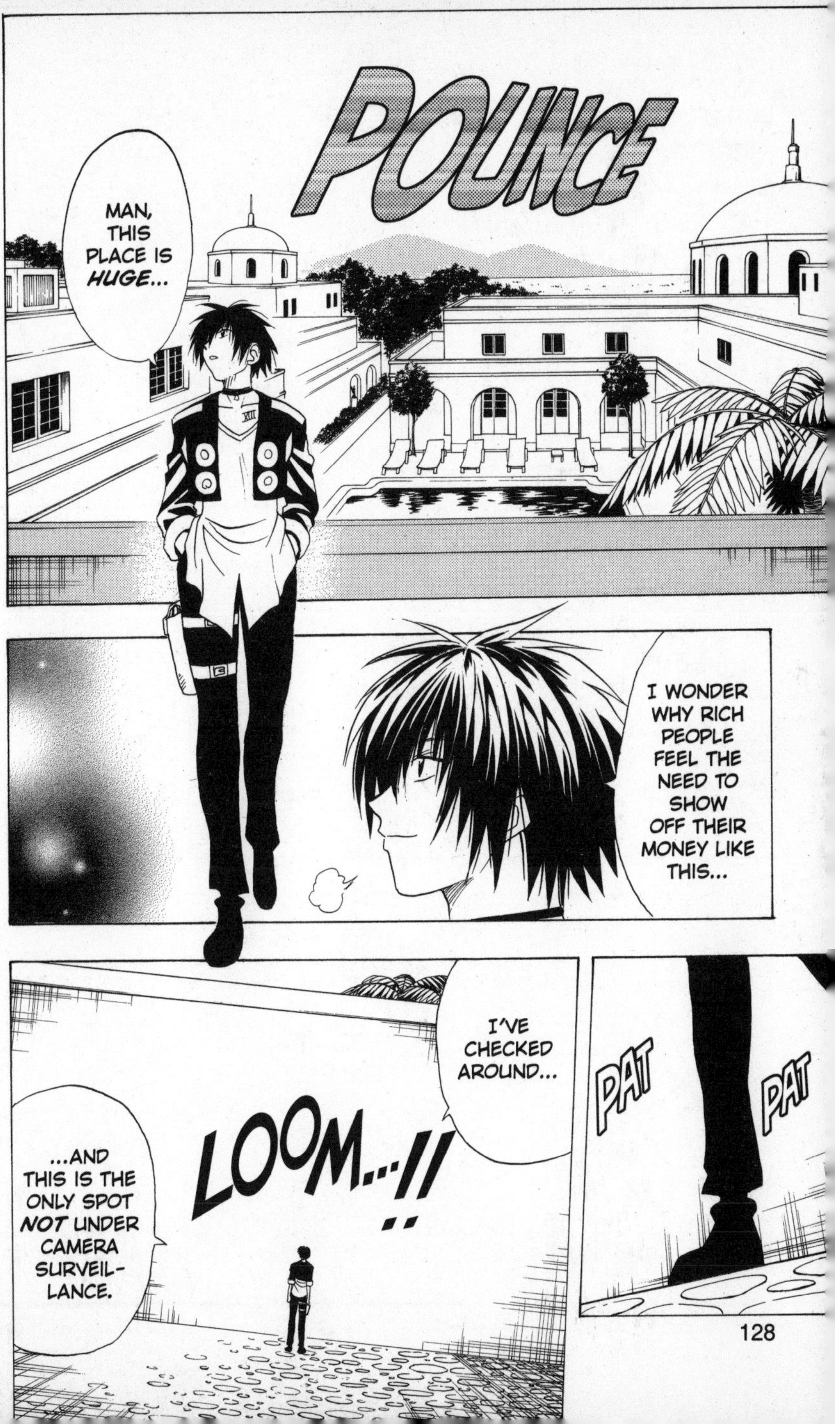
POUNCE
MAN, THIS PLACE IS HUGE...
I WONDER WHY RICH PEOPLE FEEL THE NEED TO SHOW OFF THEIR MONEY LIKE THIS...
PAT
PAT
I'VE CHECKED AROUND...
LOOM...!!
...AND THIS IS THE ONLY SPOT NOT UNDER CAMERA SURVEIL-LANCE.

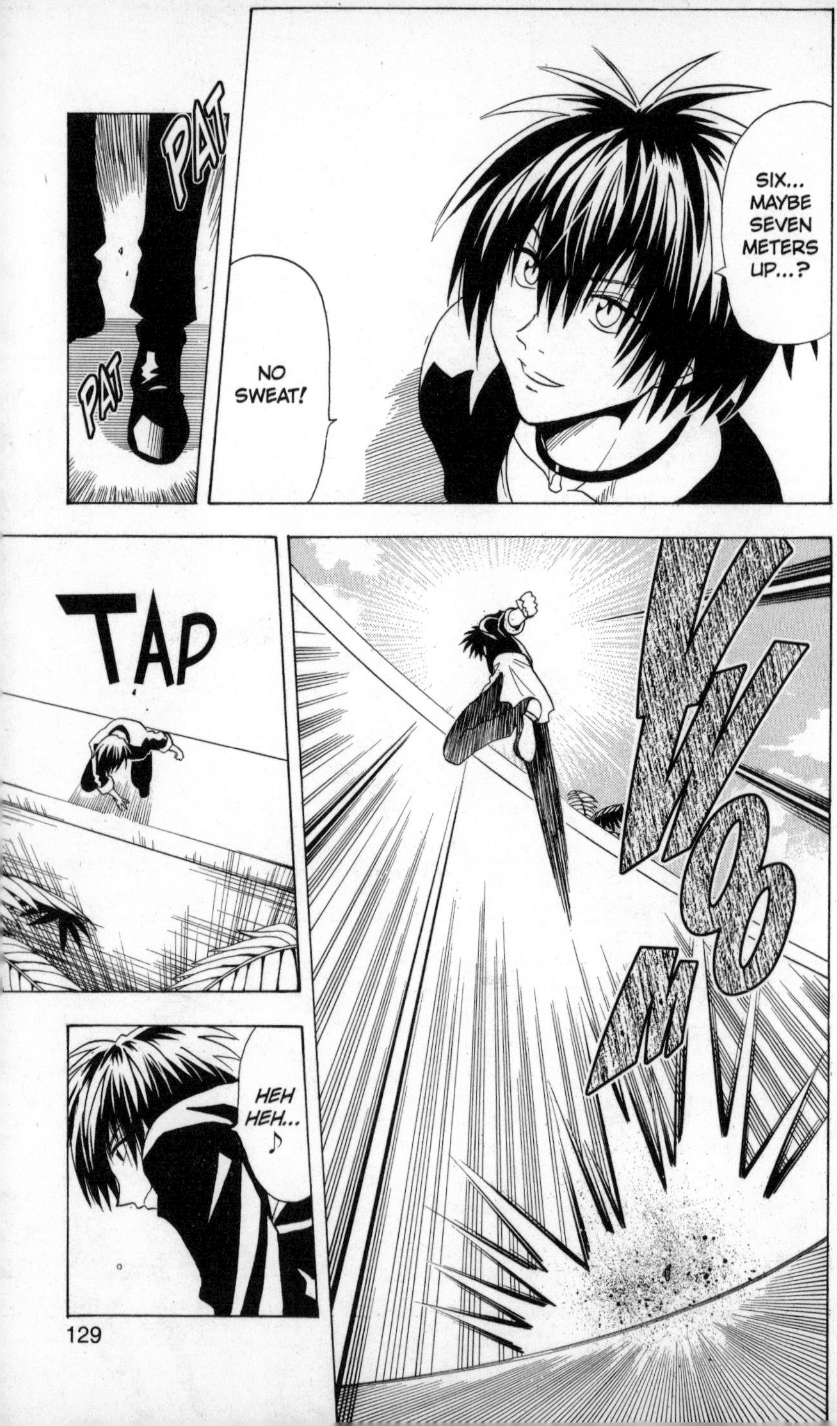
SIX... MAYBE SEVEN METERS UP...?
NO SWEAT!
PAT
PAT
WHOOM
TAP
HEH HEH... ♪

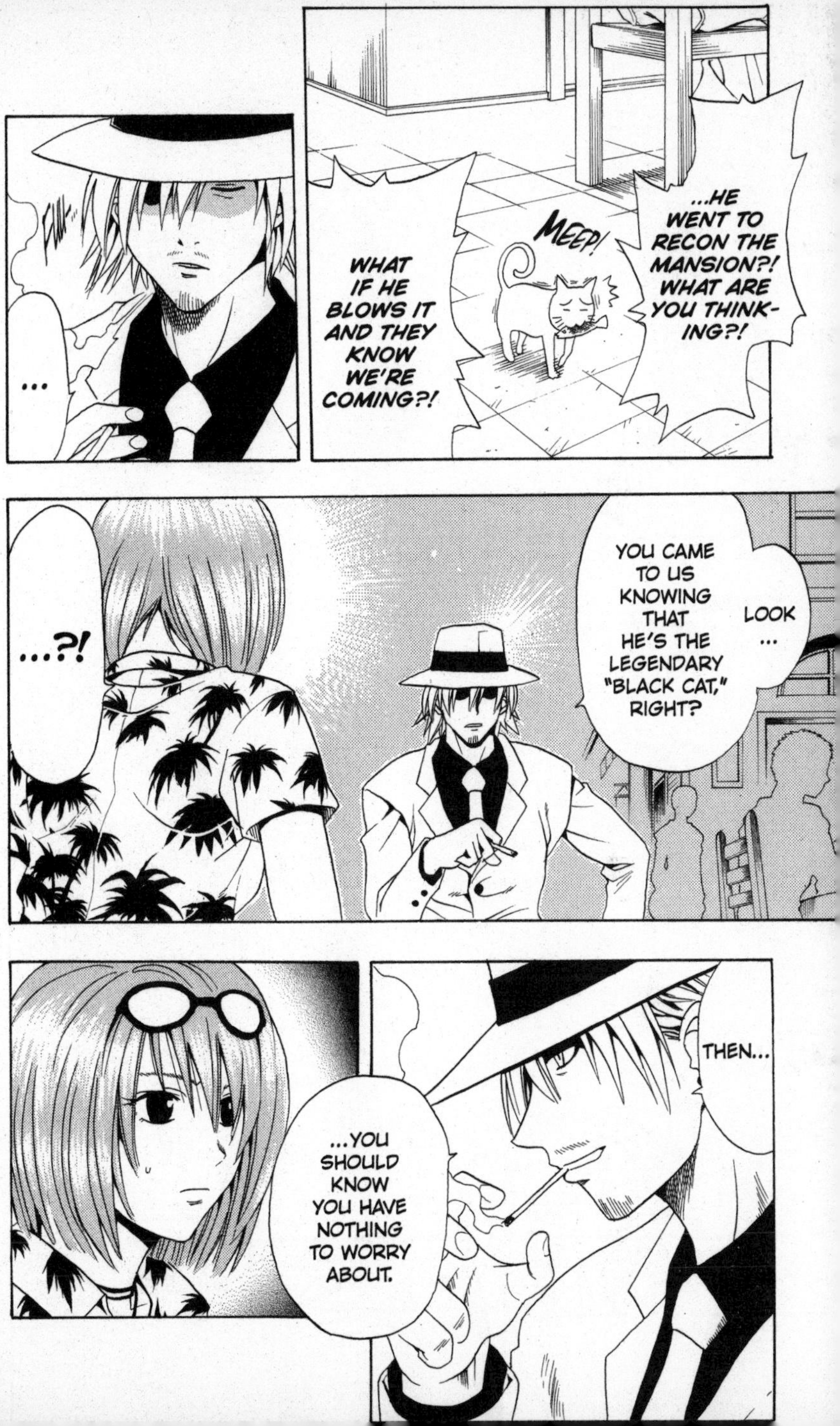
...HE WENT TO RECON THE MANSION?! WHAT ARE YOU THINKING?!
MEEP!
WHAT IF HE BLOWS IT AND THEY KNOW WE'RE COMING?!
...
LOOK...
YOU CAME TO US KNOWING THAT HE'S THE LEGENDARY "BLACK CAT," RIGHT?
...?!
THEN...
...YOU SHOULD KNOW YOU HAVE NOTHING TO WORRY ABOUT.

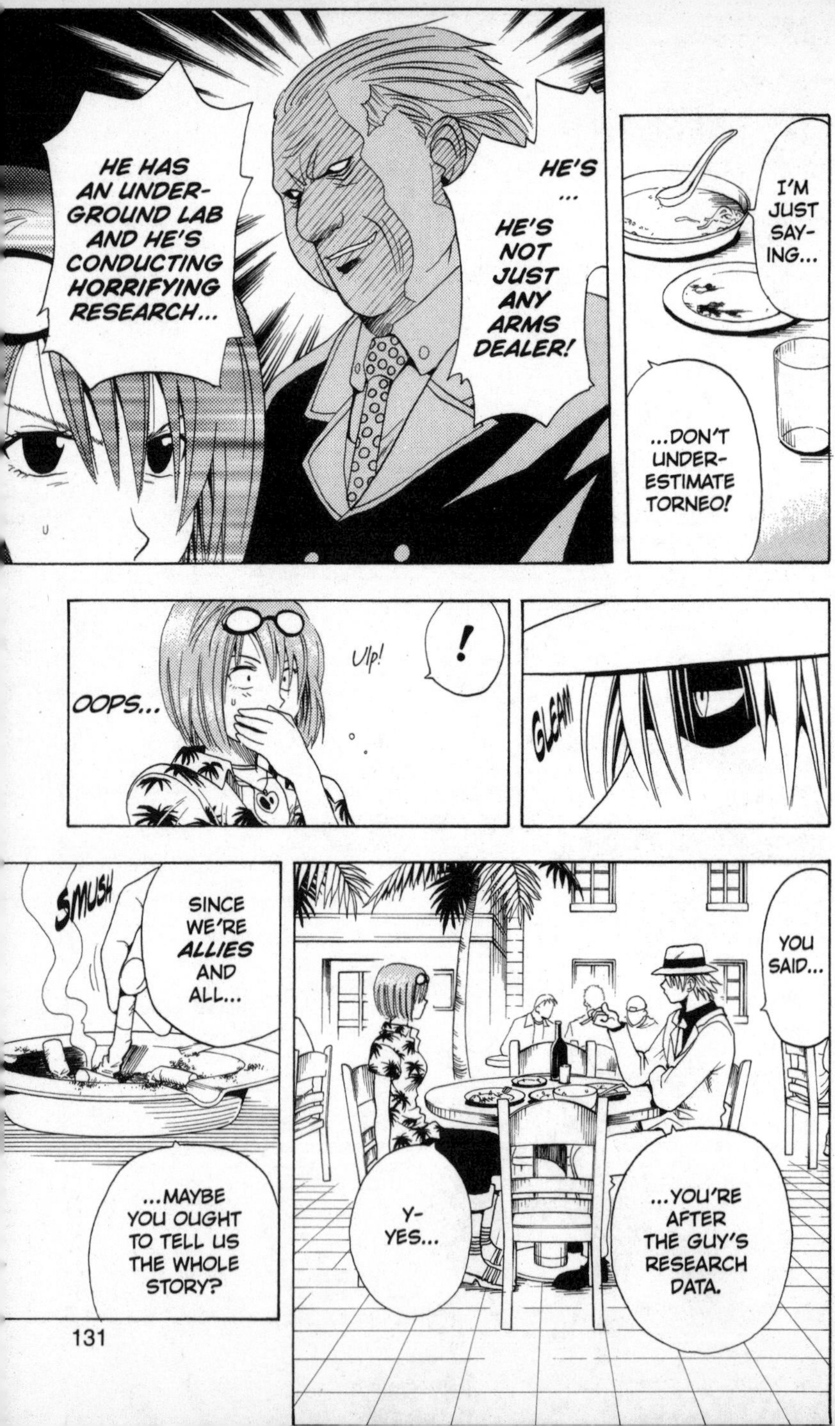
I'M JUST SAYING...
...DON'T UNDERESTIMATE TORNEO!
HE'S ...
HE'S NOT JUST ANY ARMS DEALER!
HE HAS AN UNDERGROUND LAB AND HE'S CONDUCTING HORRIFYING RESEARCH...
GLEAM
!
Ulp!
OOPS...
YOU SAID...
...YOU'RE AFTER THE GUY'S RESEARCH DATA.
Y-YES...
SMUSH
SINCE WE'RE ALLIES AND ALL...
...MAYBE YOU OUGHT TO TELL US THE WHOLE STORY?

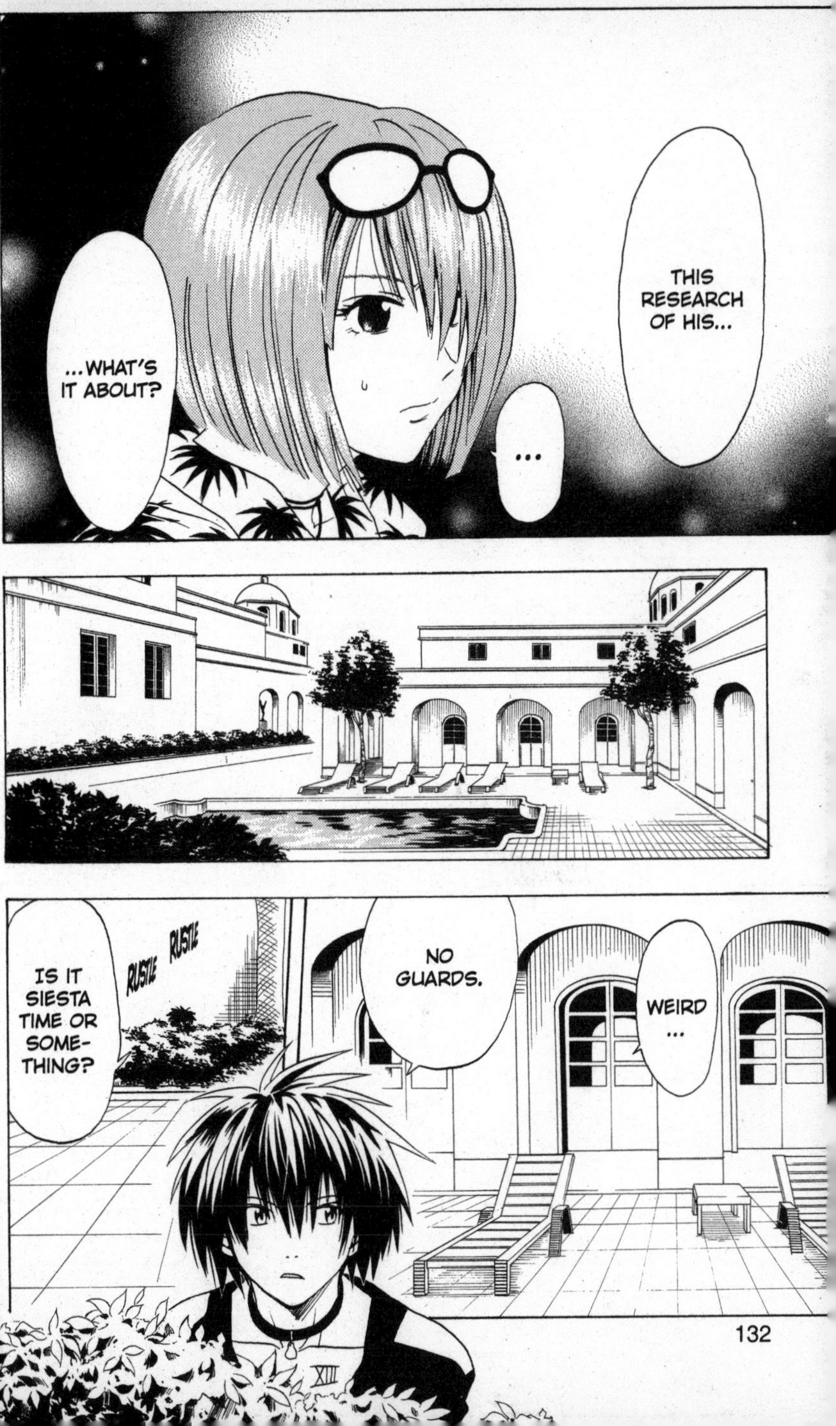
THIS RESEARCH OF HIS...
...
...WHAT'S IT ABOUT?
WEIRD...
NO GUARDS.
RUSTLE
RUSTLE
IS IT SIESTA TIME OR SOME-THING?

READ THIS WAY

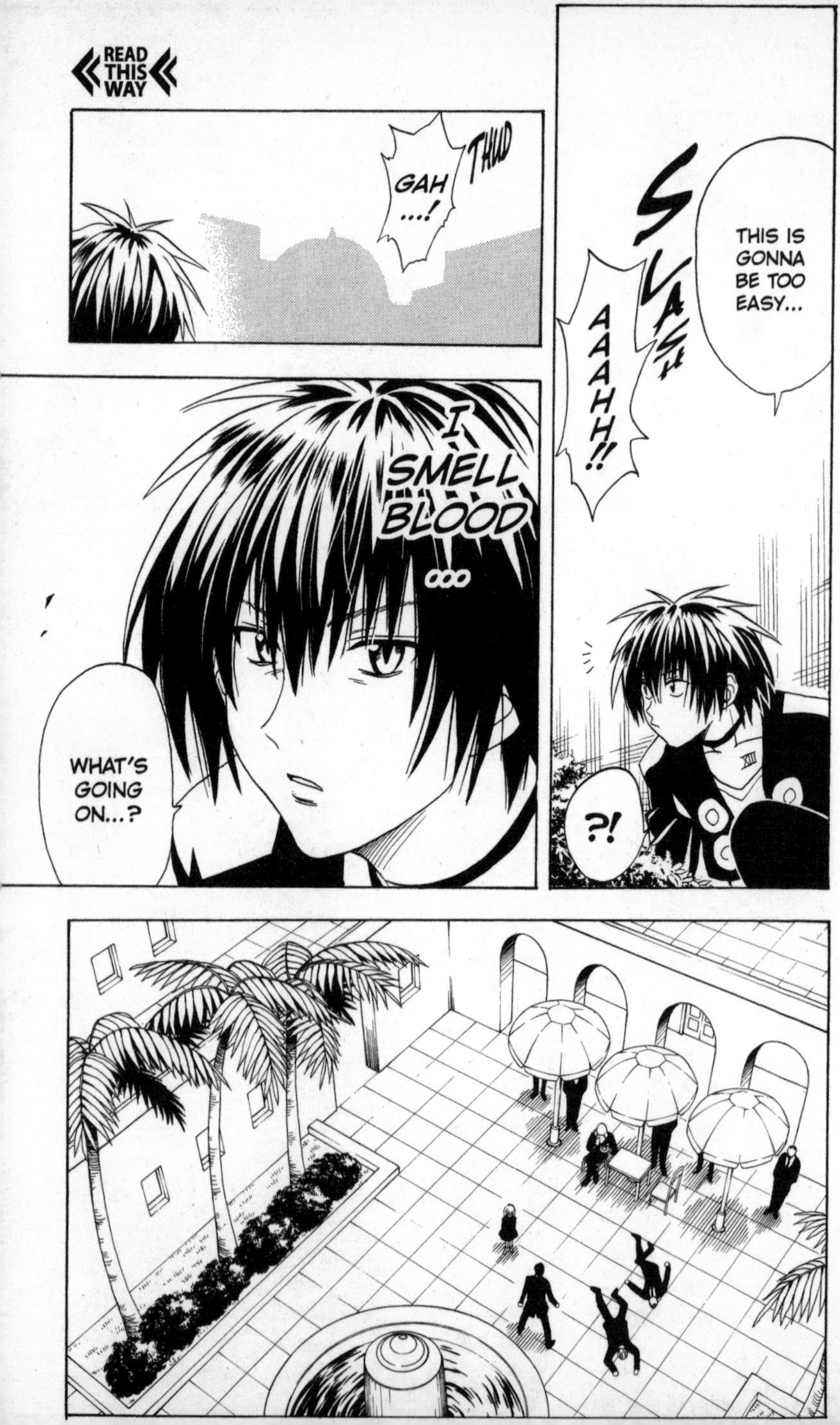
THIS IS GONNA BE TOO EASY...
SLASH
AAAHH!!
?!
GAH ...!
THUD
I SMELL BLOOD...
WHAT'S GOING ON...?

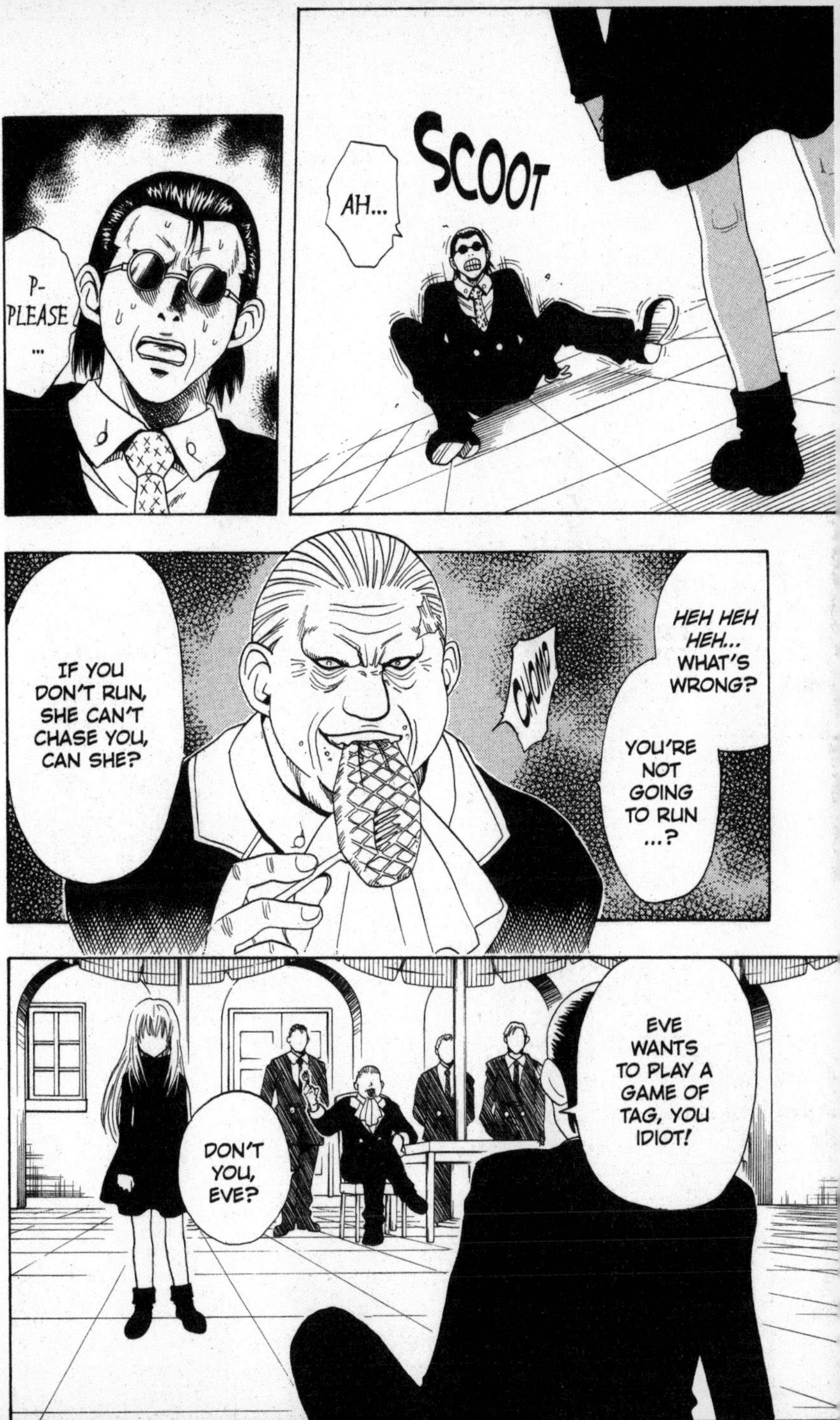
SCOOT
AH...
P-PLEASE...
CHOMP
HEH HEH HEH... WHAT'S WRONG?
YOU'RE NOT GOING TO RUN...?
IF YOU DON'T RUN, SHE CAN'T CHASE YOU, CAN SHE?
EVE WANTS TO PLAY A GAME OF TAG, YOU IDIOT!
DON'T YOU, EVE?

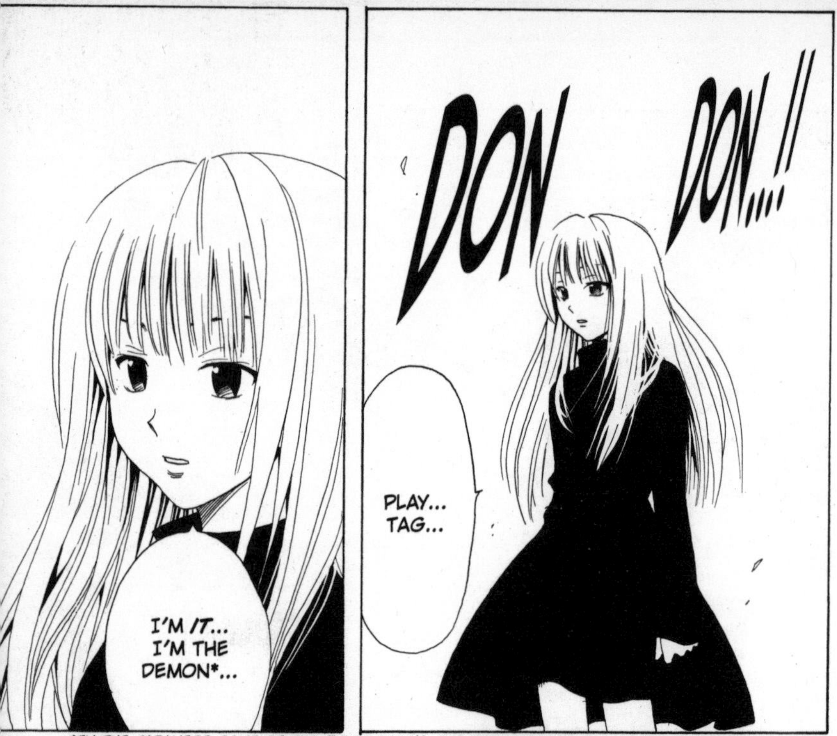
DON DON...!!
PLAY... TAG...
I'M *IT*... I'M THE DEMON*...

*IN THE JAPANESE GAME OF TAG ("ONIGOKKO"), THE PERSON WHO IS "IT" IS CALLED THE "ONI," WHICH MEANS DEMON OR MONSTER.

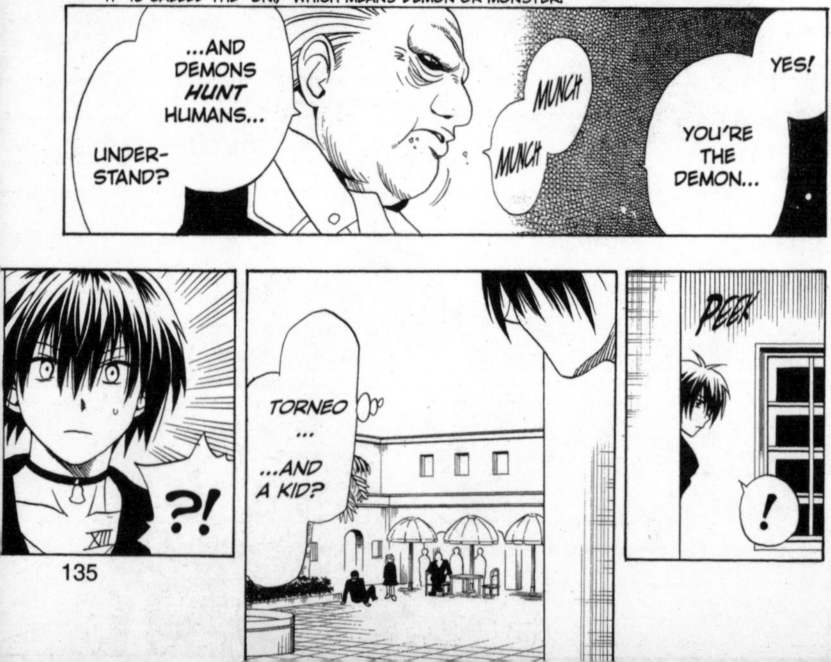
YES!
YOU'RE THE DEMON...
MUNCH
MUNCH
...AND DEMONS ***HUNT*** HUMANS...
UNDER-STAND?
PEEK
!
TORNEO ...
...AND A KID?
?!

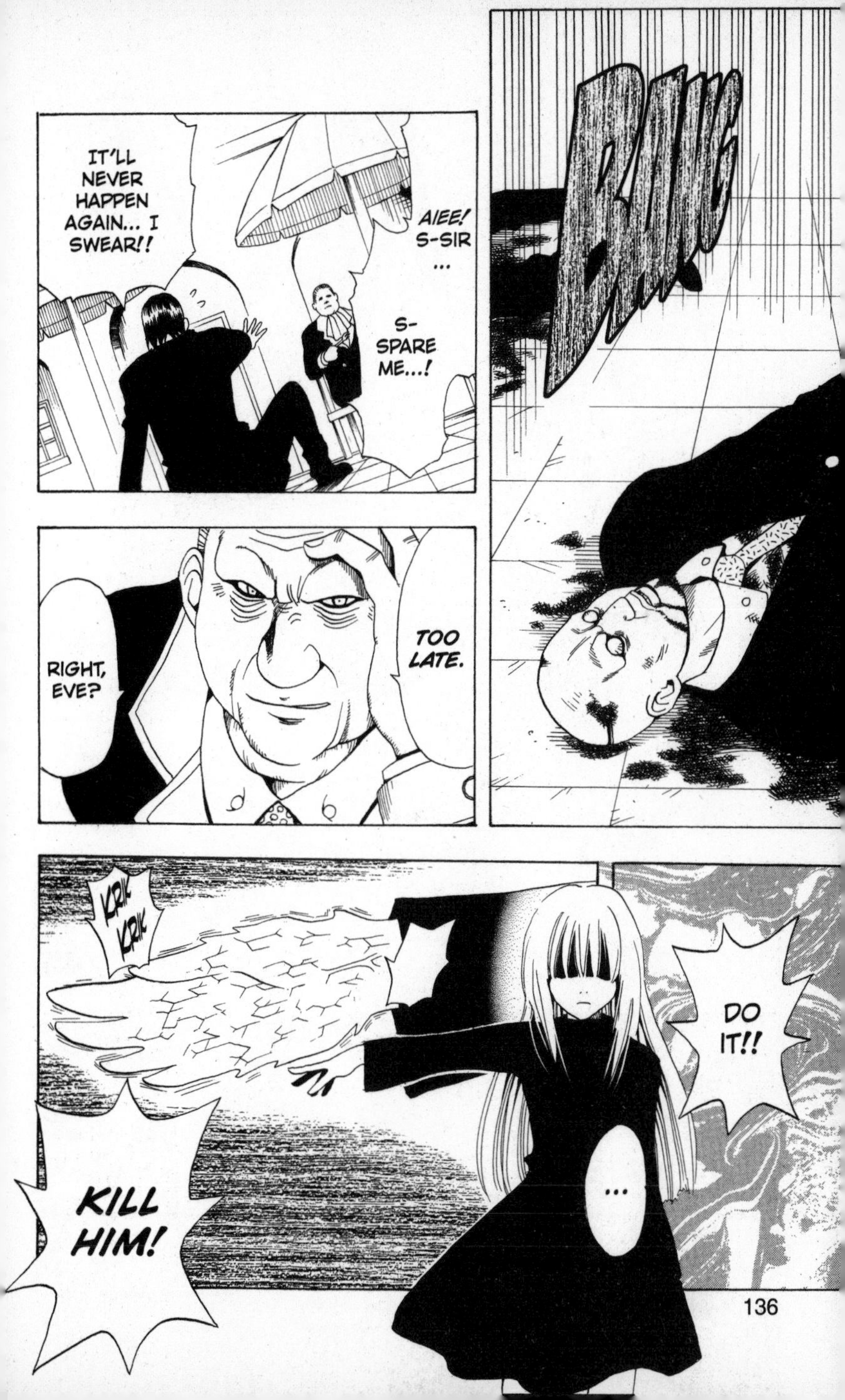

BANG
AIEE! S-SIR ...
S-SPARE ME...!
IT'LL NEVER HAPPEN AGAIN... I SWEAR!!
TOO LATE.
RIGHT, EVE?
DO IT!!
...
KRIK KRIK
KILL HIM!

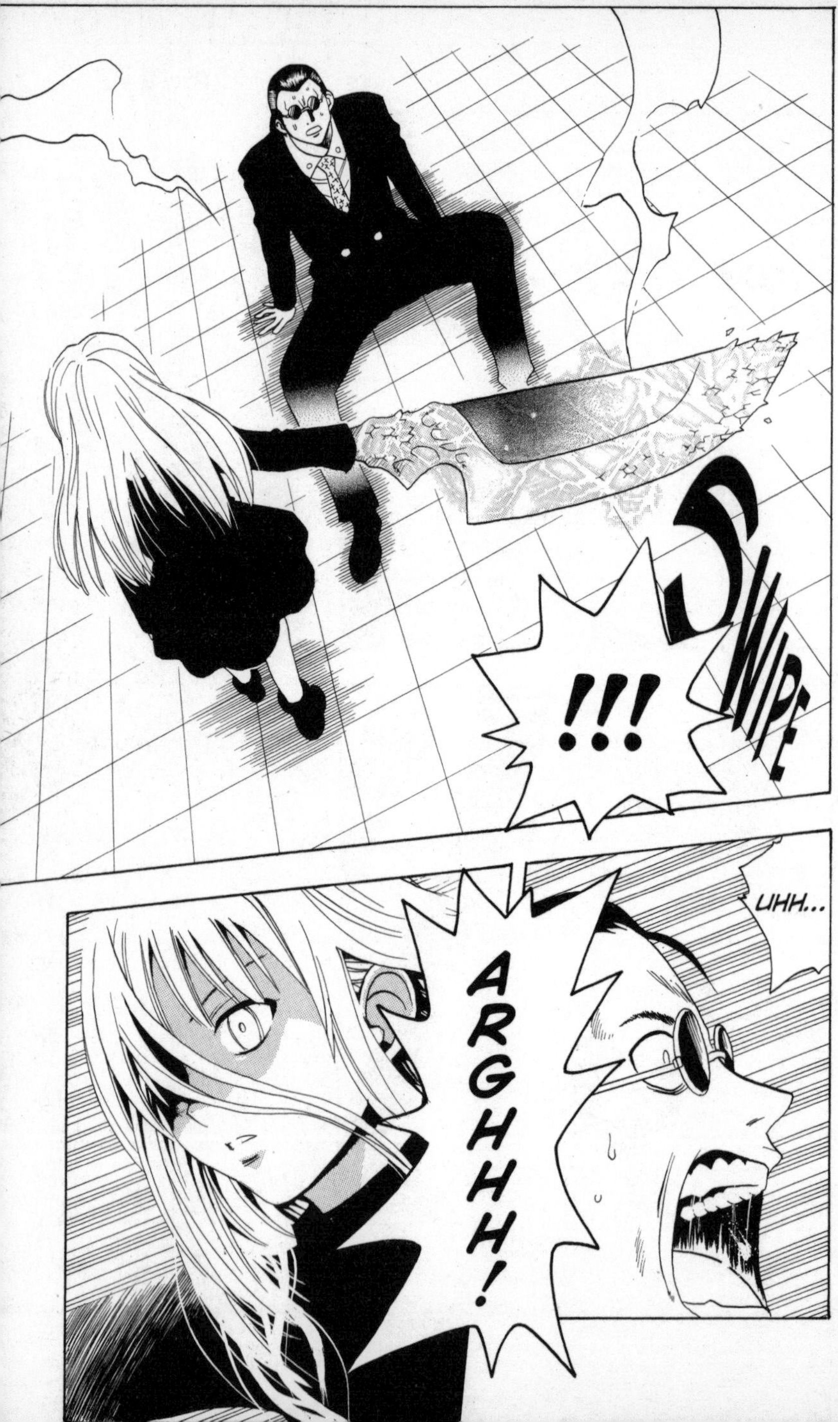
SWIPE
!!!
UHH...
ARGHHH!

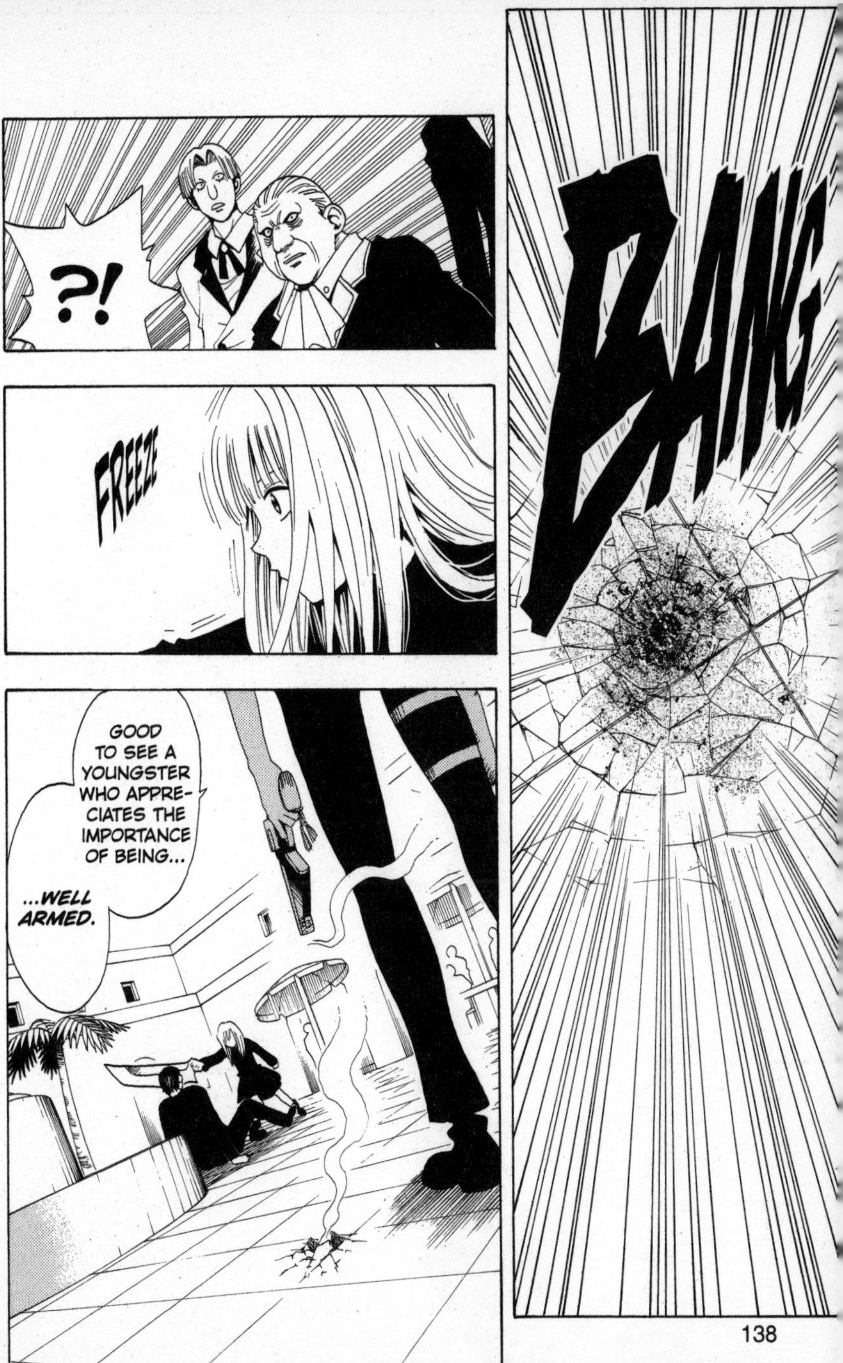
BANG
?!
FREEZE
GOOD TO SEE A YOUNGSTER WHO APPRECIATES THE IMPORTANCE OF BEING...
...WELL ARMED.

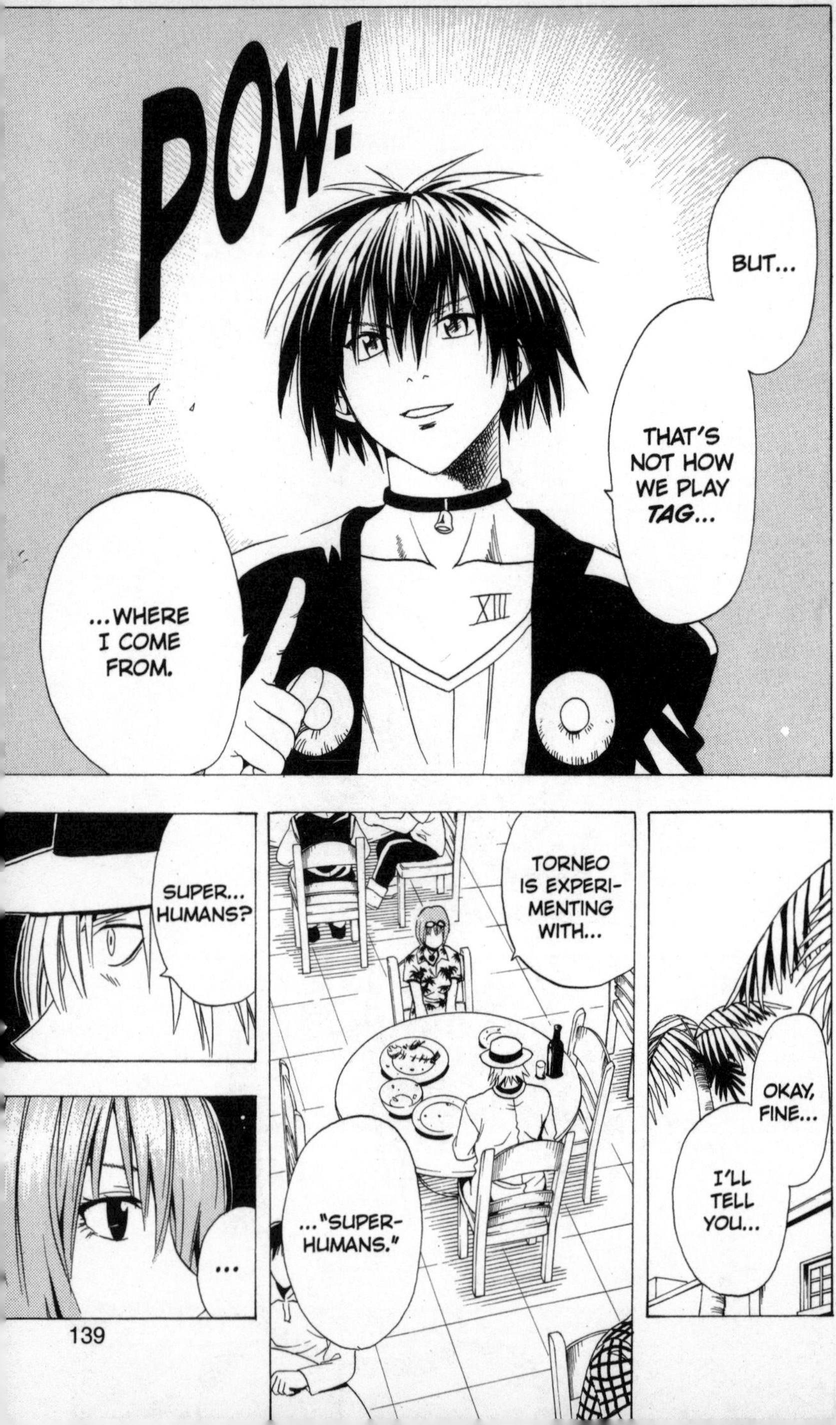
POW!
BUT...
THAT'S NOT HOW WE PLAY *TAG*...
...WHERE I COME FROM.
OKAY, FINE...
I'LL TELL YOU...
TORNEO IS EXPERIMENTING WITH...
..."SUPERHUMANS."
SUPER... HUMANS?
...

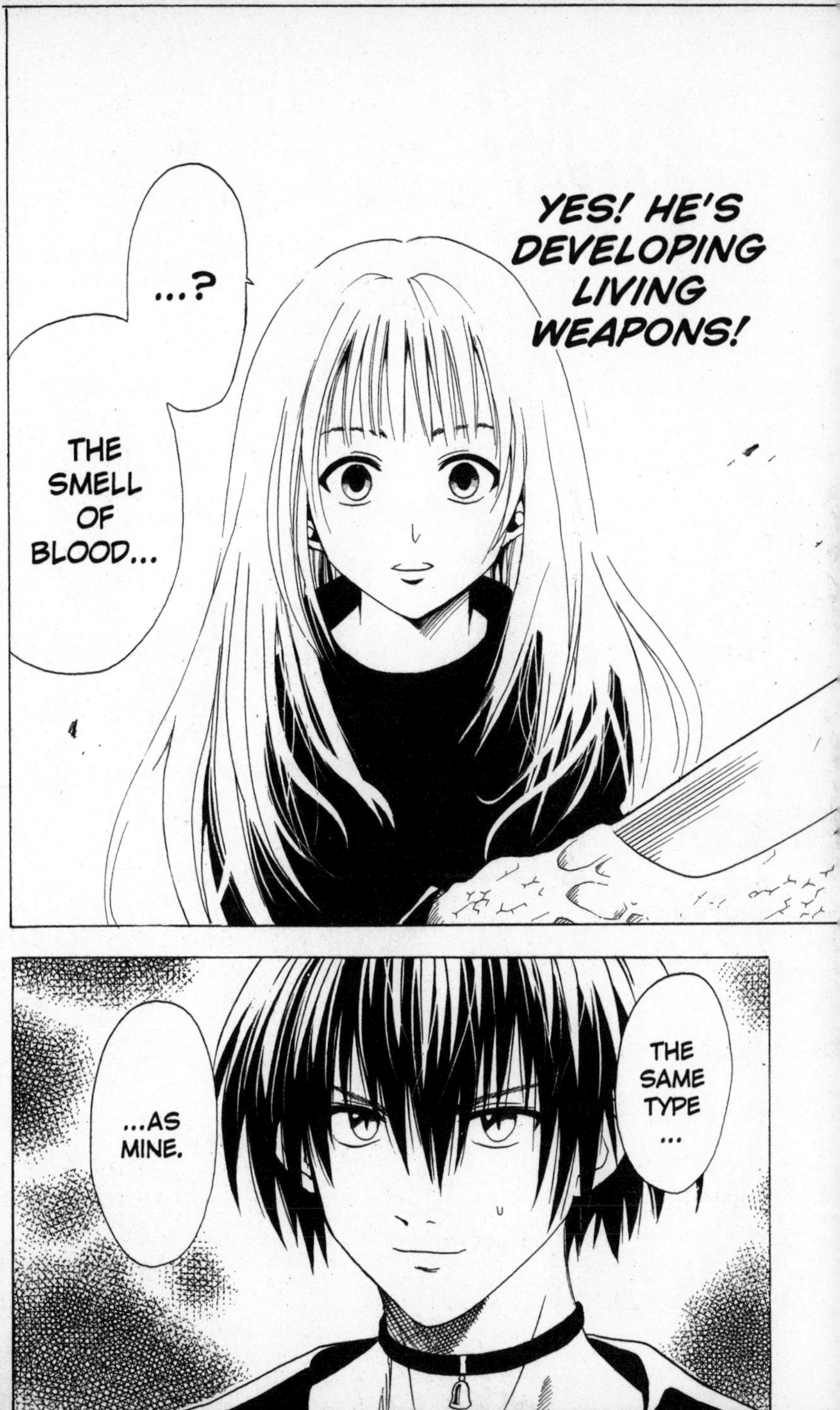
YES! HE'S DEVELOPING LIVING WEAPONS!
...?
THE SMELL OF BLOOD...
THE SAME TYPE ...
...AS MINE.

Chapter 6: Playing Tag

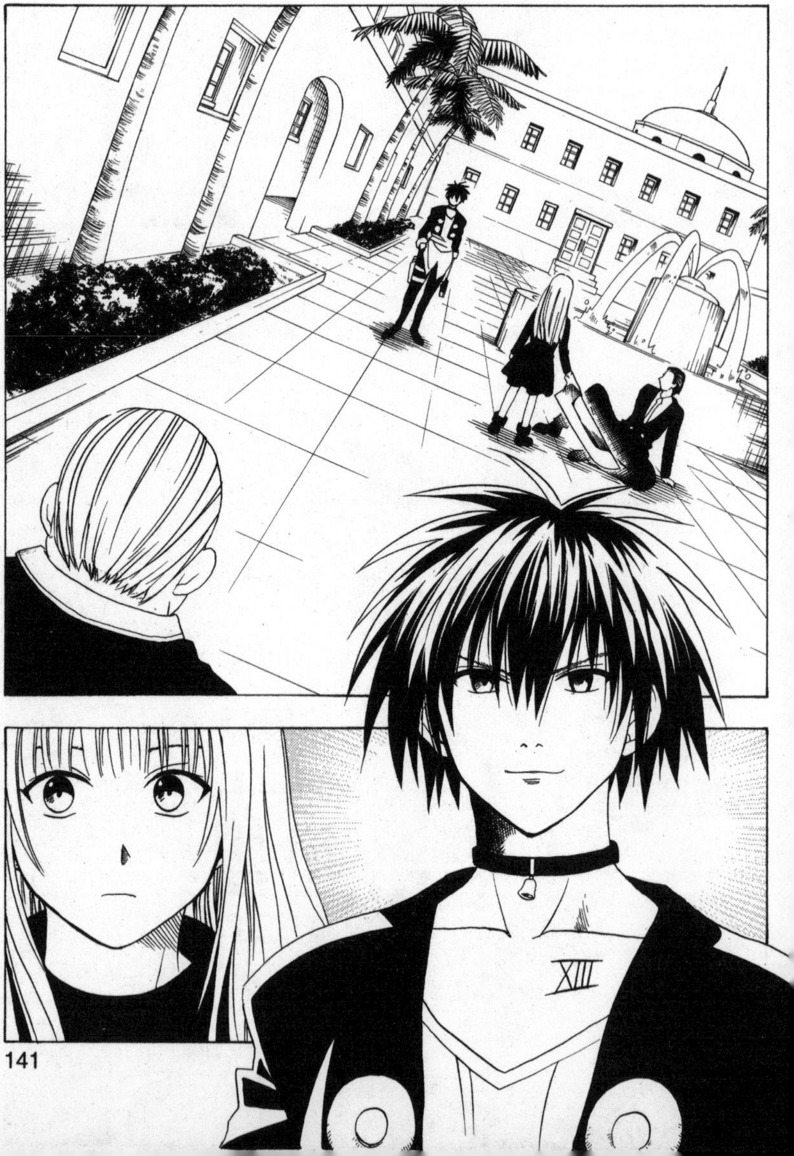
XIII

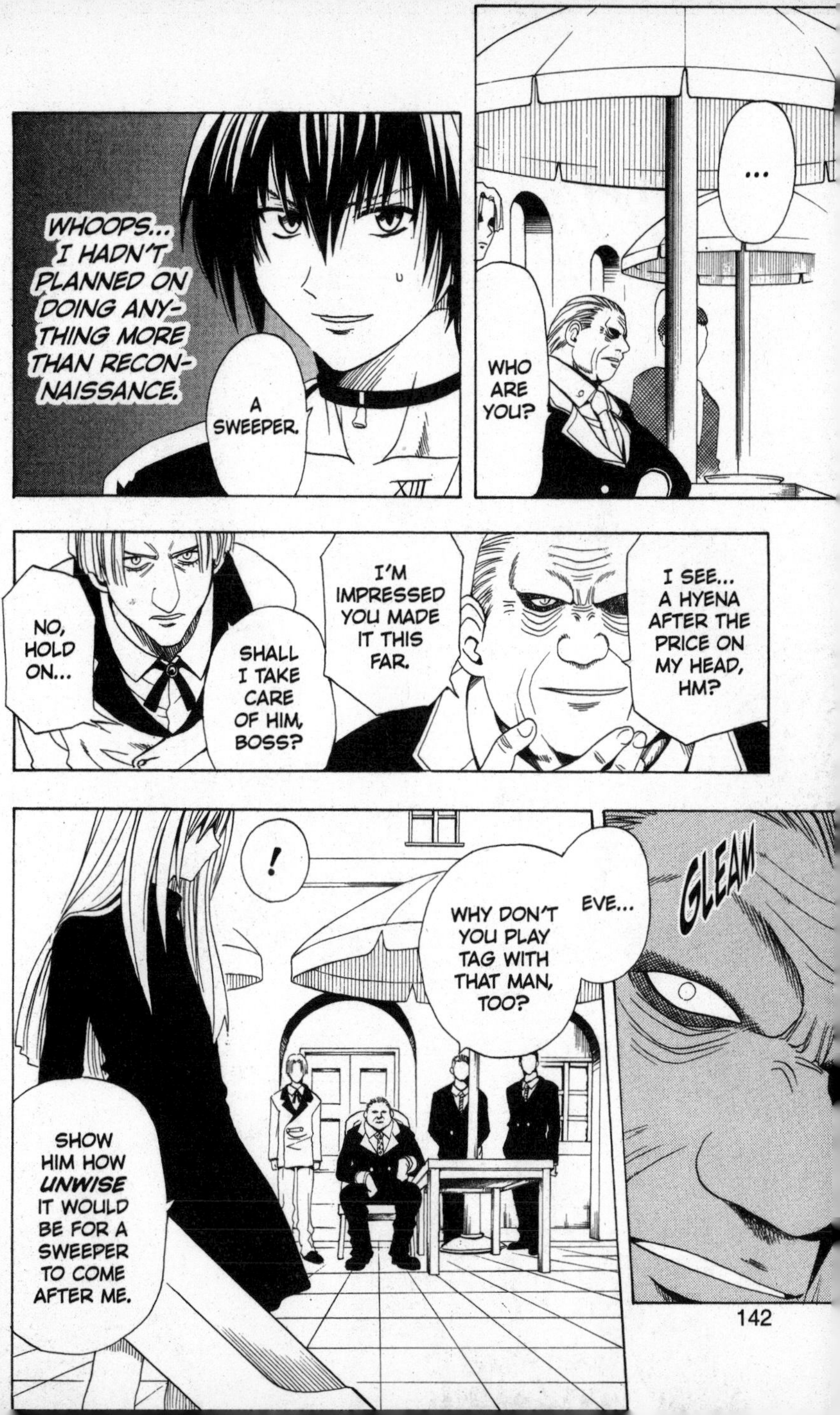
...
WHO ARE YOU?
A SWEEPER.
WHOOPS... I HADN'T PLANNED ON DOING ANYTHING MORE THAN RECONNAISSANCE.
I SEE... A HYENA AFTER THE PRICE ON MY HEAD, HM?
I'M IMPRESSED YOU MADE IT THIS FAR.
SHALL I TAKE CARE OF HIM, BOSS?
NO, HOLD ON...
GLEAM
EVE...
WHY DON'T YOU PLAY TAG WITH THAT MAN, TOO?
!
SHOW HIM HOW *UNWISE* IT WOULD BE FOR A SWEEPER TO COME AFTER ME.

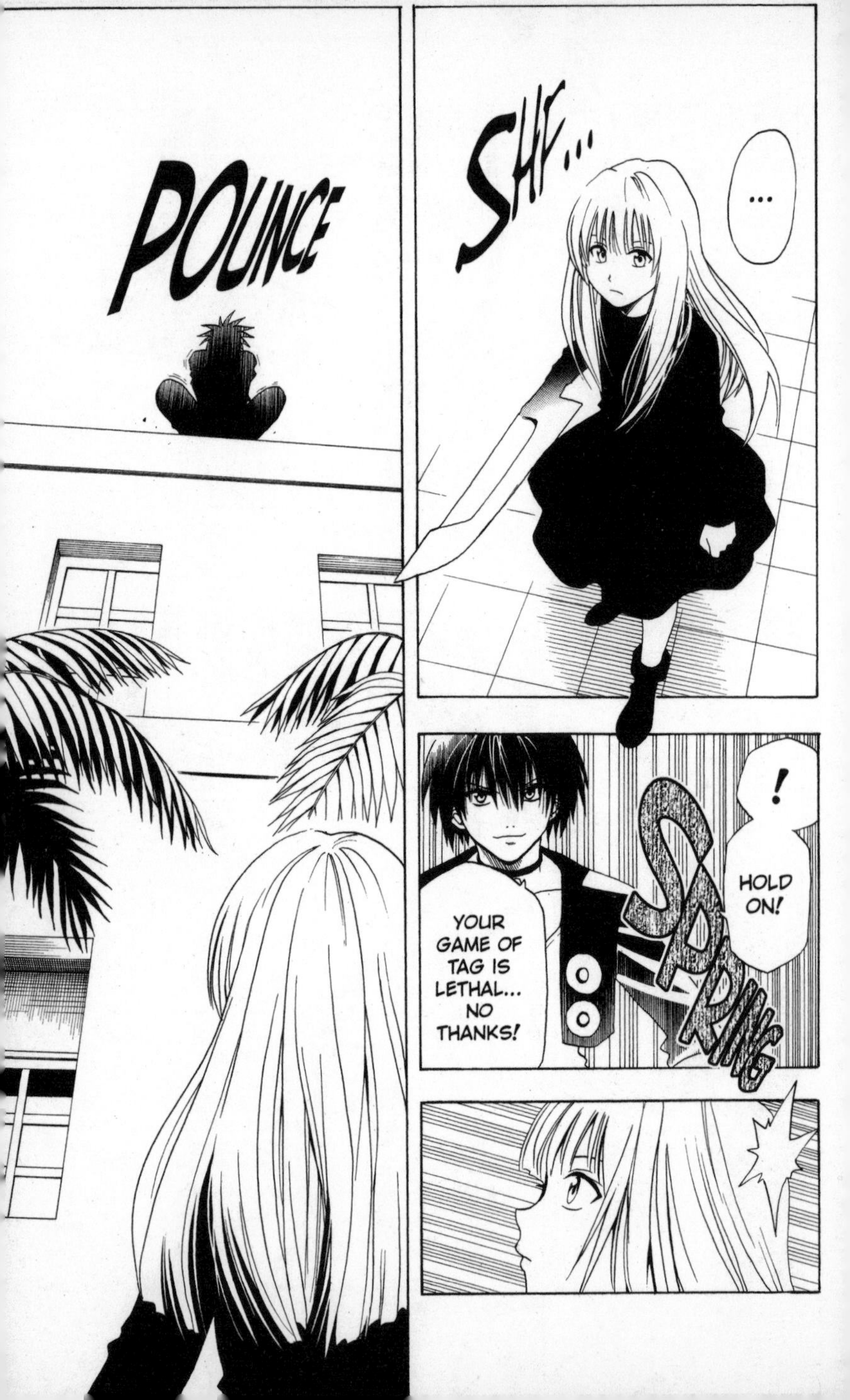
...
SHF...
!
HOLD ON!
SPRING
YOUR GAME OF TAG IS LETHAL... NO THANKS!
POUNCE

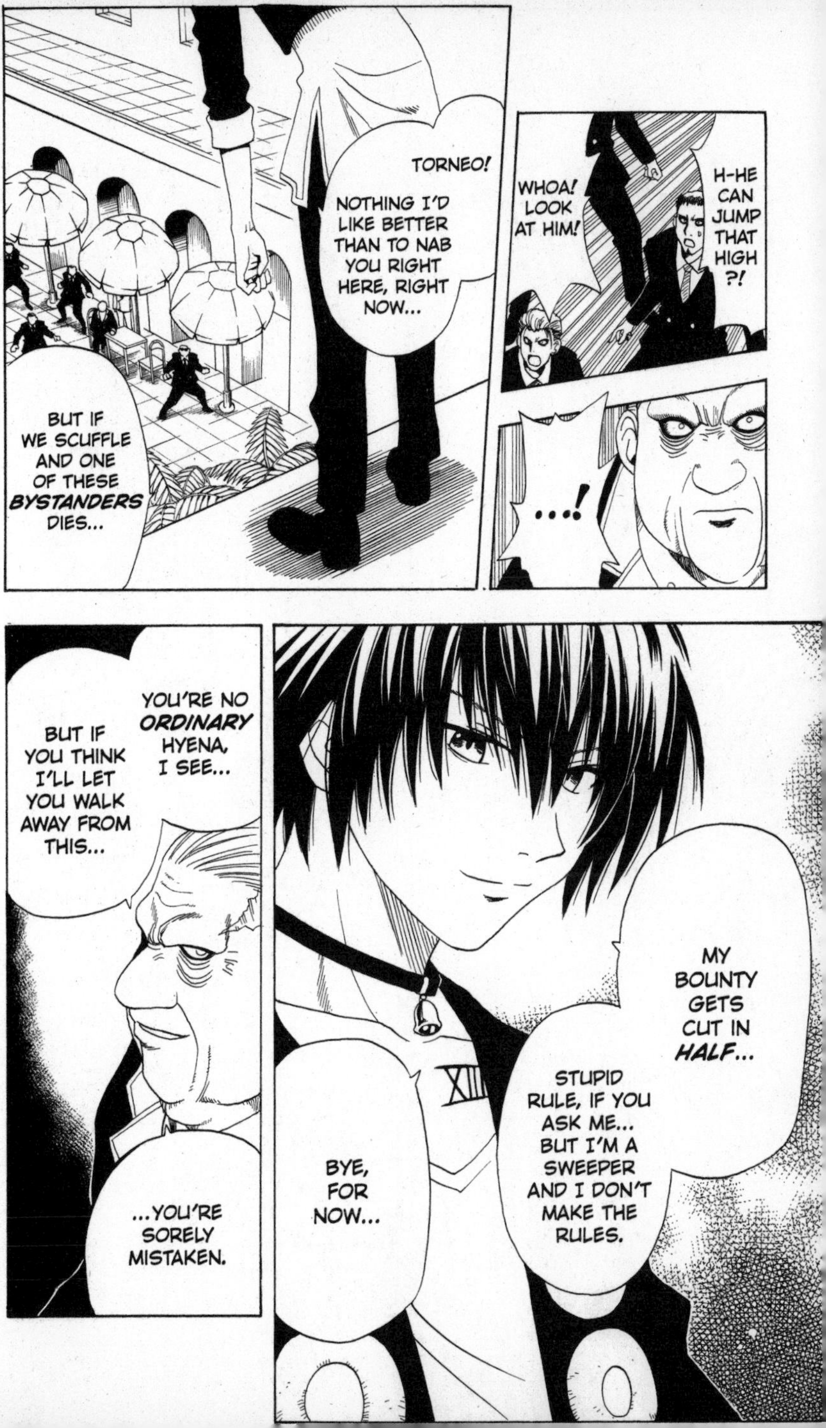
H-HE CAN JUMP THAT HIGH?!
WHOA! LOOK AT HIM!
...!
TORNEO!
NOTHING I'D LIKE BETTER THAN TO NAB YOU RIGHT HERE, RIGHT NOW...
BUT IF WE SCUFFLE AND ONE OF THESE BYSTANDERS DIES...
MY BOUNTY GETS CUT IN HALF...
STUPID RULE, IF YOU ASK ME... BUT I'M A SWEEPER AND I DON'T MAKE THE RULES.
BYE, FOR NOW...
YOU'RE NO ORDINARY HYENA, I SEE...
BUT IF YOU THINK I'LL LET YOU WALK AWAY FROM THIS...
...YOU'RE SORELY MISTAKEN.

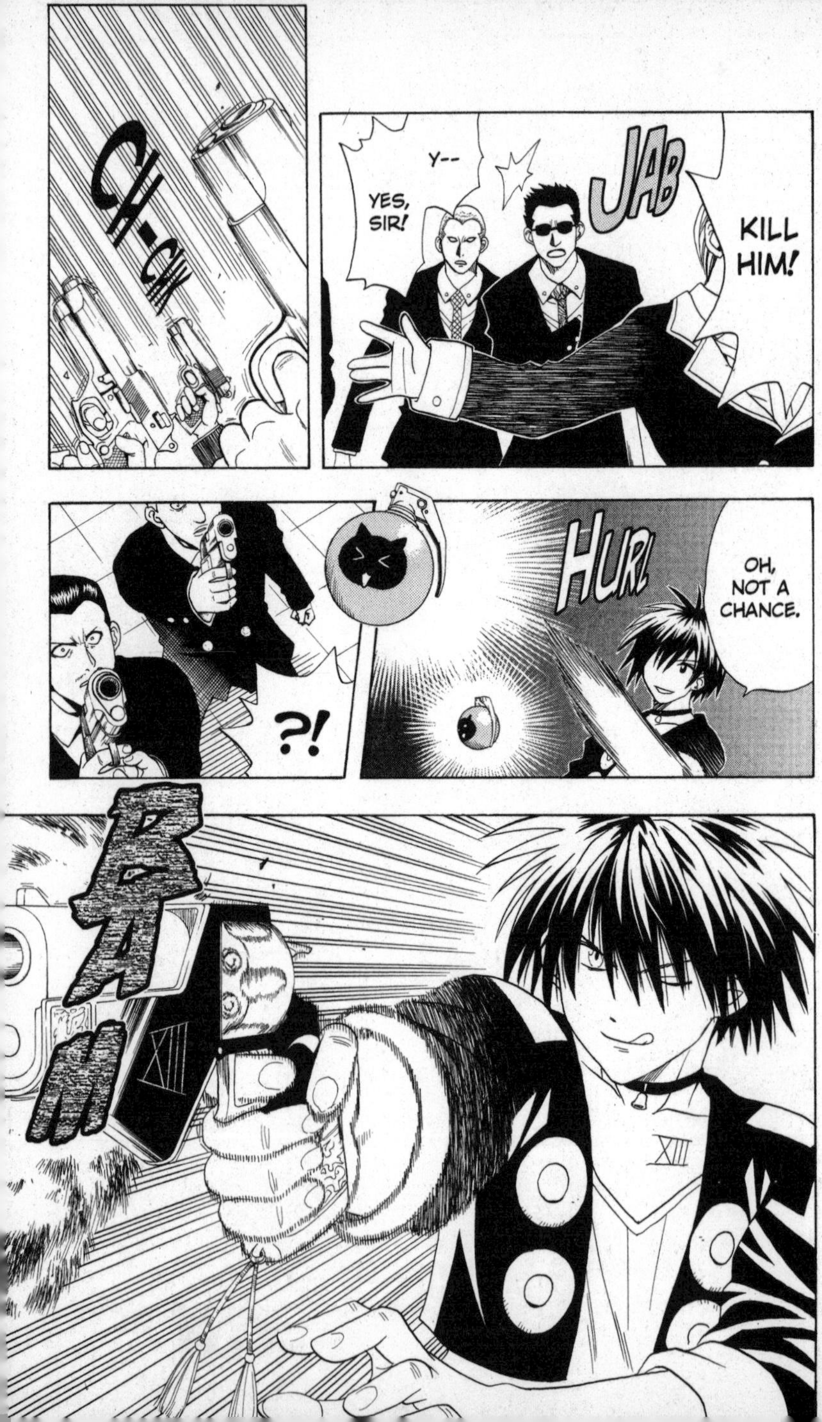
KILL HIM!
JAB
Y--
YES, SIR!
CH-CHK
OH, NOT A CHANCE.
HURL
?!
BAM

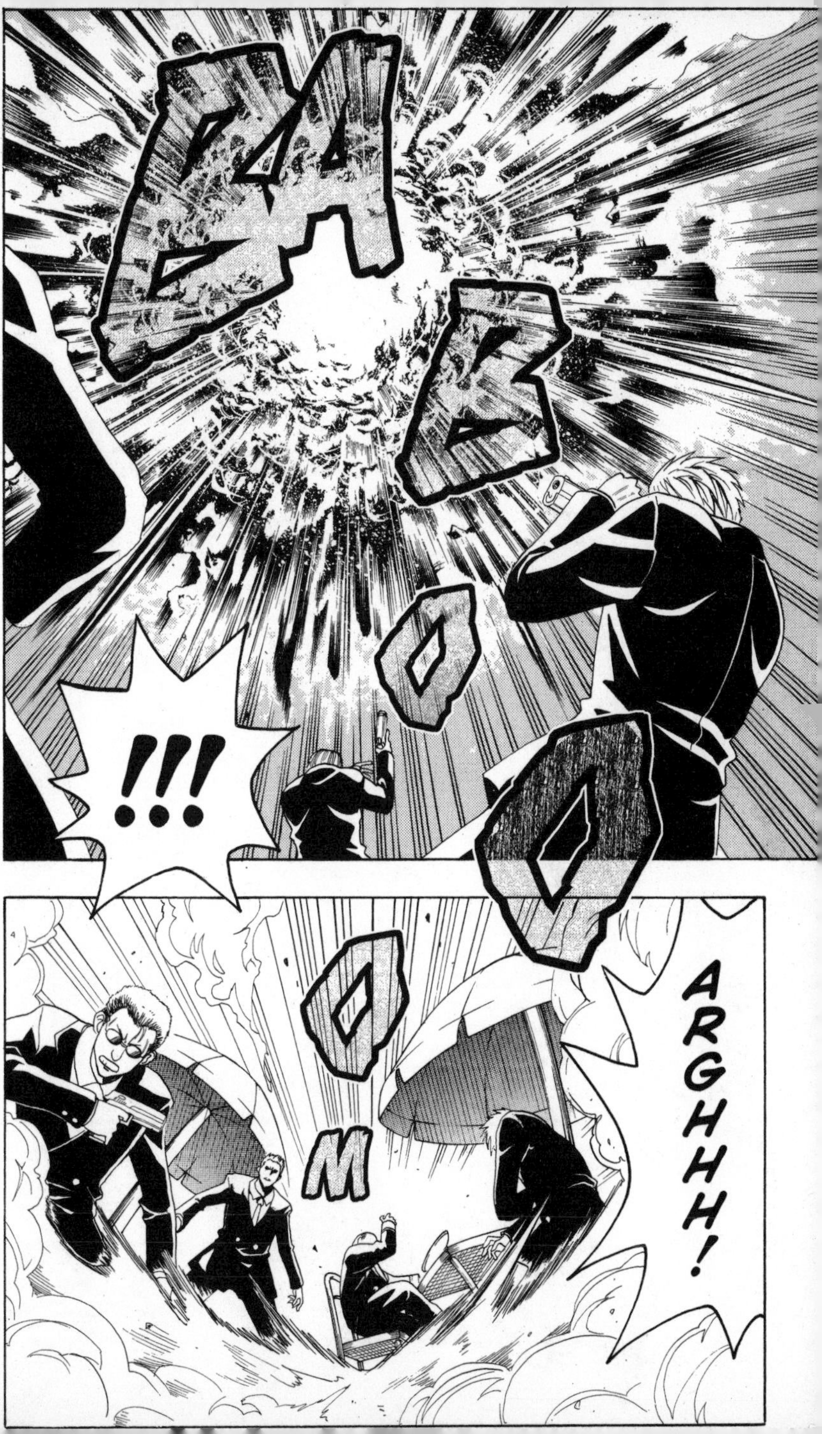
KA-BOOOOM
!!!
ARGHHH!

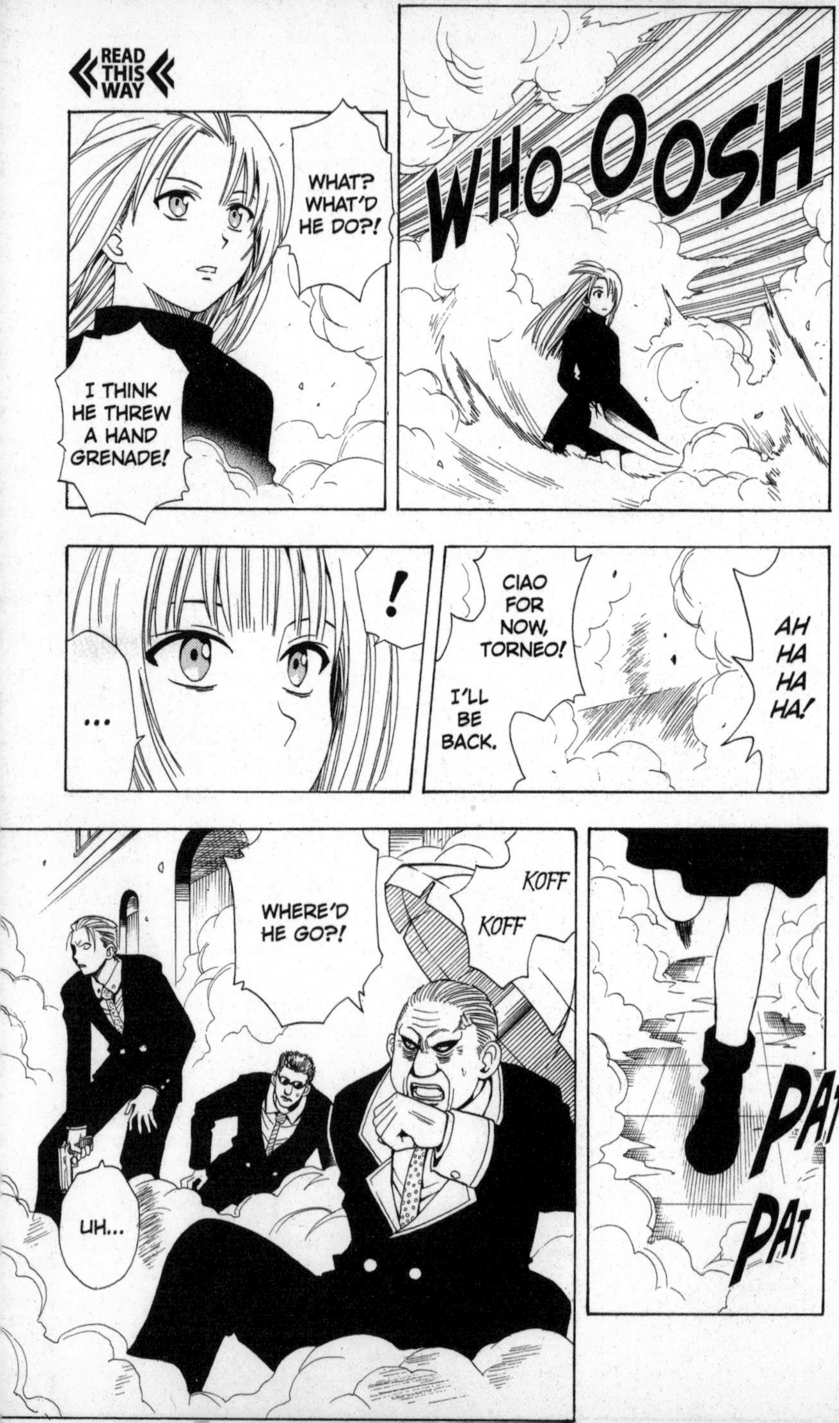
READ THIS WAY
WHOOOSH
WHAT? WHAT'D HE DO?!
I THINK HE THREW A HAND GRENADE!
AH HA HA HA!
CIAO FOR NOW, TORNEO!
I'LL BE BACK.
!
...
PAT
PAT
KOFF
KOFF
WHERE'D HE GO?!
UH...

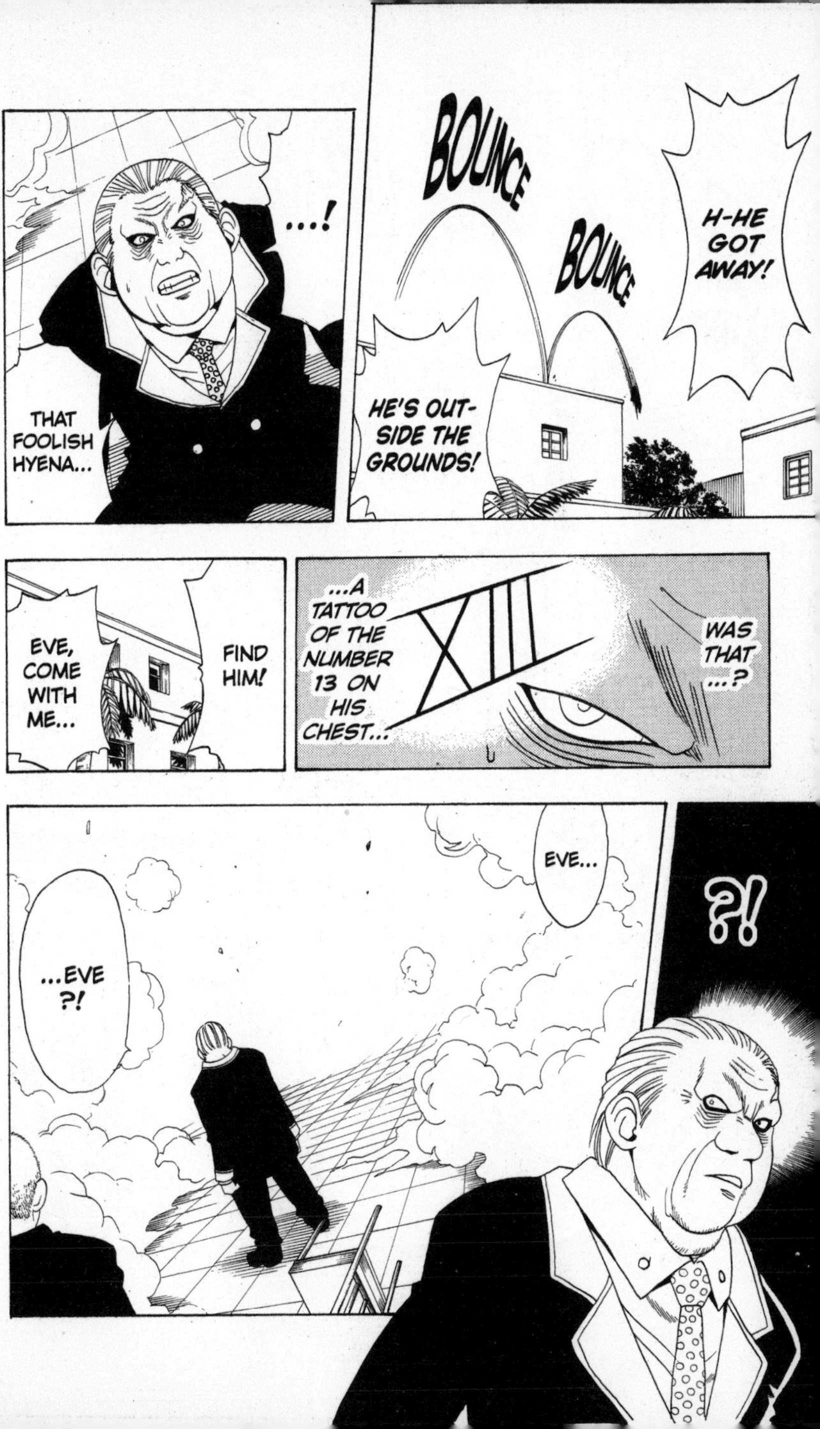
H-HE GOT AWAY!
BOUNCE
BOUNCE
HE'S OUT-SIDE THE GROUNDS!
...!
THAT FOOLISH HYENA...
WAS THAT ...?
...A TATTOO OF THE NUMBER 13 ON HIS CHEST...
FIND HIM!
EVE, COME WITH ME...
?!
EVE...
...EVE ?!

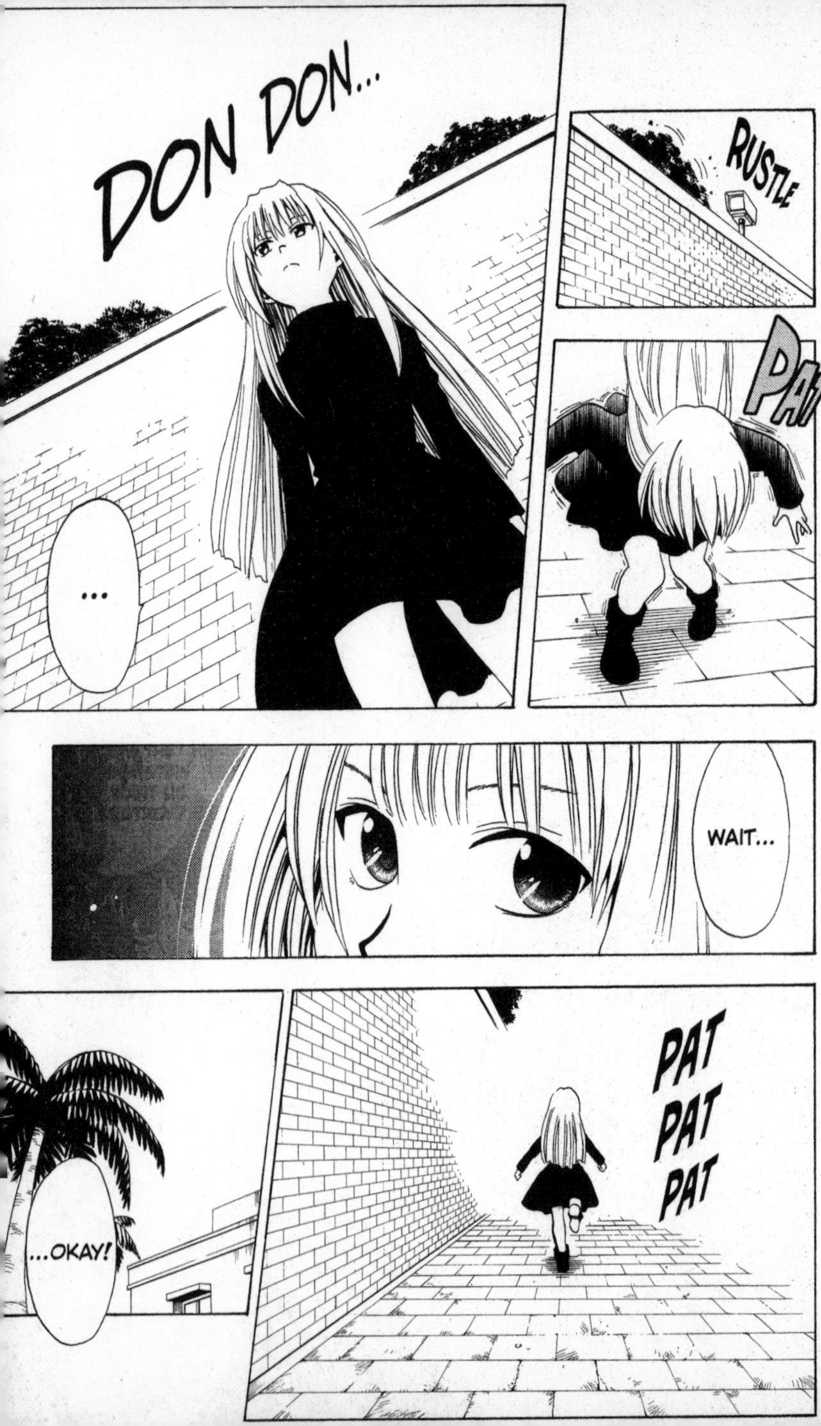
RUSTLE
PAT
DON DON...
...
WAIT...
PAT PAT PAT
...OKAY!

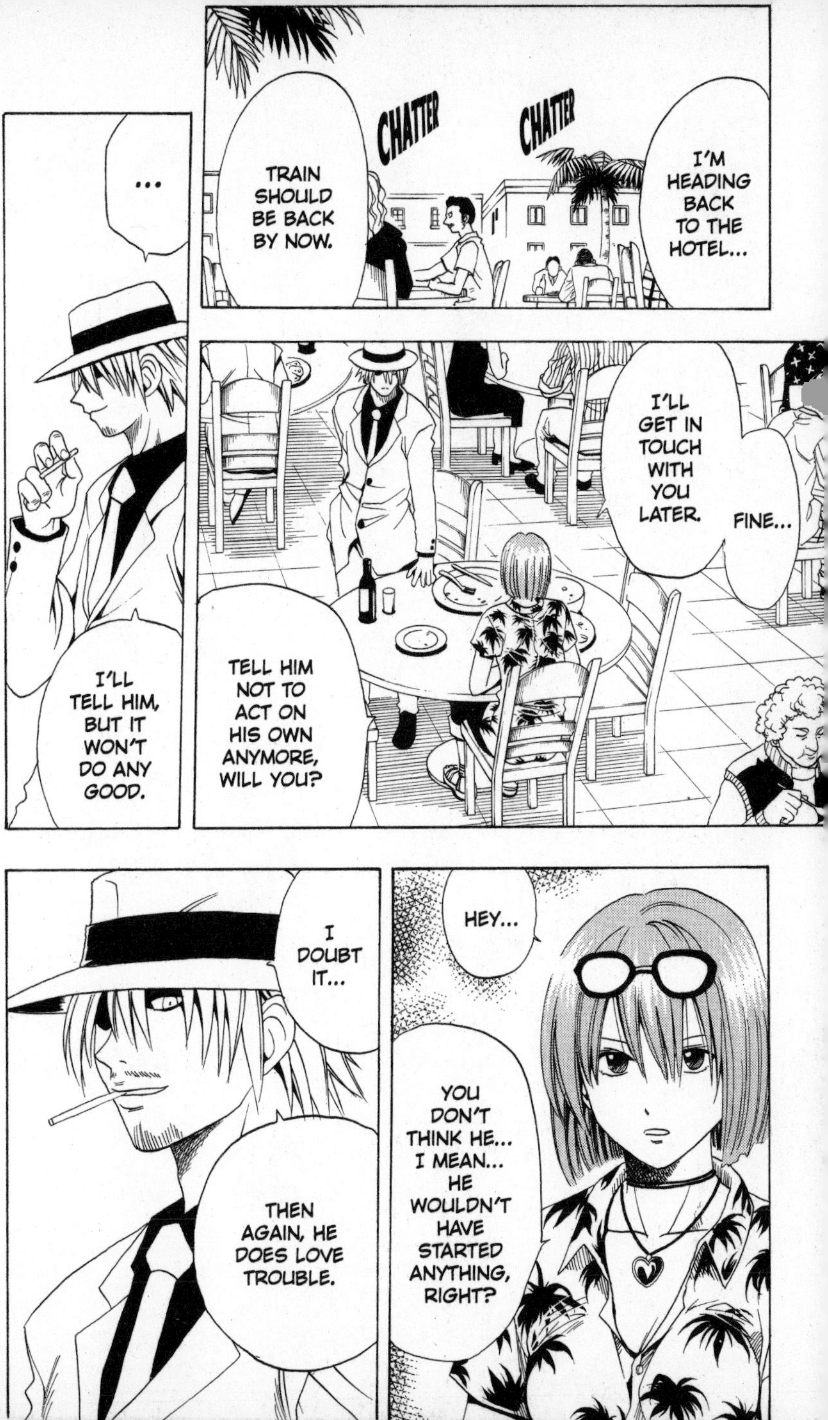
I'M HEADING BACK TO THE HOTEL...
CHATTER
CHATTER
TRAIN SHOULD BE BACK BY NOW.
I'LL GET IN TOUCH WITH YOU LATER.
FINE...
TELL HIM NOT TO ACT ON HIS OWN ANYMORE, WILL YOU?
...
I'LL TELL HIM, BUT IT WON'T DO ANY GOOD.
HEY...
YOU DON'T THINK HE... I MEAN... HE WOULDN'T HAVE STARTED ANYTHING, RIGHT?
I DOUBT IT...
THEN AGAIN, HE DOES LOVE TROUBLE.

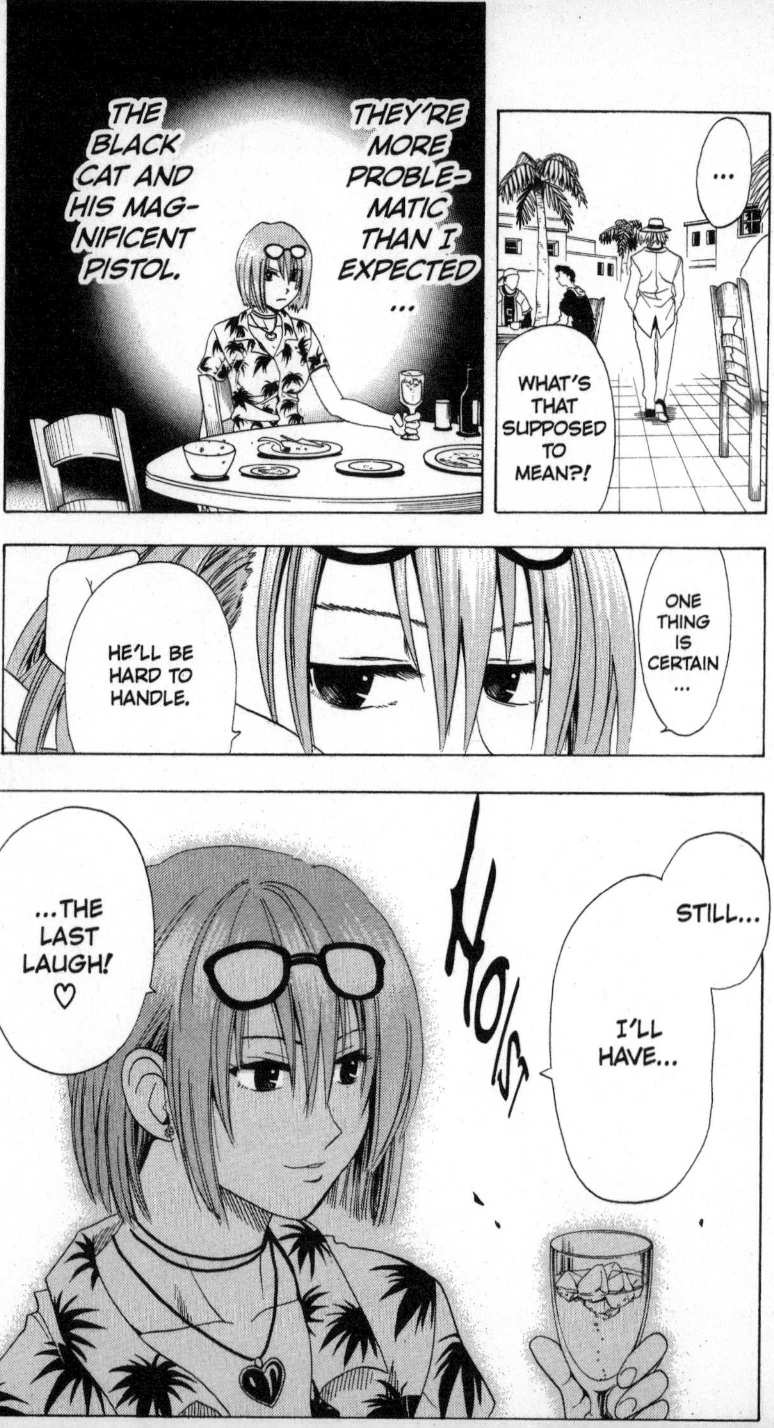
...
WHAT'S THAT SUPPOSED TO MEAN?!
THEY'RE MORE PROBLE-MATIC THAN I EXPECTED...
THE BLACK CAT AND HIS MAG-NIFICENT PISTOL.
ONE THING IS CERTAIN...
HE'LL BE HARD TO HANDLE.
STILL...
I'LL HAVE...
HOIST
...THE LAST LAUGH! ♡

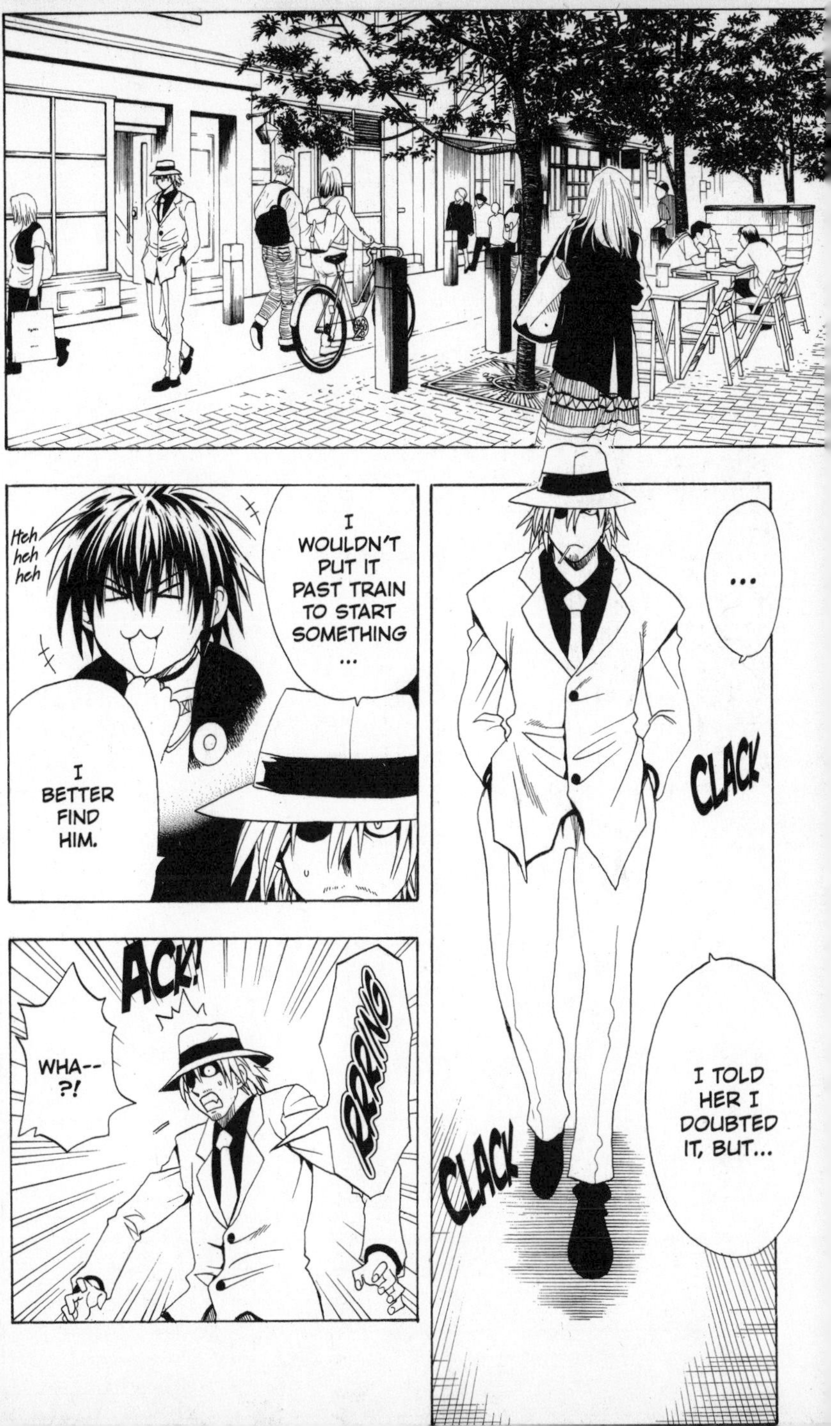
...
CLACK
I TOLD HER I DOUBTED IT, BUT...
CLACK
I WOULDN'T PUT IT PAST TRAIN TO START SOMETHING...
Heh heh heh
I BETTER FIND HIM.
BRRING
ACK!
WHA--?!

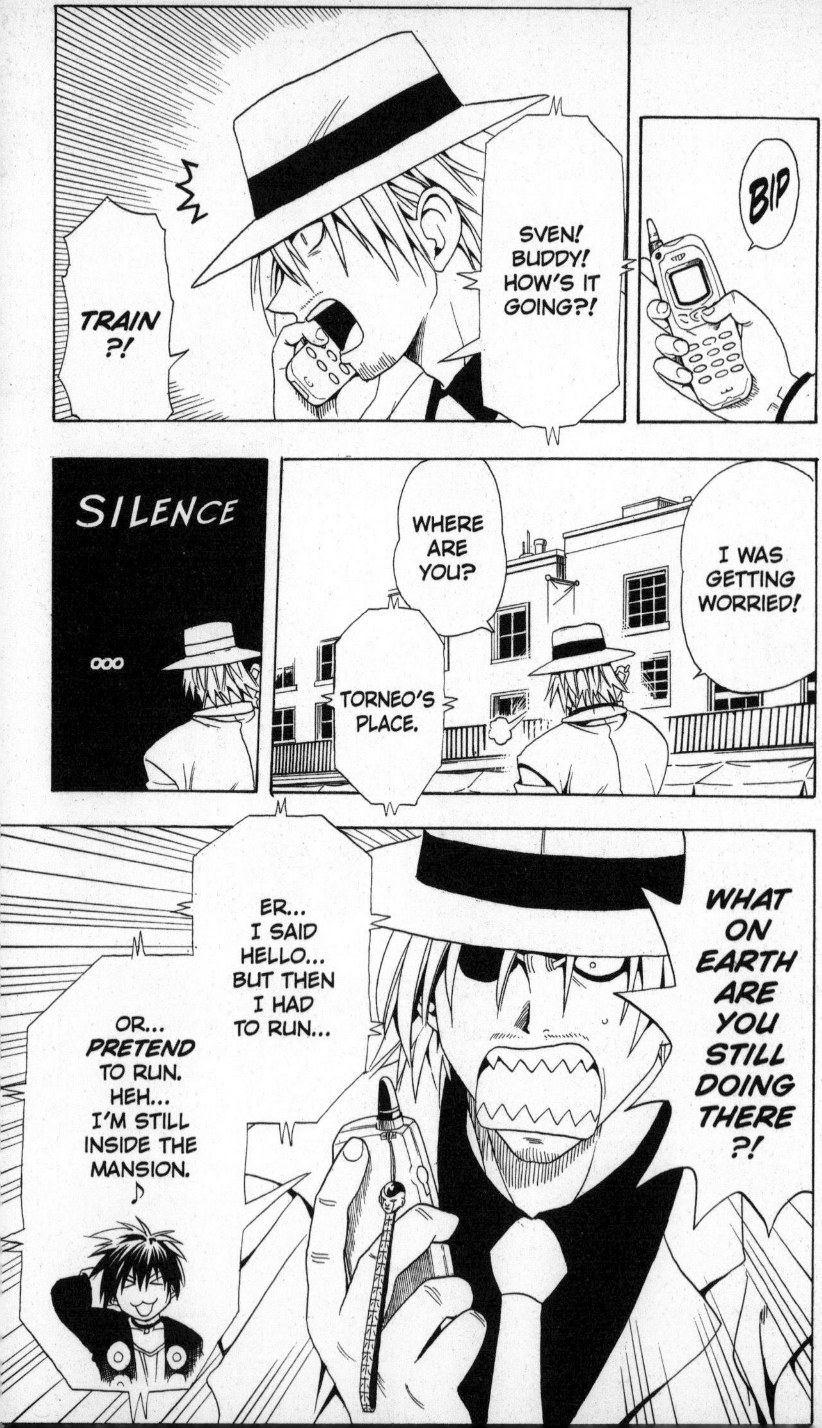
BIP
SVEN! BUDDY! HOW'S IT GOING?!
TRAIN ?!
I WAS GETTING WORRIED!
WHERE ARE YOU?
TORNEO'S PLACE.
SILENCE
ooo
WHAT ON EARTH ARE YOU STILL DOING THERE?!
ER... I SAID HELLO... BUT THEN I HAD TO RUN...
OR... PRETEND TO RUN. HEH... I'M STILL INSIDE THE MANSION. ♪

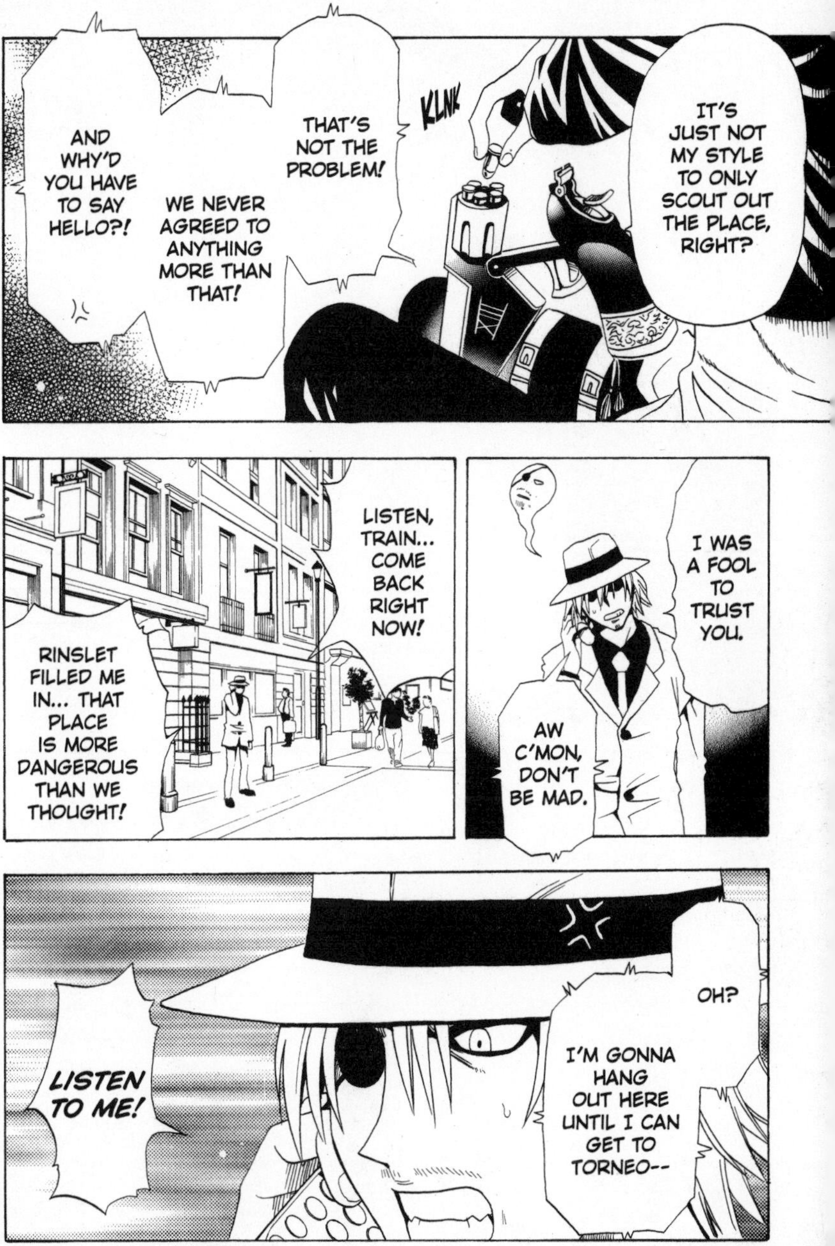
IT'S JUST NOT MY STYLE TO ONLY SCOUT OUT THE PLACE, RIGHT?
KLNK
THAT'S NOT THE PROBLEM!
WE NEVER AGREED TO ANYTHING MORE THAN THAT!
AND WHY'D YOU HAVE TO SAY HELLO?!
I WAS A FOOL TO TRUST YOU.
AW C'MON, DON'T BE MAD.
LISTEN, TRAIN... COME BACK RIGHT NOW!
RINSLET FILLED ME IN... THAT PLACE IS MORE DANGEROUS THAN WE THOUGHT!
OH?
I'M GONNA HANG OUT HERE UNTIL I CAN GET TO TORNEO--
LISTEN TO ME!

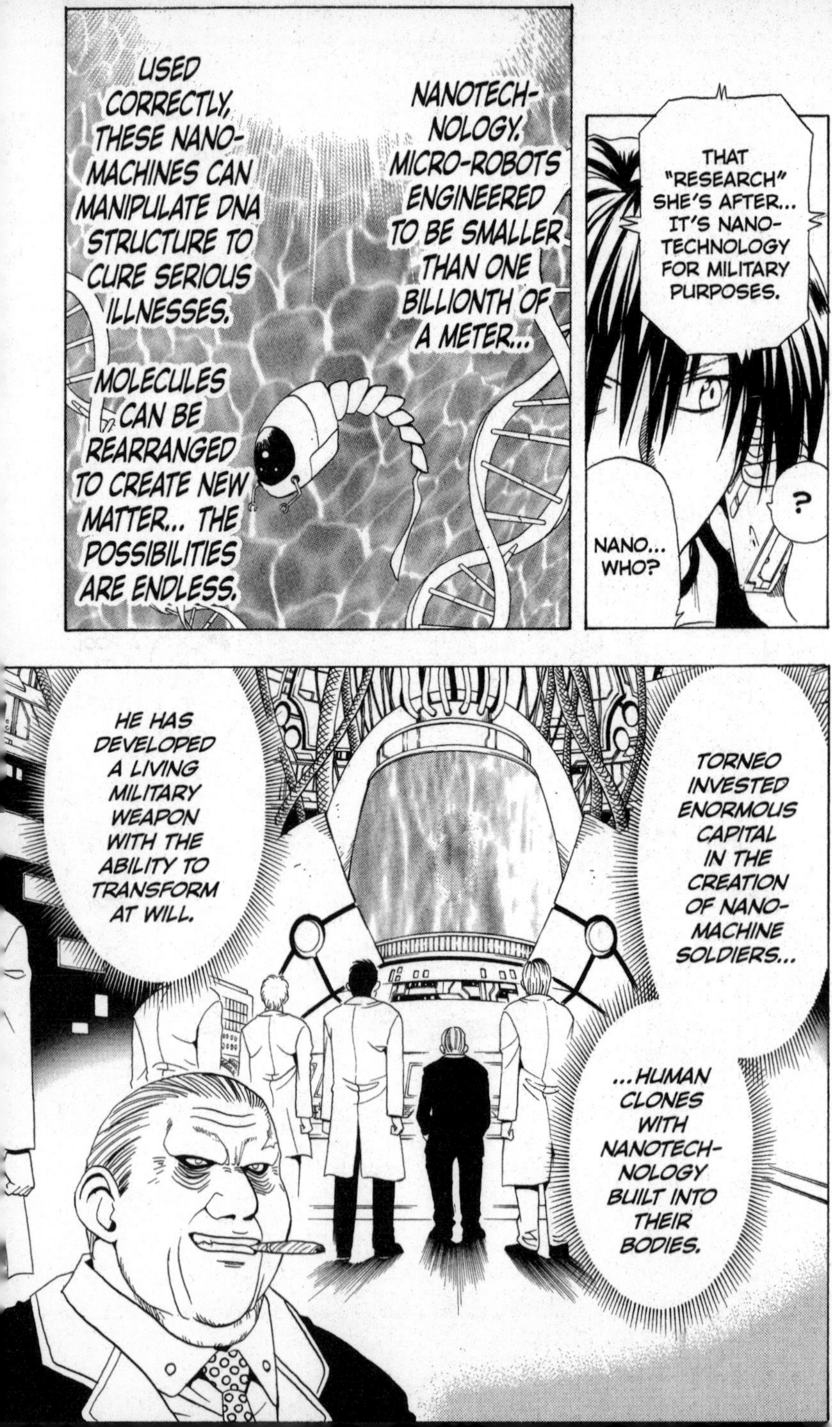
THAT "RESEARCH" SHE'S AFTER... IT'S NANO-TECHNOLOGY FOR MILITARY PURPOSES.
NANO... WHO?
?
NANOTECH-NOLOGY. MICRO-ROBOTS ENGINEERED TO BE SMALLER THAN ONE BILLIONTH OF A METER...
USED CORRECTLY, THESE NANO-MACHINES CAN MANIPULATE DNA STRUCTURE TO CURE SERIOUS ILLNESSES.
MOLECULES CAN BE REARRANGED TO CREATE NEW MATTER... THE POSSIBILITIES ARE ENDLESS.
TORNEO INVESTED ENORMOUS CAPITAL IN THE CREATION OF NANO-MACHINE SOLDIERS...
...HUMAN CLONES WITH NANOTECH-NOLOGY BUILT INTO THEIR BODIES.
HE HAS DEVELOPED A LIVING MILITARY WEAPON WITH THE ABILITY TO TRANSFORM AT WILL.

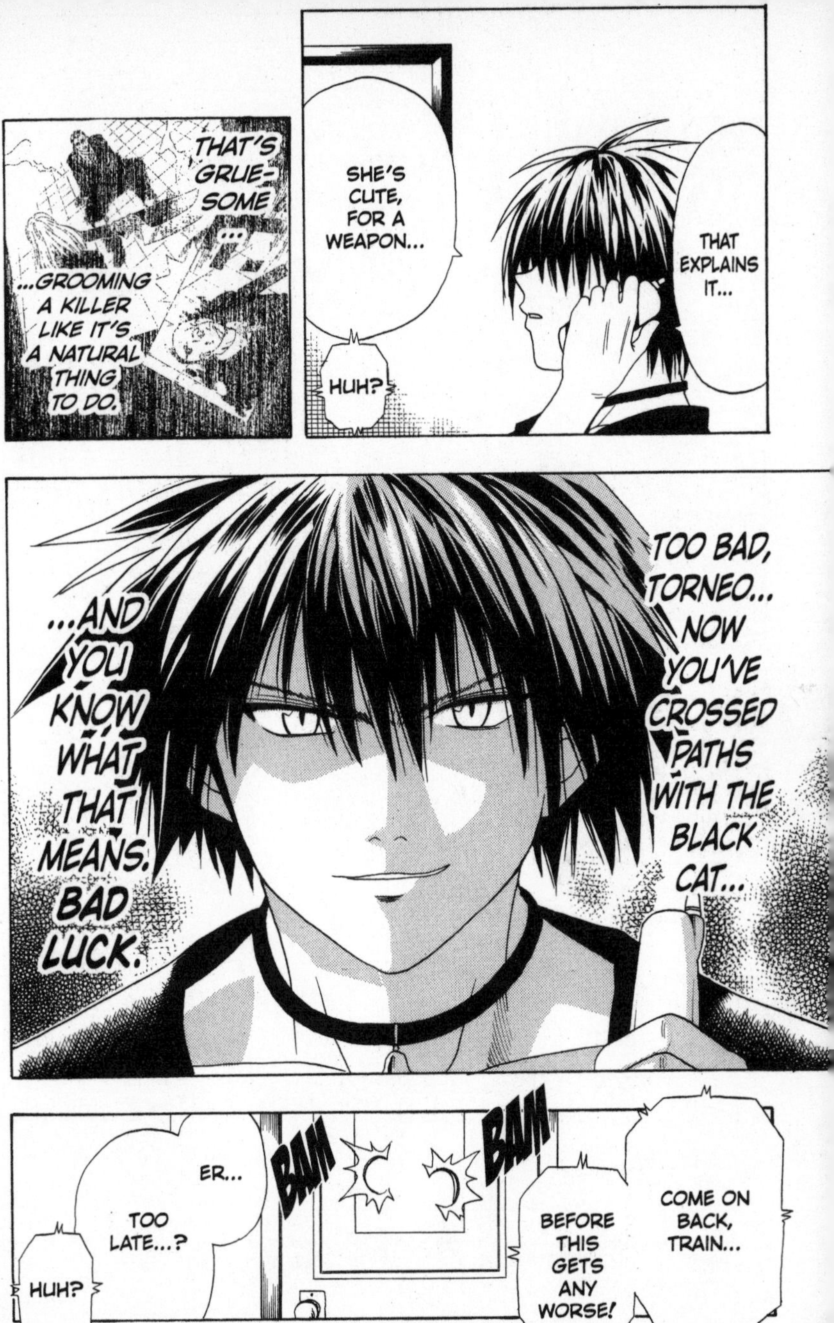
THAT EXPLAINS IT...
SHE'S CUTE, FOR A WEAPON...
HUH?
THAT'S GRUESOME...
...GROOMING A KILLER LIKE IT'S A NATURAL THING TO DO.
TOO BAD, TORNEO... NOW YOU'VE CROSSED PATHS WITH THE BLACK CAT...
...AND YOU KNOW WHAT THAT MEANS. BAD LUCK.
COME ON BACK, TRAIN...
BEFORE THIS GETS ANY WORSE!
BAM
BAM
ER... TOO LATE...?
HUH?

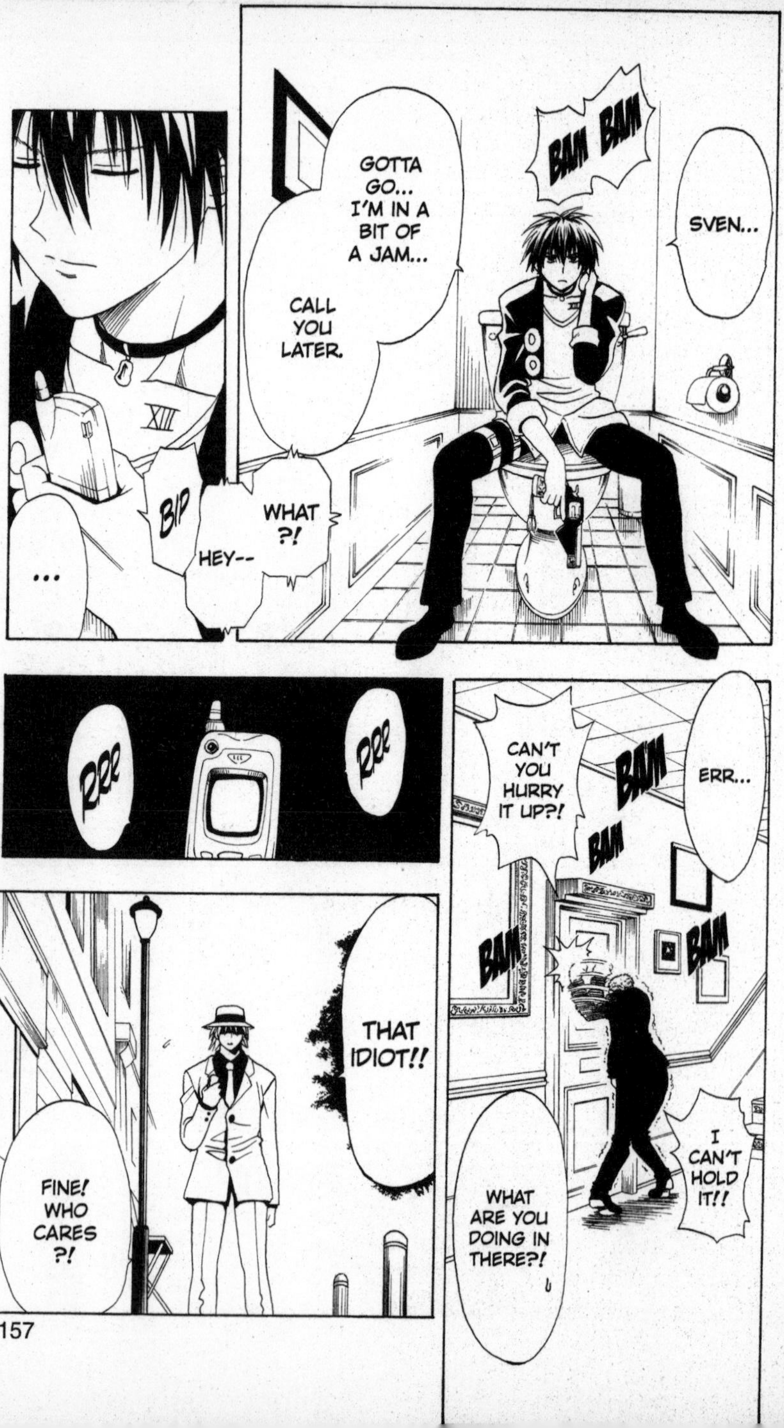
SVEN...
BAM BAM
GOTTA GO... I'M IN A BIT OF A JAM...
CALL YOU LATER.
WHAT?!
BIP
HEY--
...
ERR...
BAM BAM
CAN'T YOU HURRY IT UP?!
BAM BAM
I CAN'T HOLD IT!!
WHAT ARE YOU DOING IN THERE?!
RRR
RRR
THAT IDIOT!!
FINE! WHO CARES?!

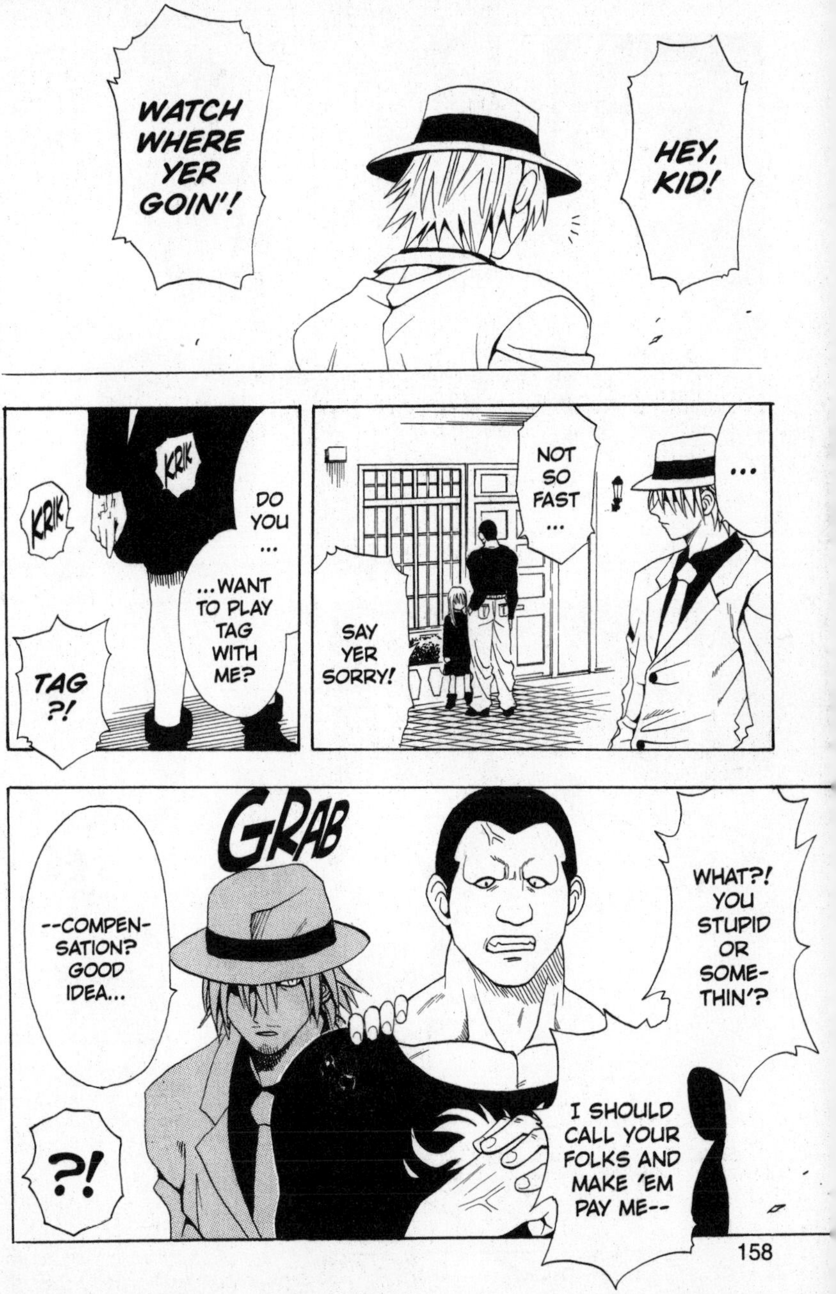

HEY, KID!
WATCH WHERE YER GOIN'!
...
NOT SO FAST ...
SAY YER SORRY!
DO YOU ...
...WANT TO PLAY TAG WITH ME?
KRIK
KRIK
TAG ?!
WHAT?! YOU STUPID OR SOME-THIN'?
I SHOULD CALL YOUR FOLKS AND MAKE 'EM PAY ME--
GRAB
--COMPEN-SATION? GOOD IDEA...
?!

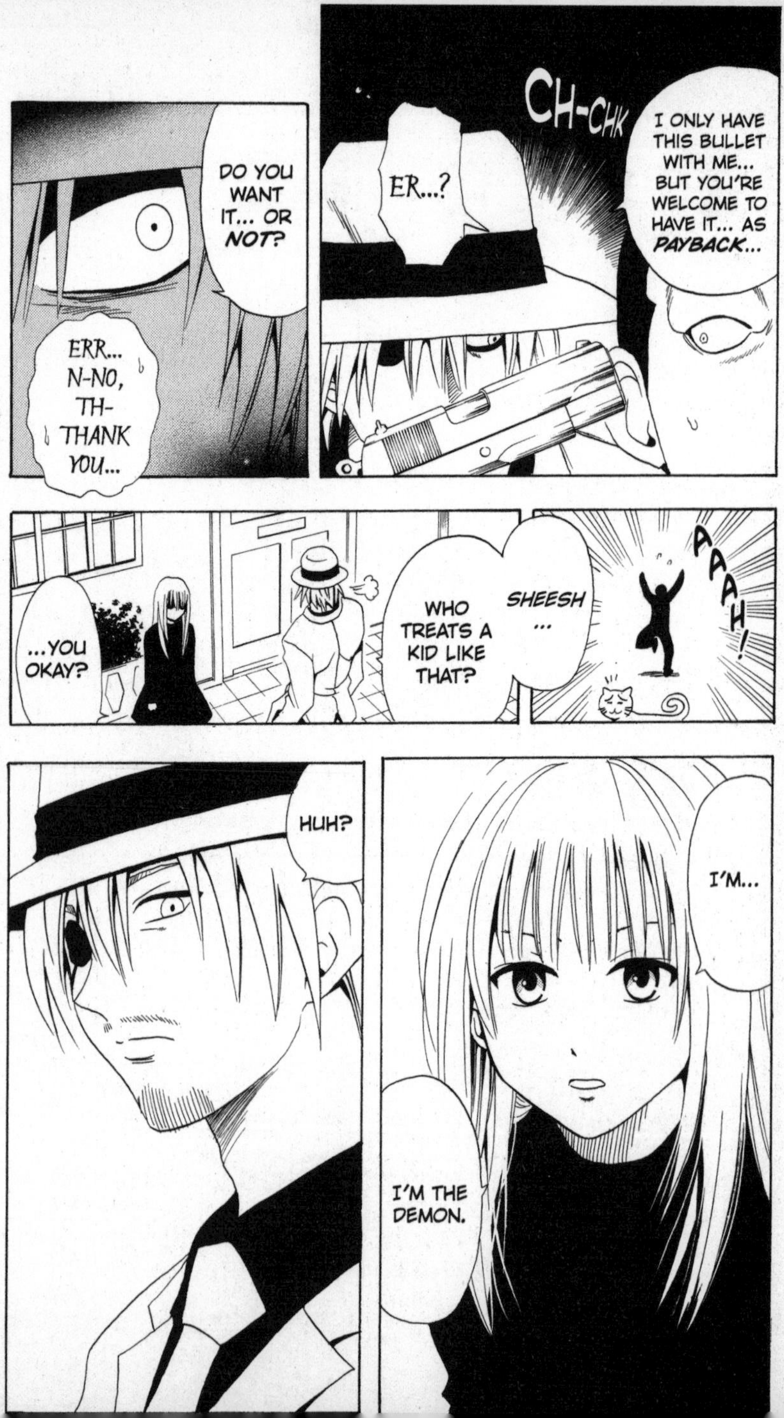
CH-CHK
I ONLY HAVE THIS BULLET WITH ME... BUT YOU'RE WELCOME TO HAVE IT... AS *PAYBACK*...
ER...?
DO YOU WANT IT... OR *NOT*?
ERR... N-NO, TH-THANK YOU...
AAAH!
SHEESH...
WHO TREATS A KID LIKE THAT?
...YOU OKAY?
I'M...
I'M THE DEMON.
HUH?

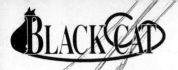

BLACK CAT

FACTOIDS

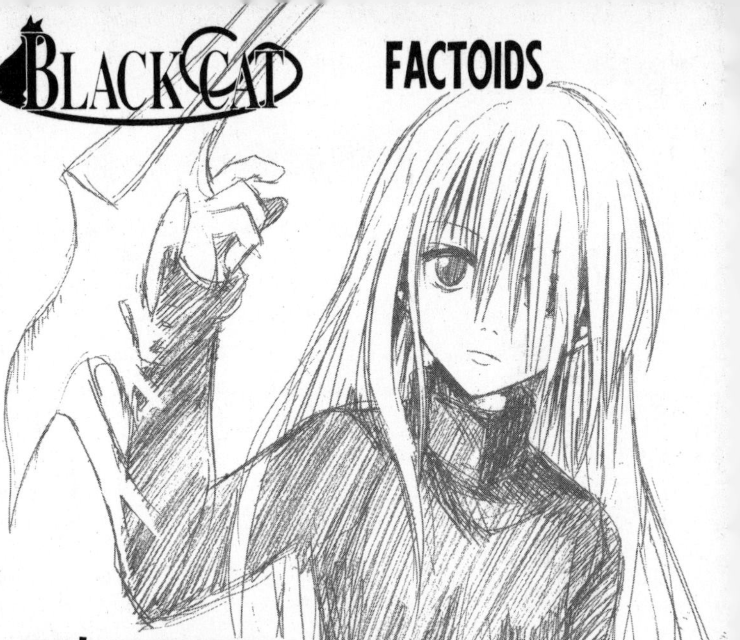

EVE'S POWERS

EVE'S BODY IS FILLED WITH COUNTLESS MICRO-MACHINES ("NANOMACHINES") THAT SHE CAN MANIPULATE VIA THOUGHT WAVES. USING THE NANOMACHINES TO REORGANIZE HER BODY ON AN ATOMIC LEVEL, SHE IS ABLE TO CHANGE HER SHAPE AND FORM AT WILL.

ULTIMATELY, EVE SHOULD BE ABLE TO MORPH ENTIRELY, BUT TO DO SO SHE'LL NEED A VERY STRONG MENTAL IMAGE OF THE END RESULT. UNTIL SHE MATURES ENOUGH FOR THAT LEVEL OF CONCENTRATION, SHE'S LIMITED TO WEAPONIZING HER ARM. (NOTE: A FULL-SCALE TRANSFORMATION WOULD BE AN ENORMOUS BURDEN ON HER PHYSICAL SELF.)

CHAPTER 7: LOST

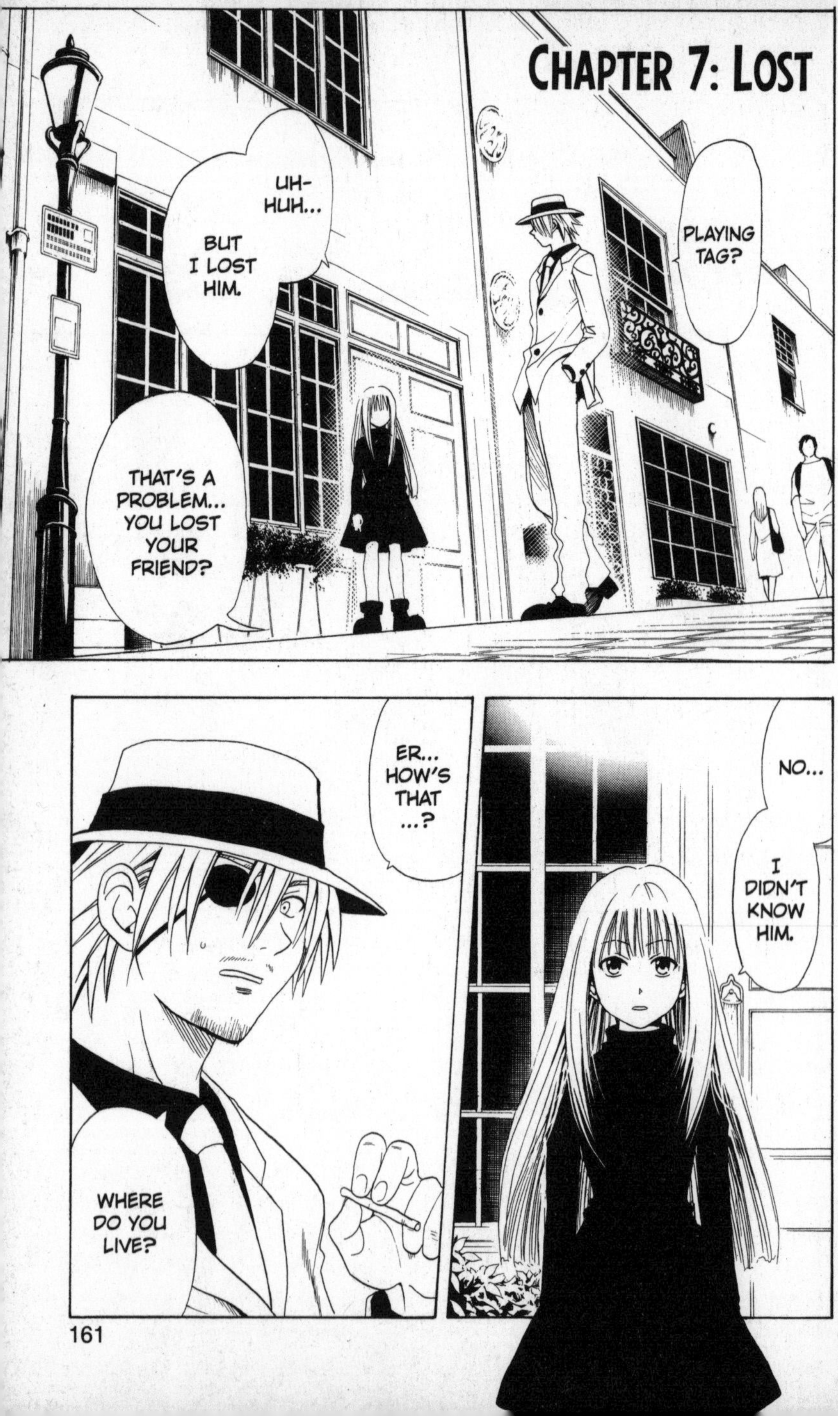
PLAYING TAG?
UH-HUH...
BUT I LOST HIM.
THAT'S A PROBLEM... YOU LOST YOUR FRIEND?
NO...
I DIDN'T KNOW HIM.
ER... HOW'S THAT ...?
WHERE DO YOU LIVE?

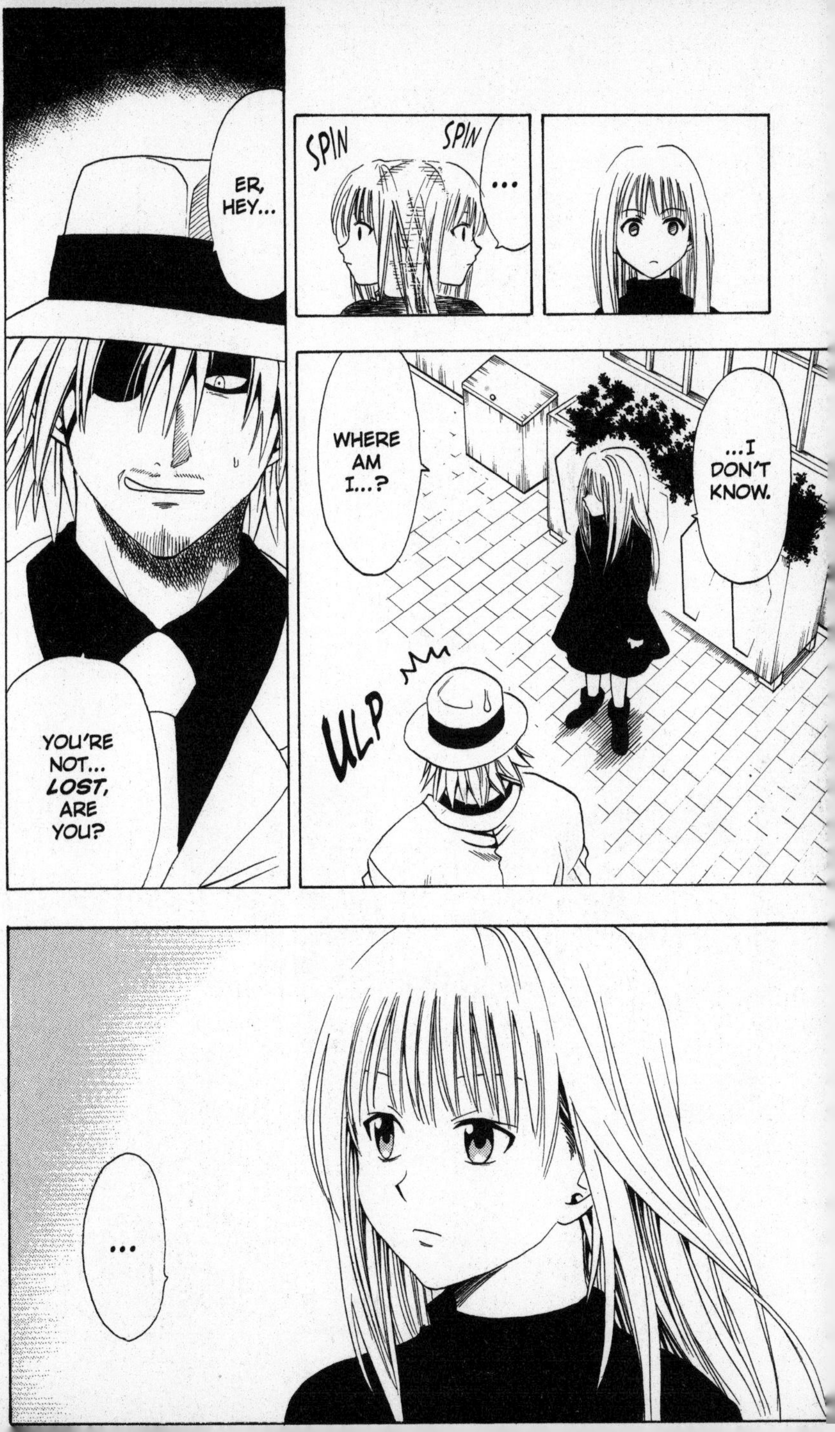
SPIN
SPIN
...
...I DON'T KNOW.
WHERE AM I...?
ULP
ER, HEY...
YOU'RE NOT... *LOST*, ARE YOU?
...

CHAPTER 7: LOST

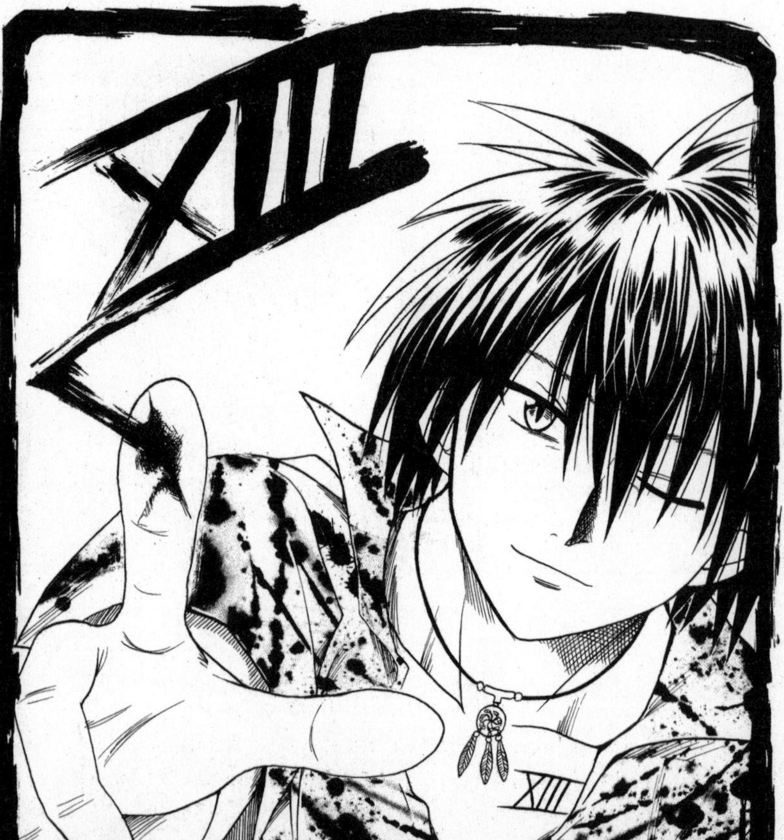

XIII
XIII

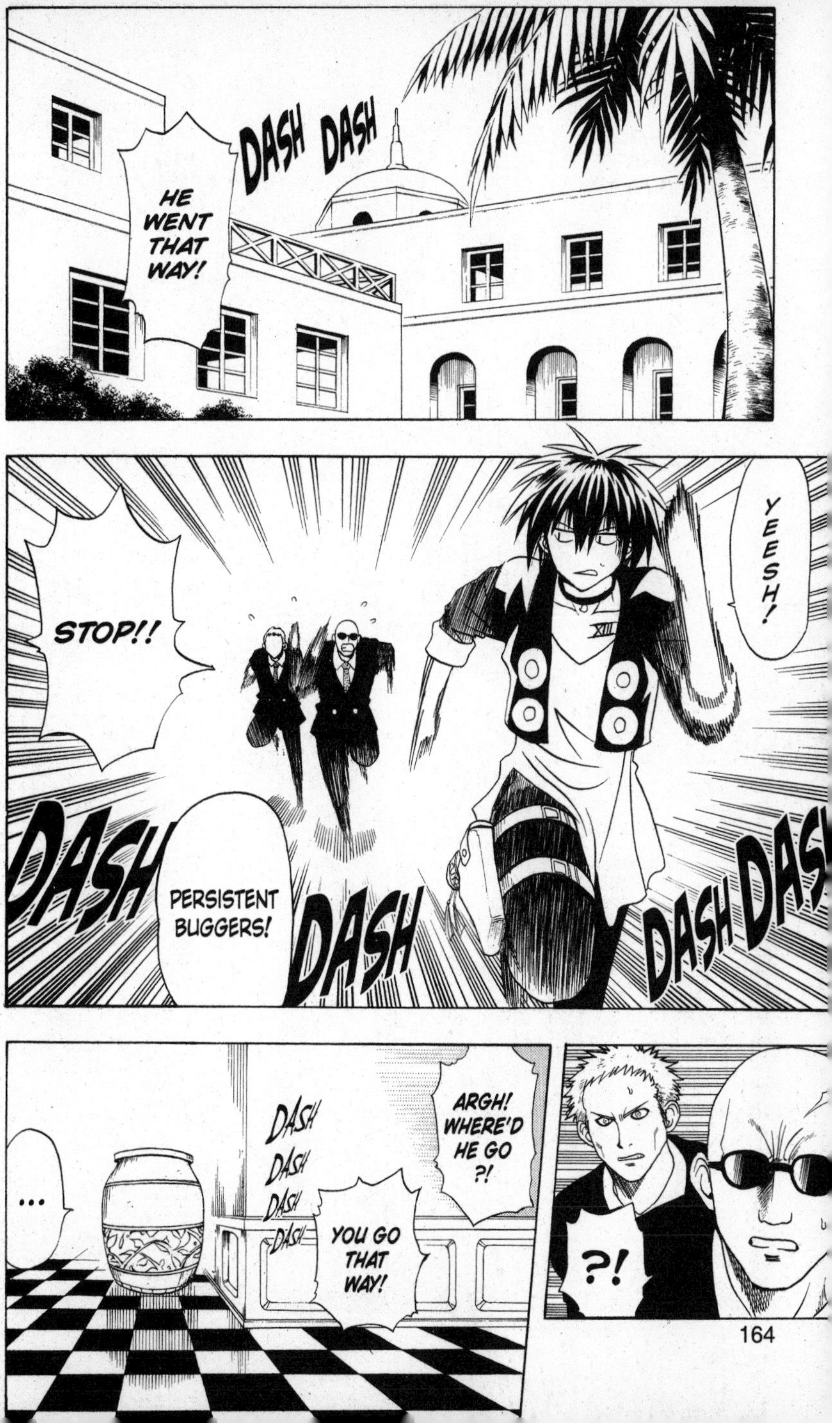
DASH DASH
HE WENT THAT WAY!
YEESH!
DASH DASH
STOP!!
PERSISTENT BUGGERS!
DASH
DASH
?!
ARGH! WHERE'D HE GO ?!
DASH DASH DASH DASH
YOU GO THAT WAY!
...

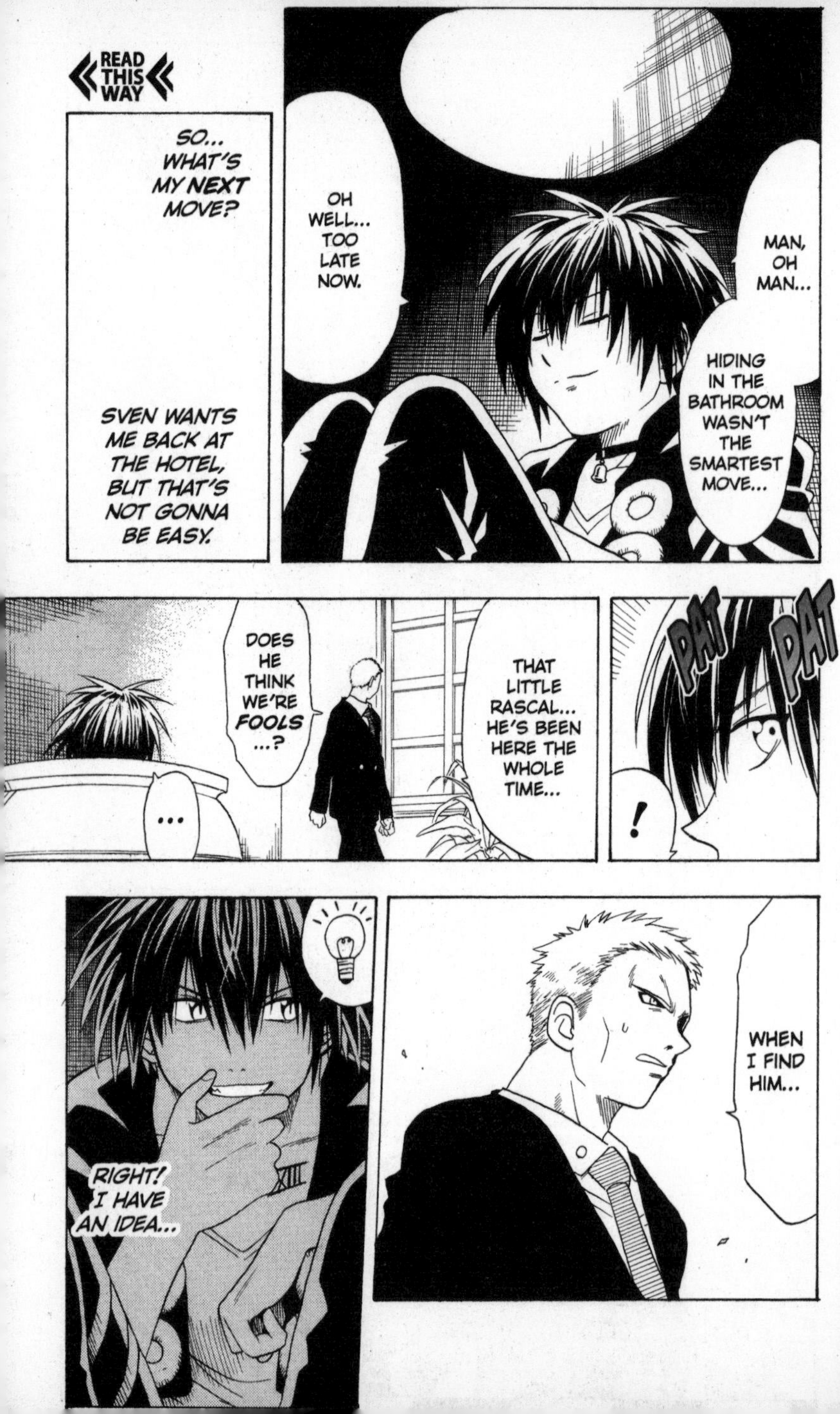
READ THIS WAY
MAN, OH MAN...
HIDING IN THE BATHROOM WASN'T THE SMARTEST MOVE...
OH WELL... TOO LATE NOW.
SO... WHAT'S MY NEXT MOVE?
SVEN WANTS ME BACK AT THE HOTEL, BUT THAT'S NOT GONNA BE EASY.
PAT PAT
!
THAT LITTLE RASCAL... HE'S BEEN HERE THE WHOLE TIME...
DOES HE THINK WE'RE FOOLS ...?
...
WHEN I FIND HIM...
RIGHT! I HAVE AN IDEA...

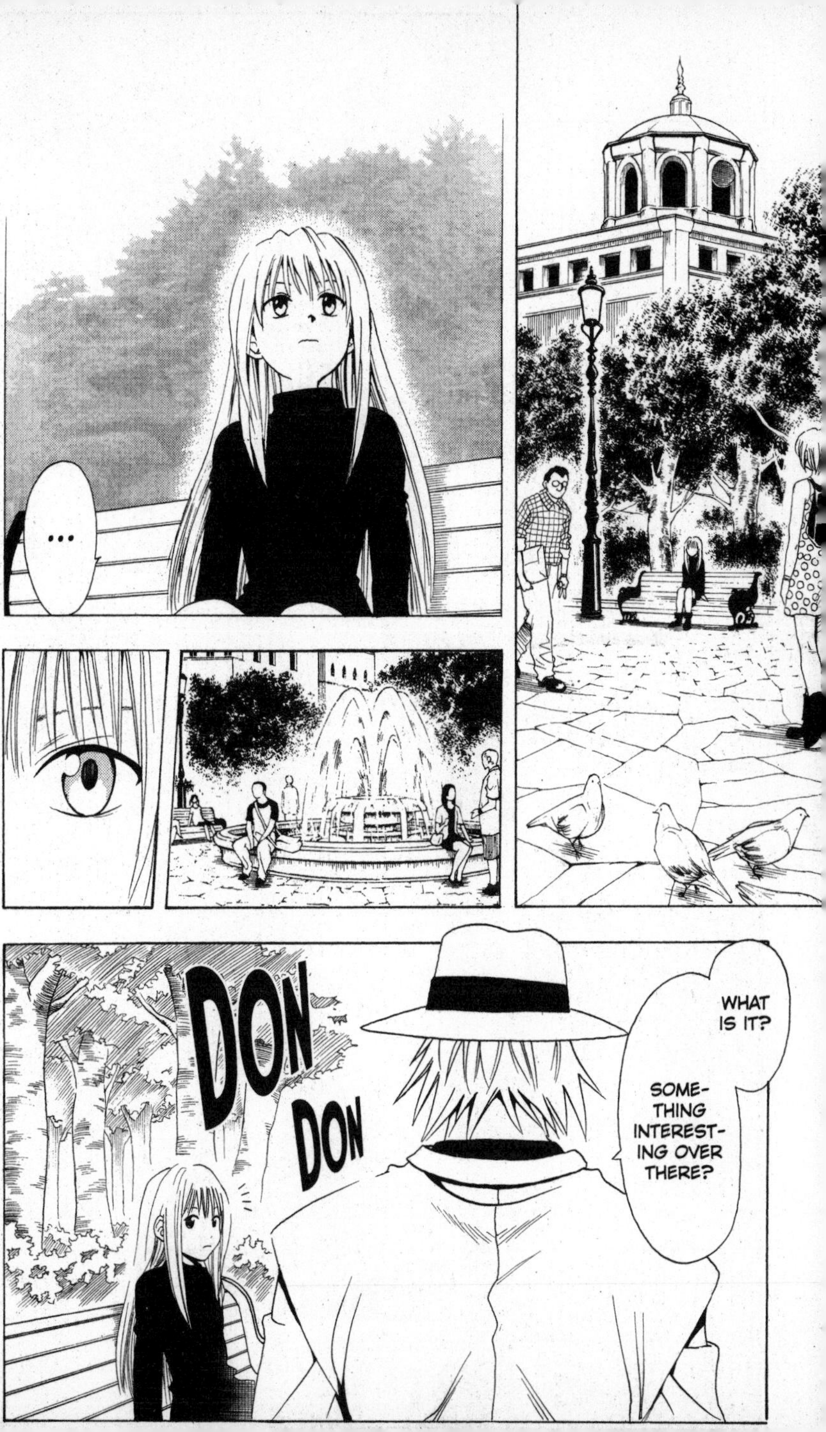
...
DON
DON
WHAT IS IT?
SOMETHING INTERESTING OVER THERE?

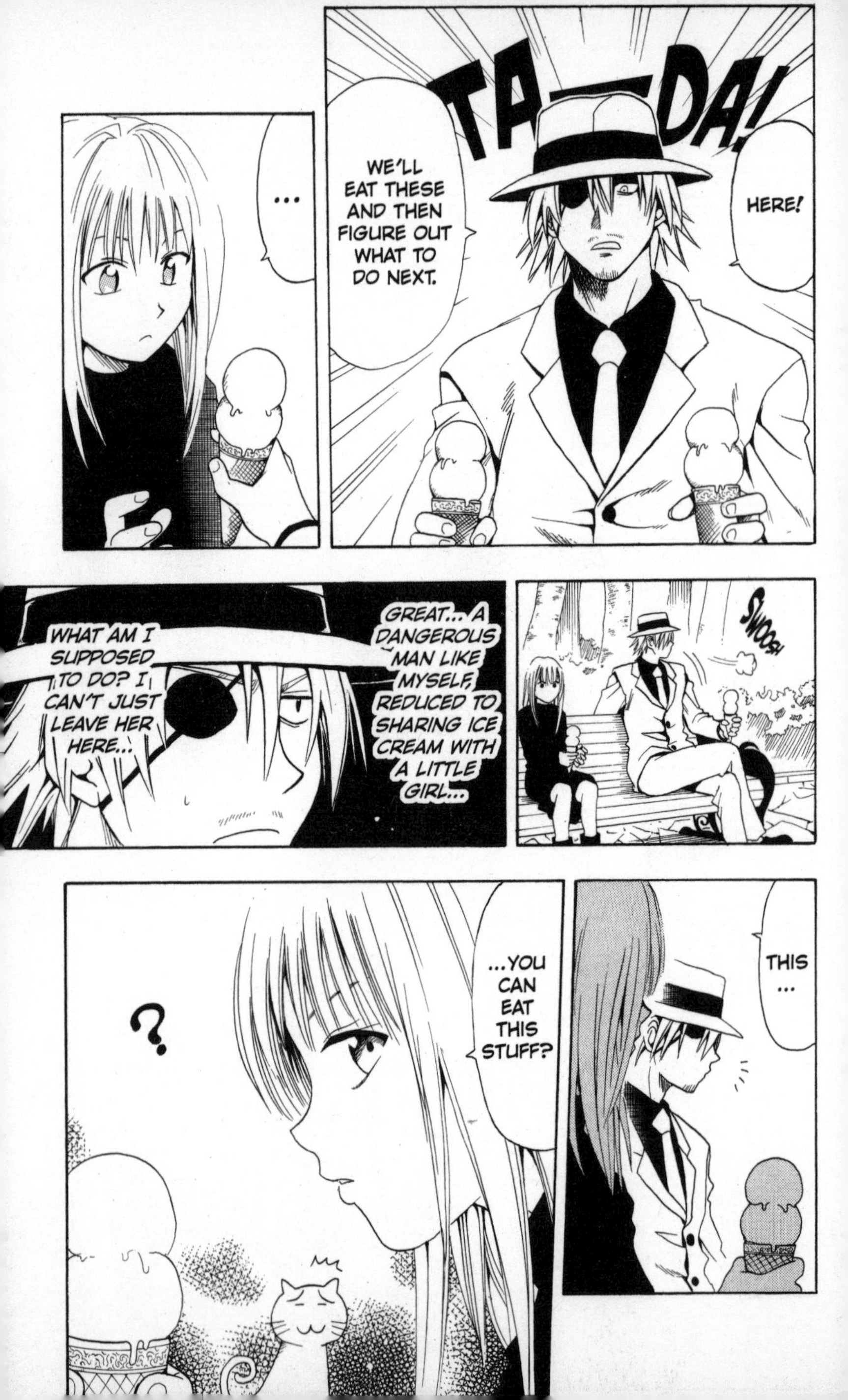
TA—DA!
HERE!
WE'LL EAT THESE AND THEN FIGURE OUT WHAT TO DO NEXT.
...
SWOOSH
GREAT... A DANGEROUS MAN LIKE MYSELF, REDUCED TO SHARING ICE CREAM WITH A LITTLE GIRL...
WHAT AM I SUPPOSED TO DO? I CAN'T JUST LEAVE HER HERE...
THIS...
...YOU CAN EAT THIS STUFF?
?

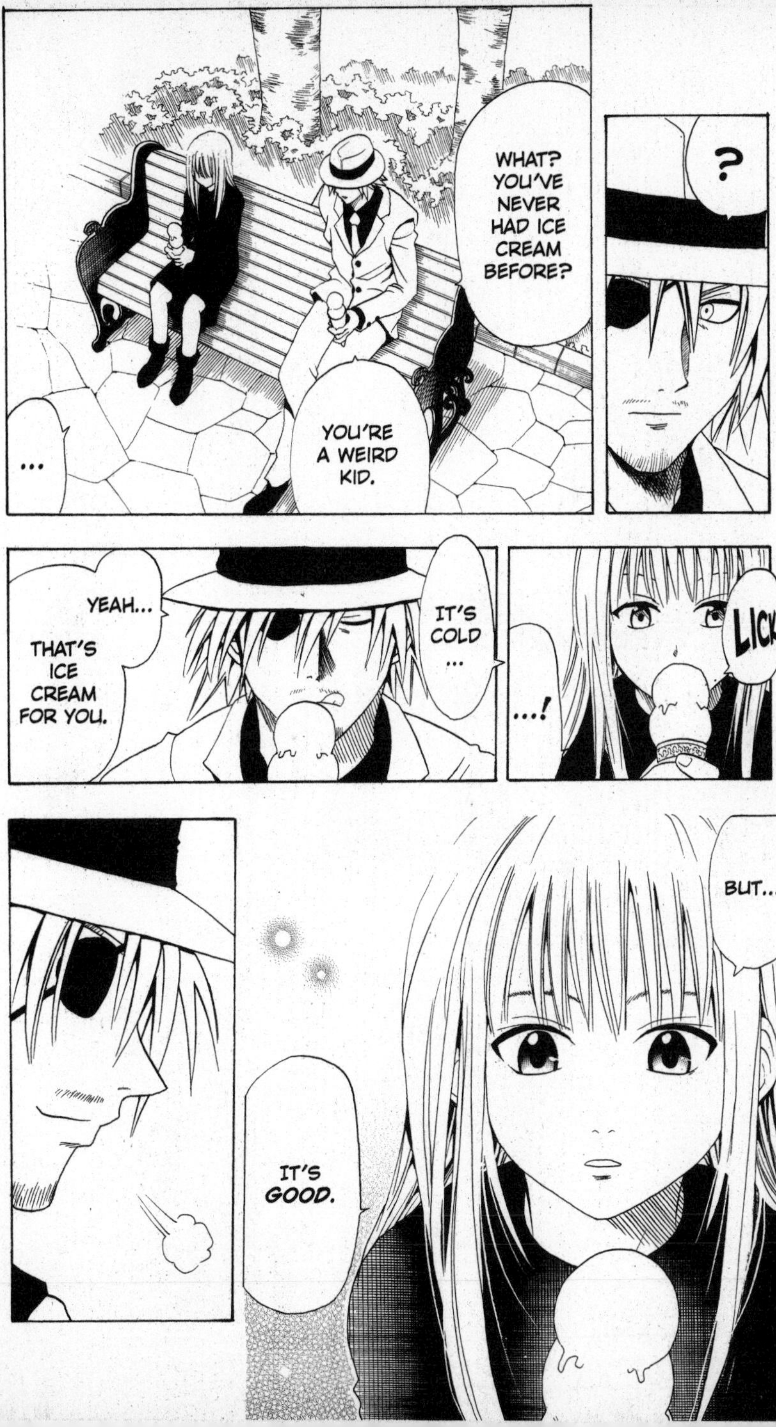
?
WHAT? YOU'VE NEVER HAD ICE CREAM BEFORE?
YOU'RE A WEIRD KID.
...
LICK
...!
IT'S COLD ...
YEAH...
THAT'S ICE CREAM FOR YOU.
BUT...
IT'S GOOD.

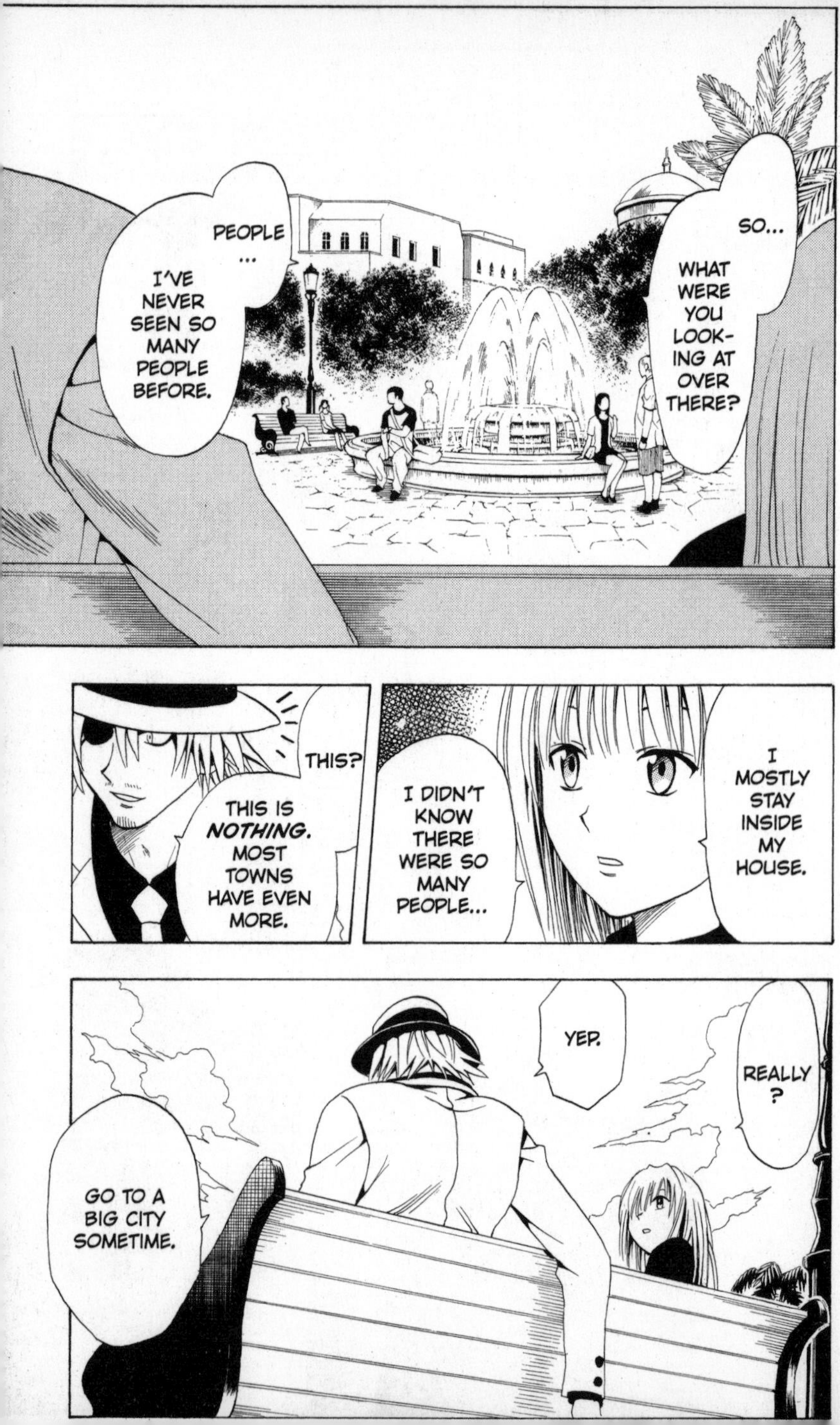
SO... WHAT WERE YOU LOOKING AT OVER THERE?
PEOPLE...
I'VE NEVER SEEN SO MANY PEOPLE BEFORE.
I MOSTLY STAY INSIDE MY HOUSE.
I DIDN'T KNOW THERE WERE SO MANY PEOPLE...
THIS?
THIS IS *NOTHING*. MOST TOWNS HAVE EVEN MORE.
REALLY?
YEP.
GO TO A BIG CITY SOMETIME.

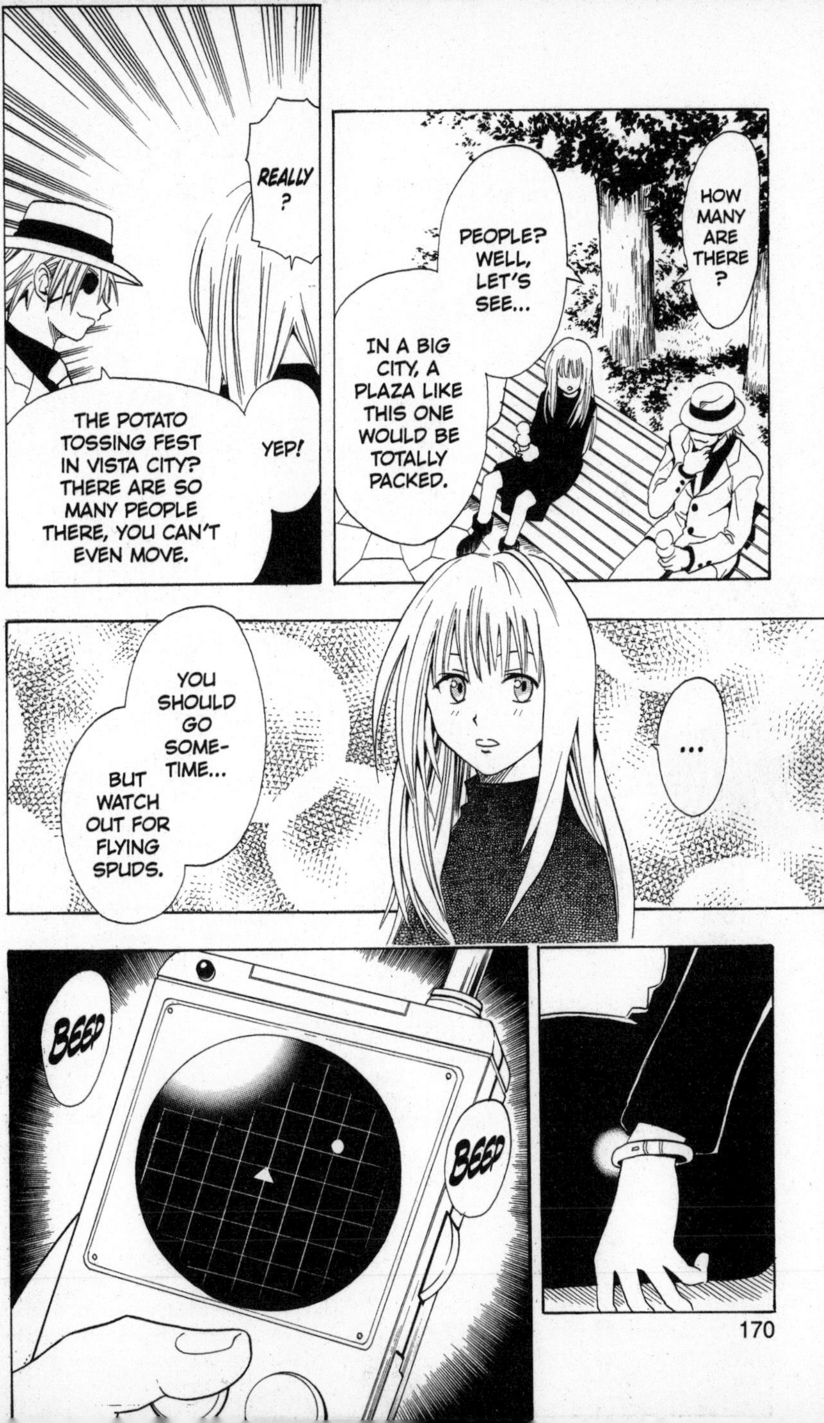
HOW MANY ARE THERE?
PEOPLE? WELL, LET'S SEE...
IN A BIG CITY, A PLAZA LIKE THIS ONE WOULD BE TOTALLY PACKED.
REALLY?
YEP!
THE POTATO TOSSING FEST IN VISTA CITY? THERE ARE SO MANY PEOPLE THERE, YOU CAN'T EVEN MOVE.
...
YOU SHOULD GO SOME-TIME...
BUT WATCH OUT FOR FLYING SPUDS.
BEEP
BEEP

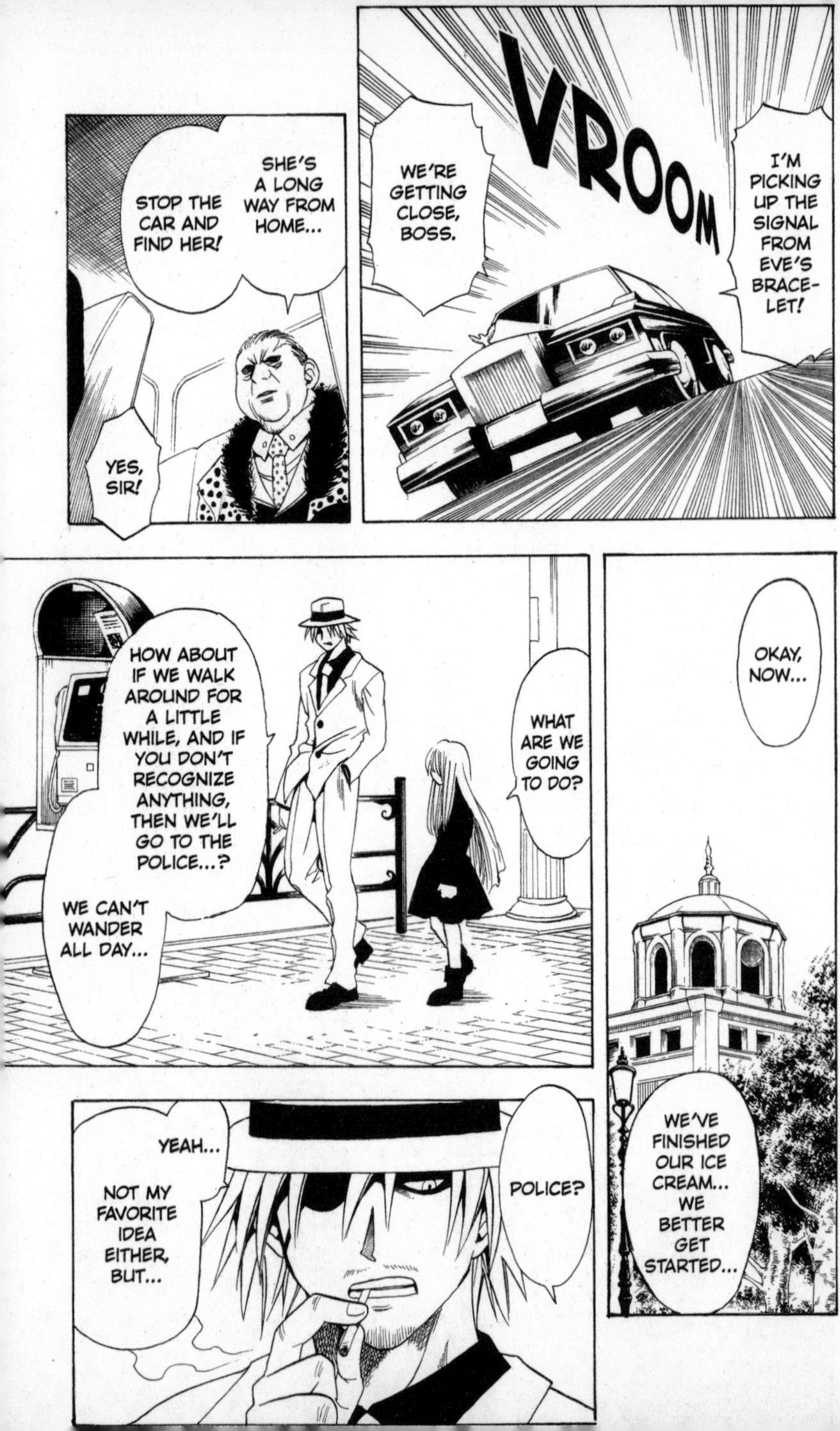
I'M PICKING UP THE SIGNAL FROM EVE'S BRACE-LET!
VROOM
WE'RE GETTING CLOSE, BOSS.
SHE'S A LONG WAY FROM HOME...
STOP THE CAR AND FIND HER!
YES, SIR!
OKAY, NOW...
WE'VE FINISHED OUR ICE CREAM... WE BETTER GET STARTED...
WHAT ARE WE GOING TO DO?
HOW ABOUT IF WE WALK AROUND FOR A LITTLE WHILE, AND IF YOU DON'T RECOGNIZE ANYTHING, THEN WE'LL GO TO THE POLICE...?
WE CAN'T WANDER ALL DAY...
POLICE?
YEAH...
NOT MY FAVORITE IDEA EITHER, BUT...

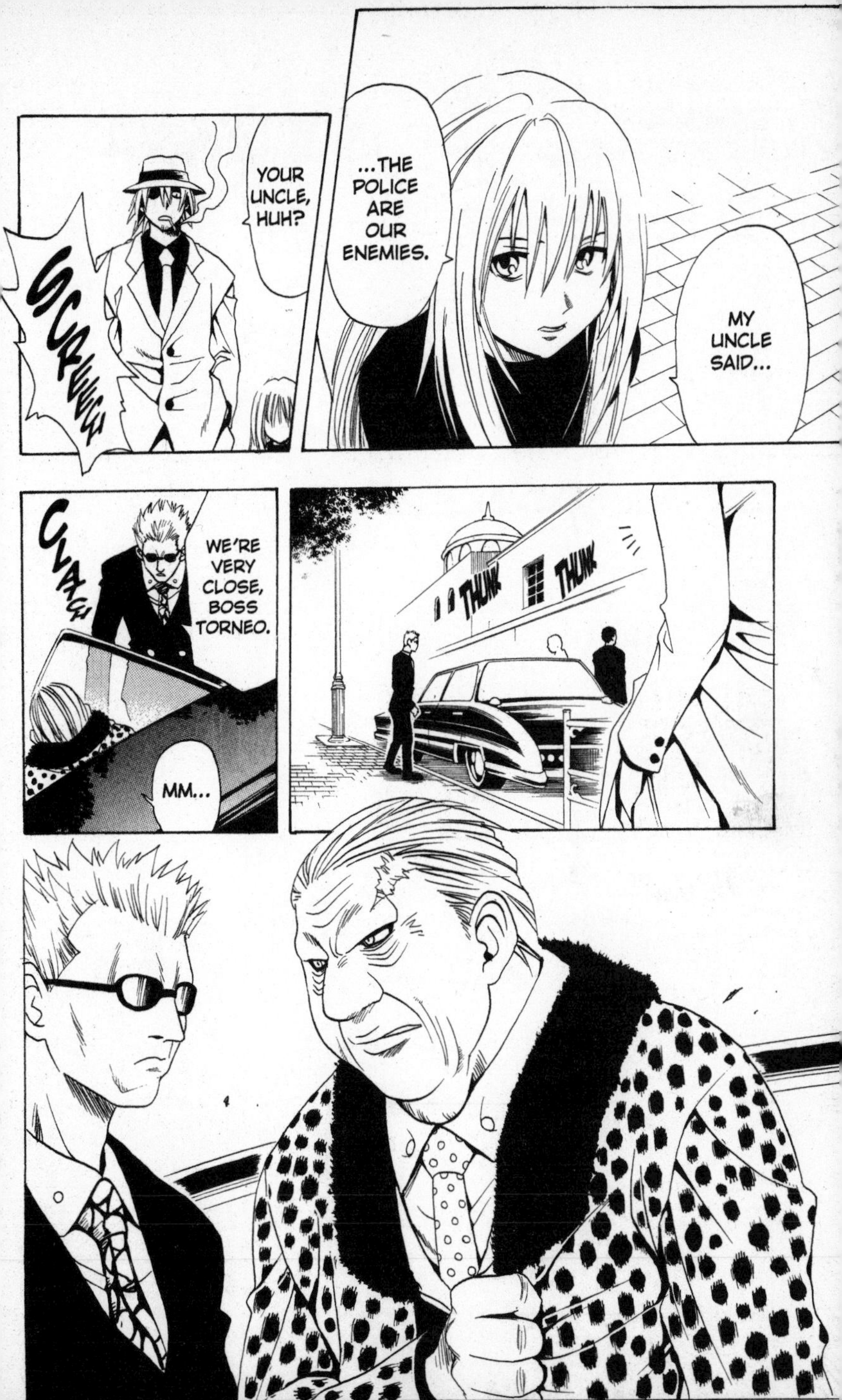
MY UNCLE SAID...
...THE POLICE ARE OUR ENEMIES.
YOUR UNCLE, HUH?
SCRUNCH
THUNK
THUNK
CLACK
WE'RE VERY CLOSE, BOSS TORNEO.
MM...

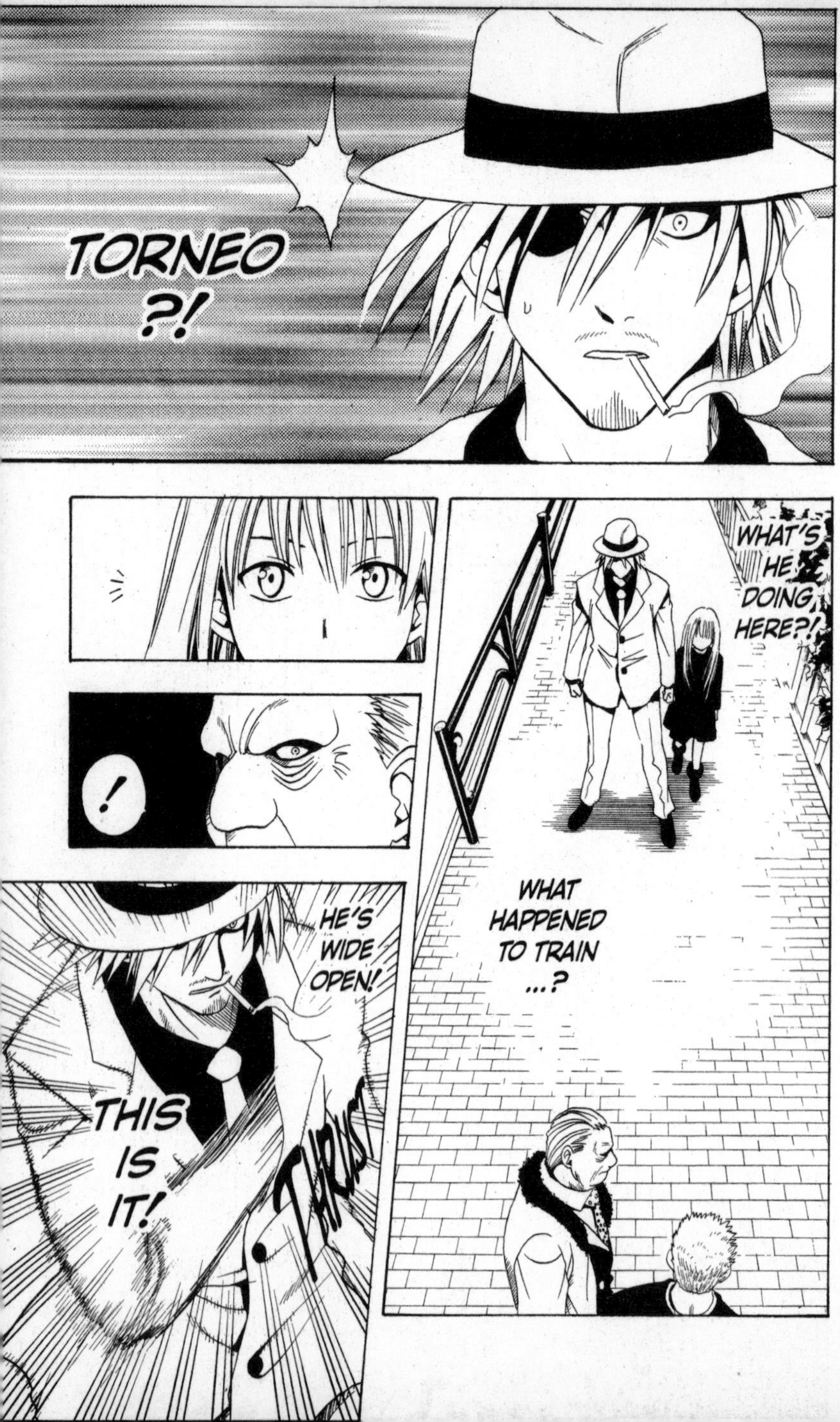
TORNEO ?!
WHAT'S HE DOING HERE?!
WHAT HAPPENED TO TRAIN ...?
!
HE'S WIDE OPEN!
THIS IS IT!
THRUST

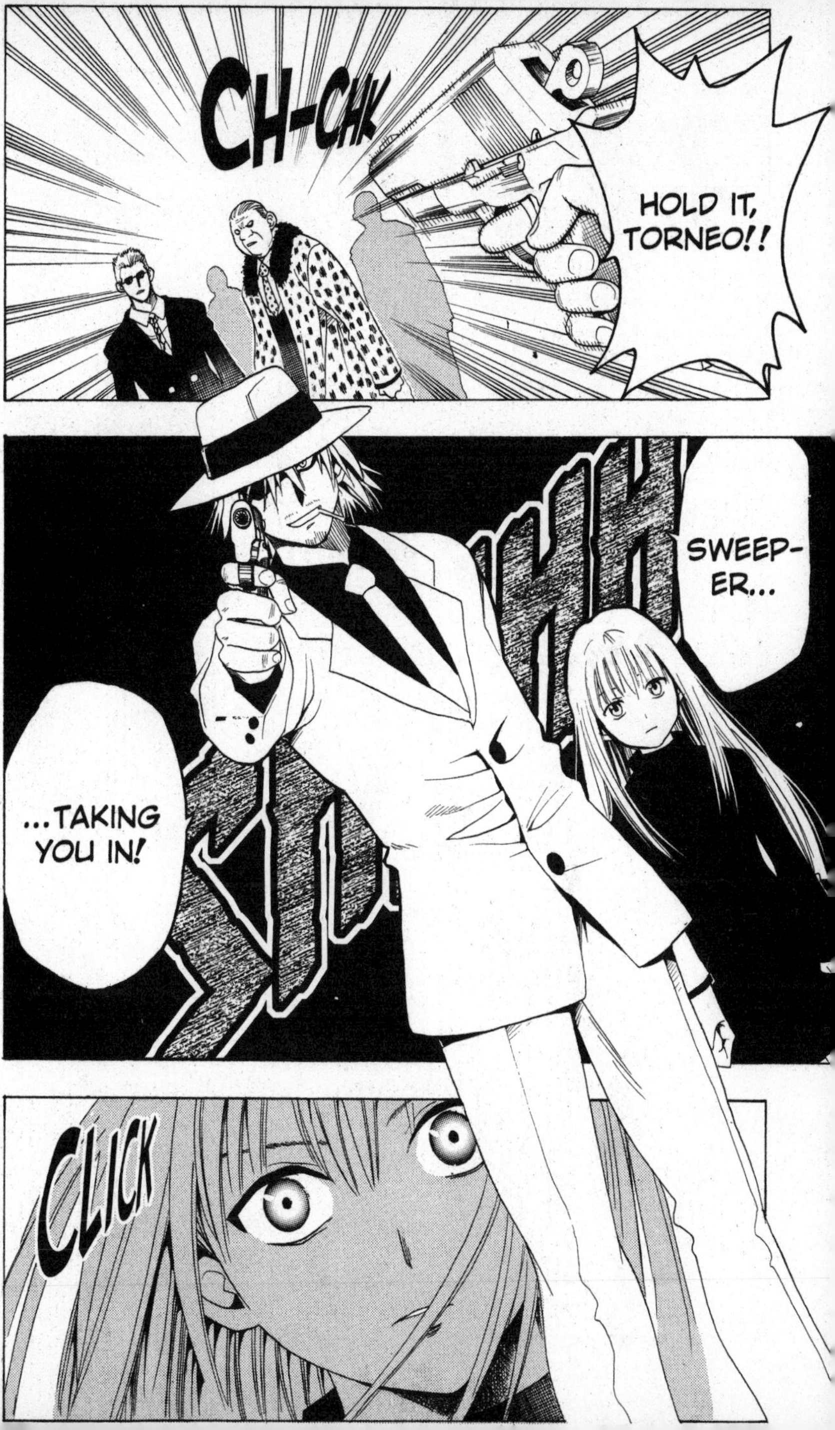
HOLD IT, TORNEO!!
CH-CHK
SWEEP-
ER...
...TAKING YOU IN!
CLICK

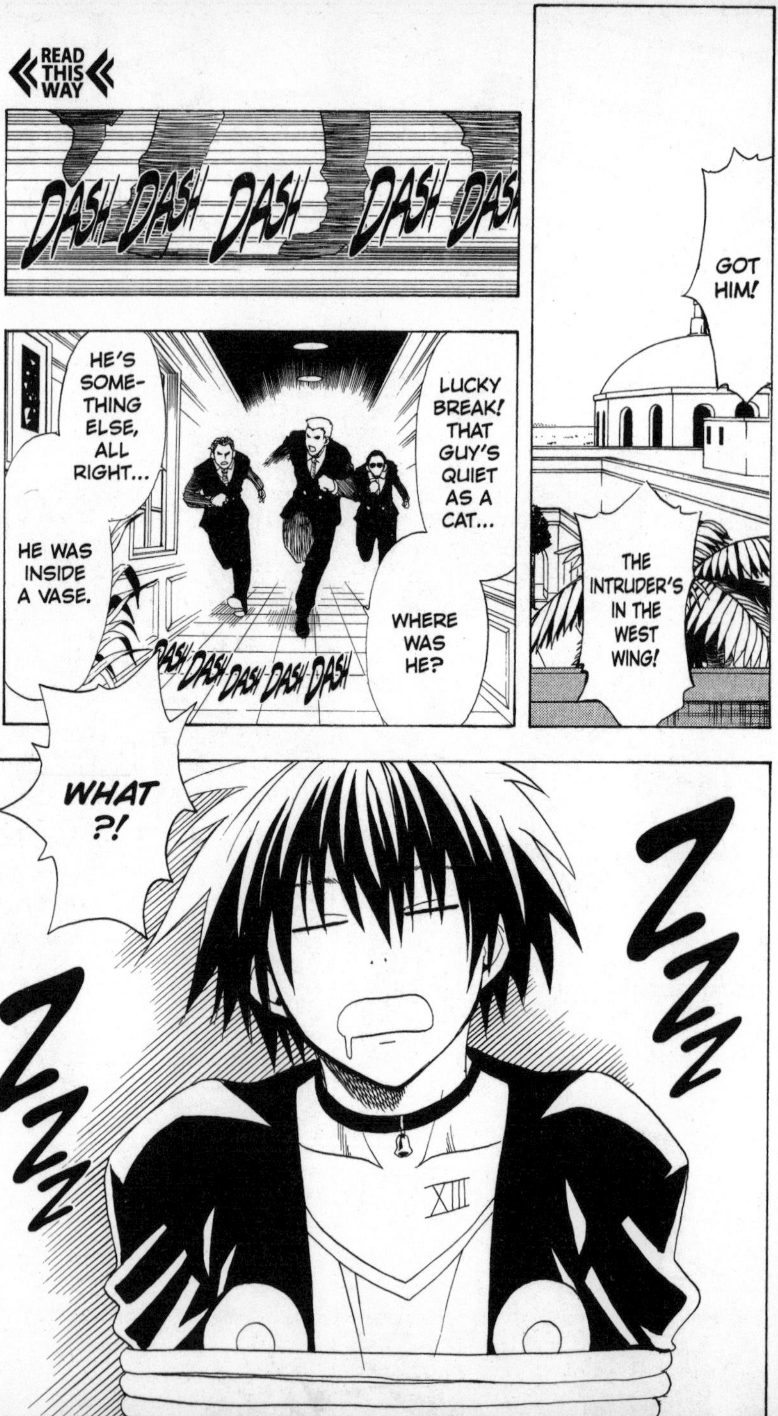
READ THIS WAY
GOT HIM!
THE INTRUDER'S IN THE WEST WING!
DASH DASH DASH DASH DASH
LUCKY BREAK! THAT GUY'S QUIET AS A CAT...
HE'S SOMETHING ELSE, ALL RIGHT...
WHERE WAS HE?
HE WAS INSIDE A VASE.
DASH DASH DASH DASH DASH
WHAT?!
ZZZ
XIII

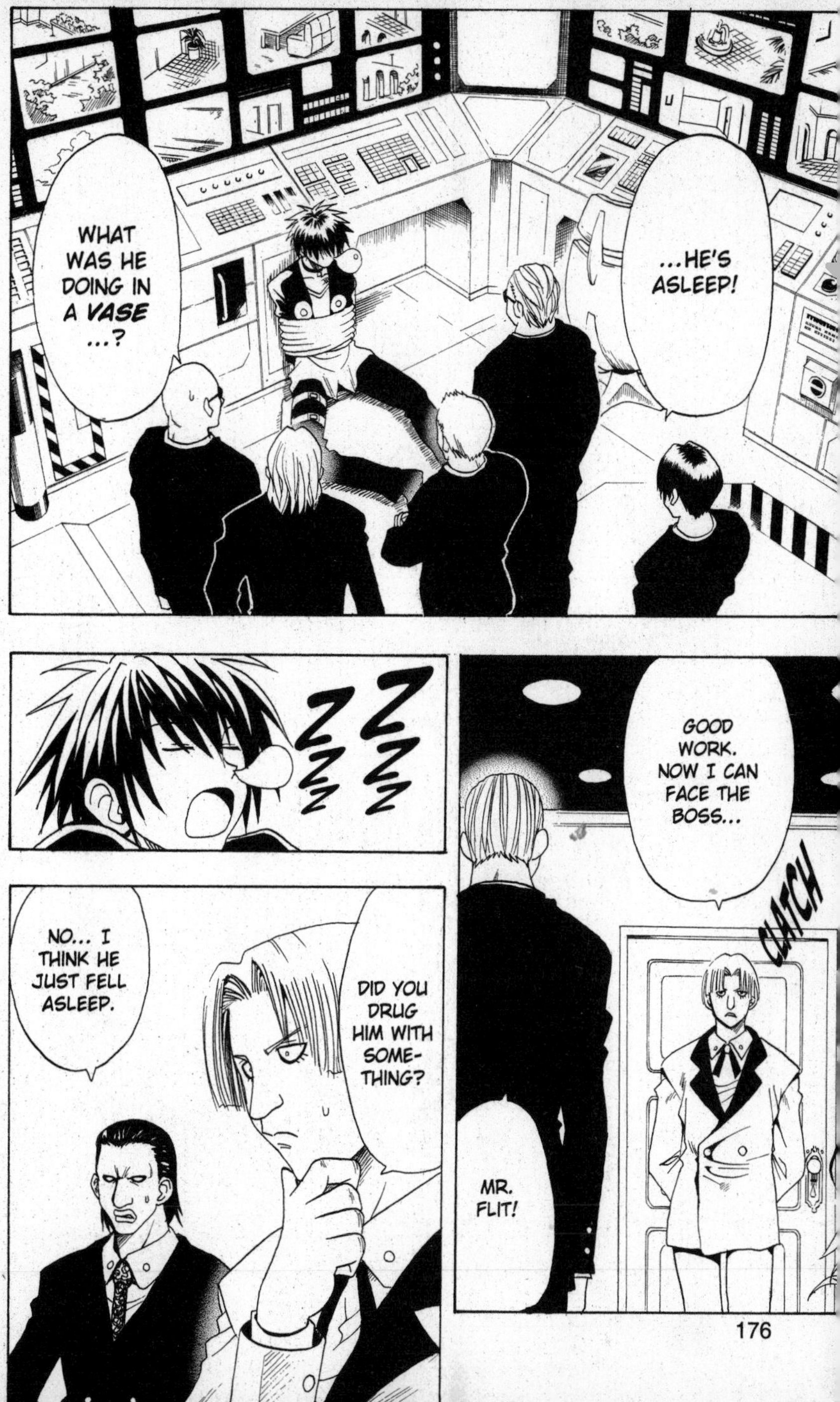
...HE'S ASLEEP!
WHAT WAS HE DOING IN A VASE ...?
GOOD WORK. NOW I CAN FACE THE BOSS...
CLATCH
MR. FLIT!
ZZZ ZZZ
DID YOU DRUG HIM WITH SOME-THING?
NO... I THINK HE JUST FELL ASLEEP.

READ THIS WAY

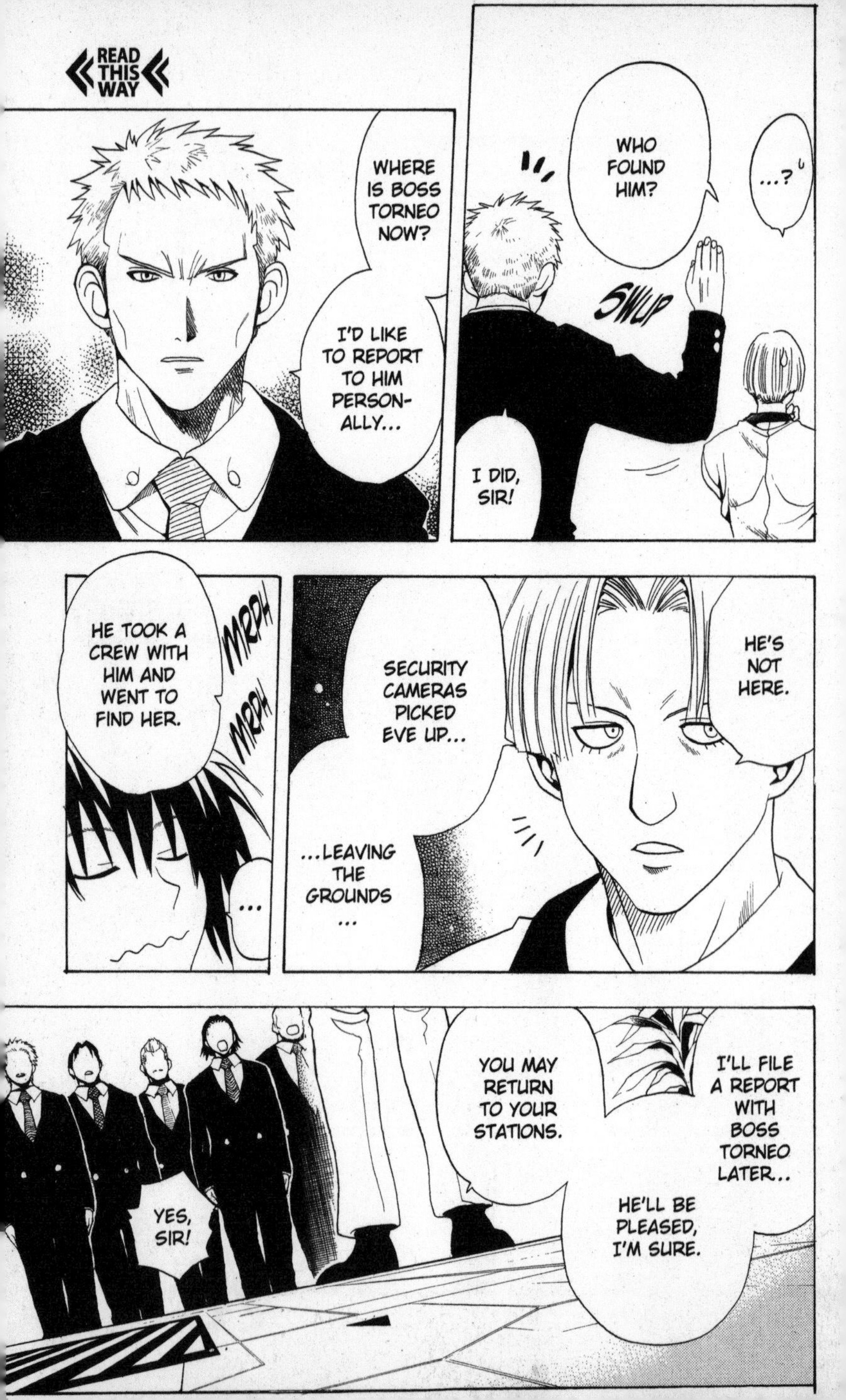
WHO FOUND HIM?
...?
SWUP
I DID, SIR!
WHERE IS BOSS TORNEO NOW?
I'D LIKE TO REPORT TO HIM PERSON-ALLY...
HE'S NOT HERE.
SECURITY CAMERAS PICKED EVE UP...
...LEAVING THE GROUNDS...
HE TOOK A CREW WITH HIM AND WENT TO FIND HER.
MRPH
MRPH
...
I'LL FILE A REPORT WITH BOSS TORNEO LATER...
YOU MAY RETURN TO YOUR STATIONS.
HE'LL BE PLEASED, I'M SURE.
YES, SIR!

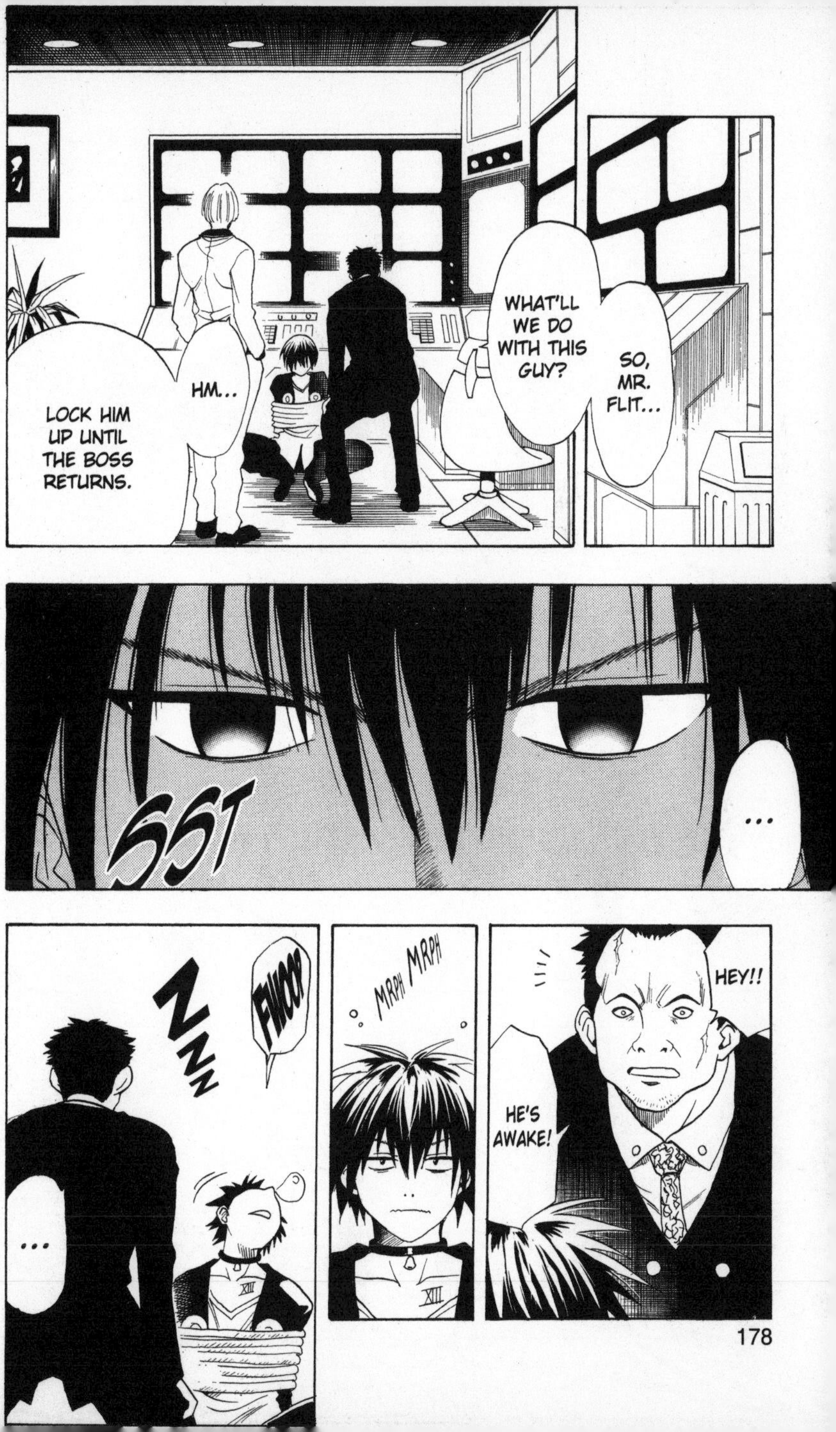
SO, MR. FLIT...
WHAT'LL WE DO WITH THIS GUY?
HM...
LOCK HIM UP UNTIL THE BOSS RETURNS.
...
SST
HEY!!
HE'S AWAKE!
MRPH MRPH
FWOOP
NNN
...

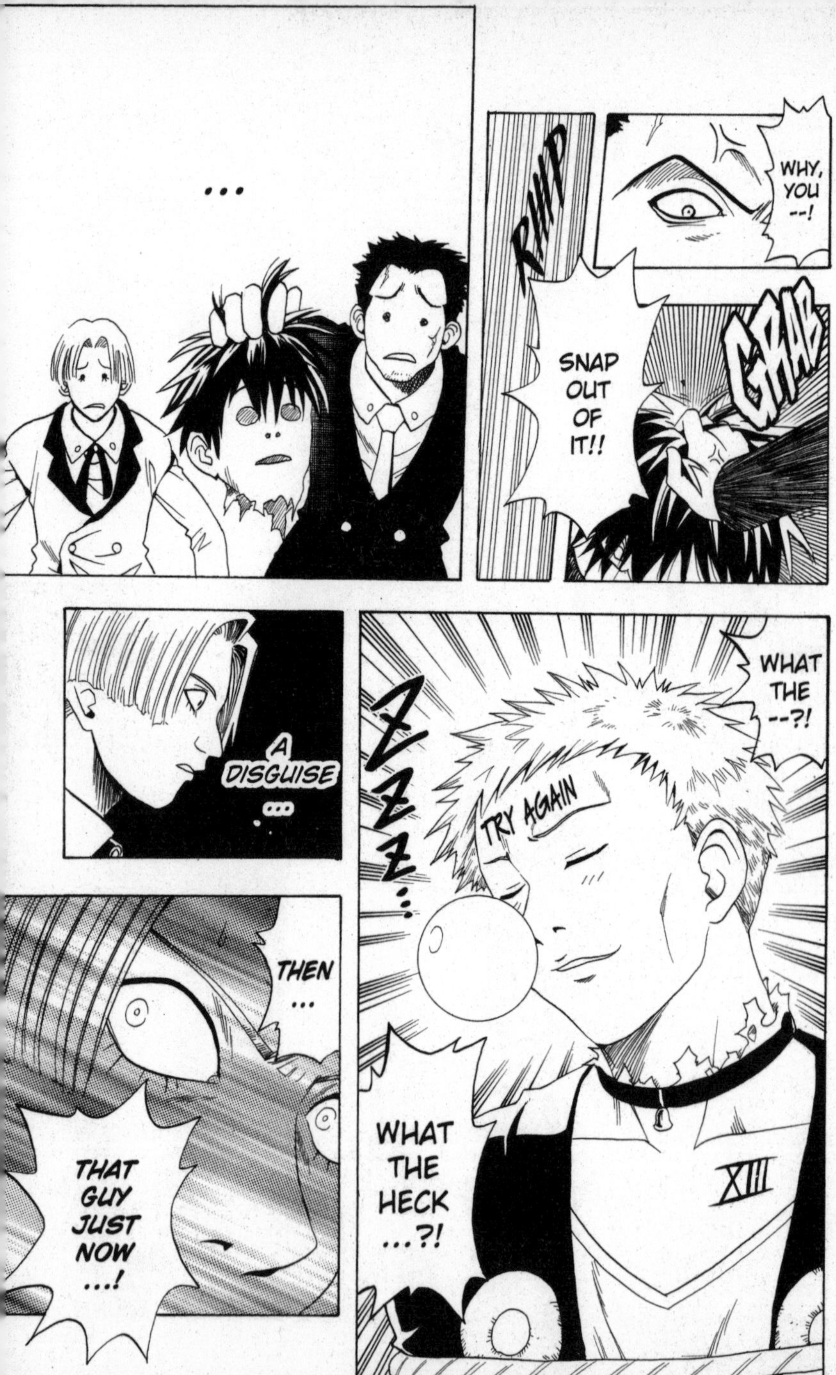
WHY, YOU --!
RHIP
GRAB
SNAP OUT OF IT!!
...
WHAT THE --?!
ZZZ...
TRY AGAIN
WHAT THE HECK ...?!
A DISGUISE ...
THEN ...
THAT GUY JUST NOW ...!

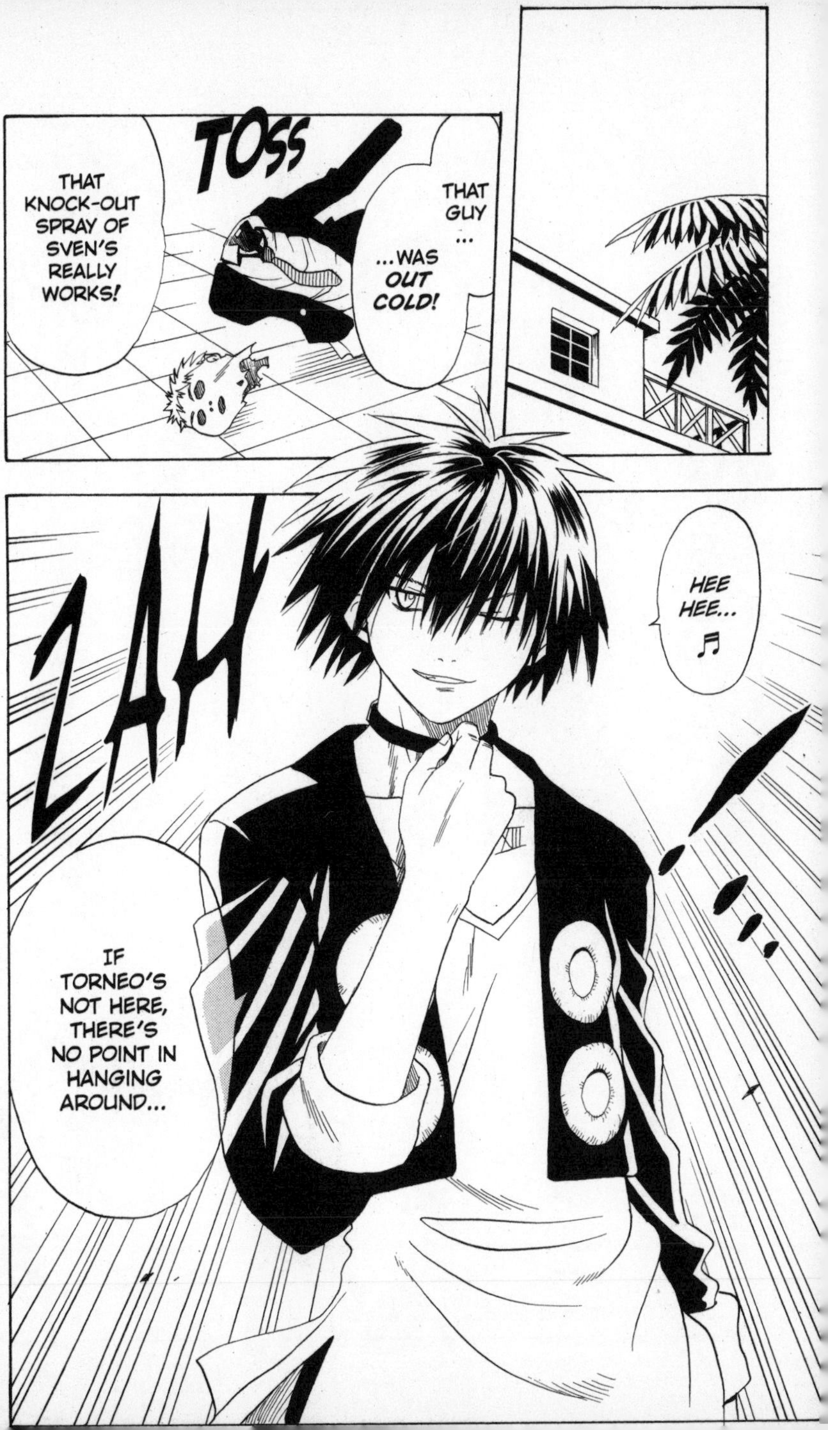
THAT GUY ...
...WAS OUT COLD!
TOSS
THAT KNOCK-OUT SPRAY OF SVEN'S REALLY WORKS!
HEE HEE... ♬
ZAH
!...
IF TORNEO'S NOT HERE, THERE'S NO POINT IN HANGING AROUND...

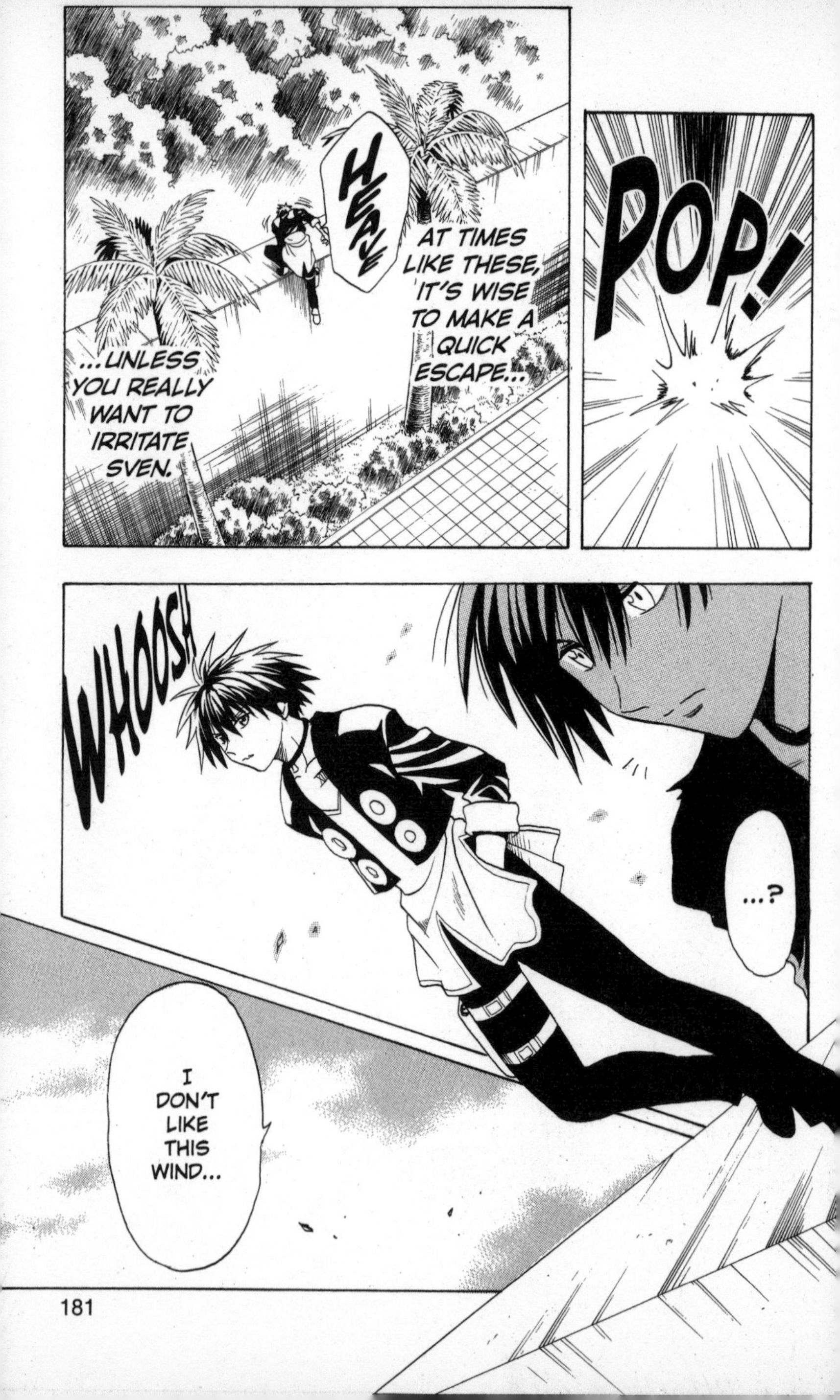
POP!
HEAVE
AT TIMES LIKE THESE, IT'S WISE TO MAKE A QUICK ESCAPE...
...UNLESS YOU REALLY WANT TO IRRITATE SVEN.
...?
WHOOSH
I DON'T LIKE THIS WIND...

Each character will be profiled starting in Volume 2!

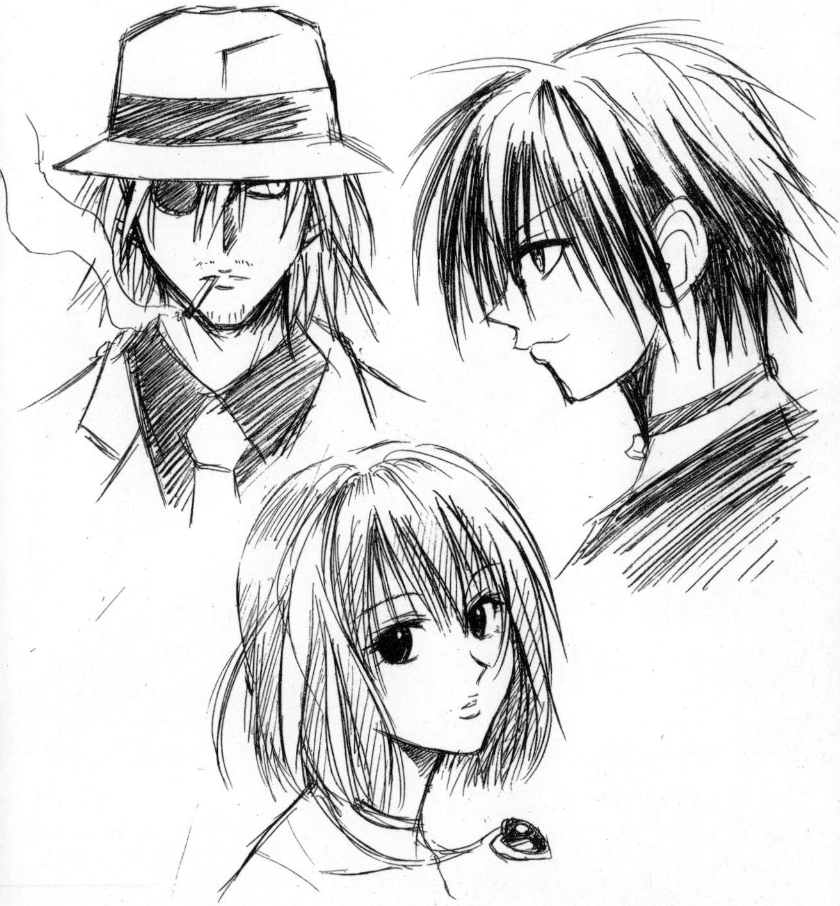

Chapter 8: Russian Roulette

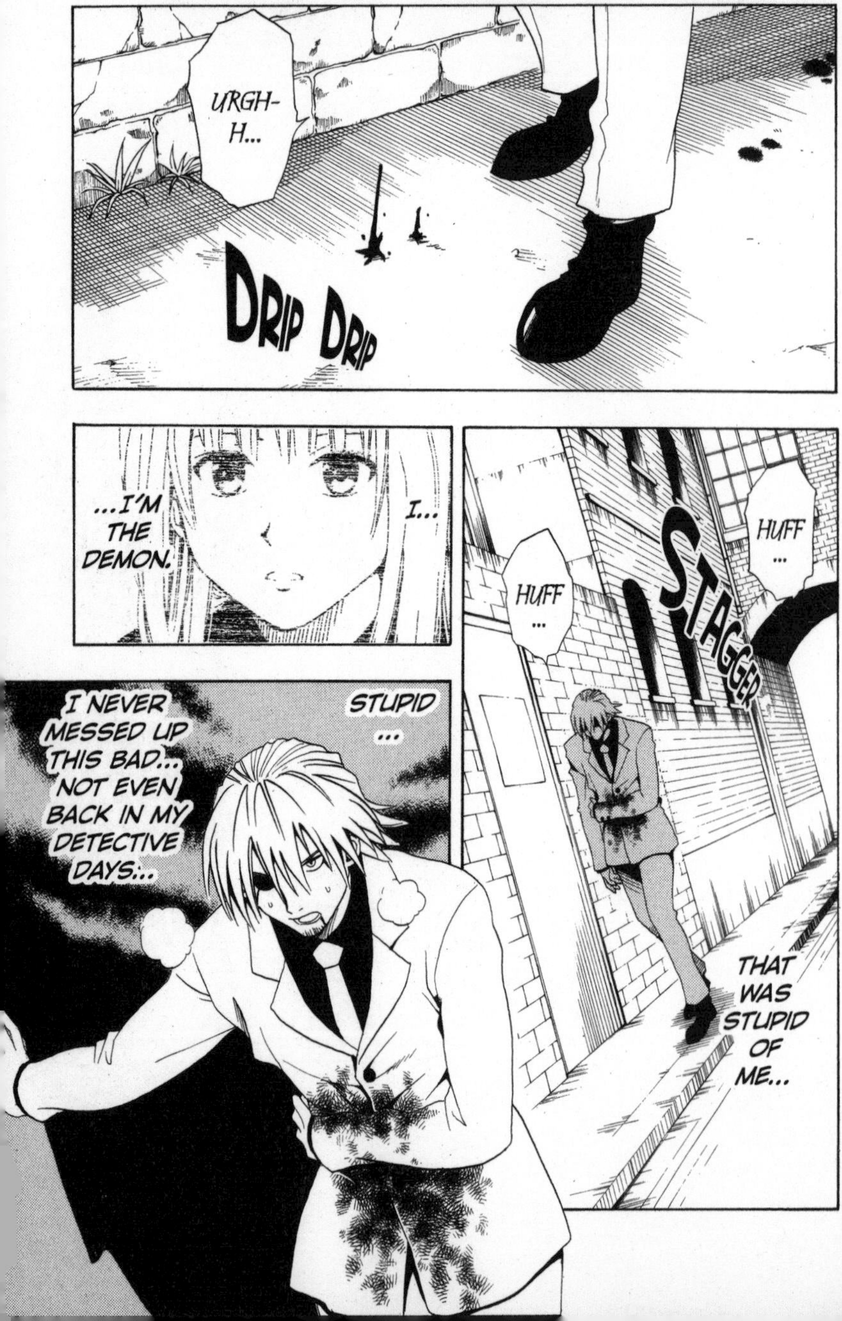

URGH-H...
DRIP DRIP
HUFF...
HUFF...
STAGGER
THAT WAS STUPID OF ME...
I...
...I'M THE DEMON.
STUPID...
I NEVER MESSED UP THIS BAD... NOT EVEN BACK IN MY DETECTIVE DAYS...

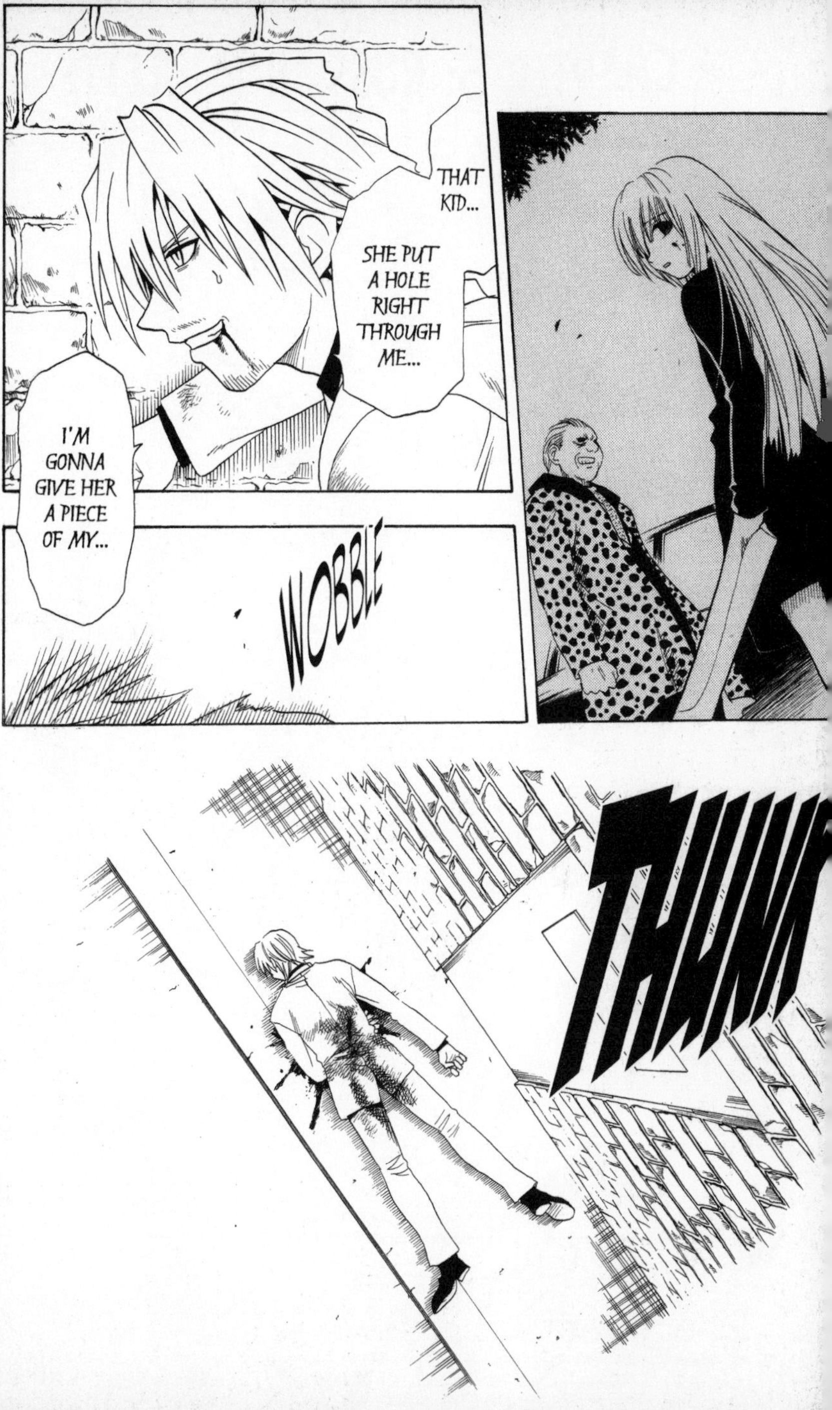
THAT KID...
SHE PUT A HOLE RIGHT THROUGH ME...
I'M GONNA GIVE HER A PIECE OF MY...
WOBBLE
THUN

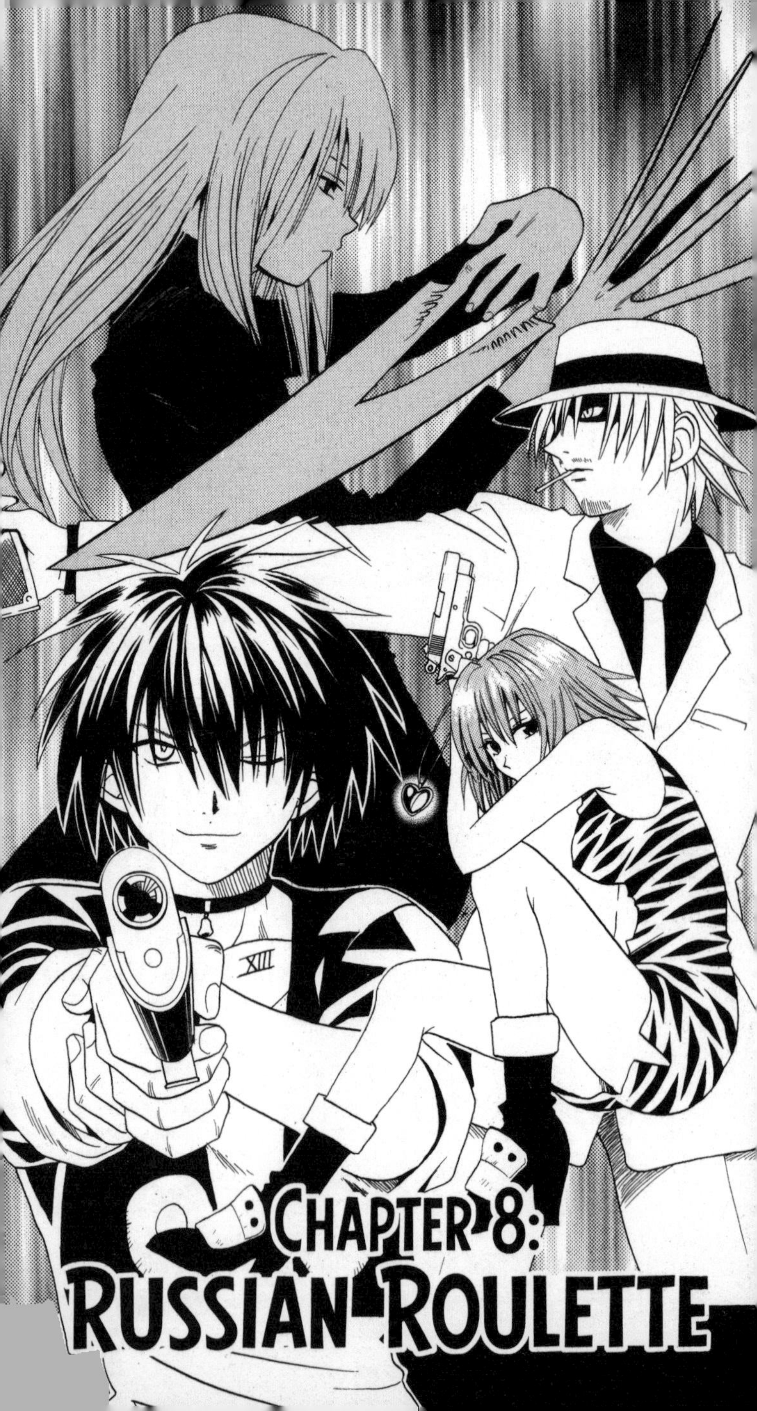

Chapter 8:
Russian Roulette

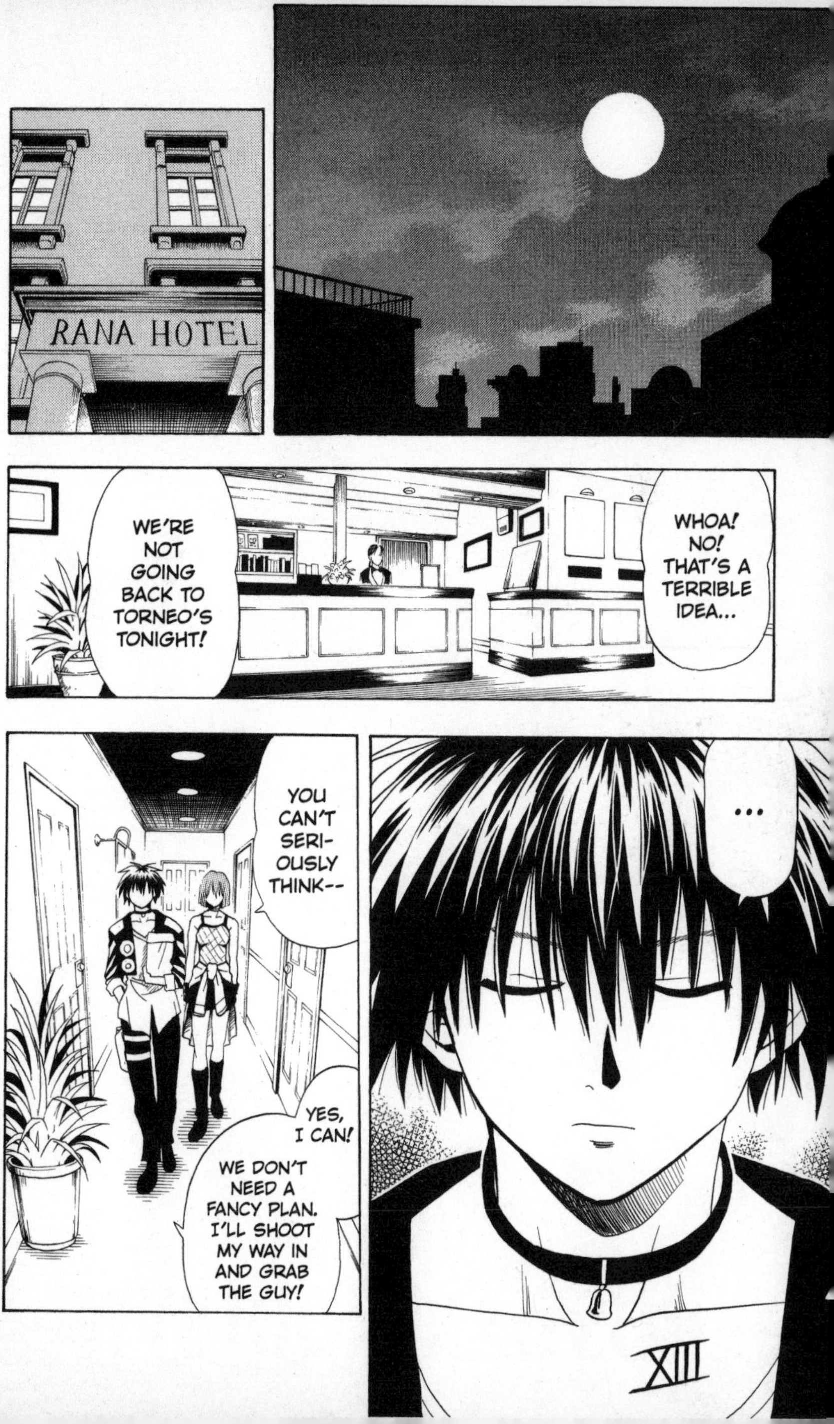
RANA HOTEL
WHOA! NO! THAT'S A TERRIBLE IDEA...
WE'RE NOT GOING BACK TO TORNEO'S TONIGHT!
...
YOU CAN'T SERI-OUSLY THINK--
YES, I CAN!
WE DON'T NEED A FANCY PLAN. I'LL SHOOT MY WAY IN AND GRAB THE GUY!
XIII

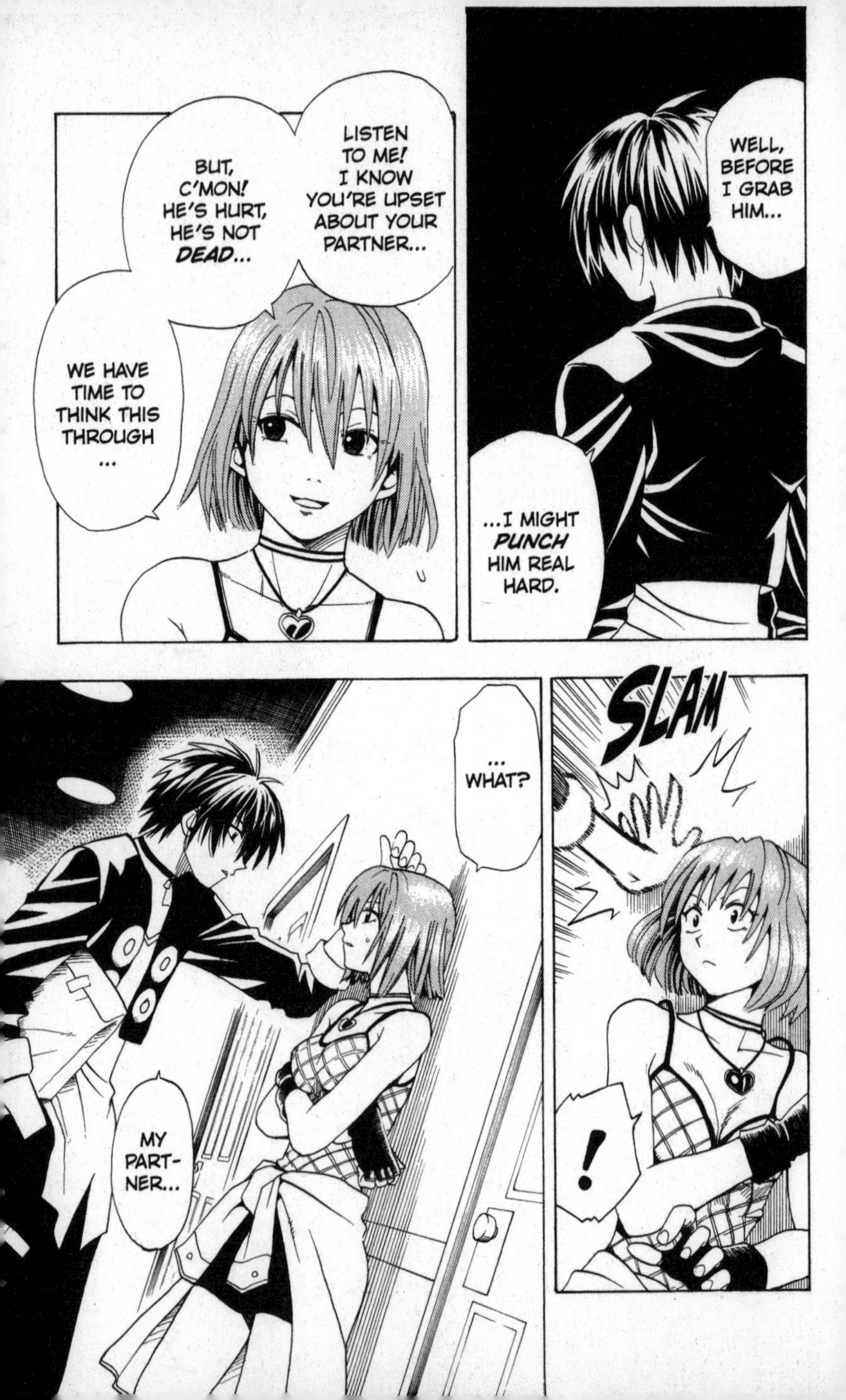
WELL, BEFORE I GRAB HIM...
...I MIGHT *PUNCH* HIM REAL HARD.
LISTEN TO ME! I KNOW YOU'RE UPSET ABOUT YOUR PARTNER...
BUT, C'MON! HE'S HURT, HE'S NOT *DEAD*...
WE HAVE TIME TO THINK THIS THROUGH ...
SLAM
!
... WHAT?
MY PARTNER...

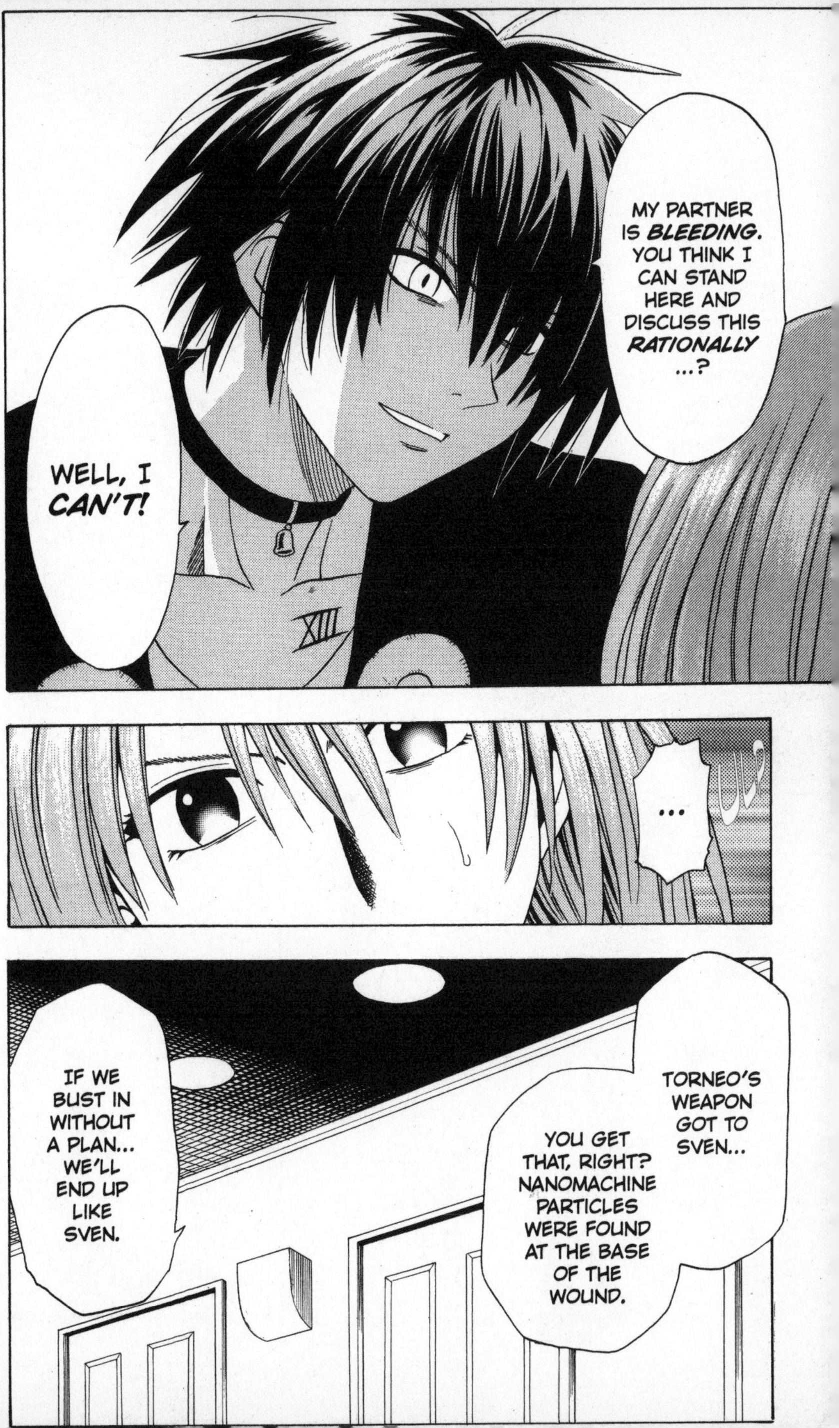
MY PARTNER IS *BLEEDING*. YOU THINK I CAN STAND HERE AND DISCUSS THIS *RATIONALLY* ...?
WELL, I *CAN'T!*
...
TORNEO'S WEAPON GOT TO SVEN...
YOU GET THAT, RIGHT? NANOMACHINE PARTICLES WERE FOUND AT THE BASE OF THE WOUND.
IF WE BUST IN WITHOUT A PLAN... WE'LL END UP LIKE SVEN.

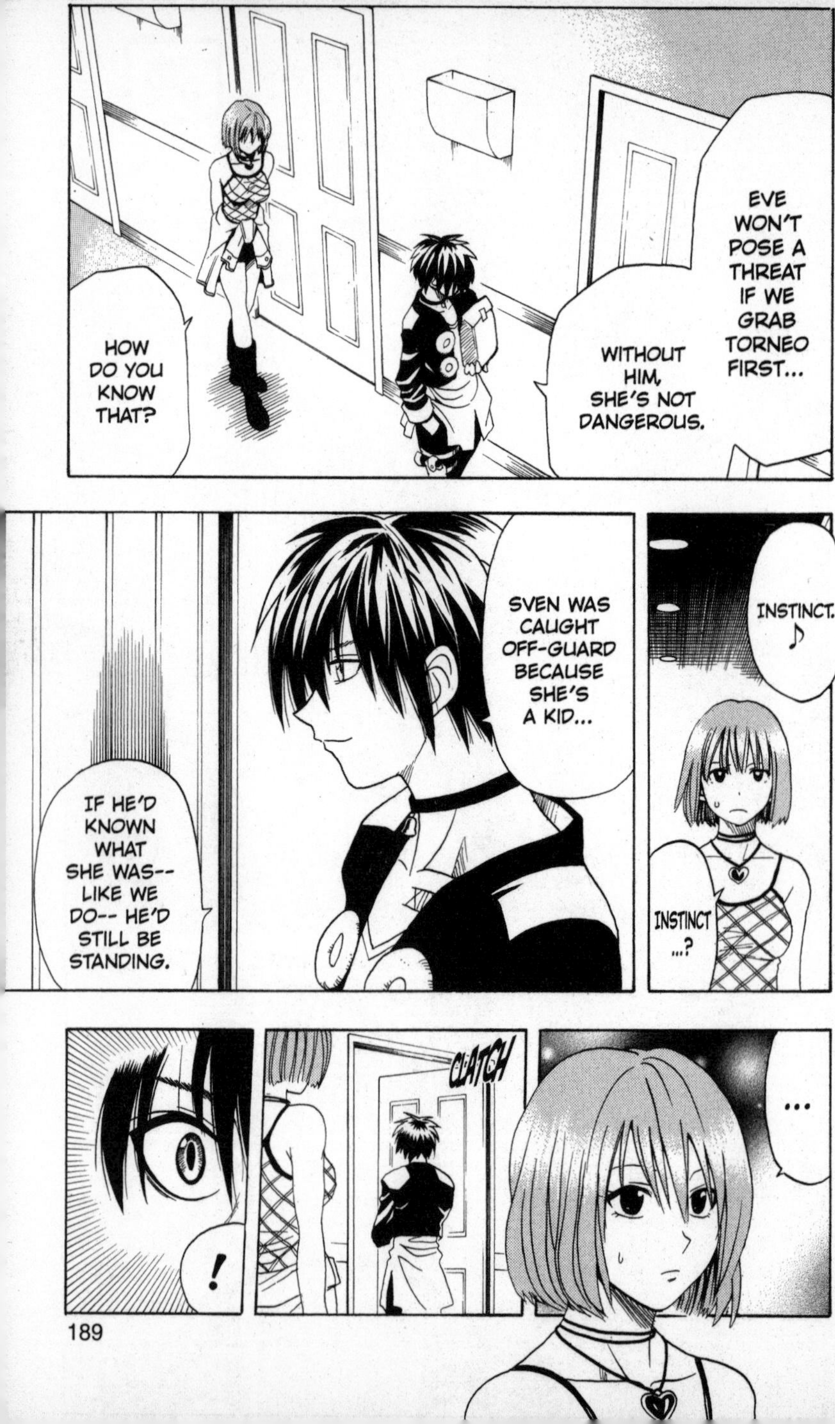
EVE WON'T POSE A THREAT IF WE GRAB TORNEO FIRST...
WITHOUT HIM, SHE'S NOT DANGEROUS.
HOW DO YOU KNOW THAT?
INSTINCT. ♪
INSTINCT ...?
SVEN WAS CAUGHT OFF-GUARD BECAUSE SHE'S A KID...
IF HE'D KNOWN WHAT SHE WAS-- LIKE WE DO-- HE'D STILL BE STANDING.
...
CLATCH
!

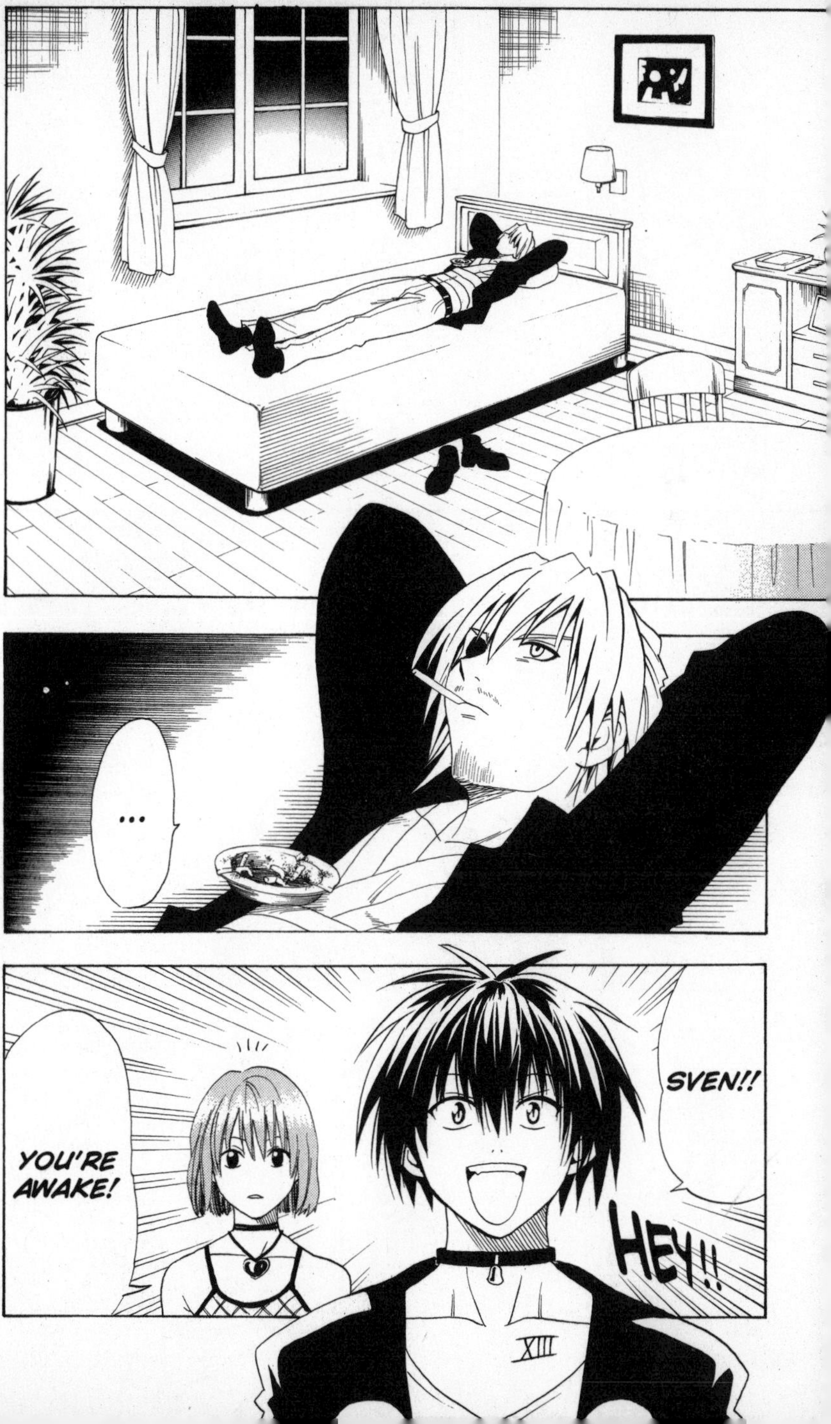
...
SVEN!!
HEY!!
YOU'RE AWAKE!

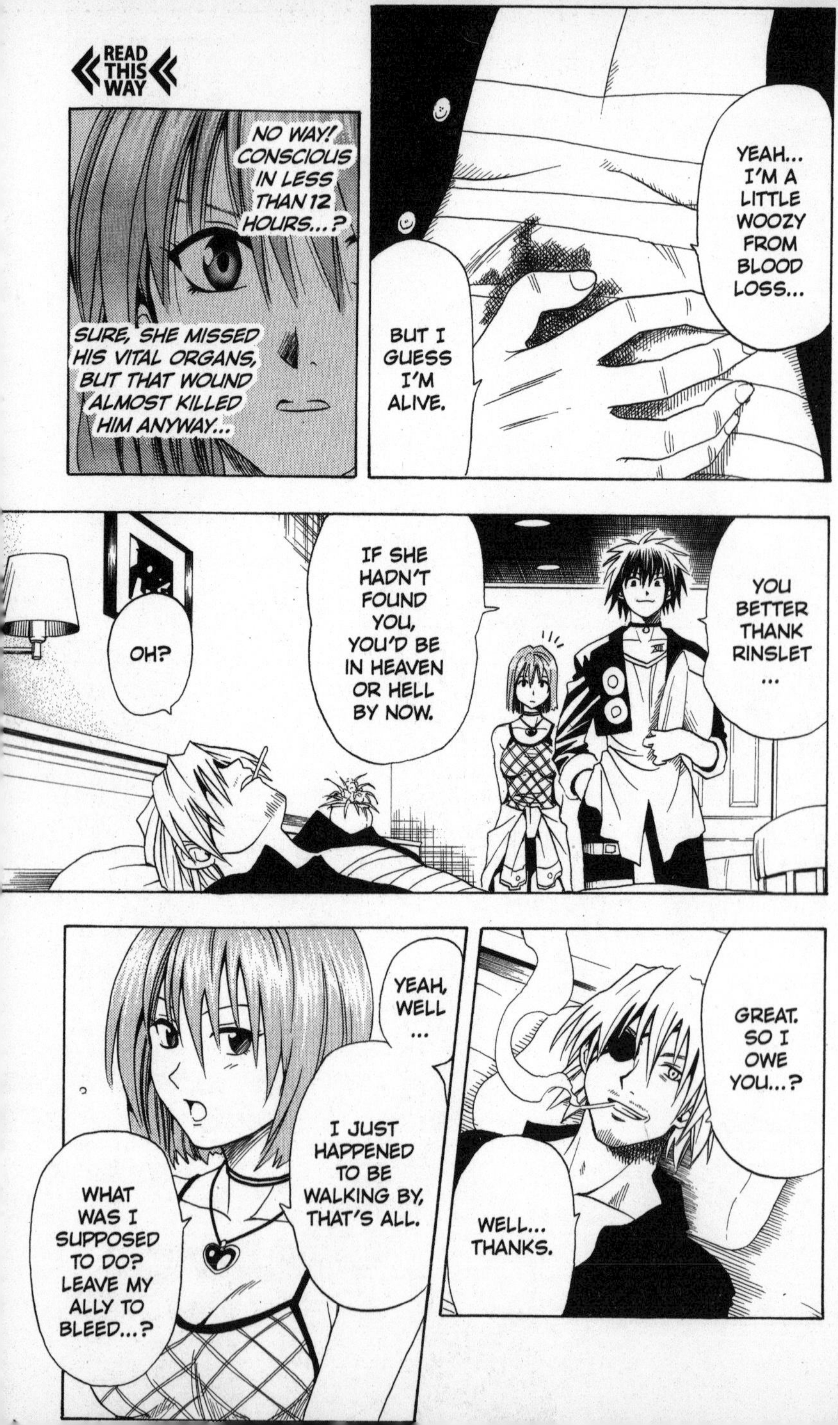
READ THIS WAY
YEAH... I'M A LITTLE WOOZY FROM BLOOD LOSS...
BUT I GUESS I'M ALIVE.
NO WAY! CONSCIOUS IN LESS THAN 12 HOURS...?
SURE, SHE MISSED HIS VITAL ORGANS, BUT THAT WOUND ALMOST KILLED HIM ANYWAY...
YOU BETTER THANK RINSLET...
IF SHE HADN'T FOUND YOU, YOU'D BE IN HEAVEN OR HELL BY NOW.
OH?
GREAT. SO I OWE YOU...?
WELL... THANKS.
YEAH, WELL...
I JUST HAPPENED TO BE WALKING BY, THAT'S ALL.
WHAT WAS I SUPPOSED TO DO? LEAVE MY ALLY TO BLEED...?

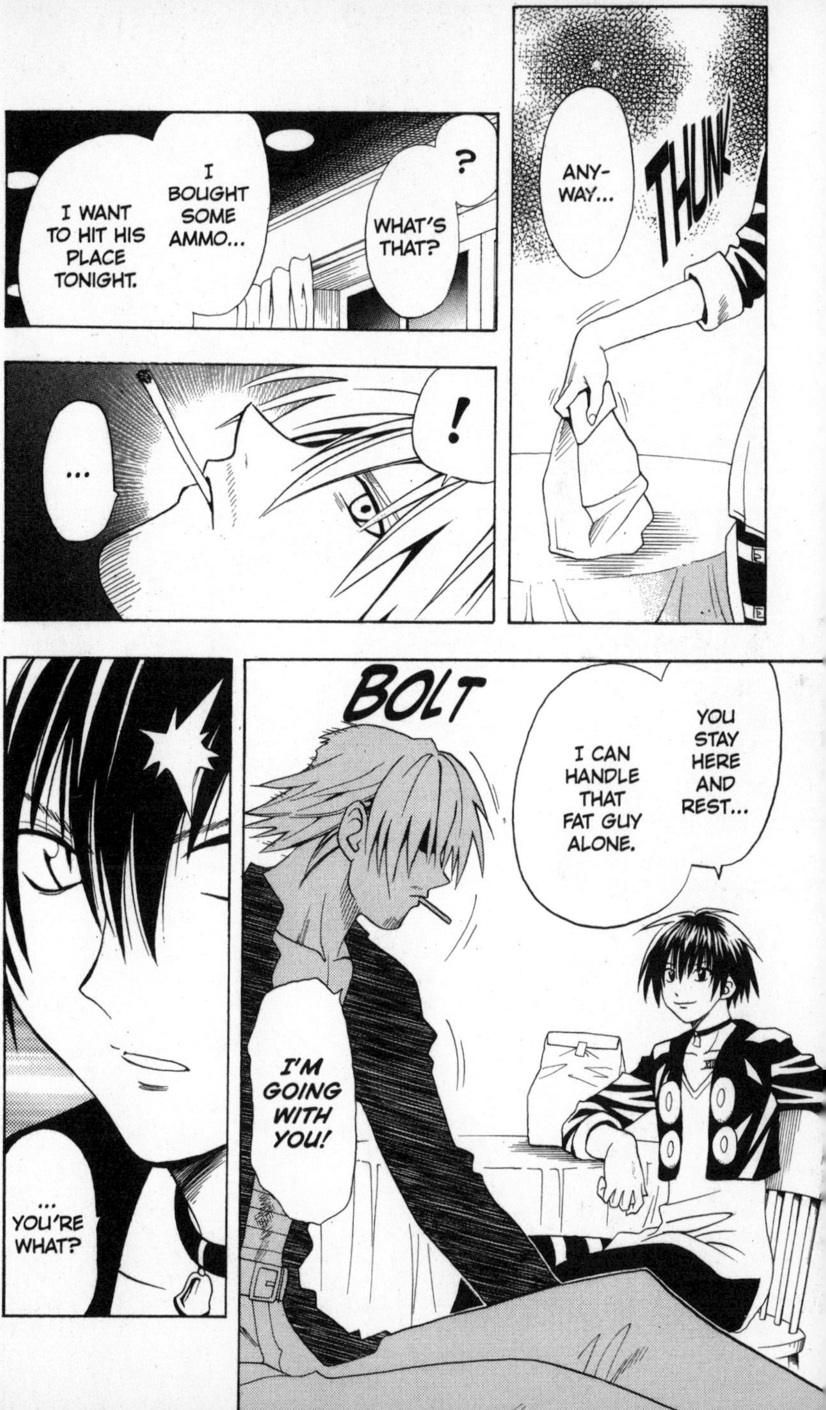
ANY-WAY...
THUNK
?
WHAT'S THAT?
I BOUGHT SOME AMMO...
I WANT TO HIT HIS PLACE TONIGHT.
!
...
YOU STAY HERE AND REST...
I CAN HANDLE THAT FAT GUY ALONE.
BOLT
I'M GOING WITH YOU!
... YOU'RE WHAT?

READ THIS WAY

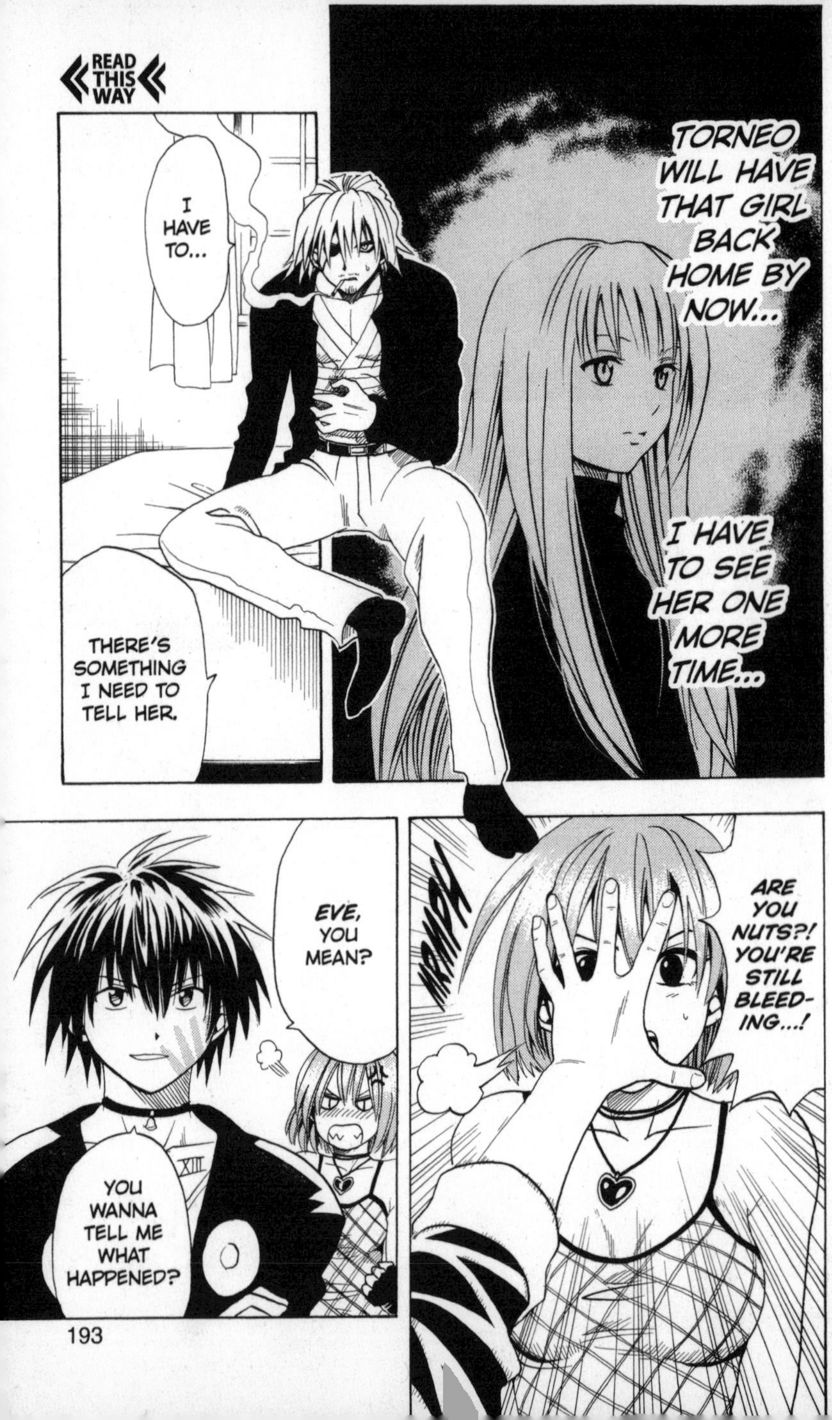
TORNEO WILL HAVE THAT GIRL BACK HOME BY NOW...
I HAVE TO SEE HER ONE MORE TIME...
I HAVE TO...
THERE'S SOMETHING I NEED TO TELL HER.
MRMPH
ARE YOU NUTS?! YOU'RE STILL BLEED-ING...!
EVE, YOU MEAN?
YOU WANNA TELL ME WHAT HAPPENED?

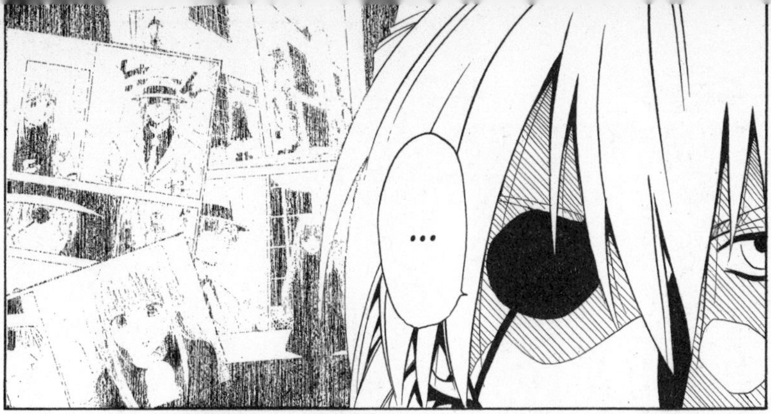
...
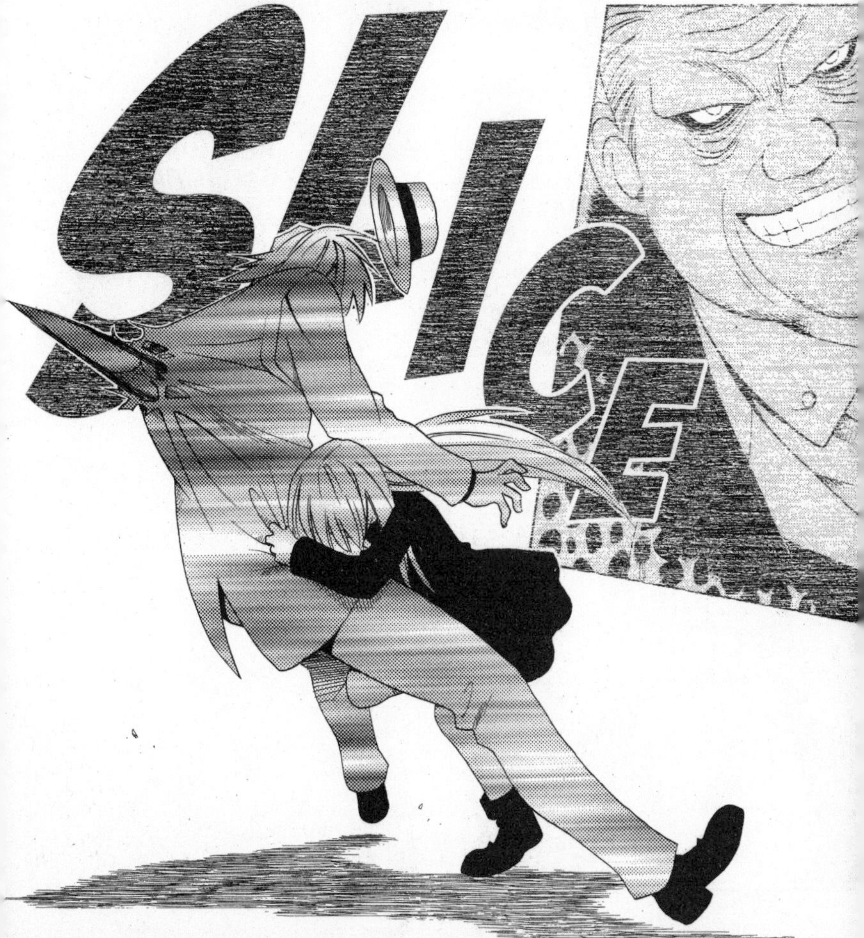
SLICE

READ THIS WAY

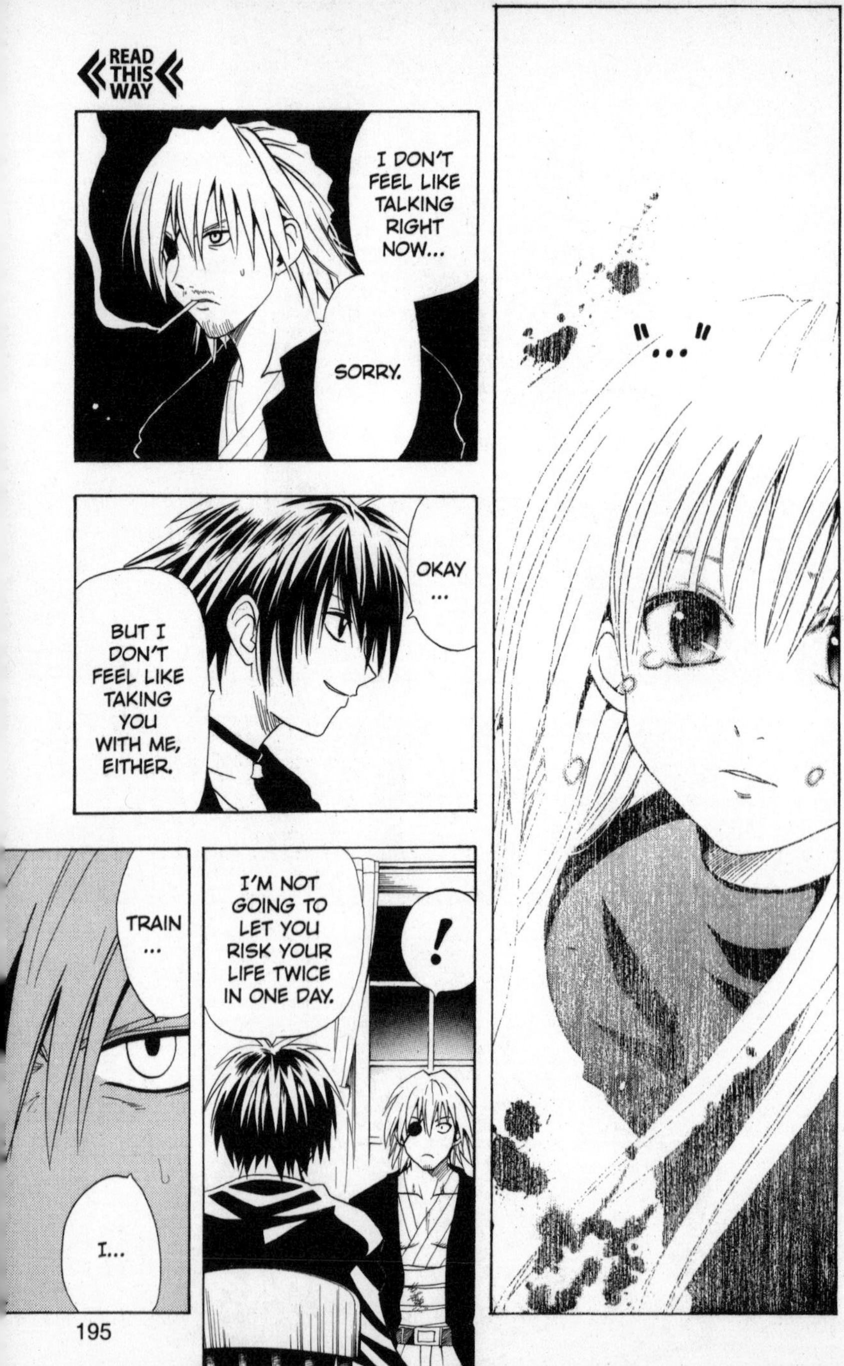
"..."
I DON'T FEEL LIKE TALKING RIGHT NOW...
SORRY.
OKAY ...
BUT I DON'T FEEL LIKE TAKING YOU WITH ME, EITHER.
I'M NOT GOING TO LET YOU RISK YOUR LIFE TWICE IN ONE DAY.
!
TRAIN ...
I...

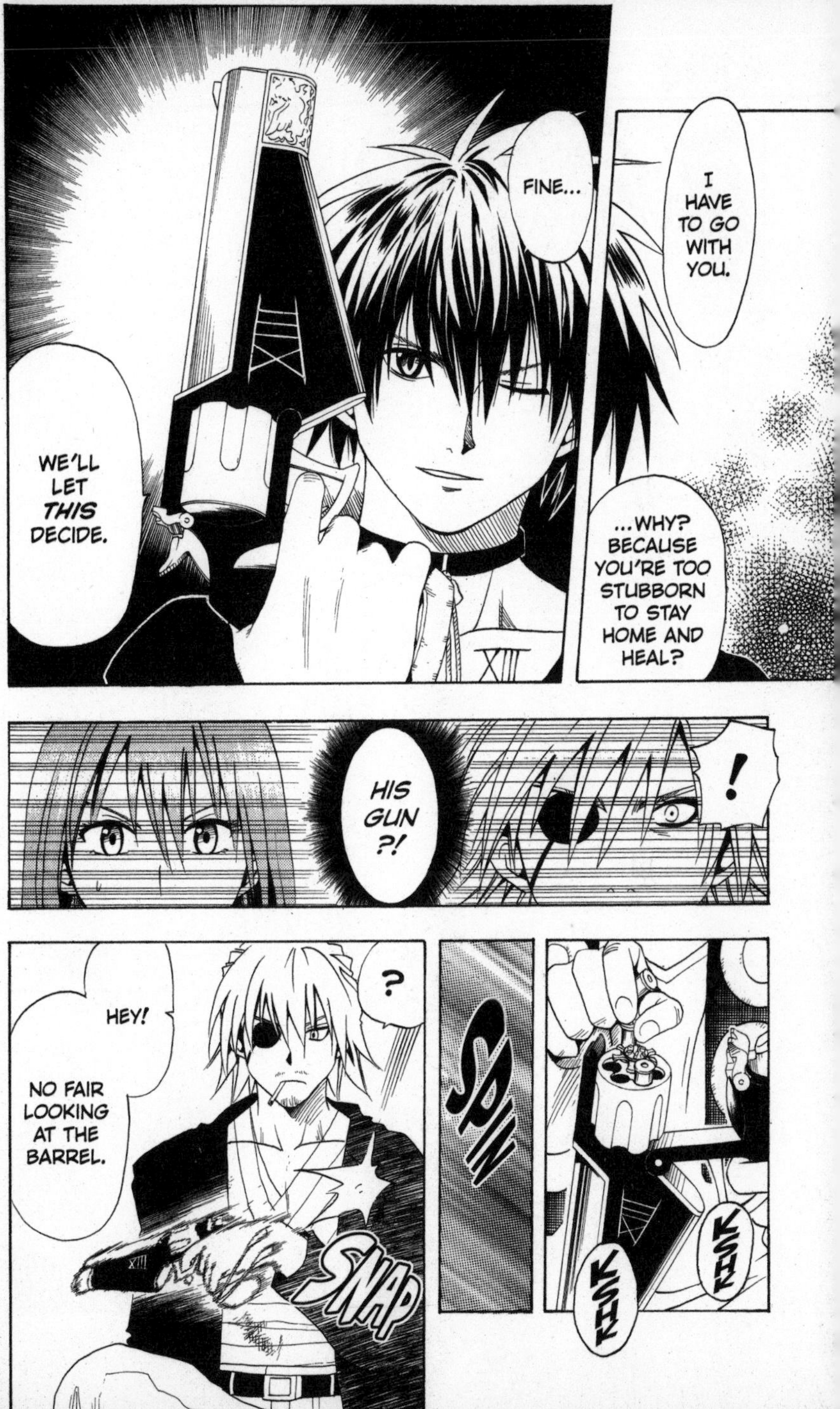
I HAVE TO GO WITH YOU.
...WHY? BECAUSE YOU'RE TOO STUBBORN TO STAY HOME AND HEAL?
FINE...
WE'LL LET *THIS* DECIDE.
!
HIS GUN?!
KSHK
KSHK
SPIN
?
HEY!
NO FAIR LOOKING AT THE BARREL.
SNAP

READ THIS WAY

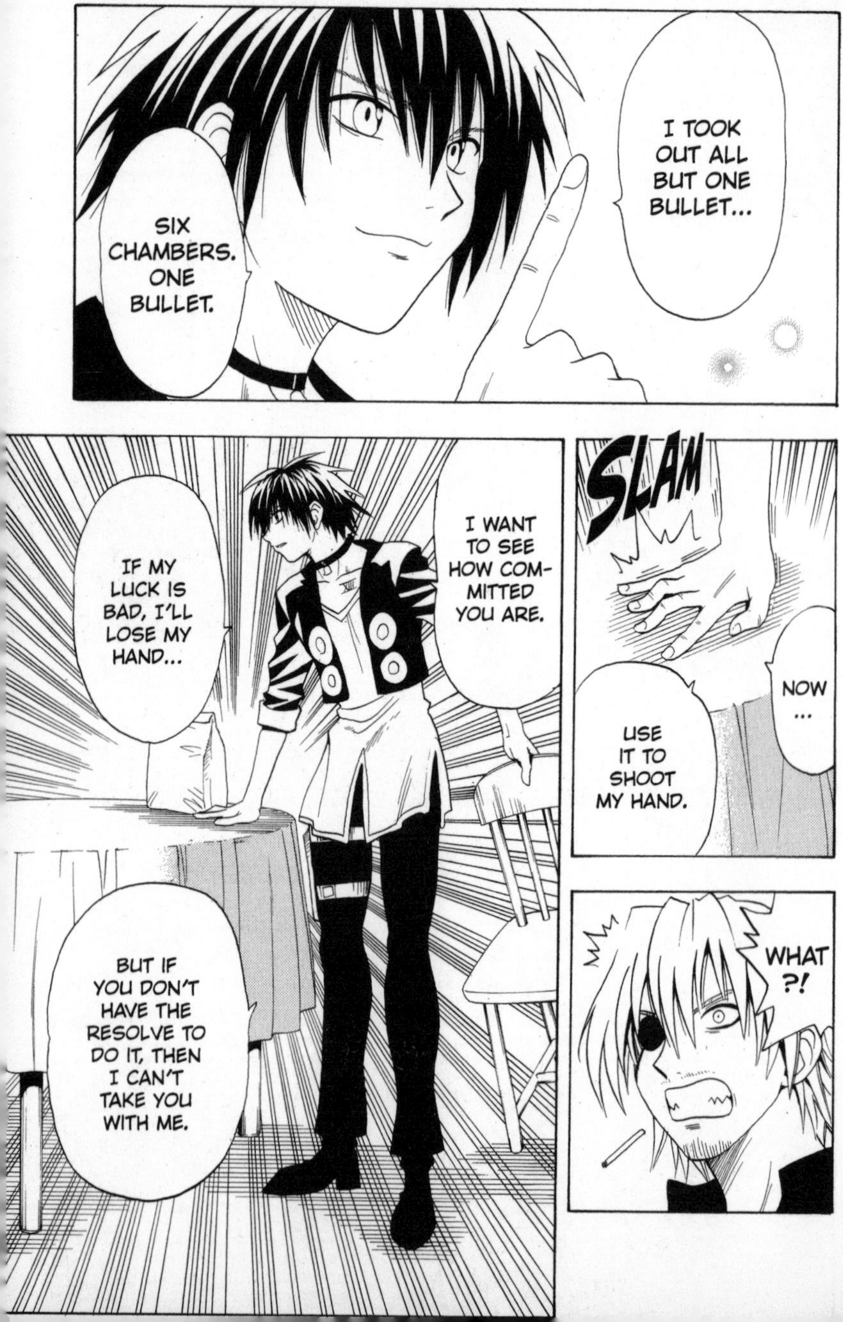
I TOOK OUT ALL BUT ONE BULLET...
SIX CHAMBERS. ONE BULLET.
SLAM
NOW...
USE IT TO SHOOT MY HAND.
WHAT?!
I WANT TO SEE HOW COMMITTED YOU ARE.
IF MY LUCK IS BAD, I'LL LOSE MY HAND...
BUT IF YOU DON'T HAVE THE RESOLVE TO DO IT, THEN I CAN'T TAKE YOU WITH ME.

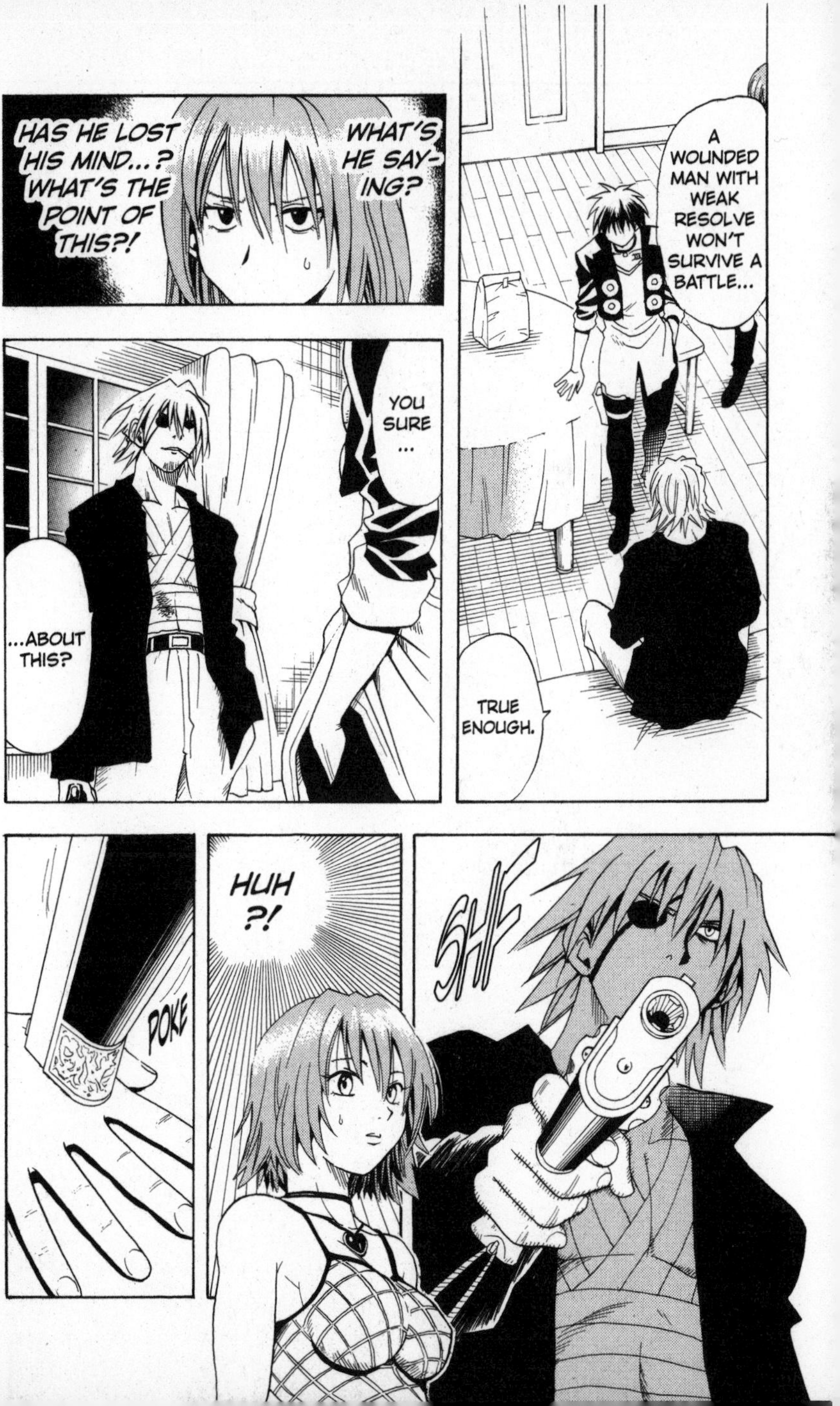
A WOUNDED MAN WITH WEAK RESOLVE WON'T SURVIVE A BATTLE...
TRUE ENOUGH.
WHAT'S HE SAY-ING?
HAS HE LOST HIS MIND...? WHAT'S THE POINT OF THIS?!
YOU SURE ...
...ABOUT THIS?
SHF
HUH ?!
POKE

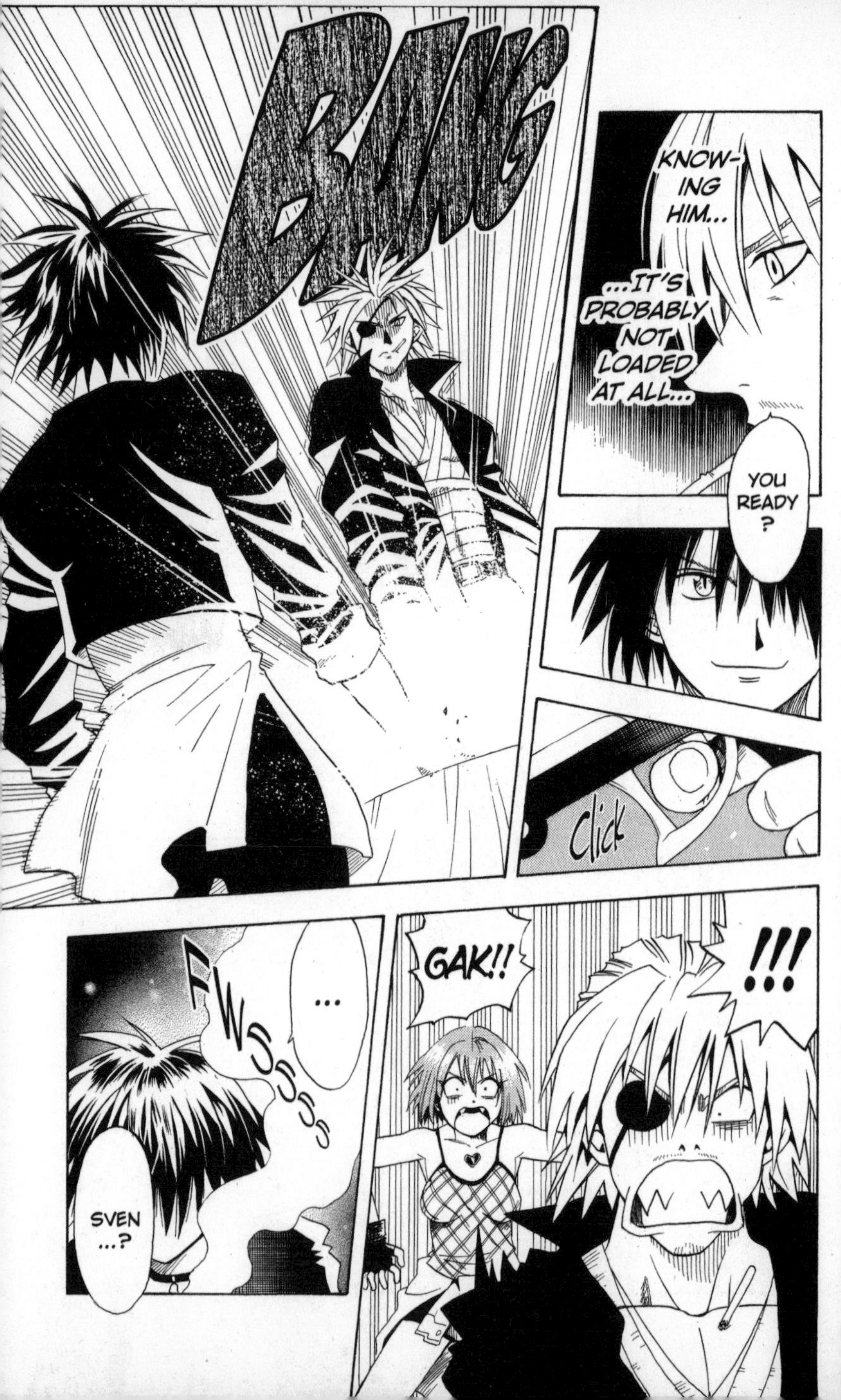
KNOWING HIM...
...IT'S PROBABLY NOT LOADED AT ALL...
YOU READY?
Click
BANG
!!!
GAK!!
...
FWSSSSS
SVEN ...?

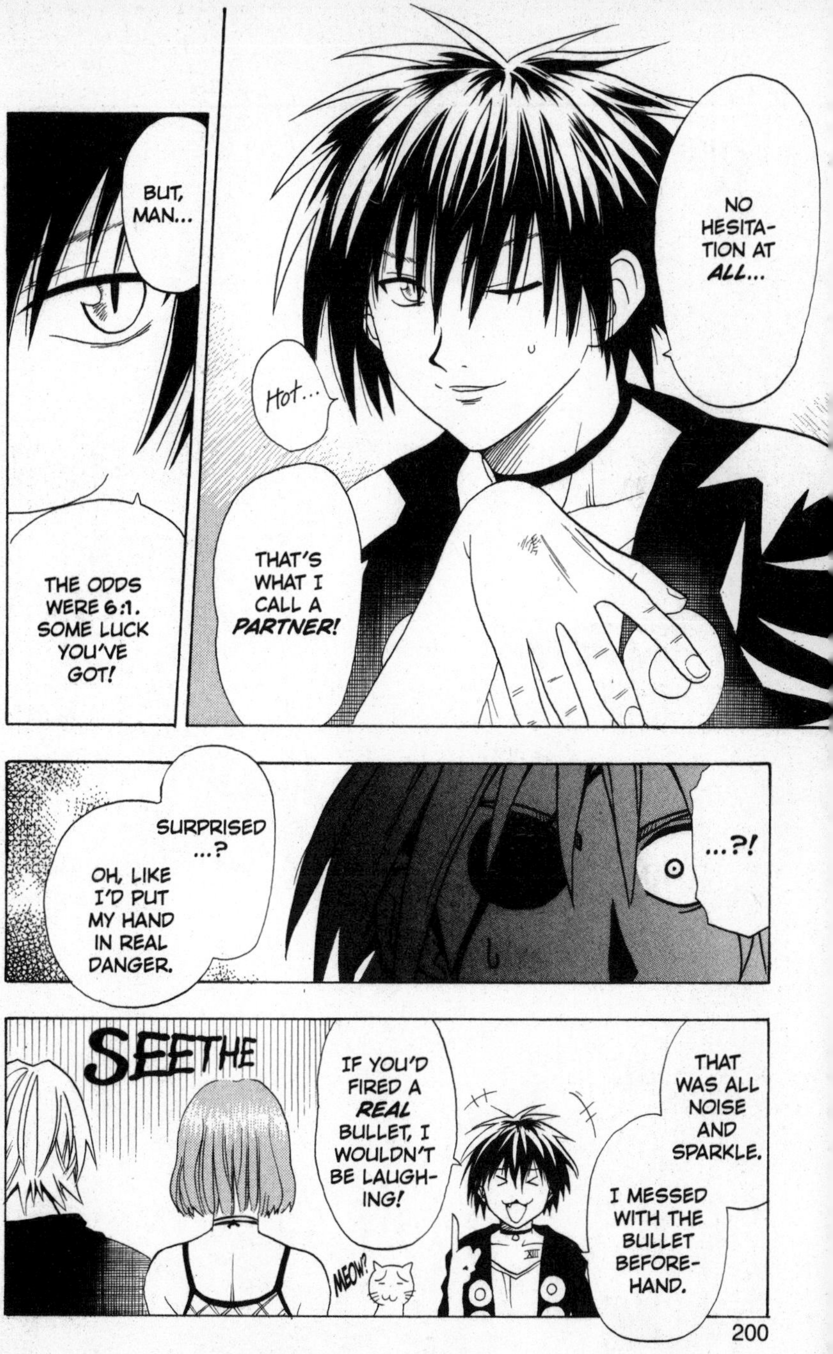
NO HESITATION AT ALL...
Hot...
THAT'S WHAT I CALL A PARTNER!
BUT, MAN...
THE ODDS WERE 6:1. SOME LUCK YOU'VE GOT!
...?!
SURPRISED ...?
OH, LIKE I'D PUT MY HAND IN REAL DANGER.
THAT WAS ALL NOISE AND SPARKLE.
I MESSED WITH THE BULLET BEFOREHAND.
IF YOU'D FIRED A REAL BULLET, I WOULDN'T BE LAUGHING!
MEOW?
SEETHE

READ THIS WAY

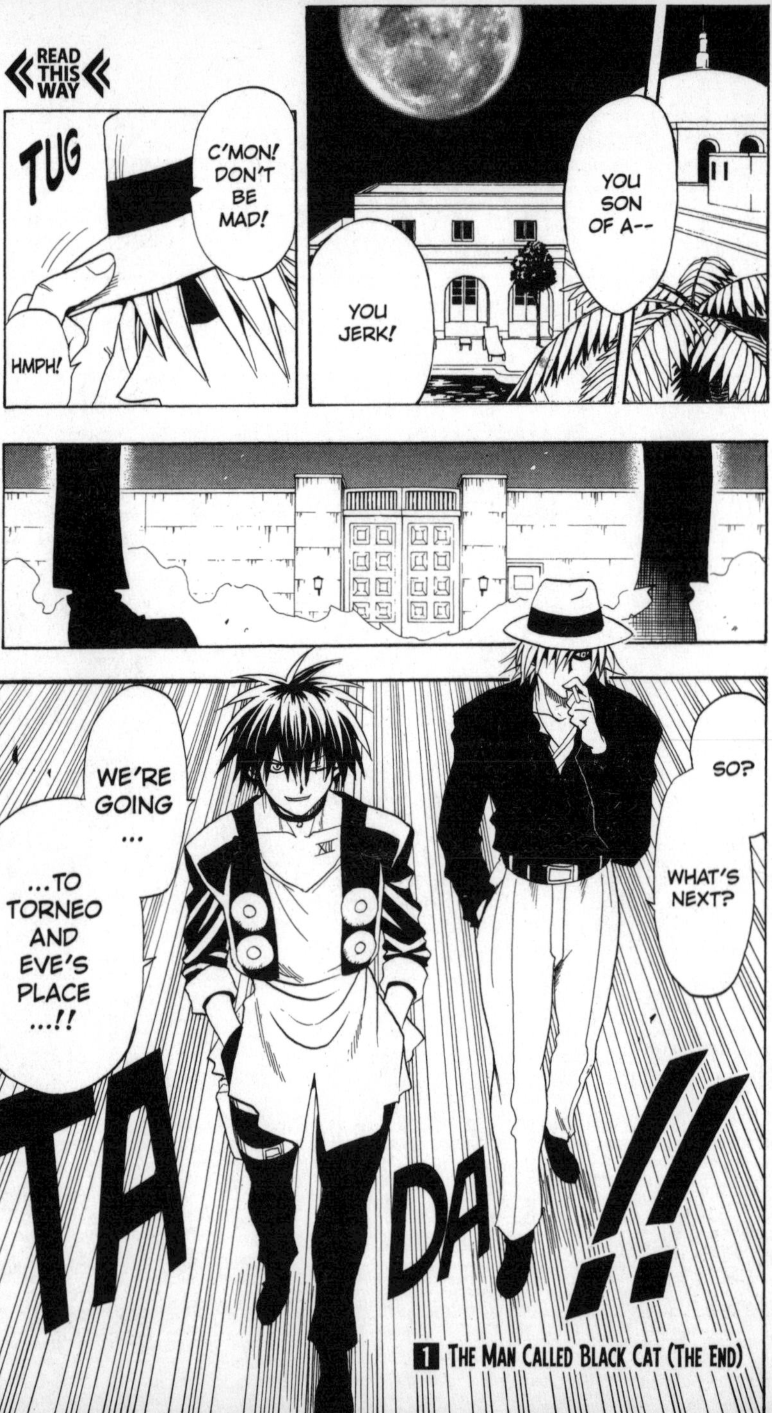
YOU SON OF A--
YOU JERK!
C'MON! DON'T BE MAD!
TUG
HMPH!
SO?
WHAT'S NEXT?
WE'RE GOING ...
...TO TORNEO AND EVE'S PLACE ...!!
TA DA!!
1 THE MAN CALLED BLACK CAT (THE END)

PRESENTED BY

KENTARO "I DREAM OF **THE GODFATHER**" YABUKI

ASSISTANTS: KATSUNORI "DRAGON" HIDA

KENTARO "JOKE WIZARD" HONNA

YUY "POISON" SHIINO

THE MEN WHO RESCUE ME WHEN TIMES ARE ROUGH!

SUPPORTERS: YOSHITAKA "THE MOBILE PUPIL" SATO

SOH "NO WAY" FUNATSU

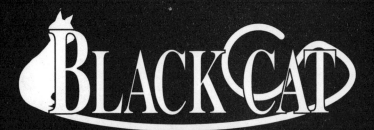

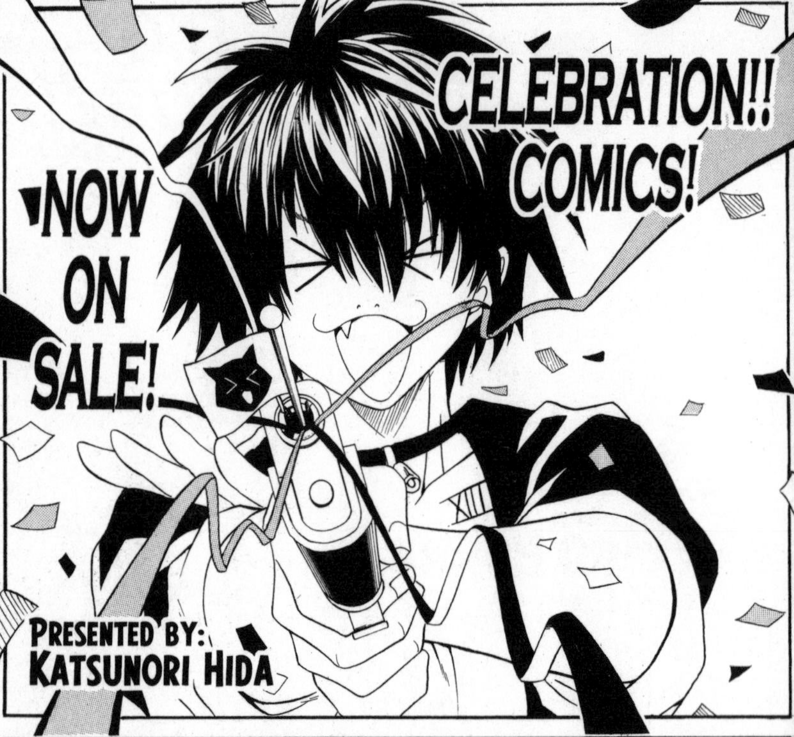
CELEBRATION!! COMICS!
NOW ON SALE!
PRESENTED BY:
KATSUNORI HIDA

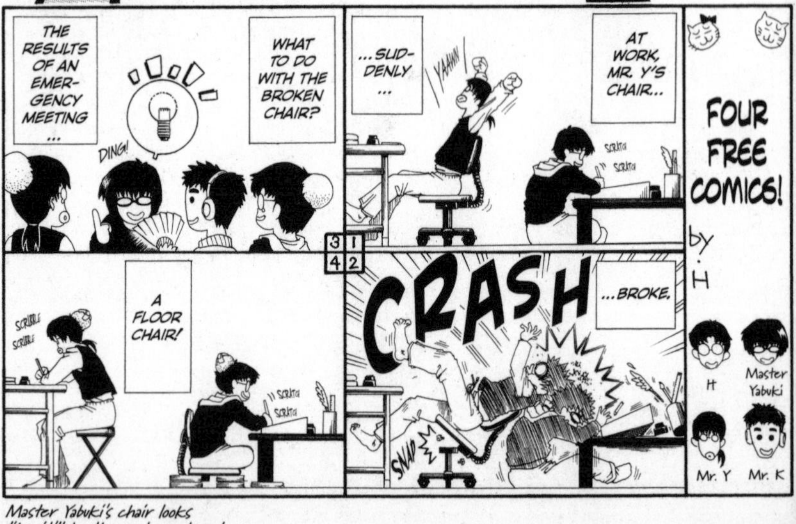
FOUR FREE COMICS!
by H
H
Master Yabuki
Mr. Y
Mr. K
AT WORK, MR. Y'S CHAIR...
...SUD-DENLY...
YAAWN
SCRITCH SCRITCH
...BROKE.
CRASH
SNAP
WHAT TO DO WITH THE BROKEN CHAIR?
THE RESULTS OF AN EMER-GENCY MEETING...
DING!
A FLOOR CHAIR!
SCRIBBLE SCRIBBLE
SCRITCH SCRITCH

Master Yabuki's chair looks like it'll be the next one to go!

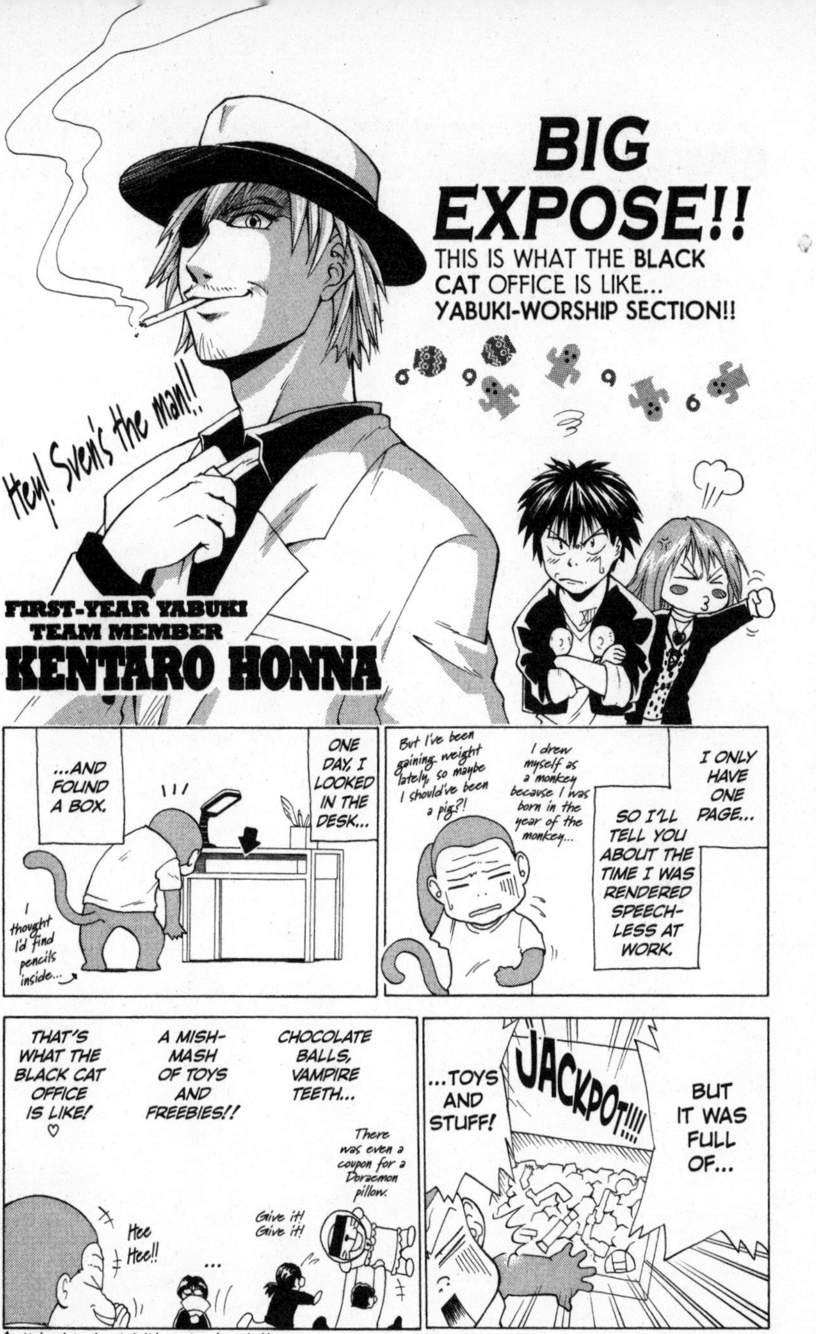
BIG EXPOSE!!
THIS IS WHAT THE BLACK CAT OFFICE IS LIKE... YABUKI-WORSHIP SECTION!!
Hey! Sven's the man!!
FIRST-YEAR YABUKI TEAM MEMBER
KENTARO HONNA
I ONLY HAVE ONE PAGE...
SO I'LL TELL YOU ABOUT THE TIME I WAS RENDERED SPEECH-LESS AT WORK.
I drew myself as a monkey because I was born in the year of the monkey...
But I've been gaining weight lately, so maybe I should've been a pig?!
ONE DAY, I LOOKED IN THE DESK...
...AND FOUND A BOX.
I thought I'd find pencils inside...
BUT IT WAS FULL OF...
JACKPOT!!!!
...TOYS AND STUFF!
CHOCOLATE BALLS, VAMPIRE TEETH...
A MISH-MASH OF TOYS AND FREEBIES!!
THAT'S WHAT THE BLACK CAT OFFICE IS LIKE! ♡
There was even a coupon for a Doraemon pillow.
Give it! Give it!
...
Hee Hee!!
He's snickering, but this monkey is no better.

Yuy Shiino's Confession File 1 — The Taboo Song of Determination

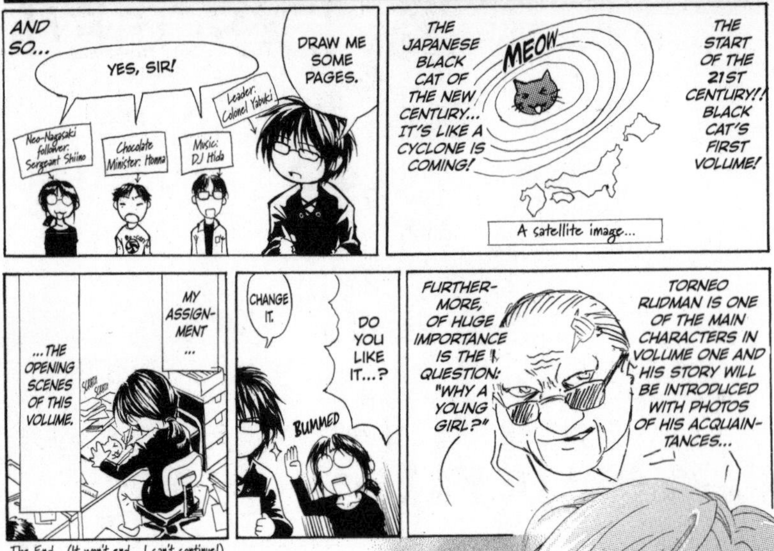
THE START OF THE 21ST CENTURY!! BLACK CAT'S FIRST VOLUME!
MEOW
THE JAPANESE BLACK CAT OF THE NEW CENTURY... IT'S LIKE A CYCLONE IS COMING!
A satellite image...
DRAW ME SOME PAGES.
Leader: Colonel Yabuki
YES, SIR!
AND SO...
Music: DJ Hida
Chocolate Minister: Honna
Neo-Nagasaki follower: Sergeant Shiino
TORNEO RUDMAN IS ONE OF THE MAIN CHARACTERS IN VOLUME ONE AND HIS STORY WILL BE INTRODUCED WITH PHOTOS OF HIS ACQUAINTANCES...
FURTHERMORE, OF HUGE IMPORTANCE IS THE QUESTION: "WHY A YOUNG GIRL?"
DO YOU LIKE IT...?
CHANGE IT.
BUMMED
MY ASSIGNMENT ...
...THE OPENING SCENES OF THIS VOLUME.

The End... (It won't end... I can't continue!)

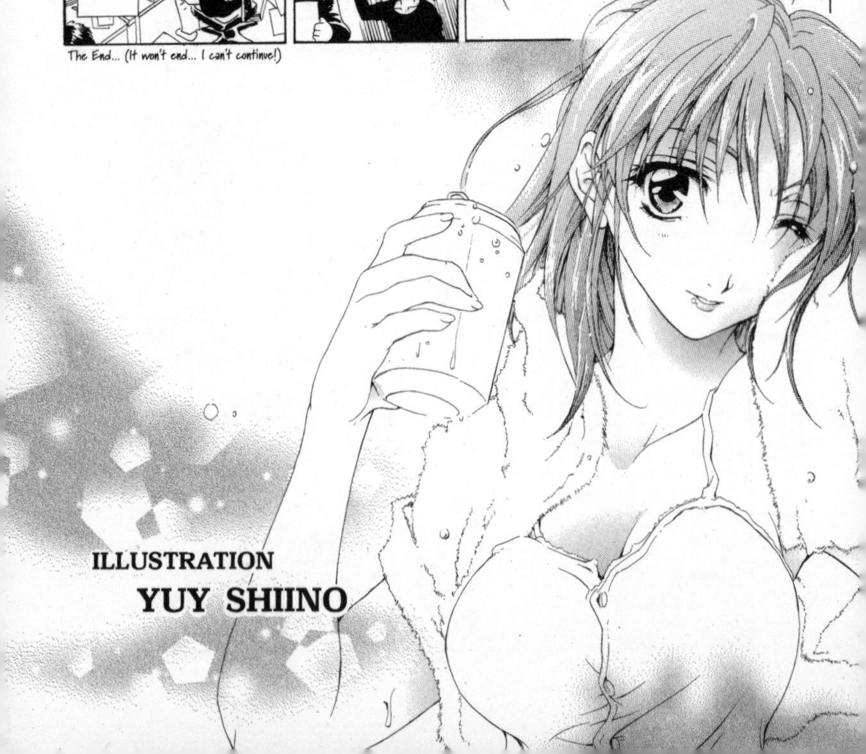

ILLUSTRATION
YUY SHIINO

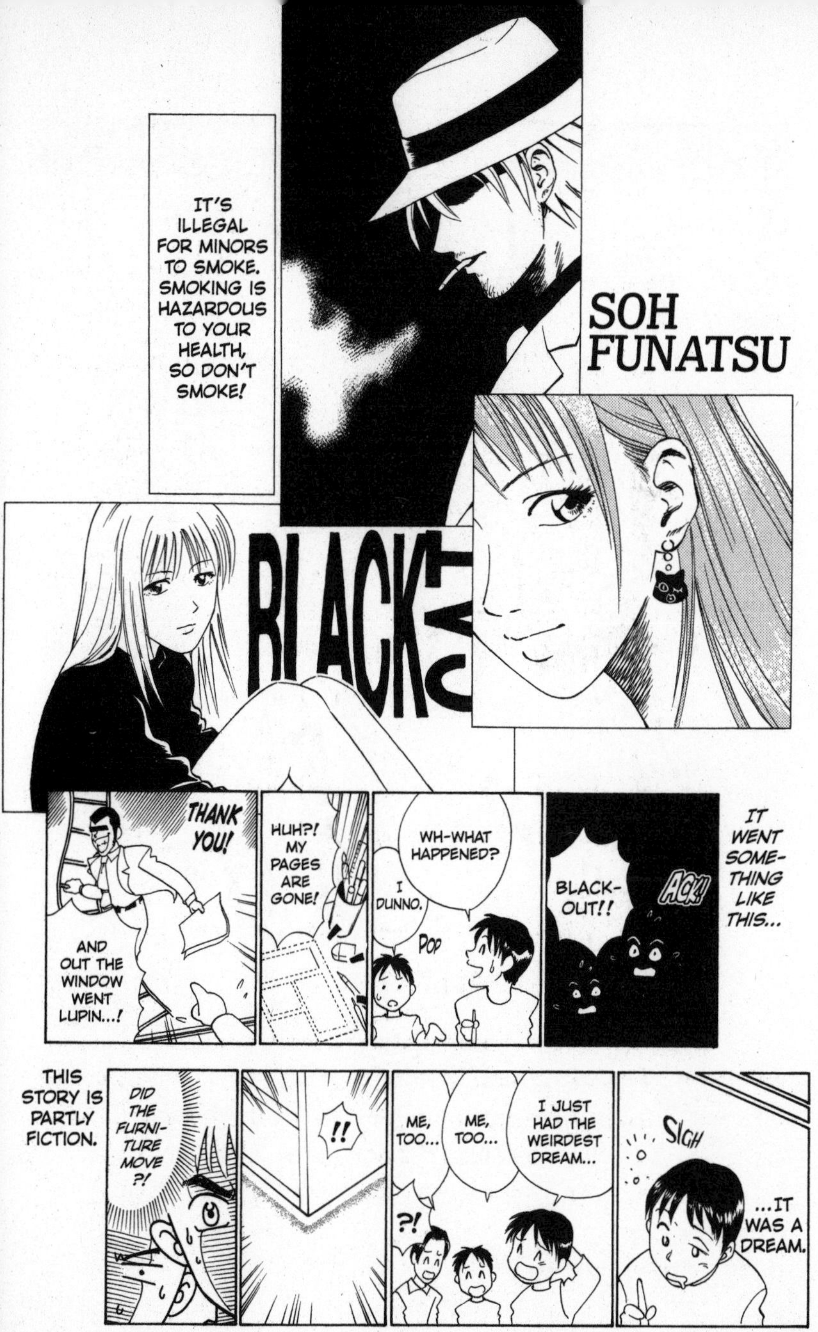
SOH FUNATSU
BLACK OUT
IT'S ILLEGAL FOR MINORS TO SMOKE. SMOKING IS HAZARDOUS TO YOUR HEALTH, SO DON'T SMOKE!
IT WENT SOMETHING LIKE THIS...
ACK!
BLACK-OUT!!
WH-WHAT HAPPENED?
I DUNNO.
POP
HUH?! MY PAGES ARE GONE!
THANK YOU!
AND OUT THE WINDOW WENT LUPIN...!
SIGH
...IT WAS A DREAM.
I JUST HAD THE WEIRDEST DREAM...
ME, TOO...
ME, TOO...
?!
!!
DID THE FURNI-TURE MOVE?!
THIS STORY IS PARTLY FICTION.

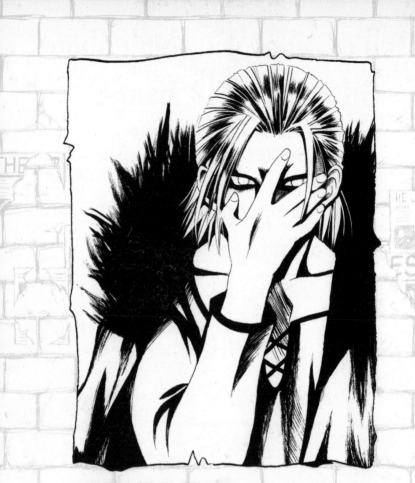

IN THE NEXT VOLUME...

Sven is determined to save Eve, but will Train really
go along with this crazy rescue mission? What kind
of shady organization are they up against? And
what will happen when Train comes face-to-face with his
mortal enemy, the man who killed his best friend?!

AVAILABLE NOW!

Tell us what you think about SHONEN JUMP

Our survey is now available online.
Go to: **www.SHONENJUMP.com/mangasurvey**

Help us make our product offering better!

THE REAL ACTION STARTS IN...

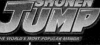

THE WORLD'S MOST POPULAR MANGA
www.shonenjump.com

ST ADVANCED

ST

VIZ MEDIA